D1535965

100 YEARS OF CONFLICT

100 YEARS OF CONFLICT 1900–2000

Edited by

SIMON TREW & GARY SHEFFIELD

Sutton Publishing

First published in 2000 by
Sutton Publishing Limited · Phoenix Mill
Thrupp · Stroud · Gloucestershire · GL5 2BU

British Library Cataloguing in Publication Data
A catalogue record for this book is available from the British Library.

ISBN 0 7509 2170 6

Typeset in 10/13 pt Sabon.
Typesetting and origination by
Sutton Publishing Limited.
Printed and bound in England
by J.H. Haynes & Co. Ltd, Sparkford.

CONTENTS

ACKNOWLEDGEMENTS

Any book like this is by its very nature a collaborative effort, involving hard work by many people. The editors would therefore like to thank those who have helped to bring it to publication. At the RMAS Mrs Marian Matthews typed a very large part of the manuscript, and without her efforts we would never have met our project deadlines; our sincerest thanks to her. Thanks also to Mrs Chris MacLennan, who helped with the typing, and the Mrs Ann Ferguson, who provided some of the illustrations. We would also like to express our gratitude to Mr Matthew Midlane, Director of Studies at the RMAS, and to the current Commandant, Major General Arthur Denaro CBE, for granting permission to use the academy logo on the front cover. At Sutton Publishing Sarah Moore did a wonderful job editing the manuscript, and was a model of friendly efficiency from start to finish. She was ably assisted by Glad Stockdale (who, among other things, produced the maps), Maria Miggiano and Catherine Watson. Jonathan Falconer (Commissioning Editor) and Peter Clifford (Publishing Director), who took on the project in the first place, were always encouraging and helpful, and saw us through several rather bleak and panic-stricken moments. We would also like to thank our wives and families, Dr Duncan Anderson and all the members of the War Studies Department at the RMAS, and those many others who gave their moral support to the project after John's death. Our love and best wishes too to Maggie, Katie and Becky Pimlott.

It is customary for editors to take full responsibility for any errors of fact or interpretation contained in a book like this, and we see no reason not to do so in this case. The first named editor, however, takes sole responsibility for any mistakes occurring in illustration captions and marginal tables.

This book is for John.

Simon Trew, Royal Military Academy Sandhurst
Gary Sheffield, Joint Services Command and Staff College,
February 2001

INTRODUCTION

In 1899 an English translation appeared of a book by a Polish banker, Ivan Bloch. The book's title posed a stark question: *Is War Now Impossible?* Bloch deduced from the changed conditions of warfare at the end of the nineteenth century that war had effectively become suicidal. Half a century later, some people likewise suggested that war was becoming obsolete. In the late 1940s the advent of the atomic bomb appeared to make warfare so dangerous that it ceased to fulfil a political function – and politics, of course, is the factor that turns mere violence into war. Both predictions were thus founded on logic, but both were wrong. Throughout the twentieth century states did not cease to appeal to the assize of arms to settle disputes. Indeed, the twentieth century was undoubtedly the bloodiest in the history of mankind. War shaped and defined the century. The two world wars led directly to the rise and fall of fascism and communism, the destruction of European empires, and the emergence of the United States as a superpower. Other conflicts brought about the victory of communism in China and Vietnam. The Cold War brought the world to the brink of destruction by nuclear weapons, but also led to the collapse of Soviet communism and the triumph of liberal democracy and free-market capitalism. War has had an enormous impact on societies and technology, for both good and evil. War is still with us. We ignore it at our peril.

There is still resistance in some quarters to the study of war as somehow immoral or at least improper. Dr John Pimlott was a living embodiment of how foolish that view is. A kind, liberal-minded and deeply humane man, John devoted his life to bringing about greater understanding of war. John was born in 1948, and was educated at Brigg Grammar School, Lincolnshire and Leicester University. He joined the War Studies Department at the Royal Military Academy Sandhurst in 1973, becoming Deputy Head of Department in 1987 and Head in 1994. John died in a tragic accident in 1997, leaving a widow, Maggie, and two grown-up daughters, Katie and Becky.

John Pimlott left a rich legacy. As a teacher, he was in a league of his own. He was a wonderfully friendly man who, despite playing up to the image of the dour Northerner, had a great sense of humour – one of the most characteristic sounds in the War Studies Department corridor was his laugh. His personality contributed to making him the great teacher that he undoubtedly was. Puffing on his pipe or gesticulating with it (more often than not it was unlit) he could keep an audience spellbound, whether they were eighteen-year-old officer cadets or generals. Generations of British

Dr John Pimlott

Army officers benefited from his lectures and seminars, and his infinite patience and willingness to devote his time, not only to his students but to anyone who had a genuine desire to learn. News of his death brought tributes from places as far afield as the United States, Norway, Australia and the Philippines.

John Pimlott's other legacy was as one of the finest popular historians and commentators on contemporary international affairs that Britain has known. He was a considerable scholar. His work on counter-insurgency is rightly regarded as seminal, and he had a major influence on the development of British Army doctrine on the subject. He also co-edited, with Stephen Badsey, an important book on the 1990–1 Gulf Crisis. However, John's *forte* was the book, article and part-work aimed at a mass audience. In the minds of some academics, there is a tension between 'scholarly' and 'popular' work. John demonstrated that the real division is between good and bad work. His writings, for example on the Middle East conflicts, were models of clarity, making a complicated subject accessible to a wider audience without compromising on the quality of his work or adopting a patronising approach. John's influence as a historian was thus much wider than most of his peers. He set formidably high standards for other writers to follow, and did the world a service in helping people to increase their understanding of war, without glamorising or trivialising it.

This book was written to honour John's memory. It is customary for scholars to honour a distinguished colleague by putting together a *Festschrift*, a collection of essays. John was the least pompous of men and we are sure that he would have appreciated the approach we have taken here, of writing a 'scholarly but accessible' book of the sort that he did so well. All the contributors are friends, colleagues and admirers of John Pimlott. Many of us have worked with him in the Sandhurst Department of War Studies. His death left a huge gap in our lives. We hope that he would have approved of this book.

ONE

THE IMPACT OF TWO REVOLUTIONS, 1789–1898

GARY SHEFFIELD

The 'long nineteenth century' between 1789 and 1914 witnessed two revolutions that were to change the face of warfare forever. The revolution that began in France in 1789 unleashed the concept of ideas as a weapon and brought profound changes to the political structure of Europe. The conflicts that began as a consequence of the French Revolution were to have an equally profound impact on the nature and conduct of war. The Industrial Revolution brought about not only technological change but also social and political change: in turn, these developments helped to transform warfare. The two revolutions made possible the total, industrialised, technologically based conflicts of the twentieth century.

THE FRENCH REVOLUTION AND THE NAPOLEONIC WARS

Total war – definable as all-out war fought for far-reaching aims, involving the mobilisation of all the resources of a state, human and economic – only really became possible in the nineteenth century. Before this time there had been wars of particular savagery, for example between 1618 and 1648 (the 'Thirty Years War'). However, the century and a half that followed was characterised by restraint in the conduct of warfare. Only one major country – Poland – disappeared from the map as a result of war; and that disappearance was the product of the peculiar circumstances faced by the Polish state.

The French Revolution was to end restraint in warfare. It began in 1789 as a reasonably limited attempt to reform the absolutist rule of the French monarchy. But by 1793 the moderates had been elbowed aside, France had become a republic proclaiming freedom, equality and brotherhood, and King Louis XVI (1754–93) had been executed on the guillotine. As a result, most of the other European powers, ruled by monarchs like

King Louis, were at war with France. The cycle of conflicts was to last until the final French defeat at Waterloo in 1815.

There was a strong element of ideology in the Revolutionary wars. As early as 1790 the British politician Edmund Burke (1729–97) foresaw that the Revolution posed a direct threat to the conservative and mostly monarchical powers of Europe. Nevertheless, the ideological aspects of the conflict should not be over-emphasised. Russia stayed out of the initial stages of the war, and Spain actually changed sides and joined the French, although admittedly not until 1795 when the worse excesses of the Revolution were over. The end of the truly revolutionary phase was underlined in 1799 when one of the Republic's more successful generals, Napoleon Bonaparte (1769–1821), mounted a coup and seized power. Napoleon went on to crown himself Emperor in 1804, and transformed France and its various conquests into an empire and satellite kingdoms. Although the ideological element never vanished, the Napoleonic Wars came to revolve around France's attempt to achieve hegemony in Europe.

In the words of the historian Hew Strachan, the importance of the French Revolution for warfare was 'intellectual and, above all, political. It established definitively a link between political rights and civic responsibilities.' Frenchmen were no longer mere subjects of the monarch. They were now citizens of the French Republic. 'The citizen, in return for the legal freedom which the state now guaranteed him, came under an obligation to shoulder a musket in defence of the nation.' The freedoms guaranteed by the French Republic might have been more apparent than real, but the concept of the 'Nation in Arms' was born. Like most innovations, this was not without precedents; indeed, recent historians have tended to stress the continuities, rather than the dissimilarities, between warfare in the eighteenth century and in the Revolutionary and Napoleonic period.

The key advantage that the French troops had over their *ancien régime* opponents was motivation. The French Revolutionary armies were the most democratic in the world. Reforms in 1790 had made it possible for men of humble background to pursue a career as an officer. During the Revolution about 6,000 noble officers fled the country, to be replaced in many cases by former NCOs. Men who did well (like Napoleon) were likely to achieve rapid promotion. Commanding generals had a rather different form of motivation: those who were defeated were liable to be recalled and executed.

The motivation of its armies notwithstanding, the Revolution seemed in grave peril in 1792. Faced by insurrections on French soil, notably a royalist uprising in the Vendée, France was also menaced by a combined Austrian and Prussian army of 34,000 men which invaded eastern France. At Valmy, on 20 September 1792, the 36,000-strong French Army drew up in a defensive position and faced the invaders. When the French general Kellermann (1735–1820) rode along the ranks to inspire the troops, the common soldiery roared back 'Vive la nation! Vive la France!' and stood firm. There was a desultory exchange of fire and the Austro-Prussian Army retreated. The 'cannonade of Valmy' was not, in truth, much of a battle, but it parried the immediate threat to the Revolution. Moreover, Valmy was of enormous symbolic importance. The rag-tag army of the Revolution had faced down the *ancien régime's* professional forces.

The execution of Louis XVI on 21 January 1793 did not actually cause the subsequent wars between Revolutionary France and much of the rest of Europe. However, it provoked a particularly violent reaction in Spain, and served as a pretext for the ending of negotiations between Britain and France over the fate of the Low Countries. With Europe's greatest economic and military powers on a collision course, the scene was set for total war. (Musée Carnavalet)

Valmy showed that not only the French government and Army, but also the French people, were waging war. What the Prussian military philosopher Carl von Clausewitz (1780–1831) later called the 'remarkable trinity' of government, army and people, united to fight a people's war, was complete in a way that had never been witnessed before but has been seen many times since.

Another important symbol of the unleashing of nationalism as a powerful popular military force was the *levée en masse* declared by Lazare Carnot (1753–1823), the French Minister of War, on 23 August 1793. Carnot's proclamation demanded that:

> From this moment on until that when the enemy is driven from the territory of the Republic, every Frenchman is permanently requisitioned for the needs of the armies. The young men will fight; the married men shall forge weapons and transport supplies; the women will make tents and clothes and will serve in the hospitals; the children will make up old linen into bandages; the old men will have themselves carried into the public squares to rouse the courage of the fighting men, to preach the unity of the Republic and hatred against Kings.

Carnot has aptly been described as 'the organiser of victory'. The *levée en masse* was a response to an immediate crisis and the French Army swelled to about a million men. By 1797 the immediate danger was over – indeed, the Republic was savouring the fruits of victory – and the size of the Army stood at about 382,000, with desertion rates climbing. Increasingly the

'No more manoeuvres, no more military art, but fire, steel and patriotism.'

Lazare Carnot, 1793

Army became less 'national', in that it contained large numbers of men who were only French because their homelands had been conquered, and for that matter many outright foreigners. But the French attempt to wage a total war was impressive, given the confines of a pre-industrial economy and society. The genie of total war was out of the bottle.

The Revolutionary and Napoleonic wars were characterised by total aims, with France using her Army to revolutionise (that is, conquer) the western German states, the Low Countries and the Italian peninsula. It was a conflict of many battles, involving the destruction of entire armies. It was war on a vast geographic scale, with the fighting on land and sea spreading from Western Europe to Russia, Egypt, Spain, India, south-east Asia and North America. The conflict also saw huge reserves of manpower deployed by the belligerents. It was, above all, a rapacious war. The Agricultural Revolution of the eighteenth century had greatly increased the productivity of the land. On campaign Napoleon's men lived mainly through organised looting of the local population. Moreover, the French made war pay for itself. They billeted troops on the territory of their vanquished foes, and pillaged not just money but art treasures and other goods, and took them back to France.

French power generally prevailed on land, but not at sea. Nelson's victory over the combined Spanish and French fleets at Trafalgar in 1805 effectively ended Napoleon's hopes of invading and conquering England. Instead, the French tried to defeat Britain by strangling its economy. The Berlin Decree of 1806 introduced the Continental System. This was an attempt to strike at the very foundations of British economic power by excluding British commerce from continental European ports (most of which lay in areas dominated by France) and mounting a blockade, albeit a largely paper one, of Britain itself. Although the Continental System failed to knock Britain out of the war, it did place her under severe pressure, causing unrest in industrial areas. This was especially true in 1812 when war broke out between Britain and the United States, thus denying Napoleon's enemy another valuable market. The British responded to the Continental System by issuing in the years 1807 to 1812 a series of Orders in Council. These set up a counter-blockade enforced by the Royal Navy, which stopped ships and confiscated contraband (a practice that was a factor in the outbreak of war with the Americans). An unanticipated by-product of these blockades was the growth of the European sugar beet industry, as British warships prevented sugar cane from the West Indies from reaching Europe.

For the Continental System to work, the entire coastline of Europe had to be closed to British traders. In practice this was impossible to achieve. The Continental System proved very unpopular and relatively easy to

THE CORPS SYSTEM

In the 1790s the French developed the use of *corps d'armée* for campaigning. These were complete armies in miniature, 14,000 to 25,000 strong, comprising artillery, infantry, cavalry and supporting troops. The corps system sounded the death-knell of the unitary army, as now forces could 'march divided, fight united' with different corps advancing along separate routes to combine on the battlefield. However, if the marches of troops were not choreographed precisely, the French could find themselves outnumbered on the battlefield. Famously, this occurred at Waterloo in 1815, when Marshal Grouchy failed to appear to reinforce Napoleon. By contrast, Blucher's Prussians arrived to support the Duke of Wellington's beleaguered forces, and tipped the balance in favour of the allies.

British subsidies to European allies, 1794–1815

£65,800,000
(in 1999 £ sterling = £50 billion)

evade; indeed, on occasions the French themselves broke their own rules. Worse, to plug a gap in the anti-British barrier, Napoleon invaded Portugal in 1807 and Spain a year later. This began the attritional Peninsular War, which lasted until 1814 and ultimately proved disastrous for France. The waging of economic warfare had become the very stuff of total war.

Another feature commonly associated with total war is the radical transformation of methods of fighting, sometimes described as a 'Revolution in Military Affairs'. If a military revolution did occur in this period, it was not based on technology. Weapons were broadly similar to those that had been in use a century before. The ordinary infantryman was armed with an inaccurate smoothbore musket, with an effective range of only 50–100 yards. Artillery was also smoothbore. The cavalry, some of whom still wore body armour, carried a sword and sometimes a lance. All armies, including – perhaps surprisingly – the French, proved conservative in their use of technology. The Austrians, Prussians and British did adopt the rifle (which was more accurate but slow to load) for certain units, with some success. Britain, the world's first industrial power, had an approach to war-making that was socially less radical but slightly more technologically based. However, the most powerful war machines in existence were heavily armed wooden sailing vessels like HMS *Victory*. Such warships represented hundreds of years of development of a basic type, not a radical new venture in technology.

On the battlefield, tactics too were generally developments of eighteenth-century practice. The French use of infantry columns for attack had its origins in earlier experiments and the ideas of theorists such as Guibert, but the method proved ideal for manoeuvring large bodies of semi-trained, if enthusiastic, troops. Initially the armies of their opponents remained faithful to the rigid linear tactics of the *ancien régime*, with mixed success. The British used the line until the very end of the war, with impressive results.

One of the reasons for British success was the adoption of light infantry as skirmishers to screen the main battle lines from enemy skirmishers. Such troops had existed in small numbers in eighteenth-century armies, but generals had been unwilling to make much use of light infantry for fear that

THE ULM CAMPAIGN, 1805

In the summer of 1805 Napoleon's main army was encamped near Boulogne, waiting for his ships to defeat Nelson's British fleet and allow an invasion of Britain. Austria took the opportunity to strike. Foolishly, instead of waiting for the arrival of their Russian allies, the main Austrian force under General Karl Mack (1752–1828) and Archduke Ferdinand (1769–1824) advanced to Ulm in southern Germany. On 25 September Napoleon turned east. The French Army, 250,000 strong, was divided into seven corps. Moving on a front of 80–100 miles, one corps plus a cavalry force advanced frontally against the Austrians through the Black Forest, effectively pinning them, while the remainder swept through Germany, shielded by cavalry screens which kept Mack guessing as to where the blow would fall. Indeed, Mack seemed mentally paralysed by the French advance: his Army remained stationary around Ulm.

Napoleon's forces gradually converged in southern Germany, crossing the Danube in early October on a 70-mile front. The French cut the Austrian lines of communication and left strong forces to guard against a possible Russian advance. At last the Austrians awoke to the danger and attempted to break out of the encirclement, but they were repulsed at Haslach (11 October) and Elchingen (14 October). On 15 October Mack surrendered his 27,000-strong force. Napoleon then advanced into Moravia and defeated the Russians and the remains of the Austrian forces at Austerlitz (2 December 1805).

Ulm is one of the great encirclement victories in history, although an opponent less supine than Mack would probably have fought his way out of trouble. Napoleon's use of corps to 'march divided, fight united' can be seen as a model of operational art. However, the battle was indecisive in its strategic effects, and new Austrian armies were soon raised to continue the war. In this sense Ulm confirmed the importance of linking individual battlefield successes to the fulfilment of an overall military–political plan. Arguably, it was Napoleon's failure to identify such a plan that was to bring about his downfall.

'Marches are war . . . aptitude for war is aptitude for movement . . . victory is to the armies that manoeuvre.'

Napoleon Bonaparte

releasing troops from close supervision would simply give them the opportunity to desert. With their high levels of morale, French Revolutionary armies had less reason to fear desertion, which fell to a mere 4 per cent in 1794. Thus they made considerable use of skirmishers, the proportion rising from 4 per cent of their infantry in 1789 to 23 per cent in 1795. French skirmishers were militarily effective and were also symbolic of the commitment of the masses which is at the centre of the idea of total war.

Today, the levels of war are recognised as the 'strategic' – concerning the fighting of wars; the 'tactical' – concerning the fighting of battles; and an intermediate level, the 'operational' (or as it was known in the late eighteenth century, the 'grand tactical'). The latter deals with the fighting of campaigns and forms the vital link between the other two. Generally speaking, in earlier hostilities each state had only one main army and wars could be decided by a single battle. But by about 1800 states were deploying several armies, sometimes in more than one theatre of operations. Defeating an enemy state simply by destroying its army in a decisive battle was becoming increasingly difficult. Instead, enemies were defeated by the cumulative result of operations. In 1814 Napoleon's victories in individual battles were not enough to save him from the consequences of constant Allied pressure.

Industrial production, 1810 (in tons)

	Great Britain	Napoleonic Europe
Coal	16m	3m
Pig iron	330,000	250,000
Woollen goods	45,000	11,000

Ultimately, Napoleon fell victim to the ever-increasing scale of warfare. A logistic system based on living off the land was reasonably effective in fertile areas like the Low Countries, western Germany or northern Italy. However, as French armies began to operate further afield, they discovered that this method did not work so well in Poland (where the French campaigned in 1807), Russia or Spain, where 'large armies starve, and small armies are defeated'. Even where it did work, depriving the local inhabitants of their food did little to reconcile them to the realities of French power.

As his forces and theatres of operations grew larger, Napoleon found it increasingly difficult to exercise control over his armies. Yet he was reluctant to delegate. From commanding about 20,000 men over a front of 80 miles in Italy in 1796, by 1812 Napoleon was attempting to command an army of 600,000 men over 500 miles. With the exception of a brief period in 1808–9, Napoleon did not command in the Iberian Peninsula in person. Instead, he attempted to direct operations from Paris, or wherever he happened to be.

Napoleon also lacked a modern general staff. The control of the French Army relied heavily on its Chief of Staff, Marshal Louis-Alexandre Berthier (1753–1815), who was by his own admission little more than a 'glorified clerk', accumulating information and executing Napoleon's orders. Berthier used a stagecoach as a travelling office, in which he had filing cabinets full of index cards, which were updated regularly with details of unit strengths and similar information. Berthier was not much of a field commander, but he was a master of the routine administration of movements, transmitting orders and securing Intelligence. Napoleon's staff system was made to work by Berthier but was simply inadequate for the mass, dispersed armies of the era of total war.

One person above all others was responsible for Napoleon's downfall:

JOMINI AND CLAUSEWITZ

Two of the most significant thinkers in the history of warfare emerged in the wake of the Napoleonic Wars. The first, Antoine-Henri Jomini (1779–1869), was a Swiss officer who served on the staff of the French Marshal Ney (1769–1815) in the Napoleonic Wars, swapping sides to join the Russians in 1813. He was a prolific writer but his most important book was *Summary of the Art of War*, published in 1838. Jomini was a social conservative who was hugely influential in his lifetime. His works looked back to the limited 'cabinet wars' of the eighteenth century. Jomini's views were, therefore, perfectly in tune with the conservative thinkers of the post-Waterloo period, not least because he attempted to break the link between Napoleonic military practice and the French Revolution. Jomini argued that Napoleon, like Frederick the Great, had deployed unchanging military principles. By reconciling the methods of the two Great Captains, Jomini played down the revolutionary sources of Napoleonic warfare. Jomini was a codifier of strategy rather than an innovator; *Summary of the Art of War* is in part a manual on how to fight wars. Much of his writing about the conduct of operations, although often expressed in a rather abstract, 'geometrical' form, retains its validity. He laid stress, for example, on exploiting interior lines of communication and threatening enemy lines of communication – concepts that are important in modern manoeuvre warfare.

Carl Maria von Clausewitz (1780–1831), author of On War, *a work described by the distinguished American strategic thinker Bernard Brodie as 'not simply the greatest but the only great book about war'. Unfortunately, the evidence of the last century suggests that Clausewitz has more often been quoted than read or understood. (Hulton Getty)*

Jomini's great rival was Carl von Clausewitz (1780–1831), a Prussian who saw much service as a regimental and staff officer during and after the Napoleonic Wars. His masterpiece, *On War*, was unfinished at his death and was published posthumously in 1832. *On War* is probably the greatest book ever written on the subject, but it is a work of philosophy rather than a 'hands-on' manual. In contrast to Jomini, Clausewitz embraced the reality of total war. In 1806 he had seen the Prussian Army and state, which looked back to the era of Frederick, destroyed by Napoleon's Army. In 1813–15 a resurgent Prussia harnessed the forces of nationalism and helped to defeat Napoleon. Clausewitz's views were unfashionable for many years after his death, but his prediction that it was foolish to write off the chances of the recurrence of total war was highly prescient.

Some of Clausewitz's writings, such as his notion of 'centres of gravity' (attacking at critical points so that maximum damage will be caused to the enemy) and friction (occurrences that prevent things from going according to plan), are related to the conduct of war. However, much of his work is concerned with the nature of war, which he saw as an inherently political activity. His most famous, and often misquoted, dictum is that 'war is the continuation of politics by other means'. He also differentiated between an 'ideal' model of conflict, 'Absolute War', and 'real' war, which was limited in its objectives and deployment of resources. Clausewitz's ideas came to international prominence as a result of Prussian victories in the German Wars of Unification in the 1860s and 1870s.

On War was not, and is not, an easy read. As a result many of Clausewitz's ideas became garbled in transmission. His views on the relationship between war and politics became inverted: Helmuth von Moltke (1800–91), Chief of the Prussian General Staff from 1857, believed 'the politician should fall silent the moment that mobilisation begins'. Similarly, while Clausewitz's stress on decisive battles and the use of mass armies was taken to heart, his insistence that defence was a naturally stronger form of warfare than attack was not. Neither was the fact that Clausewitz's apparent championing of extreme violence was related to the philosophical ideal of Absolute War, rather than the realm of actual combat. The armies of 1914 were to pay a terrible price for misinterpreting Clausewitz.

Napoleon himself. He controlled not merely the French military but also French foreign policy. Eventually his enemies realised that the Emperor was insatiable; he had no fixed goal. This led him to undertake ever greater strategic gambles, but the law of averages ensured that sooner or later one of them would not pay off. Napoleon's attempt to seize Spain in 1808 was the beginning of the end. A major advantage for the French in previous campaigns had been that while they were pursuing total war, many of their enemies had behaved in a more restrained fashion. Now Napoleon was faced by the Spanish nation in arms in a vicious struggle waged not only by regular forces but also by guerrillas. An Anglo-Portuguese army under Wellington backed the Spanish.

'We must take revenge for the many sorrows inflicted upon the nation, and for so much arrogance. If we do not, then we are miserable wretches indeed, and deserve to be shocked out of our lazy peace every two years and threatened with slavery.'

Field Marshal August von Gneisenau of Prussia, 1814

From 1812 the tide began to turn. In Spain the Allied forces took an increasingly high toll of French blood, treasure and territory. Napoleon's defeat in Russia in 1812 led to Prussia, Sweden and Austria combining against him in the following year, the coalition being aided and abetted by British gold. Napoleon's opponents had learned much from their defeats. In Austria, Archduke Charles (1771–1847) carried out a series of important military reforms. In Prussia, another group of military reformers, notably Gerhard von Scharnhorst (1755–1813), transformed the Army into a formidable instrument of war. France's opponents went on to a total war footing. Nationalism, once the preserve of the French, was now a weapon wielded by their enemies. In 1812 Russian peasant partisans harried the retreating French. The following year, 6 per cent of the population of Prussia was under arms. Furthermore, the coalition's war aims took on the character of totality, although not without some misgivings, especially on the part of the Austrians.

By 1815, the nationalism unleashed by the French Revolution had transformed the nature of warfare. Once the concern merely of governments, war was now the business of peoples. War was no longer confined to the battlefield; it had become a total activity.

THE LONG PEACE AND THE INDUSTRIAL REVOLUTION

'Thus the Industrial Revolution was born, and man emerged from his caterpillar stage, from his life on the surface of the soil, to rise, like a mechanized dragon, into a hitherto undreamt of industrial empyrean – a way of life so suddenly thrust on him that it could not fail to have cataclysmic impacts on peace and war.'

J.F.C. Fuller, The Conduct of War 1789–1961 *(1961)*

The Revolutionary and Napoleonic Wars were, predictably, followed by a reaction against the excesses of total war. Although the conservative monarchical powers had deliberately exploited nationalism, they were instinctively (and correctly) scared of it as a threat to the existing social and political order. Thus continental European states tended to return to long-service armies, albeit based on selective conscription. The Prussian system, which retained a modified and tamed form of the nation-in-arms, was an exception. Compared to previous centuries, Europe between 1815 and 1914 was relatively peaceful. The conflicts that did occur, such as the Crimean War (1853–6) and the Prussian wars against Denmark (1864), Austria (1866) and France (1870–1), tended to be short and were essentially limited. Clearly, total war was out of fashion in the second half of the nineteenth century, but it was by no means extinct.

The invention of the steam engine by James Watt (1736–1819) and others in the late eighteenth century had signalled the beginning of the

Industrial Revolution. The first surge of the Revolution, based on coal, iron and textiles and centred in Britain and Belgium, took place between roughly 1780 and 1820. From about 1840 to 1870 France, the United States and Germany began to claw back Britain's significant industrial lead. A third wave of industrialisation took place in the 1890s, notably in Russia and Sweden.

The economic transformation of Europe brought about profound social change, which in turn had important military implications. The population of the continent grew from 188 million in 1800 to 267 million fifty years later. As the number of people increased, so governments came to exercise greater control through censuses, the establishment of police forces, the development of representative bodies and the creation of state-provided welfare schemes. By 1900 armed forces had larger pools of manpower on which to draw, and individuals were less likely to be able to avoid being conscripted. Not that military service was necessarily unpopular with the masses, for the phenomenon of militaristic nationalism was now a force to be reckoned with. Contrary to the fears of conservatives, a combination of general education, trades unions and 'a cheap and lurid press' produced a European working class that, in Michael Howard's words, by 1900 'were responding at least as readily to the stimuli of nationalism as they were to those of socialism'. As the events of 1914–18 were to show, militarised nationalism was to make possible years of modern total war.

Two technological advances arising from the Industrial Revolution between them transformed the nature of war: the railway and the telegraph. The Stockton to Darlington railway, opened in 1825, was the first railway in the world to employ steam locomotives. Railways were central to the second wave of industrialisation from the 1840s to 1870s

Railways revolutionised war, facilitating the rapid mobilisation, deployment and supply of large armies over great distances. However, their fixed lines and the complexity of coordinating the movement of trains, and of men and material away from railheads, caused difficulties for those trying to exploit their potential. Their importance also made them a tempting target for the enemy. Despite overwhelming battlefield victories against the French, in 1870–1 the Prussians encountered severe problems in sustaining the siege of Paris because of their inability to use the French railway system efficiently. Later, in the South African War of 1899–1902, numerous British troops were tied down in protecting railways against attacks by Boer commandos. Here, soldiers of the Dublin Fusiliers board an armoured wagon during the South African War. (PRO)

Populations of the great powers, 1810–1900 (millions)

	1810	1900
Russia	40.7	135.6
USA	–	75.9
Austria – Hungary	–	46.7
Britain	15.0	41.1
France	29.1	38.9

and their growth in Britain, Europe and North America was phenomenal. The United States possessed less than 10,000 miles of track in 1850, about 31,000 miles ten years later, 93,000 in 1880, and 199,000 miles in 1900. In France a network of semaphore-based visual telegraphs was developed in the 1790s under the presiding genius of Claude Chappé. By the 1820s the Chappé system was beginning to be superseded by an electric system of sending messages along wires. The telegraph went hand-in-hand with the railway; indeed, without the development of the electric telegraph the development of a railway system would scarcely have been possible. By the early 1860s Britain had 15,000 miles of telegraph wire, the world's total amounting to some 150,000 miles. In 1866 a trans-Atlantic line connected Europe and North America.

The railway and the telegraph made possible the strategic movement of troops and bulk supplies at a speed that would have been unthinkable only a generation before. In 1846 a Russian corps, including horses, men and equipment, travelled 200 miles by rail in only two days. Railways made it possible to gather troops in a central position and move them to threatened areas or concentration points by train rather than dispersing them among various bases and along different routes. Thus Aldershot became the 'home' of the British Army in the 1850s. Prussia/Germany built a sophisticated network of strategic railways, which were used to excellent effect at the beginning of the 1870 Franco-German war. In 1862, during the American Civil War, Confederate forces concentrated at Corinth, Mississippi, for what became known as the Shiloh campaign. Troops were brought by rail (and in some cases river steamer) over hundreds of miles: from New Orleans, Colombus (Kentucky), Mobile (Alabama), even Charleston, on the coast of South Carolina. Significantly, a force moving on foot from Arkansas only arrived after the Battle of Shiloh had been fought. Confederate General P.G.T. Beauregard aptly commented that 'scientific discoveries affecting transportation and the communication of Intelligence' meant that commanders could now treat an entire 'theater of war as one subject of which all points were but integral parts'. Napoleon's methods, typified by Ulm, had been updated.

'Build no more fortresses, build railways.'

Helmuth von Moltke

The railway and the telegraph solved problems but they also created them. Railways could not usually be used for tactical (that is, battlefield) movement. While it was relatively easy to move vast quantities of supplies by rail, moving them from the railheads to the troops, who might well be advancing away from railway lines, presented numerous problems, particularly before the development of motorised road transport in the early years of the twentieth century. At one stage in the Austro-Prussian War of 1866 nearly 18,000 tons of Prussian supplies were stuck on the railway system. The static nature of railway track and telegraph lines made them vulnerable to attack – American Civil War cavalry proved very effective in hit-and-run raids against enemy lines of communication – and thus large numbers of troops had to be used on garrison and guard duties, away from the field armies.

'The line that connects an army with its base of supplies is the heel of Achilles – its most vulnerable point.'

John S. Mosby, Confederate Cavalry Commander, War Reminiscences *(1887)*

Moreover, for the first time monarchs, politicians and desk-bound generals could rapidly communicate with armies in the field. While this had obvious advantages, in that it gave commanders an additional means of control just at the time when armies had become too big and too dispersed to be commanded by one man in person, it also had its drawbacks. Commanders were faced with constant demands for information and bombarded with advice: at times of crisis during the American Civil War, President Abraham Lincoln (1809–65) would haunt the telegraph room at the White House, waiting for messages to come through. In 1866, an embittered Moltke muttered that 'no commander is less fortunate than he who operates with a telegraph wire stuck in his back'. This prefigured the situation in the twentieth century, when the development of even better communications made it possible for President Lyndon Johnson to interfere with extremely low level operations in Vietnam.

Length of railway (miles)

	France	German area	Russia
1840	225	291	17
1860	5,696	6,890	1,010
1880	14,347	21,027	14,208
1900	23,680	32,112	35,081
1910	25,334	39,382	43,594

Radical changes were also witnessed in the ways that armies fought on the battlefield. During the Napoleonic Wars most infantrymen had been armed with a smoothbore, muzzle-loading musket. The British model, famously known as the 'Brown Bess', had a muzzle bore of 0.75 inches and weighed 11 pounds with its bayonet fixed. The French model had a slightly smaller bore of 0.69 inches and was a little lighter. Extreme musket range was about 200 yards, effective range only 50; about three shots could be fired per minute. Pulling the trigger, which brought a hammer into contact with a piece of flint, fired the weapon. The resultant spark would touch off gunpowder, which propelled the musket ball down the barrel. In some armies skirmishing troops were armed with rifles, which had grooves on the inside of the barrel. This caused the ball to spin, improving range and accuracy – but at the cost of a slower rate of fire, as it was more difficult to force the ball down the barrel.

By the time of the Crimean War (1853–6) firearms had improved dramatically. In the 1820s the percussion cap replaced the inefficient flintlock. The Minié bullet of 1849 was easier to load and more accurate than the old musket ball, although the Minié rifle was still muzzle loaded. The Prussian Dreyse 'needle-gun' of 1841 was, however, a breech-loader, which had a high rate of fire (ten rounds per minute) and could be fired while lying down. Breech-loading rifles revolutionised the firepower available to the infantry. Every ten or so years a further-improved weapon appeared, such as the French Chassepot of 1866 and the American Winchester of 1873. In 1884 the Germans adopted an improved version of the Mauser, which used a magazine containing eight rounds. Two years later the French Lebel was introduced, which used a smokeless propellant. Until that point battles had been fought in thick fogs produced by gunpowder. By the end of the century infantrymen were armed with bolt-action, magazine-fed rifles, which used smokeless propellant and were accurate up to 2,000 metres. Infantrymen could see and fire further and more rapidly than ever before.

'It occurred to me that if I could invent a machine – a gun – that would by its rapidity of fire enable one man to do as much battle duty as a hundred, that it would, to a great extent, supersede the necessity of large armies, and consequently exposure to battle and disease would be greatly diminished.'

Richard Gatling (inventor of the Gatling machine gun), 1877

The development of artillery followed broadly the same path as infantry weapons. The most powerful field gun available to Napoleon was the 12-pounder, a muzzle-loaded smoothbore. With a maximum range of 1,800 metres, and an effective range of 900, it could fire once per minute. The Industrial Revolution made it possible to produce guns so powerful that Napoleon would have been amazed. In the 1840s breech-loading rifled artillery pieces were produced, in separate ventures, by Sardinian and Prussian inventors. Three developments in particular were important in improving artillery. The invention of the Bessemer process in 1856 allowed the production of cheap steel, and this made the mass production of high quality guns possible. Improvements in high explosive, such as picric acid (lyddite) and TNT, made shells more powerful. Finally, in 1893 the French developed a 75mm gun which employed a recoil system. This meant that after firing the gun would stay in place, rather than lurching backwards with the force of the explosion; therefore, it did not need to be resited after each shot. The 'quick-firing' or QF gun was born.

The first effective machine gun was the French *mitrailleuse*, which saw limited use in the 1870 Franco-Prussian War. Other weapons followed, such as the hand-cranked Gatling, but the first automatic weapon was built by Hiram Maxim in 1883. This could fire over 600 rounds in sixty seconds. Thus, at the end of the nineteenth century armies already possessed the two weapons – quick-firing artillery and the machine gun – that were to dominate the battlefield in the First World War.

Belt-fed Maxim machine gun, 1888. The weapon was initially used mainly in colonial warfare, where it proved devastatingly effective against native warriors, and by 1914 most European armies were reasonably well equipped with weapons based on Maxim's design.

Nevertheless, in spite of developments in the range, accuracy and killing power of modern weapons, tactics remained broadly Napoleonic until nearly the end of the century. The battles of the Mexican-American War (1846–8) and the Crimean War (1853–6) were mostly fought in ways that would have been instantly recognisable to soldiers of previous generations. The British assault on the Redan strongpoint at Sevastopol (1855), where the attackers were cut to pieces by Russian rifle and artillery fire, gave a clear pointer to the way in which the conduct of battle was changing. Some were slow to learn the lesson: the frontal attacks of Prussian infantry at Gravelotte-St Privat (1870) sustained heavy losses at the hands of the French defenders. Similarly, the Turkish defenders at the siege of Plevna (1878), armed with modern rifles, took a fearful toll of attacking Russian forces.

MOLTKE AND THE RISE OF PRUSSIA

In the early nineteenth century, staffs tended to be small and trained staff officers were rare. In the Peninsular War the Duke of Wellington (1769–1852) relied principally on Sir George Murray (1772–1846), his Quarter-Master General, while the Austrian Army in Italy, 70,000 strong, had only 11 trained staff officers. The Prussian Army began the process of creating a modern staff system. Stung by their defeat at Napoleon's hands in 1806, the Prussians carried out a series of far-reaching military reforms, including the foundation of a War College (*Kriegsakademie*). Products of the *Kriegsakademie* were an elite band, rigorously trained in staff work: administration, logistics, mobilisation and the conduct of

Helmuth Karl Bernhard, Graf von Moltke (1800–91). Reactionary, militarist and intellectual, Moltke took his profession very seriously indeed. He wrote extensively on the subject of war, and through his exploitation of Prussia's general staff system and railway network secured decisive military victories in 1866 and 1870.

operations. This was very different from Napoleon's system, which had depended heavily on the excellence of Berthier as Chief of Staff. Another development was the cultivation of *Auftragstaktik*, a command culture in which subordinate leaders were encouraged to use their initiative in support of the general thrust of the Commander-in-Chief's plan. In the aftermath of Moltke's remarkable victories, other armies followed the Prussian staff model.

The greatest Prussian general of the nineteenth century, Helmuth von Moltke (1800–91), came through this system, specialising in the military role of railways. He was appointed chief in 1857 and under Moltke the General Staff truly came of age. The excellence of their staff work gave the

'The composition of the Prussian staff will in the next war constitute the most formidable element of superiority in favour of the Prussian Army.'

Baron Stoffel, French Military Attaché in Berlin, February 1868

In the face of improved weaponry, frontal assaults had become almost suicidal by the time of the Franco-Prussian War. At Gravelotte-St Privat (18 August 1870) the elite Prussian Guard Corps launched one such attack, only to lose 8,000 men in 20 minutes, without getting within a third of a mile of the French positions. Here, German soldiers throw themselves against the enemy lines at St Privat.

THE FRANCO-PRUSSIAN WAR, 1870–1

Formally, the Franco-Prussian War began over a German royal claimant to the Spanish throne who was unacceptable to Napoleon III; in reality, the Prussian Chancellor Bismarck took the opportunity to further his ambitions in Europe, aided by ham-fisted French diplomacy. The Prussians were supported by sizeable contingents from other German states, notably Saxony and Bavaria.

The chaotic nature of French mobilisation cost them dear. One senior officer was reduced to cabling to Paris in July 1870: 'Am in Belfort; can't find brigade; can't find commanding general; what must I do; don't know where my regiments are.' This state of affairs contrasted strongly with the smoothness and efficiency of the Prussian mobilisation, which allowed them to seize the initiative and drive towards Paris, seeking the defeat of the French field armies that would be bound to defend the national capital. Moltke commanded three armies, which operated on the principle of 'march divided, fight united'; he sought, if possible, to engage the French simultaneously frontally and on their flank.

Initial clashes at Spicheren and Wörth (or Fröschwiller) on 6 August went in the Germans' favour and the French retreated. Moving on Metz, there was more heavy fighting at Mars-la-Tour, Vionville and Rezonville (16 August) and Gravelotte-St Privat (18 August). Despite stubborn French opposition and tactical errors by the Prussians, the French under Marshal Achille Bazaine (1811–88) were encircled at Metz, which eventually capitulated in October.

Marshal Marie Edmé MacMahon's (1803–93) forces, which had been beaten at Wörth, regrouped at Chalons and then set out, accompanied by the Emperor, to relieve Bazaine at Metz. Operating near the frontier of neutral Belgium, MacMahon's options were severely limited. Moltke enveloped the French forces from the south, north and west, herding MacMahon into a bend of the River Meuse at Sedan and occupying the high ground. This prompted the French General August Ducrot to utter one of the immortal (and accurate) phrases in French military history: 'We are in a chamber pot, and tomorrow we shall be crapped upon.' Mercilessly pummelled by German artillery, on 2 September 1870 Napoleon III surrendered, and the Germans then advanced on Paris.

The Prussian victories at Metz and Sedan did not end the war. Neither were the Prussians always a model of efficiency; General Karl von Steinmetz, commander of 1st Army proved to be something of a liability. Yet in the campaign of 1870 Moltke's use of strategic envelopment, his concentration of superior forces at the decisive point, and his use of his forces to pin the enemy and sweep round their flank was masterly. Moltke established a pattern of operational art that influenced German and other armies into the twentieth century. However, superficial reading of this campaign suggested that rapid victory on land was possible. In 1914 and 1941 the Germans were to pay a heavy price for believing this dangerous fallacy.

Prussians a decisive advantage when Moltke led them to war against Austria (1866) and France (1870–1). In the 'Six Weeks War' of June–July 1866 Moltke's armies inflicted a decisive defeat on the Austrians at Sadowa (or Königgrätz). The Prussian Chancellor Otto von Bismarck (1815–98) secured terms that effectively excluded Austria from political influence in Germany, yet were sufficiently lenient to avoid embittering the defeated foe (indeed, Austria and Germany were to become allies within a few years). The 1866 war stands as a model of the use of force to achieve limited political objectives.

In theory, the French should have been a much tougher opponent. In 1870 the French Army was widely believed to be one of the best in Europe; as recently as 1859 it had beaten the Austrians in a war in Italy. Yet its command and staff work, including its mobilisation procedures, was grossly inferior to that of the Prussians. There is much to be said for the idea that the war was effectively decided before a shot was fired, by the speed and efficiency with which the Prussians and their allies from the other German states brought their forces to the battlefield. French troops fought bravely, and on several occasions seemed close to victory; but ultimately they lost the initial battles and their major armies were forced to capitulate at Metz and Sedan. The Emperor Napoleon III also surrendered at Sedan.

The opposing forces, 1870

Prussia	
180,000	first-line troops
355,000	reserves
10,600,000	male population aged 15–55
France	
370,000	first-line troops
292,000	reserves
400,000	national guards
10,900,000	male population aged 15–55

Moltke had fought a technically brilliant and essentially limited war, but he was unable to translate his victories into political success. Rather, they inspired a resurgence of the revolutionary spirit of the 1790s among the French. The new French Republic raised fresh armies to defend *la patrie* against the invader, *franc-tireurs* waged guerrilla warfare against the vulnerable German lines of communication and the frustrated Germans settled down to besiege Paris. This revival of total war led ultimately to a revolution in Paris in March 1871, which was bloodily suppressed by the French Army. By this time the war with Prussia was over, and the Prussian King had been proclaimed Emperor of Germany in the Hall of Mirrors in the palace of Versailles. In contrast to the peace of 1866, in May 1871 the Germans annexed the French provinces of Alsace and parts of Lorraine. This act was instrumental in ensuring that the semi-total war of 1870–1 served as the first act in a cycle of Franco-German conflicts that lasted down to 1945.

WARFARE BEYOND EUROPE

The partial revival of total war in Europe had been preceded by a major conflict on the other side of the Atlantic. In 1861 a long-standing dispute between the slave-owning South and the 'free soil' North erupted over the election of Abraham Lincoln as President of the United States of America. From the start the war was one of ideology, a combination of the question of 'States' Rights' – whether individual states could secede from the Union – and the survival or otherwise of 'the Peculiar Institution' of Black slavery. Although both the North and the newly founded Confederate States of America initially believed that the war would be won quickly, neither side managed to deliver a decisive blow. The odds were stacked

'If destruction be our lot we must ourselves be its author and founder. As a nation of free men we must live through all time or die by suicide.'

Abraham Lincoln, 1858

William Tecumseh Sherman (1820–91) never commanded his armies in a major battle, yet is generally regarded as one of the most successful generals of the American Civil War. Introverted and nervous in manner, he was a man of the highest personal principles who tried to end the war as quickly and cheaply as possible at a time when the Confederacy was militarily defeated, yet still refused to make peace. His 'march to the sea' left an indelible impression on Georgia and the Carolinas, and to the present day his memory is detested throughout the South. (Library of Congress)

against the South, whose economic and human resources were vastly inferior to the North. However, it had some factors in its favour, including the vastness of the Confederacy – it was about the size of European Russia – the skill of its armies, and the belief that Northern will to fight was questionable. Those factors led the Southern States to believe that they had a good chance of forcing Washington to recognise their independence.

In the event the Confederacy made Herculean efforts to make the best use of its scant resources. Conscription was employed from April 1862 and about 900,000 men served in its forces. In its final days the South even freed its slaves and attempted to conscript them. But the North fielded 2,210,000 soldiers without resorting to large-scale compulsion. The Union out-built as well as out-fought the Confederacy. The numerous, well-equipped Northern troops (including many Black volunteers) who overran the Confederate heartlands in 1864–5 contrasted sharply with the ragged scarecrows on the other side, many of whom did not even possess the famous grey uniform.

The American Civil War was ultimately decided by attrition. Battles such as Shiloh (April 1862) and Gettysburg (July 1863) confirmed the pattern of European clashes – that a combination of Industrial Revolution weapons and quasi-Napoleonic tactics resulted in large butcher's bills. The premier Confederate general, Robert E. Lee (1807–70), pursued a strategy of carrying the conflict to the enemy and quickly demonstrated that he was a master of mobile warfare. Yet even his victories (such as Chancellorsville in May 1863) were costly: it has been argued that he bled the Southern armies to death and would have been better off adopting a more defensive posture. In 1864–5, under the overall command of Ulysses S. Grant (1822–85), the North pursued an attritional strategy. The US Navy was already enforcing a blockade of the Confederate coast, and Grant attacked the Confederacy from a number of directions. There were two main thrusts. In Virginia, Grant grappled with Lee in a series of bloody, attritional and inconclusive battles that none the less fixed Lee's army and forced him back to entrenchments at Petersburg. Meanwhile, General William Tecumseh Sherman (1820–91) marched through Georgia and the Carolinas, deliberately laying waste the countryside with the aim of shattering the Confederacy's will to fight. Sherman's march not only destroyed scarce resources but also severely damaged Confederate morale. Although Sherman's men did not as a rule harm the civilian population, he brought a species of total war to the Southern states. By April 1865 the economy of the Confederacy was in ruins, large areas were occupied by Northern troops, and the slaves had been freed.

When the Confederates' remaining field armies capitulated, few in the South had any taste for continuing resistance.

Although European states did not participate in any conflict on the scale of the American Civil War in the 100 years from 1815 to 1914, throughout the nineteenth century their armies and navies saw frequent action in colonial 'small wars'. These were nothing new. The eighteenth century had been marked by intense colonial rivalry between France and Britain, leading to the capture of France's North American territories in the Seven Years War (1756–63) and frequent clashes in India. The future Duke of Wellington cut his teeth as an independent commander in India, destroying the army of the Indian princes of Scinde and Berar at Assaye in 1803. However, colonial expansion entered a new phase of intensity in the nineteenth century. In 1830 France embarked on a campaign to conquer Algeria, in part to restore national pride after defeat in the Napoleonic Wars. As a general rule, however, until about 1870 European governments were reluctant to take on responsibility for further tracts of land. Conflict was often propelled by great trading organisations like the British East India Company or the initiatives of local military commanders or colonial governors. Such a man was General Louis Faidherbe, who had two periods as French governor of Senegal between 1854 and 1863.

'We are not only fighting hostile armies, but a hostile people, and must make old and young, rich and poor, feel the hard hand of war.'

General William Tecumseh Sherman, 1865

In the latter part of the century national governments came to have an increasing interest in colonial expansion. By the 1880s the government in Paris was not only condoning the expansionist policies of Faidherbe's successors but was also actually funding them. The Indian Mutiny of 1857–9 led to the British government taking over administration of India from the East India Company. 'Privatised' imperialism was losing ground to a 'nationalised' variety. Simultaneously, Russia was busy expanding its empire in Asia, and the United States was expanding at the expense of the Native American peoples and Mexico. At the very end of the century, it also acquired Cuba and the Philippines from Spain.

The popular image of colonial warfare in the nineteenth century is of well-armed European (or American) troops massacring native peoples armed with crude and primitive weapons. This has some basis in fact; the Battle of Omdurman in September 1898, in which a British-led force inflicted 25,000 casualties on a Dervish army for the loss of only 500 men, is the classic example. Similarly, many of the campaigns of the US Army on the Western frontier had the character of police actions. However, imperialist armies did not always have it their own way. Before about 1850 the technological advantage enjoyed by European forces was not always great. The British had two particularly tough struggles against well-armed, properly trained and disciplined Sikh forces in 1845–6 and 1848–9. The introduction of modern weapons into European armies from the mid-century onwards placed Asian and African armies at an ever-greater disadvantage on the battlefield, although not necessarily in guerrilla warfare. However, as the British defeat at the hands of the Zulus at Isandlwana (January 1879), and the Sioux's destruction of Custer's force at the Little Big Horn three years earlier demonstrated, given the right conditions native peoples could still win battles. Indeed, right at the end of the period the army of Ethiopia, equipped with some modern weapons, inflicted a crushing defeat on an Italian force at Adowa (March

1896). This guaranteed Ethiopian independence until Mussolini's forces conquered the country in the 1930s.

Moreover, logistics, terrain and climate hampered Western attempts to conquer native peoples. For the Ashanti campaign of 1873 the British had to impress vast numbers of Africans to carry supplies for the fighting troops. Although the British had some military success, the impact of sickness, casualties, and logistic problems forced their commander, General Garnet Wolseley (1833–1913), to agree to a compromise peace before withdrawing to his base – and this had been an exceptionally carefully planned expedition. This was often the pattern of colonial warfare – Western forces occupying bases and peripheral 'pacified' regions, often on the coast, while native peoples conducted guerrilla warfare from their positions in the interior. Given resolve and good leadership, native fighters could wage effective irregular campaigns. The Algerian Amir Abd el-Kader, with a force of 50,000, fought the French from the 1830s until 1847; at the end, the French were deploying nearly 110,000 men in Algeria. In central Asia, the guerrilla leader Yakub Beg defied Russian forces from the 1840s to the 1870s.

Much of the Western success in colonial warfare was thanks to a policy of divide and conquer. Many 'Western' armies in fact consisted of relatively small numbers of European troops and large numbers of indigenous troops under white officers. The Belgian King Leopold II's *Force Publique*, with which he ruled the Congo, consisted of 6,000 African soldiers under white officers (and some NCOs). The French raised substantial bodies of troops in west and north Africa, and elsewhere, while the security of the British Raj in India ultimately rested on the bayonets of its Indian sepoys. Only the fact that substantial bodies of Asian troops stayed loyal to the British, notably the Sikh regiments and units of Gurkhas from Nepal, enabled the British to contain and then crush the Indian Mutiny (1857–9). The Mutiny in fact took on something of the character of a nationalist revolt. In the long term the emergence of nationalism among colonial peoples was to spell the end of Western empires. Indeed, many of the liberation movements of the twentieth century were to look to the struggles of the colonial period for inspiration.

The impact of navies on colonial warfare should not be ignored. Naval power made the maintenance of imperial possessions far from the homeland possible. Some colonies were acquired largely for naval purposes: Aden, a coaling station for the Royal Navy *en route* to India, is a good example. Sailors played a vital role in many colonial campaigns, using warships in support of land forces in coastal areas, and gunboats in riverine warfare, and deploying sailors and marines to fight on land. Not surprisingly, ships of two of Europe's major naval powers played a leading role in colonial warfare. The Royal Navy carried out numerous missions, of which bombarding the Taku Forts in China in 1859 and 1860 were not untypical, while sailors from two gunboats were the first French troops to enter Timbuktu in 1893. The fledgling German Navy was crucial in the foundation of the German Empire in west and east Africa in the 1880s, while in the following decade Portuguese and *Force Publique* gunboats were used to good effect in Mozambique and the Congo respectively.

Colonial warfare had several important consequences for Western forces. In an era in which there were few major wars, it gave Western armies and navies a virtually continuous diet of action and allowed new technology (notably the machine gun) to be tested in battle. In some ways it had a malign influence, because concentration on small wars did little to prepare armies for significant conventional conflicts, as the United States Army found during the American Civil War (1861–5), and the British in the First and Second Boer Wars (1880–1 and 1899–1902). In contrast, many of the methods evolved in colonial warfare underpinned British and French counter-insurgency techniques in the twentieth century. A British officer, C.E. Callwell, published *Small Wars: their Principles and Practice* in 1896, and many of his points – the recognition that strategy had a political as well as a military dimension, for instance – had a distinctly modern ring.

'Whatever happens, we have got The Maxim gun and they have not.'

Hilaire Belloc, 'The Modern Traveller', (1898)

NAVAL WARFARE

Steam propulsion was applied to water transport as early as 1775, and by 1813 the American Robert Fulton had built the first ever steam-powered warship. However, it took decades for the sailing ship finally to be ousted from its position of prominence. This was not simply the consequence of blind conservatism. Paddle wheels were dangerously exposed to enemy fire, although the development of the steam screw or propeller in the 1830s marked a major improvement, as did the introduction of a more efficient engine. Worse was the short range of steamships, which could undertake long journeys only if they were able to put into port to take on more coal – which was a spur to the acquisition of territories overseas.

In the 1830s the French developed the Paixhans naval explosive shell, which was much more destructive than the solid shot used previously. Using shells of this type, in November 1853 Russian ships commanded by Admiral Nakhimov destroyed a Turkish flotilla at Sinope. This action underlined the extent to which technology had changed naval warfare since Trafalgar, but even more far-reaching developments were close at hand. In 1859 the French launched *La Gloire*, a wooden-hulled 'ironclad' warship, which was quickly followed by the Royal Navy's all-iron HMS *Warrior*. This ship, although steam driven, was still equipped with masts and sails. At this stage, ships mounted broadsides – in other words, guns were lined up along ships' sides. The introduction of large weapons such as the American 11-inch Dahlgren gun marked the replacement of the broadside by smaller numbers of more powerful weapons. The construction in the American Civil War of the USS *Monitor*, a freakish armoured vessel that deployed two heavy guns in a revolving turret, also pointed the way to the future of warships.

The advances made by warships over the next four decades were even more dramatic than military developments on land. The armoured, steam-powered warships with revolving turrets mounting heavy guns that fired explosive shells were to the ships of Nelson's day as a modern Tornado fighter-bomber is to a Sopwith Camel. The Battle of Lissa in July 1866, between Austrian and Italian ironclad fleets, was the last Nelsonic close-range fleet action (indeed, the ram was freely used). In future, however, battles came to be fought at ever-longer ranges.

News of the construction of the French ironclad La Gloire *caused consternation in Britain, whose relationship with France had deteriorated after the Crimean War. The result was HMS* Warrior, *an iron-hulled vessel of 9,000 tons launched in December 1860. Mounting a mixture of 110- and 68-pounder breech-loading rifled guns, and protected by a main belt of armour 4.5 inches thick,* Warrior *and her sister ship* Black Prince *were the most powerful warships then in existence. This is HMS* Warrior. *(Royal Naval Museum, 1987/403 (207))*

As guns and ammunition improved, so did ships' armour. Yet big ships were not invulnerable. This was graphically demonstrated by the event that precipitated the 1898 Spanish-American War, the sinking in Havana harbour of the battleship USS *Maine*. Although the theory was never satisfactorily proved, the US Navy blamed the disaster on a mine. Whether or not this was in fact the case, big, expensive ships were becoming increasingly vulnerable to small and cheap weapons, the torpedo and the mine, which could be fired or laid by submarines or small surface vessels.

By 1898, warfare had changed out of all recognition from that of a century earlier. The French Revolution had heralded the mobilisation of the masses and the conscription of ideas, bringing about Clausewitz's 'remarkable trinity' of government, army and people, producing total war. The Industrial Revolution had brought about advances in weaponry, improving range, accuracy and killing power, and the invention of the railway and the electric telegraph were no less important in the development of war. The Industrial Revolution also ushered in important social and political changes that were to have profound effects on the conduct of war. For those who had eyes to see, the preconditions for Armageddon were firmly in place.

T W O

THE ROAD TO STALEMATE, 1899–1914

S T E P H E N B A D S E Y

THE NEW CENTURY

As New Year's Eve was celebrated on 31 December 1899, despite all the political, social and technological changes of the previous 100 years the world was very much as it had been for centuries, hoping for peace and partly at war. But there was no war in Europe, as there had been in 1799. To prevent a major conflict the later nineteenth-century European powers had deliberately constructed an impossible puzzle made out of two rival sets of interlocking alliances. In 1879 the two empires of Germany and Austria-Hungary had allied together, joined by Italy in 1881. They were matched in 1894 by one of the most unnatural alliances in history: Republican France with Imperial Russia. The last piece fell into place when in 1904 Britain agreed to an 'Entente Cordiale' (literally a 'friendly understanding') with France, and in 1907 with Russia. The basis of this scheme was that each alliance would support its members – the 'Triple Alliance' of Germany, Austria-Hungary and Italy against the 'Triple Entente' of France, Russia and Great Britain – so that an attack on any one major power by another would produce a general European war. In Britain's case this was not a formal alliance, but it was rapidly followed by military staff talks, so that French battle plans had a role designated for the British Army which it was expected to fill (much to the surprise in 1914 of most of the British Cabinet, who were completely unaware of this commitment). Although no one knew it at the time, the twentieth century would be the first for several hundred years in which the British and French would never be officially at war with each other. The Italians were less secure in their alliance than the other major powers, and in 1914 they were to stand neutral.

Having constructed this dangerous balancing act, Europe managed it successfully for a generation, from the end of the Russo-Turkish War in 1878 to the First World War in 1914. Not only was there no war in Europe, there was also no war between the major European powers

For all the brutality of their battles, the peace conferences that followed the wars of the nineteenth century were civilised affairs. Here, Austrian and Prussian leaders negotiate an end to the war of 1866. Austria-Hungary, which fought alongside Prussia against Denmark in 1864, quickly rebuilt its relations with its northern neighbour and concluded a new alliance with Germany in 1879. (BPK, Berlin)

elsewhere in the world over their colonies, although there were plenty of war scares. The British, still expanding the largest of the colonial empires, faced possible war with France over their confrontation in southern Sudan in the 'Fashoda Incident' in 1898; with the United States over the frontier of Alaska in the same year; with Russia over Japan in 1904; and with Germany at almost regular intervals from 1897 to 1911, thanks in part to the dangerously flamboyant pronouncements of Kaiser Wilhelm II. Despite this, the partition of much of the world among the great empires in this period was marked by straight lines on the map through negotiated settlements and only rarely by fighting.

Instead, the Europeans (and the United States, which went to war with Spain in 1898) successfully exported their conflicts. There was effectively a continuous state of war somewhere throughout the world between European colonial powers (many of their troops recruited locally or despatched from other colonies) and their native opponents. Rarely did this relatively low level of violence directly affect European civil development in the colonies, or become significant enough to be called a 'war' in the history books. Between 1898 and 1902 the British fought in significant campaigns in the Sudan, Chitral, Malakand, Asante, Benin, Matabeleland and Betchuanaland, and as part of the international force to relieve the siege of Peking during the Boxer Uprising of 1900; in addition, there was the daily business of policing the British Empire. But some of these small-scale wars became notorious for their brutality, particularly in cases where the level of technological disparity meant that the war amounted to genocide, such as the near-extermination of the Herero people of German South-West Africa between 1904 and 1907 by German colonial forces.

THE FUTURE OF WAR

The nineteenth century had been the age of steam; the twentieth century was to be the age of electricity, in war as in every other aspect of society. At the start of the century there were only two environments in which war could be fought – on land and at sea – as there had been for all previous history. The invention of the diesel engine in 1901 made the ocean-going submarine practical, and the Wright brothers' first manned powered flight took place in December 1903, so introducing a third and fourth environment. By the end of the century there were six environments: on land, at sea, under the sea, in the air, in space and in the ether of the electromagnetic datasphere.

In 1914 one of the problems facing strategists seeking to understand what a major war in Europe might be like was the fact that the system of alliances had in a sense worked too well. The revolutionary changes in warfare during the nineteenth century had been dramatic enough. But

The French Canon de 75 Modèle 1897, or '75', had a range of over 4 miles and is generally regarded as the pioneer of modern field artillery. Its hydro-pneumatic recoil system allowed a rapid rate of fire, and its 16-pound shrapnel shell was lethal against troops caught in the open. Here a British medical officer interprets his Hippocratic oath rather freely by sighting a 75 during the Battle of Armentières, October 1914. (RMAS Collection)

The Short Magazine Lee-Enfield rifle was a superb weapon, and was used successfully as late as the 1980s by Afghan tribesmen during the Soviet intervention in Afghanistan. Here a British sergeant uses it as the prop for a mirror, allowing him to observe activity in the enemy's trench system during the First World War. However, given the casual attitude of the men around him, the photograph was probably posed some distance behind the front line. (IWM Q2076)

between 1878 and 1914 further developments in warfare made differences that could be guessed and theorised about, but not tested without a major war. The jump from field armies of 100,000 troops at the start of the nineteenth century to the 300,000 of the Franco-Prussian War (and more than a million Prussians and their allies of the North German Confederation under arms) had been dramatic enough. But in 1914 France, Germany, Austria-Hungary and Russia each mobilised armies of between 3 and 6 million men. The changes also included an entire new generation of weapons that would remain in service throughout the first half of the twentieth century, and would not be entirely obsolete even at its end. Among the new weapons were quick-firing artillery such as the French 75mm field gun of 1897, which could fire up to fifteen rounds a minute in an emergency, and the German 150mm field howitzer of 1913. The belt-fed Maxim machine gun with a sustained rate of fire of 250 rounds a minute appeared in 1883, invented by Sir Hiram Maxim, an American who took British citizenship; and the 1908 pattern was adopted by almost all armies (in British service as the 'Vickers-Maxim'). Bolt-action magazine rifles included the German 1898 pattern Mauser, the American 1903 pattern Springfield and the British 1907 pattern Mark III Short Magazine Lee-Enfield (the 'SMLE' or 'Smellie'). In their famous 'mad minute', fully trained British troops armed with the SMLE could fire 15 aimed rounds out to 600 yards.

THE GERMANS AND THE *VERNICHTUNGSSCHLACHT*

From the time of Frederick the Great in the eighteenth century, the Prussian Army had a reputation for the speed of its campaigning and the extreme violence of its battlefield attack. The decisive defeat of Prussia by Napoleon in the Jena campaign of 1806, which led to six years of Prussian subordination to France, only confirmed Prussian commanders in their view that a seamless and continuous campaign of manoeuvre resulting in a single decisive victory represented the highest form of military achievement. This argument was codified by Clausewitz in his writings as the *Vernichtungsschlacht* (literally the Battle of Annihilation), in which the highest objective in war was to attack and destroy the main enemy army.

The concept of the *Vernichtungsschlacht* was taken a stage further by Field Marshal Graf Helmuth von Moltke ('the Elder'), Chief of Staff of the Prussian Army, in his victories (under the titular command of the King of Prussia) in the Austro-Prussian War of 1866 and the Franco-Prussian War of 1870–1. At the time the prevailing military orthodoxy was for 'manoeuvre on interior lines', a concept popularised by the Swiss strategist Antoine Henri Jomini from his analysis of Napoleon's campaigns, whereby victory came from manoeuvring an attacking army between two enemy armies and defeating them separately before they could combine. Moltke also derived his concept of 'masses of manoeuvre' from Napoleon, but as analysed by Clausewitz, and produced the radically different approach of a strategy of envelopment, whereby one army would engage the enemy, and another join in from behind the enemy flank or rear in an attempt to surround them.

This concept of manoeuvring to surround the enemy provided an elegant solution to the later nineteenth-century problem of how to take the offensive when improved firepower was making defence with fewer troops practical. The same improvements in firepower meant that it was possible to stretch lines of troops very thinly in order to surround the enemy, and then give the latter the problem of attacking in order to break out of the trap. This enveloping manoeuvre was first demonstrated by Moltke at the Battle of Königgrätz in July 1866 against the Austrians. The style became known as the *Kesselschlacht* (a 'Kessel' is a spherical iron cooking-pot or kettle) or 'Cauldron Battle'.

The final adoption of the *Kesselschlacht* leading to the *Vernichtungsschlacht* as the standard German operational method came under Field Marshal Alfred Graf von Schlieffen (1833–1913), Chief of the German General Staff until 1905 and still influential on the 'Schlieffen Plan' until his death in 1913. Von Schlieffen advocated envelopment on both flanks, supposedly based on an analysis of Hannibal's victory over the Romans at the Battle of Cannae in 216 BC (although von Schlieffen never bothered to read the account of Cannae by the Roman historian Livy). The double envelopment or 'Cannae manoeuvre' advocated by von Schlieffen remained the preferred German operational method throughout the first half of the twentieth century, being most obviously demonstrated during 'Operation Barbarossa', the attack on the Soviet Union in 1941.

One very real argument to emerge from these new mass armies with their increased firepower was that technology had genuinely made war impossible. A controversial but very well-known book published in 1897 by a retired financier of Russian citizenship and Polish nationality, Ivan (or Jan) S. Bloch (1836–1902), *Modern Weapons and Modern War* argued that the next war would be long and inconclusive, largely because of a tactical stalemate produced in particular by massed rifle fire. Both Bloch and the British pacifist Norman Angell (1874–1967), in his book *The Great Illusion* (1910), also argued that European war would be financially, socially and politically disastrous for any country waging it.

The normal size of national field armies in peacetime, although larger than at any time in the past, was only a fraction of their fully mobilised

'The enemy front should not be the objective of the main attack. Neither the main concentration of force nor the reserves should be used against the enemy front. Only the smashing of the enemy's flanks is essential. Annihilation is complete if the enemy is also attacked from the rear.'

Field Marshal Alfred Graf von Schlieffen, Cannae *(1903)*

war strength. The French Army, for example, numbered 856,000 men compared to a fully mobilised strength of almost 4 million. In the absence of any mobilisation before 1914, it was genuinely difficult to imagine what armies of millions equipped with weapons might do on the battlefield. Armies could train or hold exercises for their headquarters staffs or for smaller numbers of troops in peacetime, but an actual full mobilisation was impossible to test. Theorists like Bloch and Angell were not ignored before 1914. Their ideas were part of a general mix that produced in many politicians and military leaders (and also some philosophers and important cultural figures) two beliefs that were not necessarily opposite. The first was that any European war between the two great alliances would be a massive upheaval, 'Armageddon', the apocalyptic final battle between good and evil as described in the Bible. The other was that the war would be short and successful, famously 'over by Christmas'. The concept of battle in 1899 was still very much that of Waterloo (or Trafalgar), the single climactic clash fought out in a day, violent and bloody but also decisive in its effects. A firm distinction was made between on the one hand campaigning to fight 'battles', which was seen as fluid and fast-moving in its results, and on the other embarking on sieges, which were seen as ponderous and slow to produce results as they had been for centuries. Indeed, one of the arguments used to show that any future war had to be short and decisive was the belief that Europe could not survive any other kind of conflict. Later in the century, similar arguments would be used to argue that nuclear wars could never be fought.

As envisaged in 1899, and practised in their annual field exercises by the Germans and French in particular, major battles would still closely resemble those of the Franco-Prussian War. Solid columns of infantry would march forward, although owing to increased gun and rifle ranges they would start to deploy into lines when perhaps more than a mile from the enemy (or where they believed the enemy to be), sending forward swarms of skirmishers. Gradually in the decade before 1914, most countries realised that the effects of firepower were so great that instead of a solid line supporting the skirmishers as in the nineteenth century, the whole infantry formation would become one thick skirmish line. Most armies also recognised the advantages of digging small scrapes or trenches when defending. But tactics remained linear, and an infantry battalion in most armies consisted entirely of riflemen, usually with two Maxim guns and no other direct fire support. Artillery remained horse drawn, and increasingly faced the problem of keeping up with the infantry to provide firepower when the horses and men had become highly vulnerable to infantry weapons. Techniques of indirect fire were rather dimly understood: artillery was hidden behind hills or in cover so that gunners could not see their target but directed their shooting through observers. This uncertain system took a long time to arrange, and although used for sieges it was seen as unsuitable for a fast-moving battle. The emphasis was on the moment when the enemy was worn down by fire, and the infantry could charge forward with the bayonet. To complete the victory, horsed cavalry would also charge against enemy infantry, cavalry or guns. Cavalry also retained its value in scouting or raiding, although in most

A fanciful vision of how traction engines might be used against the Boers during the South African War. The reality was more prosaic, such vehicles being used to tow supply wagons in areas where railways did not run.

armies cavalry carried short carbines rather than rifles, and neglected dismounted fighting.

The major problem facing armies was that although their potential size and firepower had undergone a major increase, technology had not yet provided for two other critical needs. One of these was for battlefield communications. Cities or fixed military bases were connected by telephone cables or by wireless radio sets transmitting in Morse code, but only early experimental radio sets accompanied field armies. Similarly, although the automobile made its first appearance in the 1880s, and all armies made some use of lorries and staff cars, practical cross-country vehicles did not yet exist; and nor did the infrastructure to support them, everything from good roads to petrol stations being lacking. There was great military interest in aviation, with the value of aircraft for spotting the enemy being obvious, and by 1914 all major armies had some kind of air wing, but the technology remained very underdeveloped. Despite their twentieth-century size and firepower, once they had left their railheads armies in 1914 moved at the speed of the marching man and communicated at the speed of the galloping horse, exactly like the armies of a century before. Under these circumstances, major wars fought outside

Europe between 1899 and 1914 took on considerable importance not just for their outcome, but for anyone trying to predict the nature of the next great European war.

The idea of a 'long peace' before the outbreak of the First World War is something of a myth. Between 1899 and 1914 there were two sizeable wars, the Boer War (1899–1902) and the Russo-Japanese War (1904–5), plus the First and Second Balkan Wars of 1912 and 1913 (which came too close to the start of the First World War to be properly studied outside the countries involved). Both the Boer War and the Russo-Japanese War were fought by major powers – Britain and Russia respectively – that were regarded as being European at least in a military sense. Both wars were also fought outside Europe at the end of extremely long supply lines. In the case of the British, most forces had to be sent by sea from Britain to South Africa before embarking on a campaign in a region itself almost as large as Europe. The Russians fought their war at the far end of the world's longest railway, the single-track Trans-Siberian from St Petersburg to Vladivostok (5,400 miles, begun in 1891 and only completed while the war was being fought). In both cases the enemy was not European, but had many attributes associated with European standards of warfighting and weaponry. The Boers (literally 'farmers') of South Africa were descendants of earlier settlers chiefly from the Netherlands, and they were seen as comparable to homesteaders in Canada, Australia or the American Midwest. They were also equipped with modern rifles and artillery, mainly supplied by Germany and France, that were at least as good as those of the British. Since the 1880s the Japanese had sought to modernise their country and its armed forces, consciously basing themselves on what they saw as the best European models: their army was originally trained by the Germans and their navy by the British. They also had arms and equipment as good as those of the Russians, if not better.

THE BOER WAR

The opposing forces, 1899–1902

Britain
Initially 27,000 men,
Eventually 256,000 regulars (including reservists), 45,000 militia, 56,500 Imperial Yeomanry and Volunteers, 89,500 colonial/locally raised police and troops.

Transvaal and Orange Free State
83,000 males of military age, virtually all of whom were eventually involved in the fighting.

The Boer War (or Second Anglo-Boer War, also known at the time as simply 'the South African War') of 1899–1902 appeared to contemporaries to be two almost separate wars, a European-style conflict with a colonial one succeeding it. The outbreak of hostilities resulted from tension between the expansionist plans of British imperialist politicians and financiers and the desire of the two Boer republics of the Orange Free State and the Transvaal (or 'South African Republic'), where sizeable goldfields had been discovered, to be left alone. Political demands that would have effectively meant surrender to the British were rejected by the Boers in June 1899. With forces already totalling about 27,000 in southern Africa, the British then mobilised and despatched by sea an army of 47,000 men under General Sir Redvers Buller (1839–1908), by far the largest British expeditionary army for a century.

The Boer military system was based on the 'commando', a term meaning both a man and a military unit that would become a twentieth-century byword for enterprising military skill. The commando laws required all men to serve as citizen soldiers in irregular units under elected officers, and

The Boer struggle was a genuine people's war. Here three generations of South African farmers pose for the camera. Their ages, from left to right, are 65, 15 and 43 years.

to provide their own horses and weapons. The two republics between them put about 60,000 mounted men into the field at the start of the war. True to their ideological beliefs, both sides were keen to keep this 'a white man's war'. The British did not send Indian troops to South Africa to fight, although by the war's end volunteers had come from most other parts of the empire, including Australia and Canada. Black Africans were employed throughout the war as scouts and pioneers and for other purposes, but arming non-Europeans to fight was undertaken only with reluctance.

While the bulk of the British Army under Buller was still on the high seas, the Boer republics seized the initiative by declaring war on 9 October 1899. They hoped that a quick offensive by all commandos would spark a general uprising by Boers living under British rule in the rest of southern Africa, and would allow them to capture deep-sea ports, including Cape Town, thus preventing the main British Army from ever landing. This plan only half succeeded. The Boer attack disrupted British strategy, causing problems with supply and horses that were not corrected for several months. But the commandos lacked the organisation to mount a major offensive, and instead turned separately towards the major towns close to their frontiers. This led to three sieges of British garrisons trapped in Kimberley, in Ladysmith and far to the north in Mafeking.

On arrival in South Africa, Buller had no choice but to split his forces in an attempt to relieve both Kimberley and Ladysmith. Other than a lack of

THE SECOND ANGLO-BOER WAR, 1899–1902

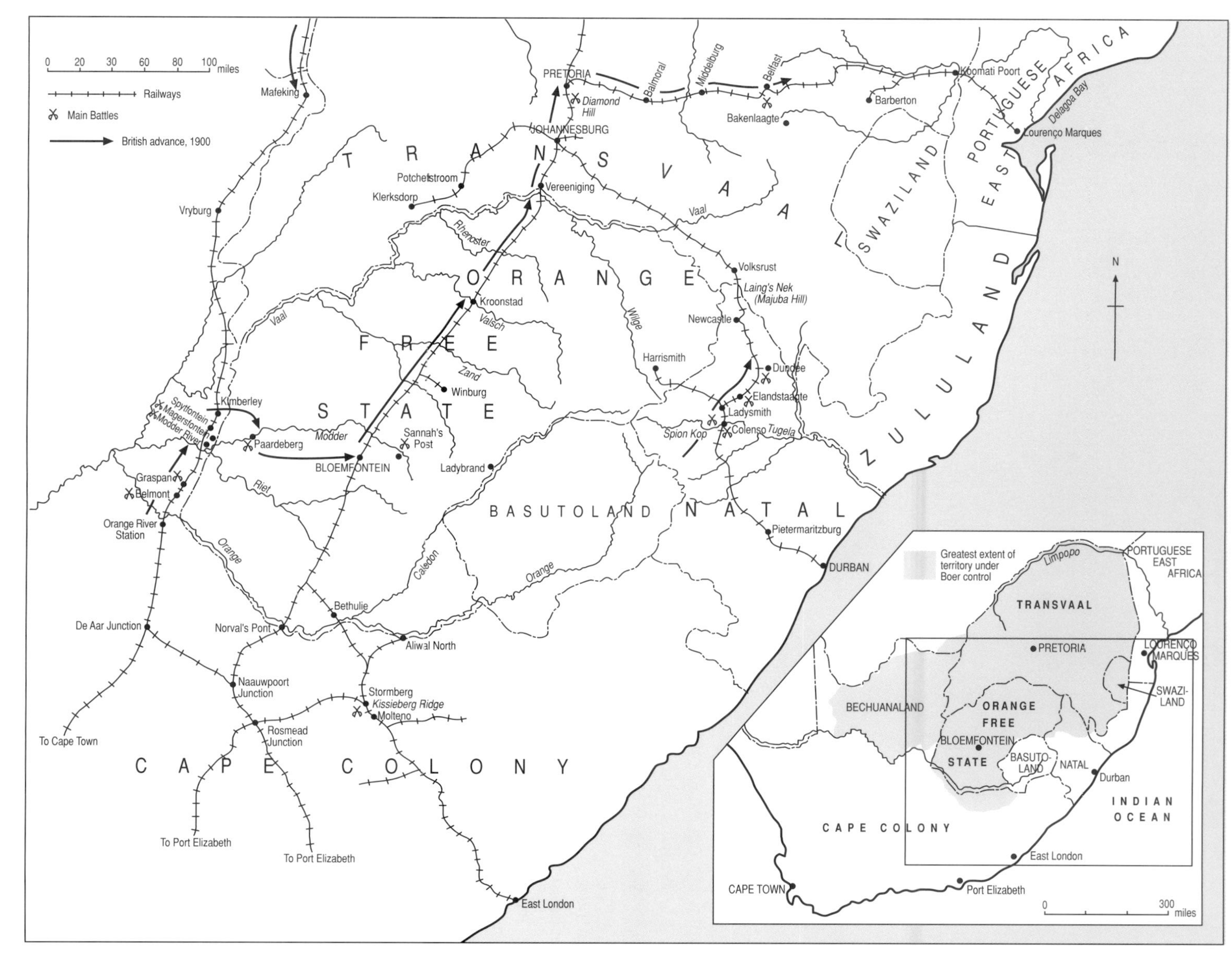

horses and wagon transport, which tied them to the railways, the main British problem was that up on the Veldt – the grassland plateau of the southern African interior – the clear air and open country meant that the Boers could see to shoot at 2,000 yards, virtually the maximum range of their rifles. This unique problem was coupled with the Boers' good understanding of the ground and a traditional style of fighting (developed against charging foot-warriors such as the Zulu) of digging concealed trenches and ambushing the enemy. Early battles generally went the British way, but suggested that the Boers were not going to be simply brushed aside by the mighty British Empire.

On 28 November the western British forces advancing towards Kimberley suffered a major defeat at Modder River, attempting a frontal dawn attack with inadequate preparation that got caught in marching column too close to the concealed Boer trenches. This shock defeat set the pattern for three more defeats of three separate British armies in quick succession throughout 'Black Week': the battles of Stormberg in Cape Colony on 10 December, Magersfontein north of Modder River the next day, and then Buller himself defeated at Colenso on 15 December while attempting to relieve Ladysmith. In each case poorly prepared British advances ran into deadly Boer rifle fire from well-concealed positions. The same devastating Boer firepower was seen in Buller's defeat at the Battle of Spion Kop on 23 January 1900, commemorated in the name of the main stand in more than one British football ground.

The shock of Black Week went all round the world. Although the total of British dead from all three battles was only about 380 men, what mattered was the defeat of modern European-style armies by apparently untrained irregulars. This was the Boer high point, but the British did not respond by offering peace, deciding instead that a swift victory was politically essential. Although Buller remained in command opposite Ladysmith, Field Marshal Lord Roberts (1832–1914) was sent out to take overall command in South Africa, together with reinforcements. Roberts in turn took charge of the western forces opposite Kimberley, drastically increasing the number of horsed troops and sacrificing the organisation of his transport system in order to get enough wagons together to get away from the railway. The cavalry, who were encouraged to carry rifles to give them better firepower, were also concentrated together under Roberts, along with volunteer riders from Britain (the 'Imperial Yeomanry') and around the empire.

Roberts' ensuing campaign was certainly spectacular, and one of the most remarkable examples of military manoeuvre in the twentieth century. Starting in February 1900 he outflanked the opposing Boers to relieve Kimberley, and then drove them back along the main railway in one battle after another, capturing the Orange Free State capital of Bloemfontein on 13 March, Johannesburg on 31 May and the Transvaal capital of Pretoria on 5 June. In the process, Buller relieved the siege of Ladysmith on 28 February, while Mafeking was also relieved on 16 May. Roberts made no attempt to hold other towns or the wider countryside in his advance, which was governed by the political need to reach the two Boer capitals quickly. His supply system failed under the strain, and a decisive final battle against the commandos always eluded him. By the time Pretoria was captured the

'Black Week', 10–17 December 1899

Battle	British losses			Boer losses killed and wounded
	killed	wounded	prisoners	
Stormberg 10 Dec	135		600	negligible
Magersfontein 11 Dec	220	690	–	297
Colenso 15 Dec	143	756	220	27

'The week which extended from December 10th to December 17th 1899 was the blackest one known during our generation, and the most disastrous for British arms during this century.'

Arthur Conan Doyle,
The Great Boer War
(1900)

British forces in southern Africa were themselves on the verge of collapse from disease, horse-sickness and supply problems, and needed months to recover their full fighting ability. More British soldiers died from disease in the war than from enemy action. Nevertheless, having annexed both republics to the British Empire, in November Roberts announced that the war was won and went home to a hero's welcome.

The Anglo-Boer War, 11 October 1899–31 May 1902: the cost

British
7,582 killed/died of wounds; 13,139 died of disease; 31,429 wounded injured/prisoners

Financial cost: £222 million, of which £3 million was compensation paid to the Boers for destroyed farms. The level of income tax in Britain almost doubled as a result of the war.

Boers
4,000 (estimated) killed/died of wounds; 33,000 (estimated) prisoners; 20,000 (estimated) civilians died of disease and neglect in concentration camps.

Most European military observers, including the British themselves, agreed with Roberts' assessment and focused their attention almost entirely on this period of set-piece battles and manoeuvre. But in fact the nature of the Boer War had changed even before Roberts left South Africa, and fighting continued for another eighteen months. About 20,000 Boers refused to accept peace, and instead adopted a guerrilla strategy based on their high mobility on horseback and on support from the farms and homesteads of the Veldt. The British resorted first to farm burning, and then to relocating Boer and African women and children in tented camps – the infamous 'concentration camps' in which disease and squalor were rife, and in which many died from disease and neglect.

By early 1901 British strategy had become based on blockhouses of stone and corrugated iron placed along the main railway lines, which absorbed over 50,000 British troops and 16,000 Africans. Using these as fixed points, rifle-armed, mounted British 'columns' of about brigade size (themselves looking and acting very much like commandos) swept the countryside in attempts to trap the last remaining Boers. Peace was negotiated at Vereeniging on 30 May 1902, with the Boers agreeing to absorption into the British Empire in return for moderate terms. The best of the Boer commando leaders, such as Christiaan de Wet and Koos de la Rey, eluded capture to the very end. The British victory had required 448,435 troops of which just over half were regulars from Britain itself, and the rest volunteers from Britain and its empire.

The experience of the Boer War suggested that in the future battles would be fought by troops dispersed and entrenched on battlefields many miles wide, but also that battle would be dominated by long-range rifle fire and that mobility on horseback would be important. The British in the war's aftermath worked to introduce reforms into their army, including equipping all their cavalry with rifles rather than carbines, making them unique in Europe. The British declined to introduce conscription, but did introduce a general staff; and the experience of South Africa helped make their army the best for its size in Europe in 1914. The moderate settlement to the Boer War went some way to prevent any more than a tiny uprising against the British in South Africa in 1914, while many more South Africans volunteered to fight for the British Empire.

THE RUSSO-JAPANESE WAR

The Russo-Japanese War of 1904–5 was much more than a naval war, although its critical battles were fleet actions, and control of the sea helped determine how much both sides could reinforce or move their land forces. However, European armies (including the British) also sent observers to watch its land battles and draw conclusions. Unlike the Boer War, which

had been one of long rifle ranges, open country and often of movement, this was a conflict of trenches and tunnelling which reminded some observers of the Crimean War (1853–6). Here, the distinction between sieges and battles sometimes seemed to have little meaning.

The Russo-Japanese War began as the result of rival imperial ambitions, with both Russia and Japan hoping to establish a presence in the Far East at the expense of the declining Manchu Empire of China, which also

The opposing forces, 1904–5

Russia
Initially 83,000 field and 50,000 garrison troops. This force increased steadily as troops arrived from western Russia, allowing the Russians to deploy almost 400,000 men for the Battle of Mukden, February 1905.

Japanese
Around 90,000 men by summer 1904; 320,000 men for Battle of Mukden.

The Russo-Japanese War, 8 February 1904–6 September 1905: the cost

Russia
At least 220,000 killed, wounded and missing.

Japanese
At least 180,000 killed, wounded and missing.

controlled Manchuria itself and claimed ill-defined control of Korea. As a result of their victory in the Sino-Japanese War of 1894–5, the Japanese had been granted rights in Korea by the Chinese and Japan claimed that Russia had violated these. A treaty signed between Japan and Great Britain in 1902 meant that no other power could come to Russia's aid without the British coming to assist Japan too. The principal land campaign was fought in Manchuria between the regional capital of Mukden and the Kwantung peninsula, on which lay the Russian naval base of Port Arthur (Korea and China, in whose territory the war took place, were both technically neutral throughout). Again, it was widely assumed at the war's start that a Russian army would brush aside the Japanese, who in keeping with the racial ideas of the day were seen as inferior because they were Asiatics.

The war began with a surprise Japanese naval attack against the Russian Pacific Fleet at Port Arthur on 8 February 1904. Over the next five months the Japanese landed about 90,000 men on the mainland. One army of 40,000 moved up through Korea, forcing the line of the River Yalu to enter Manchuria in May, so threatening Mukden. Also in May, a second Japanese army landed in southern Manchuria. Leaving part of its force under General Nogi to lay siege to Port Arthur, the main body of this force under Marshal Oyama advanced up the peninsula towards Mukden. Together these armies faced Russian forces numbering about 148,000 under General Aleksey Nikolayevich Kuropatkin (1848–1925), 41,000 of which were tied down as the garrison of Port Arthur.

The first major battle came on 25 August as the Japanese forces under Marshal Oyama fought and defeated Kuropatkin's forces at the Battle of Liaoyang, which lasted eight days, after which Kuropatkin fell back to Mukden. The fighting around Port Arthur then lasted through to the winter, a semi-siege without either Russian naval or land forces interfering. Repeated Japanese attempts to break the Russian entrenched defences by frontal charges all resulted in failure, and Japanese heavy artillery and entrenching work proved the critical factor. Finally, after the loss in December of Hill 203, the dominating ground to the north-west, the Russians surrendered Port Arthur on 2 January 1905.

Elsewhere in Manchuria the more open country seemed to lend itself to Russian mounted manoeuvres, but both the regular Russian cavalry and the famous Cossacks, far from home at the end of long supply lines, proved a failure and a disappointment. With the troops that had besieged Port Arthur now available to him, in February 1905 Oyama attacked Kuropatkin's positions at Mukden with 320,000 men against 380,000 in a battle that lasted for two weeks on a front of 40 miles. It led to the city's capture on 10 March. The war was ended by the Treaty of Portsmouth (New Hampshire) on 6 September, in which Russia acknowledged the Japanese victory and conceded Port Arthur as well as much of its position in the Far East.

Generally, most observers regarded the Russian performance in the war as so poor that any conclusions had to be doubtful. But although the Russians attempted to reform their army after the humiliation of defeat by Japan, they were much less successful than the British had been. The habit of Russian soldiers in 1914 of digging protection for themselves whenever possible, acquired from fighting in Manchuria, was seen as evidence

THE CULT OF THE OFFENSIVE: GERMANY AND FRANCE

The experience of both the Boer War (1899–1902) and the Russo-Japanese War (1904–5) suggested to European observers that battle had become so violent and intense that conscript soldiers would fail after more than a few days' fighting, opening the way for a general enemy collapse and for a decisive victory. It seemed impossible also that even the most advanced industrial states could supply weapons and ammunition at the rate that they had been consumed in the fighting in Manchuria, or that any country could afford the cost of such a war – £220 million to the British taxpayer for South Africa, and 255,888,951 roubles to their Russian counterparts for the naval Battle of Tshushima alone. At the time these all seemed good arguments for the theory that a future European war would have to be short, and would have to be fought by attacking quickly to win victory. Both wars showed the near-impossibility of infantry attacking into the face of entrenched rifle fire; but this was seen as largely a matter of lack of courage on the infantry's part. It was hard for the Germans and French in particular to admit that their own men could not out-perform undertrained British volunteer 'militia', or industrially backward Russians, or Asiatic Japanese. But the real answer to the question why the commanding generals of Europe did not prepare better for the First World War is that they did not want to do so: a slow-moving, stalemated war of entrenchments and artillery was not the war that they wanted to fight.

The Silesia manoeuvres, 1913. Formations like these would survive no more than a few seconds on the battlefields of the following summer. (RMAS Collection)

In 1914 the German Army was regarded as predominant in Europe, not only as a result of its victories over the French in 1870–1, but because of its military training and institutions which had been copied by almost all other countries. The German General Staff, in particular, had many imitators, although its central idea that the staff provided a separate elite within the army was seldom realised in other countries. German infantry were well trained, although like all the armies of Europe that had not directly experienced recent warfare, the Germans undervalued the effect of firepower. German cavalry were inadequately armed and overloaded, making them poor scouts, but even as late as 1913 in the annual 'Kaiser Manoeuvres' in Silesia, massed cavalry charges against entrenched infantry positions were still being practised. German artillery was excellent and their commanders tended to rely heavily on artillery support in attacking. In particular their heavier howitzers, which were intended for siege work or capturing fortifications, proved of great value in trench warfare. The dark side of the German military reputation was a fearsome 'Prussian discipline', a belief in militarism (the valuing of military behaviour for its own sake) and an accompanying contempt for others. The Kaiser's injunction to the German contingent for the Peking relief expedition in 1900, to behave in China as the Huns of antiquity had done, provided an appropriate nickname for German troops.

European military attitudes were conditioned not just by admiration for the German Army and imitation of its methods, but also by German concepts of the nature of war and how it should be fought. These derived ultimately from the ideas of the Prussian soldier-philosopher General Carl von Clausewitz, popularised throughout military Europe after the Prussian victories over the Austrians and French. Britain did not produce one major original military thinker between 1900 and 1914, and the work of French theorists was derived very much from Clausewitz's ideas, as interpreted by their German predecessors. But the 'Neo-Clausewitzians' differed from Clausewitz himself by their belief in the importance of the offensive, which was seen not only as a method of fighting but also as an attitude of mind.

It was the French, rather than the Germans, who took the 'cult of the offensive' to extremes before 1914, notably two of their most influential military teachers, Colonel François de Grandmaison and Colonel Ferdinand Foch (1851–1929), who believed that France had been defeated in 1870 through the failure of morale that was only to be regained by attacking. All European armies subscribed to some extent to the idea that the method by which the firepower of the defensive could be overcome was largely a psychological one: that troops could be trained and motivated to endure heavy losses and still keep going. These beliefs proved correct in the sense that troops on the Western Front in the First World War largely accepted heavy losses and poor conditions for years without significant protest. But the French, of all the armies of Europe, placed least emphasis on the new strength of defensive firepower, even returning to the denser infantry attacking formations of a generation earlier, supported by their quick-firing 75mm guns which were built to move as rapidly as possible. French troops marched to war in 1914 wearing blue tunics and red trousers (with white gloves for the officers) as a symbol of attacking pride; while twelve of their cavalry regiments were charging cuirassiers with metal breastplate, sword and pistol armed like their ancestors in Napoleonic service.

of timidity and lack of offensive spirit; while the Cossacks even had their firearms taken away for a while in an effort to improve their aggressiveness.

The Russo-Japanese War, in which battles had much greater troop densities than those in South Africa, helped restore the role of the infantry and particularly the artillery to prominence in European thinking. This war also showed that a 'battle' could last considerably more than one day, and revealed the great physical and mental strain under which troops at the front would have to fight. In all armies, the generals did not really trust their conscript soldiers, regarding them as undertrained civilians in uniform and believing in their hearts that it took several years' service to make a real soldier. Indeed, throughout the twentieth century, senior officers persistently underestimated the courage and skills of civilians at war.

'Combat . . . has for its end to break by force the will of the enemy and to impose on him our own. Only the offensive permits the obtaining of decisive results. The passive defence is doomed to certain defeat; it is to be rejected absolutely.'

French Field Service Regulations, 1895

1914

When war came in 1914 the individual plans of all the major European powers were different in detail, but the same in their underlying ideas. Each was based on the rapid call-up and mobilisation of very large conscript armies, and their equally rapid despatch to the front by pre-arranged railway timetables. The single significant exception was the British, who were without conscription but mobilised and deployed rapidly their own main army, the 100,000-strong British Expeditionary Force or BEF. What was to happen after the armies left their railheads and finished deploying was much less certain in any of the plans. It was not at all clear that armies of such size could even be controlled with the staff methods and communications available; and the less-well-trained staffs like the Russians and Austrians almost seemed to have ceased to try. What was certain was that every country believed hesitation was fatal, and could lead to armies being caught by a surprise attack while still forming or even in barracks. The train timetables also gave commanding generals very little choice of action. Austria-Hungary, which declared war on Serbia on 28 July, almost succeeded in demonstrating how an army's own

German infantry pour across the fields of Lorraine, August 1914. The Schlieffen Plan was highly ambitious, and demanded impressive marching performances from the troops undertaking it. Nevertheless, even by living off the land the Germans could not avoid requiring their soldiers to carry large amounts of equipment on their backs, as the full – and heavy – packs of these men indicate. (RMAS Collection)

commanders could reduce it to chaos by their indecision over the use of railways. The Austrians' plan was for their strongest army to deploy in Galicia against the Russians as a precaution, whether or not they actually declared war; a smaller army would attack Serbia, while a reserve army could support either move depending on circumstances. With Russia not declaring war and mobilising until 31 July, the Austrian reserve army was originally despatched to the Balkans, and spent several days shuttling back and forth on its trains before ending up in Galicia against the Russians. This was as far as Austrian plans went; they were aghast to have started a general European war with all the implications for their ramshackle empire, and were among the first to suggest a negotiated peace in the following year.

'Remember that the German people are the chosen people of God. On me, the German Emperor, the spirit of God has descended. I am His sword, His weapon and His vice-regent. Woe to the disobedient and death to cowards and unbelievers.'

Kaiser Wilhelm II, September 1914

On 1 August Germany also mobilised its forces in support of Austria-Hungary and declared war on Russia, in response to which France mobilised next day and declared war on Germany. Great Britain declared war on Germany on 4 August following the German invasion of Belgium. If Austria had begun the war, Germany's plans made sure that it would become Europe-wide. Only for Germany did mobilisation automatically mean an attack on another country, and since that country was France, German mobilisation spread the war from eastern to western Europe.

German war plans were based on the belief that they could not win a long two-front war against Russia and France. Russia, with the larger army, would take six weeks longer than France to mobilise; and that period was the German window of opportunity in which to defeat France completely, while minimum German forces held in the east against the Russians. The Russians had two main plans: 'Plan G' for a defensive war against both the German and Austrian main armies and 'Plan A' for the war that actually happened. Plan A called for the major Russian offensive to be made against the Austrians in Galicia, but also for a second offensive to be made into north-east Germany while the main German forces were in the west fighting the French. The French war plan, 'Plan 17', played into German hands by calling for attacks by the bulk of the French forces against the common frontier with Germany in an effort to recapture Alsace-Lorraine, annexed by Germany after the French defeat of 1870–1. The German plan had first been proposed in 1905 by Field Marshal Alfred Graf von Schlieffen (1833–1913), Chief of the General Staff, and was carried out by his successor in the post, Colonel General Helmuth von Moltke (1848–1916) (known as 'Moltke the Younger'). It envisaged holding or minor attacks against the French Plan 17, while the main German armies outflanked the French in the west by coming through neutral Belgium. In order to provide enough troops for this massive wheeling move, the Germans used their second-line infantry divisions, made up of reservists who had been out of the Army for some years, as front-line troops, a risk that the French had not predicted in their own pre-war planning.

The events of the 1914 campaign, in all cases and on all fronts, showed that the ability of the offensive to overcome the defensive had been over-estimated, that there were limits to how far and fast men could march to battle, and that even the most impressive victory in battle was no longer decisive. Once away from their railheads, the armies of Europe staggered across the countryside like gigantic, fierce, murderous animals, each almost blind and barely able to move forward under its own weight, but capable of tearing to pieces anything that fell within its reach. At a range of 10 miles, an army might not see the enemy at all. But at 1 mile or less its firepower was such that most of the tactical manoeuvres practised before the war resulted only in massive casualties for both sides, with the advantage strongly favouring the defence. In the Balkans, the Austrians were unable even to defeat the Serbs, who in December went on to the offensive and briefly drove their enemies back. In Galicia lack of information and poor reconnaissance on both sides produced a confused series of battles in late summer, counted as Russian victories. This was more than balanced by a spectacular German victory against the attacking Russians at the double battle of Tannenberg and Masurian Lakes in August and September, which involved the encirclement and destruction of one entire Russian army. In earlier wars a victory like Tannenberg would have been decisive, but in the context of the armies and resources of twentieth-century states it was only an incident.

The most spectacular failure of attempts to win a quick victory came in the west, where the German plan broke down under the accumulated pressure of events and enemy action. Anxious before the war over possible delays in their advance through Belgium, the Germans had planned a deliberate campaign of terror to suppress popular guerrilla uprisings, known as *Schrecklichkeit* (translated into English at the time as 'frightfulness'). Nevertheless, Belgian forces slowed up the German advance, in particular with British help in the defence of Antwerp until 9 October. By sheer coincidence the British Expeditionary Force ('contemptibly small' according to the Kaiser, hence the troops' nickname of 'the Old Contemptibles') found itself in the path of the main attack by the German 1st Army, and played a small but important part in imposing more delay on the Germans at the Battle of Mons on 23 August, the first British battle in Europe since Waterloo ninety-nine years before. This, together with their own much heavier fighting in the Battle of the Frontiers gave the French time to assess the German strategy and to redirect their own forces. Despite their heavy losses the French were able to regroup and counter-attack in September east of Paris at the First Battle of the Marne, halting the German advance. Still trying to win by manoeuvre, both sides then tried to outflank the other to the west in a series of battles misleadingly known as 'the race to the sea', involving moving forces by train. In October advancing French and British forces joined Belgian and British forces retreating from Antwerp to hold the last little corner of Belgium at Ypres.

The fighting in Belgium at the end of 1914, known to the British as the First Battle of Ypres, set the pattern for the next three years of war. As soldiers and their commanders abandoned major attacks in the open in favour of digging trench defences to make maximum use of their weapons, firepower was enough to prevent ordinary movement above ground in daylight by the enemy and to break up all but the most determined and well-supported attacks. For the first time in the history of warfare, both sides had enough troops under arms to present a continuous front clean across Belgium and northern France from the North Sea to the Swiss frontier. As the lines solidified and the troops dug in for winter the

Western Front chronology, 1914

3–20 Aug	German 1st, 2nd and 3rd armies overrun a large part of Belgium.
14–25 Aug	Battle of the Frontiers. French offensive in Lorraine and the Ardennes repulsed by Germans, who inflict 300,000 casualties on the French.
23 Aug	Battle of Mons. BEF fights successful delaying action.
25–7 Aug	BEF fights a second successful action at Le Cateau.
29 Aug	Battle of Guise: tactically successful French counterattack on German 2nd Army.
5–10 Sept	First Battle of the Marne. German 1st, 2nd and 3rd armies halted by French and BEF, and forced to retreat.
15–18 Sept	First Battle of the Aisne. Unsuccessful Allied attempt to outflank and then break through German line on the River Aisne.
19 Sept–24 Nov	The 'Race to the Sea'.

'I think the battle of the Aisne is very typical of what battles in the future are most likely to resemble. Siege operations will enter largely into the tactical problems – the spade will be as great a necessity as the rifle, and the heaviest calibres and types of artillery will be brought up in support of either side.'

Field Marshal Sir John French, Commander of the BEF, 1914

General Alexander von Kluck's German 1st Army entered Brussels on 20 August 1914. At this early stage the Germans already faced difficulties in feeding their horses, and at the Battle of the Marne (in September) the exhaustion of their horses was to be a significant factor in explaining the German defeat. Here, artillery passes through the Belgian capital, 26 August. (RMAS Collection)

Germans had the advantage, holding almost all of Belgium and important areas of northern France, but this was a long way from the quick and total victory they had expected.

One of the tragedies of the First World War was that, in deflecting crisis after crisis for a generation, the diplomats of Europe had been either too successful or not quite successful enough. By only a few years, 1914 was absolutely the wrong time to have a war. For the first time in the whole of human history, it was just possible for the highest developed levels of civilisation – the industrialised states of Europe – to keep millions of men under arms living in holes in the ground. In the soil of Europe itself, Britain, France and Germany could keep them there clothed, fed and free from lethal epidemic diseases, day and night, all the year round without respite. The men, although subject to strong military discipline, also had sufficient patriotism and faith in their respective causes to stay in those holes in the ground. What was lacking was the sometimes quite small developments in military ideas, technology and tactics, all of which would come within a decade, that could get the soldiers out of their holes when required and let them advance against the enemy with a reasonable chance of success.

THE FAILURE OF THE SCHLIEFFEN PLAN

Almost no other campaign produced as much analysis and argument after the First World War as the failed German offensive of August 1914 under Colonel General Helmuth von Moltke ('the Younger', to distinguish him from his famous uncle). These arguments in turn raised the issue of whether the Schlieffen Plan in any form could have worked at all. The whole German military style from the nineteenth century through to the end of the Second World War emphasised 'operational' thinking at the expense of both military Intelligence and logistics (transport and supply), on the assumption that a paramount 'will to win' could overcome any deficiencies, including a chaotic supply system.

The Schlieffen Plan demanded rates of advance through the heat of August of more than 15 miles a day from the leading troops of the outer wheel, sometimes stretching to 25 miles a day. Even by wheeling east of Paris, at the Battle of the Marne in September the troops of German 1st and 2nd armies were already exhausted. It is hard to see how they could have reached the Channel ports first and then continued onwards to wheel west of Paris as the original plan required, or how they could have continued to advance without several days' rest if they had won on the Marne.

All the German armies depended on supplies coming from their railheads, which were moved forward behind the troops in the advance. But by the time it reached the Marne the outermost German formation, the 1st Army, was over 100 miles from its railhead. Generally speaking, ammunition and food were not a problem, but from the start of the campaign fodder for the horses could not be supplied at sufficient rates. Horses for transport and gun haulage began to starve and fall ill, and at the Marne even the heavy artillery was affected. Even more importantly, the German cavalry, which were supposed to scout ahead of the army and report on enemy positions, were rendered largely ineffective from the very start by fodder shortages and overwork that wore out even the horseshoes. Not knowing where the enemy was, and allowing the French and British to retreat and regroup largely unmolested, were major factors in the German defeat.

Even had they won the Battle of the Marne, the Germans could not have continued their advance without a major halt to sort out their supply and transport problems, and to rest their men and horses. This suggests that with a semi-modern army still largely dependent on marching men and horses, von Schlieffen had aimed to achieve too much.

Viewed in this way, the traditional question 'What were the causes of the First World War' turns out to be the wrong question, asked in the wrong way. The nature of the First World War was shaped, more than any other factor, by the discovery a few months after it began that it could not be fought and won by the methods that politicians and generals had hoped before 1914 might produce a quick victory. After the failed attacks of early 1915, it was accepted by all but the most stubborn political and military leaders that the size, motivation and firepower of modern armies,

REPORTING THE WARS: COMMUNICATIONS, CENSORSHIP AND THE PRESS

The First World War was not simply about firepower and technology, but about entire societies, the way in which ordinary people understood war, and how governments believed that they would react to it when it came. The start of the twentieth century was accompanied in most European countries by a general increase both in mass popular literacy and in political awareness, often also marked by an extension of the right to vote. By 1900 most politicians were conscious of the fact that they were dealing with a new kind of mass politics and a new 'public opinion'.

This new politics was accompanied especially in Britain and in the United States by the rise of the 'press baron', the newspaper owner who was also a major political figure. It was commonly believed that the Spanish-American War of 1898 was provoked by a press campaign led by the newspaper magnate William Randolph Hearst (1863–1951). In Britain in 1896 Alfred Harmsworth (later Lord Northcliffe) (1865–1922) founded the *Daily Mail* as the first mass-circulation newspaper deliberately aimed at a working-class market. Harmsworth's success allowed him to buy *The Times* in 1908, and gave him and others like him considerable power and influence.

The new technologies that went into weapons of war also gave rise to new forms of communication, with great potential both for warfare and for the commercial media. Journalism was transformed by mass production, new paper manufacturing technology and new forms of printing. Developments in the optical and chemical industry that produced twentieth-century artillery also produced the first practical popular cameras in the 1880s, and by 1896 the practical cine-camera. By 1914 in Britain the cinema was by far the most

War correspondents, 'those newly invented curse to armies who eat the rations of the fighting man and do not work at all' (Field Marshal Viscount Wolseley), await Lord Roberts' entry to Kroonstad, May 1900.

popular form of mass entertainment, with 20 million attendances a week from a population of 43 million. Although wireless was in its infancy, the first speech transmission by radio waves was achieved by Fessenden in the United States in 1900, and the first telegraph transmission across the Atlantic by Marconi from Britain a year later. By this date the British Empire was linked together by underwater telegraph cables stretching out as far as Australia, allowing communication from London to the furthest colonies within a day. In 1910 the notorious British poisoner Dr Henry Crippen, trying to escape to the United States by steamship, was foiled when a radio message was sent to the ship's captain in mid-Atlantic. In 1915 Alexander Graham Bell successfully demonstrated a transcontinental telephone call from New York to San Francisco.

'The British public likes to read sensational news and the best war correspondent is he who can tell the most thrilling lies.'

Earl Haig, 1898, on the Sudan campaign

Regulation of the methods by which later nineteenth-century colonial military campaigns had been reported had in most countries depended heavily on informal arrangements between commanding generals and the journalists, and had been very small-scale affairs. The experience of the Boer War and the Russo-Japanese War (in which the Japanese had maintained a tight censorship on reporting of their movements and the Russians had not) convinced most major governments that in future the reporting of wars needed to be regulated and controlled to prevent high-speed communications giving information to the enemy. The British Official Secrets Act of 1911 was one symptom of the growing trend towards official regulation. Provisions were made by the major powers for the introduction of press censorship in wartime. The military view, which prevailed briefly in 1914, was that the press had no place on a modern battlefield and should be excluded altogether. The issues first raised between 1900 and 1914 of the relationship between the mass media, censorship, public opinion and warfare continued to feature in every major war of the twentieth century.

backed by the industrial production of the most advanced of the European states, had produced a defence so strong that not even the best attacking troops could break it with the means available to them. To do so would take the reorganisation of entire societies for war, and the creation of mass armies and killing power on a scale utterly unknown to the pre-industrial world. It would take the development of entirely new forms of war under the sea, in the air and even in the ether through radio waves. It would take millions spent in cash and credit, and more importantly millions of dead and wounded. The principal 'cause' of the First World War, in this sense, was the tactical deadlock of the trenches; and the principal cause of its end was the resolution of that problem over the next four years.

THREE

THE BIRTH OF MODERN LAND WARFARE: THE WESTERN FRONT 1914–18

ANDREW WIEST

'Everybody will be entrenched in the next war. It will be a great war of entrenchments. The spade will be as indispensable to a soldier as his rifle.'

I.S. Bloch, Is War Now Impossible? *(1899)*

Though the idea is still controversial in some circles, most military historians now consider the First World War to be the first truly modern war. Other contenders, such as the American Civil War and the Franco-Prussian War, had aspects of modernity, but these conflicts represented the beginning of military change, not its completion. The First World War was different in both form and substance from what had gone before. The conflict changed forever the way nations prosecuted war. As this first truly industrial war inched slowly toward the Clausewitzian paradigm of totality, the combatant nations had to call upon their people, industry and treasure to a degree never before witnessed in their efforts to achieve victory. Tactically the conflict represented a significant departure from previous wars in which generals presided over battlefields they could see and, in the main, control. Commanders in the First World War had to deal with a system of trenches that spanned hundreds of miles. In addition the battles of the First World War were simply on a different scale to anything ever seen before. The Battle of Verdun in 1916 lasted nearly ten months and claimed nearly 800,000 casualties. At the same time, just 100 miles to the north, the Battle of the Somme raged for six months and claimed 1 million casualties. Neither Napoleon nor Robert E. Lee would have recognised the Somme – aeroplanes flew overhead and tanks slowly rumbled past. The battlefield was gargantuan, the casualties horrific, the weapons new, the tactics untried, the communications partly old-style, partly experimental. It was a different war, a modern war that called for undreamed of sacrifices on the part of soldier and civilian alike.

THE OPENING STAGES

Many in Europe welcomed the onset of the First World War, or at the very least, had little reason to fear the coming cataclysm. Recent military experience, most notably the Franco-Prussian War, seemed to indicate that the war would be quick and decisive and that the troops would be 'home by Christmas'. Soldiers marched off to the conflict cheered by huge crowds and intent upon bringing glory, honour and victory to themselves and their respective nations. However, the war was not quick and decisive. Instead, it was protracted, and seemed to destroy an entire generation of Europe's best and brightest. Indeed, the war would call into question the very ideas of glory, honour and victory.

Advances in both agricultural and industrial production made it possible by 1914 to raise, equip and sustain mass armies at war. Never before had a nation been able to keep an army numbering millions in the field for over four years. By 1914 seven countries were able to accomplish such a feat. The new industrialised war pitted nation against nation, not merely army against army. Seemingly limitless supplies of men fell victim to the steel embrace of limitless supplies of munitions. In some ways the First World War can be envisioned as a mighty factory constantly at work over three continents. Its finished product was death and mutilation. The industrial machine worked horrifically well, claiming the lives of over 19 million people.

Two new machines came to dominate the factory of death: the machine gun and the quick-firing artillery piece. Both were, in the main, untried and misunderstood by military leaders in every major combatant nation. The commanders of the First World War, for the most part, were nineteenth-century gentlemen with little knowledge that would serve to prepare them for industrial war. Its ferocity and technical nature took them unawares.

The first of the new weapons, the modern machine gun, was invented by Hiram Maxim in 1883 and used the recoil of the weapon to load the next round. Though machine guns saw some service in the Russo-Japanese War and colonial conflicts, their first extensive use came in the First World War. Machine guns at this time fired about 600 rounds per minute. Though many generals were loathe to admit it, the new weapon revolutionised war, for it could replace the firepower of over forty trained riflemen, who could fire something like thirteen aimed rounds per minute. In addition the machine gun did not really have to be aimed. Machine guns working in pairs with interlocking zones of fire could simply traverse back and forth at a fixed height and devastate all in their path. The defensive fire of machine guns would dominate the Western Front for several years.

Artillery also made the nature of the First World War fundamentally different from what had gone before. In the American Civil War artillery pieces fired ordnance that exploded into five chunks of shrapnel. The range of this artillery was limited to line of sight. The Industrial Revolution, in the form of improved metallurgy and explosives, made artillery much more lethal. Improved barrels led to greater range. First World War artillery pieces fired from miles behind the lines. They could

Populations of the great powers, 1913 (millions)

Russia	175.1
USA	97.3
Germany	66.9
Austria-Hungary	52.1
Japan	51.3
Britain (incl. Ireland)	45.6
France	39.7
Italy	35.1

'Machine guns play a great part – almost a decisive part under some conditions – in modern war.'

General Douglas Haig, final despatch after the Battle of the Somme, 1916

Heavy machine guns like this German schwere Maschinengewehr *08 could inflict fearful casualties on an assaulting force as it crossed no-man's-land. Fed by 250-round fabric belts of ammunition, a rate of fire of over 400 bullets per minute could easily be achieved by the sMG 08. However, the cumbersome nature of such weapons and their prodigious consumption of ammunition made them virtually useless in the offensive, although as the war progressed indirect machine-gun fire did help attackers to suppress enemy defences. Given the amount of natural cover and the composition of this photograph, it was almost certainly taken well away from the battlefield. (IWM Q23709)*

deliver airburst shrapnel shells that peppered exposed troops with 1,000 deadly lead pellets. They could also fire steel-tipped high-explosive shells that devastated all but the most strongly built defensive emplacements. The new artillery pieces were also very accurate and quick-firing. When used in association with machine guns, artillery could rain a deadly 'storm of steel' upon an enemy advancing over open terrain, allowing defenders to massacre attackers with impunity.

Many commanders on both sides understood the heightened lethality of modern weaponry. It was their belief, though, that such innovations would lead to greater decisiveness in war. No army could stand up to such modern weaponry for long. The nation with the highest morale, greatest élan and most offensively orientated plan would win a quick and devastating victory. Each of the major powers proceeded with their own offensive plans in 1914. The French Plan 17 attempted to seize Alsace-Lorraine from Germany, but the Germans countered with the audacious Schlieffen Plan aimed at the destruction of the entire French Army. The French, though surprised, were able to react swiftly enough with the aid of their imperturbable leader General Joseph Joffre (1852–1931).

The French reaction to the threat of German invasion and the Battle of the Frontiers is very revealing. Joffre was able to move troops laterally, using rail lines, much more quickly than the Germans could advance on foot. In addition Joffre was able to utilise intact phone and telegraph lines to communicate with his forces. The advancing Germans had to rely upon despatch riders to communicate, and they often lost track of their advancing forces. The state of communications in the First World War, therefore, favoured the defender. Attackers moved forward at a snail's pace, and had no true method of communication. Defenders could react quickly using modern communications and railways. Thus defenders could out-think and out-pace attackers. Joffre made this evident when the French and British forces recovered from their initial shock, redeployed and then won the First Battle of the Marne (September 1914).

For the remainder of 1914 armies on the Western Front occupied themselves in attempting to outflank each other to the north in the 'race to the sea'. Their other chief occupation was digging in. By the end of the year the front stretched from the English Channel to Switzerland, and the conflict had stagnated into trench warfare. The new phase of the war is boring and not very glorious to many laymen. A fresh look, however, reveals that the generals of the First World War faced a problem that seemingly had no solution. In a concentrated period of military innovation and modernisation, however, they found the solution to the riddle of trench deadlock and laid the foundations for every war since.

The inability to interdict railway traffic behind the tactical battle zone caused great difficulties for any force seeking to break through the enemy's defences. Almost without exception, attackers found that by the time they had ground their way through the opponent's trench system, fresh forces were in place to oppose them. Even in 1918, when ground attack and bomber aircraft were available, the sophistication of Western Europe's railway network made this an insoluble problem. (IWM Q327)

The riddle was rather simple in nature. Once the enemy had dug in, how did you evict him from his trench systems? It must be remembered that the enemy had to be evicted from his defensive emplacements. Nations, even strong ones, rarely win wars through purely defensive actions. Politicians, the public and generals demanded victory, and victory was attained only by attacking. The problem remained, though, of how the armies were to put this simple idea into effect in 1915.

TRENCHES

Trenches were usually 8 feet deep and ran in a zigzag pattern for defensive purposes. Defenders did not have one trench; far from it. Defensive systems were up to 10 miles from the front line to the rear and were made up of a rabbit warren of lines, fortifications, communication trenches, dugouts, bunkers and barbed-wire entanglements. They ran for over 400 miles, but consisted of many thousands of miles of trench. Within their impressive systems of fortifications the defenders could call upon the strength of machine guns and artillery to destroy enemy troops foolhardy enough to show themselves in the area between the opposing trench systems known as 'no-man's-land'. In addition communications aided the defender. Messages could flash that an attack had taken place and reinforcements could be rushed to the scene long before any attacking army could break through the complicated defences. All of the advantages in the First World War were with the defenders. However, the generals had to attack to win. The responses to this dilemma were sometimes futile, sometimes gallant and sometimes simply murderous.

Trench life was mostly boring, monotonous and uncomfortable. This was especially true in British and French positions, which tended to be on lower ground than German trenches, and which remained undeveloped by comparison with those of their enemies because of the Allied commanders' determination to advance. Here, a British soldier peers through a periscope into no-man's-land, waiting for something to happen. (IWM Q4654)

Generals in every combatant nation tried to break the trench stalemate. They relied upon their pre-war training and the weapons at hand in their first, futile attempts to achieve victory. These nineteenth-century gentlemen officers had been educated for dashing, mobile war, and had precious little experience of static trench warfare. To make matters worse, attacking armies were at a distinct tactical disadvantage, for the weaponry at hand best suited the defender. Standard-issue infantry weapons, the rifle and the bayonet, would have little effect on an enemy dug in and employing machine guns and artillery. Thus the infantry, the 'queen of the battlefield' in previous wars, could achieve little in trench warfare. The cavalry too were unsuited for such a confrontation. Machine guns, deadly in defence, were heavy and cumbersome and could play only a small role in an attack. The only weapon in the attacker's arsenal that seemed to hold offensive promise was artillery. It, however, was being used in a new way. The improvement in artillery range meant that the guns fired from well behind the lines. This 'indirect fire' was untried and inaccurate. For the first time on a large scale artillery was firing at what it could not see. Such tactics called for a level of technical expertise that did not exist at the beginning of the war. This detail, though, did not stop commanders relying on this powerful, if flawed, weapon in 1915 and 1916. The generals had to change and become modern, technically proficient men. Science too had to help answer the riddle of trench warfare. While these changes were taking place, though, the twin horrors of the First World War, Verdun and the Somme took place. These battles were indeed so tragic in nature that most historians and laymen have been blinded to the quiet revolution in warfare that took place during this time.

'How I should love to have a real "go" at them in the open with lots of cavalry and horse artillery and run them to earth.'

Field Marshal Sir John French, commander of the BEF, 1915

The year 1915 was one of experimentation and the first true tests of trench warfare. The Germans chose to stand on the defensive in France and Belgium and attempted to deal a death blow to Russia in the east. The British experimented by using their traditional naval mastery to circumvent the Western Front. The British and Australian & New Zealand (ANZAC) forces that landed on the Gallipoli peninsula in Turkey fought gallantly, but their efforts were in vain and the Allies would be forced to seek their eventual victory in France. On the Western Front the bulk of the fighting initially fell to the French. However, the British experience in the west serves best to demonstrate the nature of the continuing struggle.

Britain entered the conflict with a small, professional army that was in many ways a colonial police force. Though the battles of Mons and Le Cateau in 1914 showed that it was very skilful, this tiny army could not stand against the conscript juggernauts of continental Europe. Then Britain called for every man to do his duty and the response was overwhelming. Hundreds of thousands flocked to the recruiting offices to join the forces. Britain thus raised its first mass army and prepared for the first time to face a continental foe in full land battle. Even this, though, was not enough. The tremendous losses of 1915 and 1916 forced Britain to adopt conscription for the first time in her long military history.

On the Western Front in 1915 the British Expeditionary Force (BEF) took part in several, and in the light of later developments, minor offensives. The most notable attacks took place at Aubers Ridge (May) and Loos (September). Though military lessons were gleaned from these

Western Front chronology, 1915

20 Dec 1914–30 March 1915	First Battle of Champagne. French and British launch unsuccessful frontal assaults against German line in northern France.
22 April–25 May	Second Battle of Ypres. German attack and British counterattacks around Ypres, Belgium; small territorial gain by Germans. (Also, first confirmed use of poison gas on Western Front – by Germans).
9–26 May	Failed British attack at Festubert (Aubers Ridge).
16 May–30 June	Failed French attack on Vimy Ridge.
25 Sept–6 Nov	Failed French offensives in Champagne and on Vimy Ridge. Failed British attack at Loos (25 Sept–14 Oct).
17 Dec	General Sir Douglas Haig replaces Field Marshal Sir John French as commander of BEF.

battles, their major importance lies elsewhere. Before the war Britain had been a state built upon the liberal economic traditions of Adam Smith. Such ideas were so deeply ingrained in the British psyche that the government planned to allow 'business as usual' in wartime. In other words Britain would rely on the law of supply and demand to equip and sustain her army. Such reliance was misguided and belied a fundamental misunderstanding of the nature of modern war. Newspapers reported, with an element of truth, that the BEF had not achieved victory in the battles of spring 1915 because of a shortage of shells. The ensuing 'shell scandal' forced Britain to take stock of her political and economic situation. As a result the government formed the Ministry of Munitions to take control of all aspects of military supply. This and other moves, including the introduction of conscription in May 1916, compelled the liberal British to accept an extension of state control over economy and society. The needs of total war forced Britain to abandon long-established traditions, helping to bring about the collapse of the Liberal Party and the rise of Labour. Thus even Britain, protected as it was by the Channel and the Royal Navy, could not avoid the repercussions of a modern nation at war. Russia, France and Germany would fare much worse.

'Men died in heaps upon the Aubers Ridge ten days ago, because the field guns were short, and gravely short, of high explosive shells.'

The Times, *1915*

THE WAR INTENSIFIES

Although events in 1915 were important, they paled in comparison to the titanic struggle on the Western Front in 1916. The battles of Verdun and the Somme would last for months and the horrific casualties suffered there would haunt an entire generation. The principal architects of the battles, Erich von Falkenhayn (1861–1922) for the Germans and Douglas Haig (1861–1928) for the British, believed that they were in possession of the answer to trench warfare – masses of artillery and huge numbers of men. Falkenhayn, in his planning for the German attack at Verdun, boiled war down to its essence – attrition. He hoped to ring the exposed French salient around the historic city of Verdun with thousands of artillery pieces. He would then unleash unrelenting firepower upon French manpower. He claimed that he never wanted to seize the fortress of Verdun itself. Rather, his goal was to drag the French Army through a meat grinder and 'bleed France white'.

General Douglas Haig (centre), General Joseph Joffre (left) and General Ferdinand Foch (right) leave Beauqesne Chateau after lunching with King George V, 12 August 1916. Their cheerful expressions are in stark contrast to those of their soldiers, dying in their thousands on the Somme and at Verdun. (RMAS Collection)

Haig's planning for the Somme used the same ingredients but followed a different recipe. He was a commander from the old school, a cavalryman who longed for open warfare and decisive battles. He realised that the infantry, with its low offensive capabilities, could not achieve such results. He did, however, hope that the cavalry would have a glorious role in his decisive battle. Artillery, though, was again to be the main weapon. The BEF would amass so much artillery and then shell the battlefield so intensively that no German could survive. The infantry would then walk across no-man's-land and occupy the trenches full of German dead. If all went well the cavalry would gallop through the infantry and unhinge the entire German position. The result would be the decisive defeat of the enemy.

Although they chose to use artillery in different ways, both generals failed to understand the strengths and weaknesses of these marvels of modern technology. In essence they misunderstood modern war. Both generals asked the artillery, only one facet of a modern armed force, to carry the weight of the entire battle. This meant that artillery had to achieve three goals. First it had to flatten the enemy's first line of defence,

VERDUN, 21 FEBRUARY–18 DECEMBER 1916

At Verdun the Germans, under the command of Erich von Falkenhayn, ringed the French fortress city with 1,200 artillery pieces. Of these 850 guns were 'heavies', meaning that they fired large, high-explosive shells that could penetrate all but the most sturdy defensive emplacements. The Germans hoped that such a concentration of firepower would devastate the defenders in a contest between steel and flesh. As the Germans prepared to launch their maelstrom of fire, the French played into their hands.

Verdun is a city near the Franco-German border straddling a traditional German invasion route. For this reason the French had constructed a series of very strong forts and defensive works surrounding the city, making it the most defensible place on earth. However, the French commander, General Joffre, believed in the offensive. As a result he paid scant attention to the defensive fortifications around Verdun, leaving them undermanned and in a general state of disrepair.

At 0715 hours on 21 February 1916 the Germans unleashed their bombardment. Their guns fired a million shells into an area of the French line only 12 miles square. Only the strength of modern industry made such a horror possible. At a very important point in the French defences near the Bois de Caures the Germans concentrated an amazing 80,000 shells upon an area of the French line only 500 by 1,000 yards in size. The slaughter was prodigious, but some defenders survived.

Consequently, the German advance on Verdun was tortuously slow. The gallant, if undermanned, French defenders made good use of their surviving machine guns and artillery pieces to make the Germans pay dearly for each advance. The very fact that the Germans moved forward illustrates a mistake made by von Falkenhayn. His original plan had called for a struggle between German steel and French flesh. However, the pressures of war were too great and the Germans attempted to seize the city of Verdun itself. In so doing the Germans doomed their own offensive, for all of the tactical advantages in the First World War lay with the defender.

'No retreat at Verdun. We fight to the end.'

General Joseph Joffre, 1916

By late April Joffre had sent reinforcements to the area and French forces at Verdun equalled those of the Germans. As a result, continued German attacks netted little in the way of territorial gain and cost a prohibitive number of casualties. The riddle of the First World War had not been solved. The Germans had poured shellfire into unprepared and poorly supplied French defenders on 21 February. They had achieved great gains, even seizing the forts of Douaumont and Vaux, but they had not broken through the French lines. Nor had they inflicted sufficient attrition on the French to bring them to the point of surrender. Although Joffre made serious mistakes, he had been able to use the advantages of defence to stem the German advance. Verdun became a stalemate. The battle finally ended in December, by which time the original front lines had moved little. The casualty lists astounded a world that had expected glorious and quick victory: over 800,000 men fell at Verdun.

Heavy artillery such as this British 15-inch howitzer came to dominate the battles on the Western Front. In 1914 the British had only 6 heavy batteries, compared to 72 field batteries. By November 1918 they had 440 and 568 heavy and field batteries respectively, and the ratio of gunners to infantry participating in major battles was almost one to one. The picture was much the same in the French and German armies. (IWM Q4196)

the deadly entanglements of barbed wire. Next it had to destroy the entirety of the enemy's intricate trench system and silence his deadly machine guns. Last, but certainly not least, it had to destroy the enemy artillery that stood ready to rain death upon attacking infantry in no-man's-land. The tasks were too varied and difficult, the scientific approach to gunnery was still in its infancy, and artillery would fail to win the day.

Partly in response to French appeals for aid, Haig's British forces launched their own offensive in July 1916: the Battle of the Somme. As already stated, Haig relied in the main on the simple idea that massive firepower could flatten all enemy resistance and the infantry could then walk across and occupy the ruined German trenches. To this end the BEF amassed over 1,400 artillery pieces for the bombardment of the German lines. On 24 June 1916 these guns opened up with a hurricane of fire on the German defensive emplacements. In the next week a total of 1½ million shells rained down upon the Germans on a front of 18 miles. Impressive as it was, however, the British shelling was doomed to failure.

The British at the Somme, like all other combatant nations in this first modern, industrial war, made some fundamental mistakes that illustrate a failure to grasp how the nature of conflict had changed. Of the British artillery pieces, 1,000 were field guns. These guns were light and mobile, but could not fire shells large enough to destroy the German trenches, or far enough to duel with German artillery. To make matters worse, of the 1½ million shells fired in the preliminary bombardment, 1 million were shrapnel shells. Such shells could devastate an army in the open, but did precious little to the Germans sheltering in their deep dugouts. These figures meant that some 400 heavier artillery pieces firing some 500,000 high-explosive shells did the bulk of the real work. But the problems did not stop there. The manufacture of high-explosive shells is a complex and very exacting science. The most difficult part of the shell to make is the fuse, and British fuses were of poor quality in 1916. As many as 30 per cent of British shells fired during the bombardment were duds, and others did not explode at the required time. Finally, much of the British bombardment was hopelessly inaccurate. In the First World War artillery generally operated out of sight of its target using what is known as indirect fire. Some artillery pieces fired at ranges of up to 15,000 yards from their target. The artillery relied on forward observation officers in the front line to register the fall of shot and adjust fire. Such a scheme was impractical because no reliable form of communication connected the batteries to their observers, and the observer's field of vision was extremely limited. In essence, artillery in 1916 fired blind.

As a result of artillery shortcomings, when the British went over the top to face the foe on 1 July 1916, some of the defenders were still alive. They readied their machine guns, called for artillery support and cut down the British infantry in swathes. The British fought gallantly, but the effort was mostly futile. The artillery had failed, and the infantry could have little impact on entrenched defenders. In most areas the British did not even dent the German front-line trenches, much less effect a breakthrough. During this single day of fighting the British suffered over 57,000 casualties. The defensive remained stronger than the offensive. The riddle of trench warfare lived on.

Although the first day of the Battle of the Somme was a failure, the British remained on the offensive. Haig continued to hope that his hammer blows might force the Germans to break and restore a war of movement. However, the British Commander-in-Chief began to move more towards deliberate attrition as the answer. The Germans, once again using the advantages of the defensive, rushed reinforcements to the scene. However, their offensive efforts at Verdun kept the forces available to defend on the Somme at a dangerously low level. As a result the Germans adopted a defensive posture in both battles, putting an end to their effort to 'bleed France white'.

The fundamental reality of the First World War had not changed. The German lines at the Somme never broke and the defensive remained

PROBLEMS WITH ARTILLERY

Although artillery was modern, the men using it were not. In 1916 artillerymen did not yet know how the conditions around them could have an effect on the accuracy of their fire. Little was known regarding how wear on a barrel or weather conditions could change the flight and trajectory of a shell. Later studies revealed the extent of the inaccuracy such mistakes forced upon a bombardment. If a gun using indirect fire fired 100 shells at a fixed target in 1916, 50 of those shells would miss their target entirely. The remaining shells would fall into a zone 40 yards long and 5 yards wide. These impacts were considered 'hits', but even these hits were of little value. Trenches were but a yard in width, and machine gun nests were only a little larger. Thus the vast majority of 'hits' did little damage to entrenched defenders. When all shells are considered, only around 2 shells out of 100 would be direct hits. Only a very tiny percentage of those hits would be so accurate as to penetrate the trench and destroy a bunker under it. Add to this the fact that one of those two direct hits might well be a dud, and the ineffectiveness of artillery bombardments in the first half of the war is easy to understand.

Over the top. British infantry walk to their death, 1 July 1916. (IWM Q1142)

supreme. Continued attacks by the BEF achieved little, and casualty lists grew longer. By the end of the six-month struggle (13 November), the trench lines had moved only 7 miles and nearly 1 million men had become casualties. Such meagre results, when compared to the quick movements of the Franco-Prussian War, or the dramatic 'Blitzkrieg' of the Second World War, seem quite senseless and futile. This dichotomy has forced historical examination of the First World War to focus on the grim horror of the Somme and its twin, Verdun. The astounding innovations that were to come have been generally ignored in the rush to condemn the war and its commanders. However, within two years of the Somme the British would solve the riddle, and bring about the greatest victory in British military history.

THE SCALE OF THE WAR

The battles of Verdun and the Somme brought the world into a new era of total, industrial war. The two battles lasted a combined sixteen months and cost nearly 2 million casualties. When normal wastage along the remainder of the front is added, the number of casualties on the Western Front in 1916 rises to over 2½ million. The amount of munitions expended during the two battles is staggering. The two sides fired off a total of more than 35 million shells and 60 million machine gun rounds. A vast amount of industrial might was mobilised to supply the armies with everything from the countless bullets they fired to the food they ate to the beer they consumed. In the end, the battles of 1916 cost more than the yearly gross national products of most countries in the world. Such immense numbers represent another revolution in war. The First World War was the first modern total war. The societies and industries in all combatant nations had to work and sacrifice for the war effort on an unprecedented scale. Europe had reached a new, horrific level of warfare that was only to be exceeded by the Second World War.

THE DEADLOCK BREAKS

The year 1917 was one of trial and disappointment, which saw no country master the art of modern warfare. Russia, possibly the weakest of the great powers, cracked under the strain of modern war and the defeats her armies had suffered, and succumbed to revolution. The Germans, usually considered to be the strongest of the combatant nations, had taken such heavy casualties in 1916 that they had to fall back to more defensible positions on the Western Front to avoid suffering such losses again. In addition Germany was in such dire straits that its government chose to launch an unrestricted submarine (U-boat) campaign in the hope of crushing the British war effort through economic strangulation. The Germans knew that such a move might force the United States, hitherto a neutral giant, into the conflict. Such a gamble illustrates the desperate state of German affairs in 1917 and the country's inability to grasp the fundamental nature of modern, industrial warfare. One simply does not voluntarily force the greatest latent industrial power in the world into war. Though sometimes close run, the German effort to defeat the British failed. The gamble failed too when the United States declared war on Germany in April 1917.

The French also faced an important decision in 1917. Their experience at Verdun had been trying for the Army and for the entire nation. General

*The destruction of natural and man-made drainage systems by prolonged artillery bombardments compounded the misery of life on the Western Front and had a severely detrimental effect on tactical mobility. Here a wiring party of British troops crosses a water obstacle. (*Illustrated London News*)*

Robert Nivelle (1856–1924) became French Commander-in-Chief and adhered to an offensive strategy. When faced with the spectre of a war-weary France, Nivelle responded by planning a glorious campaign designed to win the war so quickly that France would not have time to follow Russia into societal collapse. Nivelle's offensive was based on the old formula of deploying overwhelming artillery fire and huge numbers of men. In many ways he had not moved beyond the ideas of 1916, and his men paid the price. The French attack began on 16 April 1917, one week after a subsidiary British offensive had opened at Arras. The Germans, aware of Nivelle's planning, repulsed the assault and inflicted 120,000 casualties upon the French. It seemed to be the killing fields of Verdun over again, and as a result the morale of the French Army broke. Nivelle subsequently lost his position as Commander-in-Chief and was replaced by General Philippe Pétain (1856–1951).

The British undertook the main offensive effort of 1917 on the Western Front at the Third Battle of Ypres. The battle began on 31 July and did not conclude until mid-November. Again the trenches moved little, and the losses were very high, somewhere in the region of 800,000 total casualties. Like the Somme, historians and laymen remember this battle (popularly known as 'Passchendaele') for its futility. Again Haig hoped for a breakthrough brought on by a heavy artillery bombardment. When that did not come to pass the battle settled down to the dreaded attrition. Closer

An American soldier demonstrates to his British friends what he intends doing to the first German he meets, 1918. By the end of the war there were over one and a half million US soldiers on the Western Front, which was even more than the number of men fielded by the British. The imminent arrival of US forces was a decisive factor in persuading the Germans to launch an offensive in spring 1918, although the most impressive successes in the Allied counter-offensive of summer and autumn were achieved by British and Empire troops. (IWM Q8847)

scrutiny, though, reveals a battle in which the British often moved forward with relative ease, bearing in mind the traditional defensive dominance. Especially in the second phase of the battle, under the local command of General Sir Herbert Plumer (1857–1932), the BEF made significant advances in tactics, which was to serve it well in 1918. However, the great historical black cloud that is Passchendaele swallowed all possible bright spots, leaving just an image of futility. It is only in recent years that revisionist historians have begun to look at the military changes made during 1917 that eventually led to the stunning British victories of 1918.

The coming of the new year saw many changes in the First World War. Russia had been knocked out of the conflict, allowing the Germans to shift forces west for one last attempt at total victory. In addition the United States was by spring 1918 sending large numbers of troops to France. These men still required additional training, but they were only the thin end of the wedge, for millions of 'Yanks' were on the way. There was to be a showdown: could Germany force a conclusion before the forces of the United States arrived in overwhelming numbers? The year 1918 would witness a change in the very way in which war was fought. The nations doing battle on the Western Front had been learning the art of modern war for nearly four years. In 1918 science and tactics would come together in a way that was revolutionary.

NEW INFANTRY WEAPONS

By 1918 science and invention, the hallmarks of 'modern' war, had begun to provide solutions to the riddle of trench warfare. On the Somme, only two years earlier, infantry had been seen as almost powerless against an entrenched enemy. However, by 1918 the infantry soldier was once again a force with which to be reckoned. There were now truly portable machine guns (for example, the British Lewis gun) that gave advancing infantry more firepower. In addition infantry could now carry their own artillery in the form of hand grenades and mortars. Such weaponry enabled the infantry to deal with an enemy strongpoint or machine gun nest on their own, rather than having to halt their forward momentum to wait for artillery assistance. Finally, infantry in 1918 also carried more exotic weaponry such as flamethrowers and bangalore torpedoes. Such changes meant that infantry could once again assume a major role on the battlefield.

The Germans are generally credited with being the first to experiment (on the Eastern Front) with new, updated infantry tactics, which are often associated with the name of General Oskar Hutier (1857–1934). The tactics called for the infantry to attack in bursts, rushing from cover to cover, rather than in waves. In the van of the attack were German storm troops. Their job was to use their firepower and speed to probe the enemy for weakness. Once located, the storm troops would infiltrate through the weak spot and advance to depth. Such tactics, it was hoped, would shock and dislocate the enemy defensive system and lead to the capture of the enemy's supporting artillery. It was a far cry from the waves advancing at the Somme. Using their new-found firepower, infantry would probe and advance quickly, avoiding the strongest points and leaving them for second echelon forces to mop up at a later, more convenient time. It is often forgotten that French and British tactics developed more or less in parallel.

On 21 March 1918 the Germans, under the command of General Paul von Hindenburg (1847–1934) and General Erich Ludendorff (1865–1937), launched Operation 'Michael' and achieved surprise against the British 5th Army. The Hutier tactics, aided by British mistakes, immediately proved

'Every position must be held to the last man: there must be no retirement. With our backs to the wall, and believing in the justice of our cause, each one of us must fight on to the end.'

Field Marshal Douglas Haig, order of the day, 12 April 1918

their worth. The 5th Army fought stubbornly but suffered a great reverse and by 6 April the Germans had advanced an amazing 40 miles. It appeared to be a great victory, but the advance ended in the same fate as the German push of 1914. After a few initial errors the Allies rushed reinforcements to the scene and eventually stemmed the German tide. Again the Allies could communicate and move laterally more quickly than the Germans could move forward. In addition, the great advance cost the Germans over 200,000 men, a price they could ill afford after nearly four years of war.

After the failure of Operation 'Michael', the Germans launched additional attacks both north and south of their original offensive. These later attacks met with more mixed results. However, an assault on French lines near the Chemin des Dames led to another great advance and brought the Germans near the River Marne yet again. Once he had achieved this success Ludendorff placed the remainder of his efforts there to try to crush the Allied line and advance on Paris. Try as they might, though, the German attacks could not break the Allied defensive line. The rules of the First World War were still in place, and though tactically proficient, the Germans had not yet solved the riddle of trench warfare. To make matters worse for the Germans, their strength was waning, and by the onset of summer the initiative had passed to the Allies.

The British too had been making major tactical advances, as their fleeting success at Cambrai on 20 November 1917, when tanks were used *en masse* for the first time, demonstrated. They used sophisticated new infantry tactics, coupled with major changes in the ability and role of artillery. On the Somme artillery could not easily hit what it could not see. Scientific developments had changed this relationship by 1918. Gunners had learned to compensate for the effects that weather and barrel wear had on the flight of a shell. British industry had become proficient in the manufacture of reliable fuses and shells. Such advances made artillery much more accurate and lethal, while other advances allowed it to hit unseen targets. Since 1915 spotter aircraft had circled the battlefield using radio to adjust the fire of artillery batteries. In another very important development, aircraft using cameras with special lenses to compensate for the curvature of the earth photographed the entire German defensive system in France. The British then used the detailed photographs to compile a very accurate map of the German lines. Artillery could fire using only the map as a guide. Before this innovation the guns had to fire before an attack in order to set their range, thus sacrificing surprise. Now British artillery could remain silent until the very moment of attack and then unleash a hail of unexpected and precise fire upon the enemy. Finally, the British had developed ways to locate hidden enemy artillery. These techniques of 'flash spotting' and 'sound ranging' called for spotters to locate the muzzle flash of an enemy artillery piece. Next, sophisticated microphones would pick up the sound of the shell being fired. The differences between the speed of light and sound enabled the discovery of the location of the German battery. Thus science enabled the British artilleryman of 1918 to hit what he could not see with stunning accuracy. The British nation, from worker to scientist to soldier, had come together to overcome the weaknesses of artillery. As a result, modern artillery and warfare were born.

First World War tanks were unreliable, slow and extremely uncomfortable for their crews. However, at the tactical level they could provide a degree of intimate support to other arms, and most importantly – as illustrated here – they could crush barbed-wire obstacles, creating gaps through which infantry could exploit. (RMAS Collection)

Although armoured, tanks were vulnerable to enemy fire of almost any kind. 'Bullet splash', whereby rivets and flakes of metal would be sent spinning through the interior of the vehicle by the impact of enemy rounds on the outside, caused many casualties, and even the lightest artillery pieces could easily penetrate the skin of the tank. By 1918 dedicated anti-armour weapons were also appearing, such as this German anti-tank rifle. Given its obvious weight and size, being ordered to carry it into action must have been less than popular. (RMAS Collection)

THE WESTERN FRONT, 1914–18

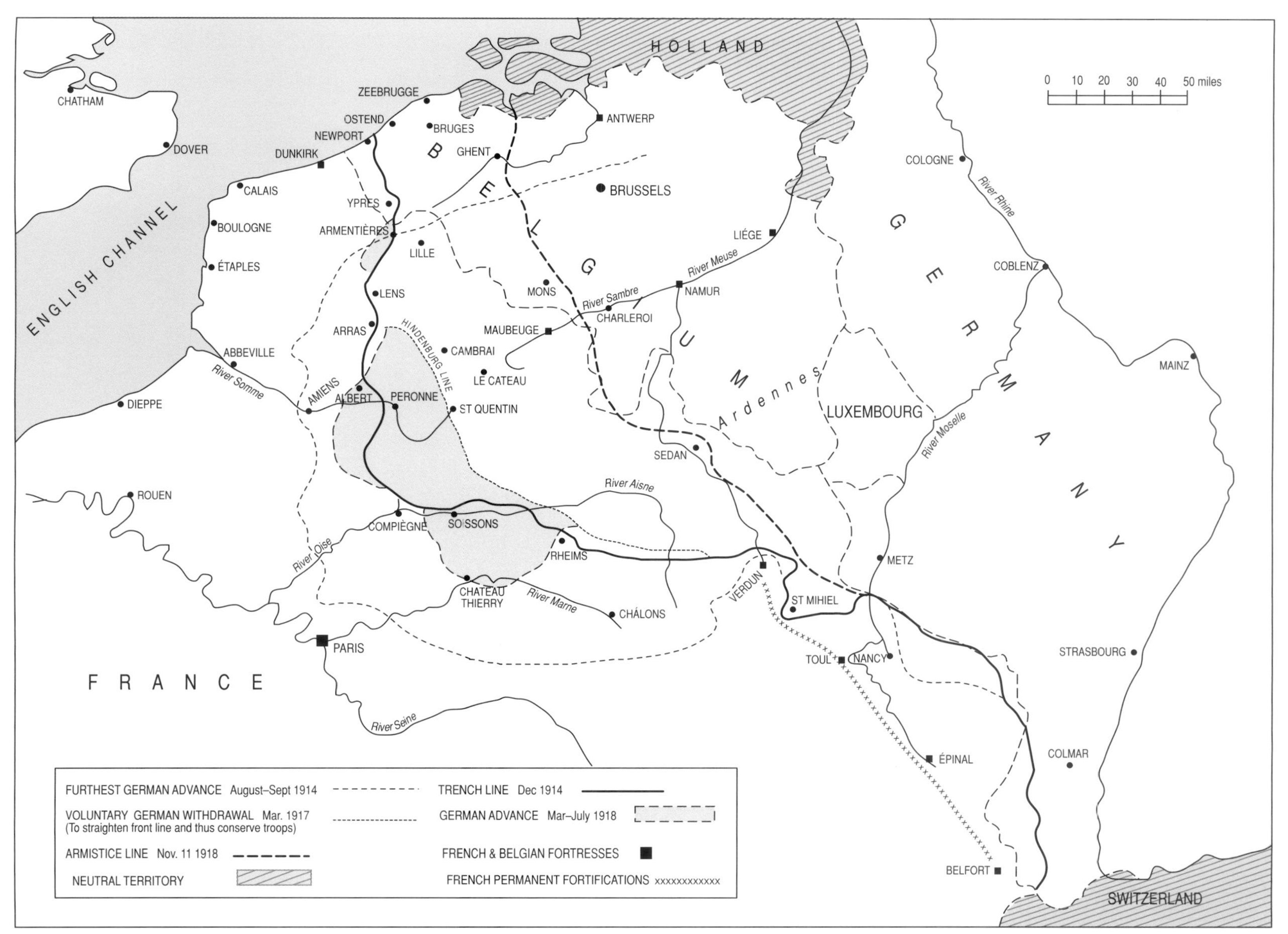

The British had learned from their mistakes, and their offensive plan for 1918 is a thing of modernist military beauty. In previous battles the British had been too reliant upon artillery to win the day. This was not the case in 1918. Haig and his commanders planned the coming battles using unprecedented levels of all-arms coordination. The modern battlefield is a symphony of war, and a commander, like a conductor, must use all the elements of a modern armed force seamlessly to achieve victory. The new plan called on infantry to use modern infiltration tactics. Where the Germans had been elitist and trained only a small proportion of their army in such tactics, all British infantry received such training. The role of the artillery too had changed. At the Somme the artillery had to do it all. In 1918 artillery was much more effective, and was called upon to do less. Artillery no longer had to defeat the enemy, only force him to keep his head down until the newly powerful infantry arrived at his trenches. In addition, the artillery had to deal with the opposing guns. British artillerymen could perform these duties with relative ease in 1918. The British also used massed tank formations to help breach the enemy trench systems and destroy bunkers and machine gun nests. Finally, air superiority allowed the British to use aerial communications and interdiction raids to augment the offensive.

British forces, among them strong formations of Canadians and Australians, launched a major attack on 8 August near Amiens. In preparation for the assault the British employed false radio traffic to deceive the Germans as to their intentions. In additional efforts to achieve surprise, British artillery did not fire ranging rounds prior to the battle. Finally, while the British amassed their tank forces, airplanes swooped over the German lines to cover the engine noise of the rumbling vehicles. The secrecy worked and the Germans were caught unawares when the artillery barrage began. The artillery struck with deadly accuracy. As soon as the shelling began, the infantry rushed forward under its cover accompanied by 400 tanks. The swift blow pinned the Germans in place as the infantry found and exploited weak points to advance to depth. The slow-moving tanks created havoc, while artillery and air strikes silenced German artillery and took a heavy toll of German reinforcements moving forward to the front lines. The British had launched a well-coordinated whirlwind of battle, and the Germans broke. By 12 August the British had advanced over 15 miles and had inflicted terrible casualties upon the German defenders. In a development of the greatest importance the Germans suffered

TANKS

Science and technology provided the British with an important innovation – the tank. The story of the development of the weapon is indicative of a truly modern war. Britain needed a way to overcome the enemy's defensive dominance. The military-industrial complex noted the battlefield requirement and designed a weapon suited to that need. Never before in warfare had such a marriage of battlefront and home front, fighting need and technological answer, taken place.

Tanks first saw wartime service in September 1916 at the Battle of the Somme, but they were too few in number to change its outcome. By 1918, though, the British possessed hundreds of the vehicles. Though numerous, the tank was still a rather ineffective weapon. In 1918 the British in the main used Mark V tanks, which had a top speed of barely 5 miles per hour, were poorly armoured, had little firepower and were prone to breakdown. Thus the tank was not yet a decisive weapon; that would have to wait until the Second World War. However, the development of the tank is illustrative of the modern nature of the First World War, and tanks would play an important role in the Allied victory in 1918.

'August 8th [1918] was the black day of the German Army in the history of this war.'

General Erich Ludendorff, My War Memories *(1919)*

significantly higher numbers of casualties than the British. Such a result was astounding in a war in which the defenders had possessed all of the advantages. Science, professionalism and all-arms coordination had shifted the balance of the First World War narrowly in favour of the attacker. The riddle was being solved.

Nevertheless, a major problem still existed for the British. The Germans could still move laterally and reinforce the affected area more quickly than the British forces could move forward to exploit their success. Like the German attack in 1918, the British assault bogged down. Rather than try to press forward once the advantage had been lost, as Ludendorff had earlier, Haig called an end to his attack at Amiens once the balance had shifted in favour of the defender. The battle had reached its logical conclusion, and there would be no clear breakthrough, so Haig called a halt. Not quite one week later, on 18 August, the British renewed their offensive to the north of Amiens, repeating their earlier performance. German reinforcements, which had been in the Amiens sector, were now rushed north to face the new offensive. When they arrived in force Haig ended the assault in that area, and the French under Pétain attacked further south, forcing the Germans to react yet again. The Allies had struck upon a war-winning operational method to go with their new tactics. A breakthrough was not possible due to German speed in reinforcement. However, new methods made it possible to rip away great chunks of the German lines before they could react. Attacks up and down the line kept the Germans guessing. As a result of an attack at Amiens the Germans would weaken their Flanders sector, making a British attack there easier. Once that attack began the Germans weakened their Champagne sector, allowing a French attack there. The Allies were no longer fighting battles for their own sake. With the French Marshal Ferdinand Foch now coordinating the actions of all the Allied armies, one battle logically led to and helped prepare the way for another. Battlefield successes, none of which was strategically decisive in its own right, were strung together into a seamless tapestry. This series of victories is usually referred to as the 'Hundred Days'. The British had discovered the operational level of war and solved the riddle of trench warfare in the process.

'The edifice begins to crumble. Everyone advance.'

Marshal Ferdinand Foch, despatch to British GHQ, 1918

The Hundred Days, along with the general privations that modern war forced upon its populous, forced Germany to sue for peace in November 1918. The German Army and the German nation had been decisively defeated in the first truly modern war. The sheer size and lethality of the First World War set it apart from all others that came before. Nations fought each other as nations, spending their fortunes and dedicating their entire populations to the destruction of the enemy. Industries ran at full capacity for years to sustain the insatiable demands of the battlefields. Nations had to call upon all of their resources, including female labour, to meet the crisis. A meaningful way to judge the importance of a war is to note the changes that it brought to the world. In this sense the First World War again ranks as a truly modern, total war, for the conflict transformed the political make-up of the world. Austria and Russia crumbled under the strain and were destroyed in the crucible of war. Germany was rent asunder, and left to grope its way toward eventual revenge. France and Britain, though victorious, saw the strain of a modern nation at war

The cost of the First World War (all figures estimates)

	Mobilised (millions)	Military battle deaths (millions)	Military wounded (millions)	Civilian dead (millions)	Economic and financial cost ($ millions)
Principal Allies					
France	8.41	1.36	4.27	0.04	49,877
British Empire	8.90	0.90	2.09	0.03	51,975
Russia	12.00	1.70	4.95	2.00	25,600
Italy	5.61	0.46	0.95	?	18,143
USA	4.35	0.05	0.20	?	32,320
Belgium	0.27	0.01	0.04	0.03	10,195
Serbia	0.70	0.04	0.13	0.65	2,400
Central Powers					
Germany	11.00	1.80	4.25	0.76	58,072
Austria-Hungary	7.80	0.92	3.62	0.30	23,706
Turkey	2.85	0.32	0.40	2.15 (mainly Armenians killed by Turks)	3,445
Bulgaria	1.20	0.07	0.15	0.27	1,015

change their societies in many ways. From votes for women to the rise of the welfare state, much altered even for the winners. Only the United States, a latecomer to the war, profited from the conflict. Even so, Americans would find their world transformed by the war, for the United States was now a reluctant world superpower.

In a more narrow military sense the First World War was also modern and revolutionary. Gone were the ideas and rules that had dominated military thinking from the time of Napoleon. Modernity, in the form of industrial might and the firepower of new weaponry, had transformed the battlefield. Each nation in the conflict saw its preconceived notions of war shattered on the barbed wire of Verdun and the Somme. As a result generals had to jettison the old ways of thinking about conflict and develop new tactics and doctrine. In the space of two years commanders on both sides of the front, especially the British, had succeeded in redefining war. Firepower, science and professionalism now dominated. Morale and spirit remained, but had been placed in perspective. The battles of 1918 were thoroughly modern. The tactics used by the British at Amiens set the stage for 'Blitzkrieg', Soviet Deep Battle and even the Gulf War. The manner in which the British fought from victory to victory set the stage for the development of the operational level of war. For good or ill the age of Napoleon, Lee and von Moltke the Elder had passed. Modernity had triumphed.

FOUR

NAVAL WARFARE, 1900–19

ANDREW LAMBERT

In many ways naval warfare between 1900 and 1919 served to re-educate navies, and the statesmen who used them, in the realities of warfare. For a number of reasons they had expected war at sea to be quick and decisive, both of itself and as the dominant factor in great power relations. Their expectations were of a single fleet battle that solved everything, without involving merchant shipping, civilians or collateral damage. Sadly, this was an illusion based on wishful thinking and wilful ignorance. Naval warfare between 1914 and 1918 reminded the optimists that reality is less simple and far less pleasant. The First World War at sea was a grim attritional struggle in which new strategies and new weapons were countered by old strategies and new weapons. The results were neither clear-cut nor glorious, but they were decisive. Unfortunately the contest was so lacking in glamour that naval power, the backbone of the British Empire, was not only removed from the exaggerated position in which it had been placed by pre-war sea power enthusiasts, but demoted to a position below its true worth by the focus on the human cost of the Western Front.

Alfred Thayer Mahan (1840–1914), prolific author of books and articles on sea power and naval history. Mahan was disliked by his fellow US naval officers for his apparent arrogance, yet remained tremendously influential both during and after his lifetime. His most important works reflected his respect for Britain's naval and imperial achievement, but he was also determined to persuade his own government to adopt a more positive attitude to the potential of sea power, an aim in which he eventually succeeded. (US National Archives)

COLONIES AND BATTLESHIPS

In 1900 naval power was the growth area in global defence spending. Any nation with pretensions to significance was buying into the sea power concept so cogently argued by Captain Alfred T. Mahan (1840–1914) of the United States Navy, whose book *The Influence of Sea Power Upon History, 1660–1783* was published in 1890. Mahan used history to show how the acquisition, maintenance and exploitation of battlefleet-based naval mastery led to the growth and triumph of empires, as exemplified by the current global dominance of Britain. The failure of Britain's rivals, notably France, was attributed to the failure of their governments to maintain strong navies, and their repeated decision to pursue attritional commerce raiding strategies instead of seeking to secure sea control through battlefleet action. While the target of the book was American politicians and naval officers, some of whom still favoured the American commerce raiding strategy used in the War of 1812, its impact was truly global. By 1900 it had been widely translated and had been taken up by British statesmen, the German Emperor, an American President and many more world leaders.

'It is not the taking of individual ships or convoys, be they few or many, that strikes down the money power of a nation; it is the possession of that overbearing power on the sea which drives the enemy's flag from it, or allows it to appear only as the fugitive; and by controlling the great common, closes the highway which moves commerce to and from the enemy's shores.'

Alfred T. Mahan, The Influence of Sea Power Upon History *(1890)*

Sea power was popular because all the major nations were engaged in the final rounds of imperial acquisition, with colonies as a vital status symbol. Africa and Asia were in the process of being divided, with precious few sovereign states able to assert their independence. The only Asian state to make the transformation to great power status, Japan, effectively joined the Western game, seizing territory from its neighbours. Imperialist states sought to control other countries to secure access to markets, vital raw materials, and areas into which they could decant surplus population without losing the people. For this purpose naval power was seen as the key to securing access to the colonies, and was supported by commercial and industrial interests. Unfortunately, the rhetoric of empire was more effective than the reality. Few states profited from their new lands, and fewer still could consider their empire secure.

Mahan's sea power was not open to all. Rather, it was a very singular form of power, one in which forces were capable of moving around the world, translating command of the sea from one area to another. The British Empire, which possessed a unique chain of bases across the entire globe, could move fleets with relative ease. These bases were all connected by submarine telegraph cables, and contained unrivalled supplies of best steam coal from South Wales. The Royal Navy was also effectively as strong as the next two (or even three) navies put together in terms of its number of modern effective warships. No nation could consider its overseas territory safe against such power. In 1898 the Anglo-French clash over the headwaters of the Nile had been resolved without war because France recognised she could not defeat Britain, and to fight would be to invite the destruction of her overseas empire. As the Kaiser observed, 'the poor French, they have not read their Mahan!'

HMS Majestic, *the classic pre-Dreadnought battleship.* Majestic *was launched in 1895 and mounted four 12-inch and twelve 6-inch guns. Constructed in response to the growing naval strength of France and Russia, the Majestics comprised the largest class of battleships (nine vessels) ever built. HMS* Majestic *herself was sunk off Gallipoli by a German submarine on 27 May 1915 with the loss of forty lives. (Royal Naval Museum, 1987/477 (14))*

Contemporary ideas on the nature of war at sea had been shaped by decades of relative inactivity. During this period technology had advanced without being subjected to the ultimate test of war. By the early 1890s the pace of advance in new systems had slowed appreciably, reaching something of a plateau with what later became known as the 'pre-Dreadnought'-type ships. Typical 'pre-Dreadnoughts' were steel-hulled, used coal-fired triple-expansion steam engines, mounted breech-loading artillery, with guns of 6-inch calibre and below capable of quick firing, were protected by alloy steel armour, and fitted with torpedoes.

Battleships displaced about 14,000 tons, steamed at up to 18 knots, mounted four 12-inch guns and twelve to fourteen 6-inch weapons, with smaller guns to drive off torpedo boats. Cruisers were generally smaller and faster, designed for fleet action or scouting, with torpedo boats for local defence and limited fleet service. The only recent naval wars, the Sino-Japanese of 1894 and the Spanish-American of 1898, had seen decisive fleet actions in which better equipped and larger Japanese and American forces had annihilated their weak and badly handled enemies, leading to the capture of territory. Modern sea power had produced rapid and decisive results.

However, expectations that this would continue to be the case were unrealistic. Wars between major powers over issues of the most profound importance have never been settled by a single battle or campaign. It took Britain and France twenty-two years to resolve their differences over Europe between 1793 and 1815. Even Trafalgar, the most 'decisive' victory at sea, had not been enough, and Napoleon was finally worn down by economic attrition. Mahan had pointed this out in his second sea power volume in 1892, but his conclusions were largely ignored. In part this reflected the educational and organisational weaknesses of contemporary navies. While armies adopted the Prussian/German staff system and planned for war, navies tended to focus on technical issues. The Royal Navy was content to apply strategies that had worked in previous wars, without adopting a planning staff or an educational system that would equip officers for such a role in wartime. Other navies were little better prepared. In 1900 nations that could not afford (or did not require) ocean-going battlefleets could choose alternative forms of naval power. Coast defence using short-range small battleships, torpedo boats, mines and shore batteries could secure local waters, and protect vulnerable coastal cities – or even colonial territory, within limits. Commerce destroying, using fast cruisers to run down merchant shipping, still had its devotees in France, but elsewhere it had been abandoned. The universal acceptance of sea power led minor nations to copy the great: three South American navies built Dreadnought battleships between 1906 and 1914. Not one of these ships ever fired a shot against their neighbours, although the Brazilian and Chilean ships fired on their own people.

After 1900 the final wave of imperialism took off, with the imperialists beginning to fight among themselves over conquered territory. The British were able to resolve their dispute with the South African republics in the Second Boer War (1899–1902) because they had undisputed command of the sea, both to move troops and supplies to the theatre, and to deter foreign intervention. This war, like many other British colonial conflicts, also provided a baptism of fire for young naval officers, albeit on land. For a generation they had been denied such experience at sea. The last British fleet action against serious opponents had been Trafalgar in 1805, and the last ship-to-ship encounter with equals against the Americans in 1815.

In 1904 Russia and Japan went to war over Korea and Manchuria (see map, p. 33). The clash was between the unlimited military resources of Russia, deployed via the Trans-Siberian railway, and Japan's smaller army, which could be moved to the theatre quickly by sea, provided the Japanese had command of the Sea of Japan and Yellow Sea. The Japanese had six modern British-built battleships, eight heavy cruisers and other craft. Russia had a fleet of seven battleships and four heavy cruisers based at Port Arthur and Vladivostok, on either side of the Korean peninsula.

The Japanese opened the war with a pre-emptive strike on 8 February 1904 when ten destroyers attacked the Russian fleet at Port Arthur. Caught unprepared, the Russians had three major units disabled, and although no heavy ships were lost, repairs would take some time. This gave the Japanese the initiative and they sank two isolated Russian warships at Chemulpo before landing their troops. To secure command of the sea the Japanese elected to lay siege to the isolated base at Port Arthur, while keeping the fleet pinned inside with minefields and a blockade. Mines proved to be the biggest ship killers, sinking one Russian and two Japanese battleships. Eventually the Russians recognised they would have to move their fleet to Vladivostok. The Russian fleet left harbour on 10 August and had to accept a battle because it lacked the speed to escape. At the end of a long-range engagement, mostly fought at 8,000 yards, the Russians were doing well, holding off the Japanese under Admiral Heihachiro Togo (1846–1934). Then, just as the sun was setting, two 12-inch shells hit the bridge of the Russian flagship, killing the Admiral, leaving her out of control, and throwing the Russian line into confusion. Finally the Russians scuttled home, to be sunk later by Japanese land-based howitzers. Raids by the Russian cruisers from Vladivostok proved annoying, until the ships were caught by a superior force on 14 August and badly beaten. This allowed Japanese troopships to ply the seas, and their armies won the battles in Manchuria.

While the Russo-Japanese War was still raging naval power was about to make another quantum leap. Several key technologies matured in the decade before 1910, enabling guns to be fired and controlled at ever longer ranges, while improved torpedoes forced battleships to fight further and further apart. The result was HMS *Dreadnought*, the first of a new

HMS Dreadnought, *the first 'all big gun' battleship.* Dreadnought *displaced 21,845 tons at full load and used a turbine powerplant instead of the less efficient and more unreliable reciprocating engines that equipped her predecessors. With her powerful armament, high speed and thick armour she rendered all existing capital ships obsolete. Ironically,* Dreadnought *never fired a shot in anger at a surface target during the First World War (although she did sink a U-boat), and the vessel was scrapped in 1923. (Portsmouth Central Library)*

TSUSHIMA

With the war on land going badly the Tsar elected to send his Baltic Fleet to the Far East, to save Port Arthur. Impressive on paper, this fleet of eight battleships and several heavy cruisers was largely made up of obsolescent ships, although it did include four new battleships. Their round-the-world voyage was an epic of ill-advised endeavour, for they arrived in the Straits of Tsushima in no condition for battle against the rested and refreshed Japanese.

Having located the Russians before dawn on 27 May 1905 Vice-Admiral Togo used his superior fleet speed to cross the Russian line of advance, and keep crossing it despite Russian attempts to engage broadside on. Battle opened at 1408 hours, at ranges around 7,000 yards. Although the Russians scored some hits, the concentrated Japanese gunfire shattered the leading Russian vessels, and one after another they turned over and sank, exploded or were left dead in the water. That night destroyers closed in to finish off the cripples, and by daybreak only a few old vessels, with one modern battleship, were left huddled together, surrounded by the Japanese and incapable of effective resistance. Wisely they surrendered. A handful of smaller ships escaped, including two light cruisers, an armed yacht and six destroyers. Total Russian casualties were 11,500 killed, wounded and captured. The Japanese lost 600 killed. In effect the entire Russian Navy, the third largest in the world, had been destroyed. After Tsushima the Russians accepted their defeat, signed away Korea and Manchuria and retired to lick their wounds. Tsushima joined Trafalgar as the pinnacle of modern naval achievement. The Japanese flagship, the *Mikasa*, has been preserved as a national monument.

> *'The* Mikasa *and the eleven others of the main force had taken years of labour to design and build, and yet they were used for only half an hour of decisive battle. We, too, studied the art of war and trained ourselves in it, but it was put to use for only that short period. Though the decisive battle took such a short time, it required ten years of preparation.'*
>
> *Admiral Heihachiro Togo*

The Japanese battleship Mikasa, *flagship of Vice-Admiral Togo at the Battle of Tsushima. Built in a British yard, as were most Japanese vessels,* Mikasa *was an extremely well-armoured ship capable of absorbing as well as delivering great punishment. Although sunk by an internal explosion in 1905,* Mikasa *was raised and restored to active service. She is now on permanent display as the last surviving pre-Dreadnought battleship. (NHC-Photo NH44621)*

generation of warships. She weighed 17,800 tons, mounted ten 12-inch guns and was driven by new turbine engines at up to 21 knots. While America and Japan had been thinking about such ships, the British First Sea Lord, Admiral Sir John Fisher (1841–1920), had built one in the truly astounding time of only a year and a day.

Fisher's move revolutionised the naval balance, and introduced a new, higher form of competition. In effect he threw down the gauntlet to other navies. If they wanted to remain in the first rank of naval strength they had to build Dreadnoughts, which were larger and more costly than older types of vessel. This would simplify Britain's global position by reducing the number of navies with first-class ships, and allow her to focus on those that made a serious response to *Dreadnought*. In the event only two nations met the challenge, the United States – which built steadily but slowly, and was not considered a rival by Britain – and Imperial Germany. No other power built more than half a dozen Dreadnoughts before 1914.

Admiral-of-the-Fleet Sir John Fisher, First Sea Lord from 1904 to 1910. Fisher was a man of great energy and determination who did much to prepare the Royal Navy for war in 1914. His educational reforms also ensured an enduring legacy, the positive effects of which were fully felt during the Second World War. (Royal Naval Museum)

GERMANY'S CHALLENGE

The German Navy had been revitalised and reoriented in 1898 by Navy Secretary Admiral Alfred Tirpitz (1849–1930). Tirpitz used his political skill to secure a fixed naval establishment in that year, and subsequently raised it in 1900 and again in 1906 to meet the *Dreadnought*. Under Kaiser Wilhelm II Imperial Germany sought global power, and saw Britain as an obstacle to her ambitions. Tirpitz's new navy was designed to operate in the North Sea, rather than protect German colonies and trade. It was intended to act as a political tool, securing Britain's acquiescence in German imperial and European policies by threatening her naval dominance. It was not intended that the fleet should actually fight. This policy called into question the very basis of British power, her naval mastery. After 1815 British policy had aimed at the preservation of peace and a European balance of power as the ideal conditions for trade. Britain's strategy had been based on the deterrent threat of an overwhelming naval force, and her ability to engage any other power in a long and ultimately unwinnable war of economic attrition. If a rival power had a fleet capable of questioning British naval mastery, even if it was not big enough to win, then deterrence was less credible.

By 1904 Britain had noticed the German challenge, symbolised by her new navy, and settled her own differences with France. In 1904–5 Britain deterred German threats against France by a clear statement of political

'All the years of my reign my colleagues, the Monarchs of Europe, have paid no attention to what I have to say. Soon, with my great Navy to endorse my words, they will be more respectful.'

Kaiser Wilhelm II of Germany

support and the movement of naval forces into the Baltic, where the fleet threatened vital German interests, notably iron ore shipments from Sweden. Fisher skilfully played on German fears of a pre-emptive strike along the lines of Port Arthur, by talking of 'Copenhagening' the German fleet – a reference to the British attack in 1807 that captured the entire Danish Navy in time of peace. This threat forced the Germans to divert a large part of their naval budget into coast defences, as their war-gaming indicated that a British attack would be likely to succeed. The legacy of Trafalgar, an unbroken run of successes dating back 200 years, gave the Royal Navy a moral superiority that no amount of training and drill could overcome.

While Tirpitz met the Dreadnought challenge, increasing his budget to buy bigger ships and to widen the Kiel Canal, his fixed fleet establishment left him hostage to British decision-makers. German industry had only enough turret-erecting shops to build the mountings for four capital ships (battleships or battlecruisers) per year. Britain, with a large warship-building industry, much of it for export, could accelerate construction more easily. Britain had invariably met challenges like Tirpitz's by engaging in a naval arms race. Here superior industrial capacity, political commitment and financial strength ensured that Britain won through. By building Dreadnoughts Tirpitz had entered a naval race with Britain. Fisher, who wanted to deter war through superior strength, accepted the challenge. He built his ships as cheaply as possible, to get the best value from his limited budget. British ships cost little more than half their German contemporaries. Then in 1908–9 he used his mastery of the press and propaganda to build eight capital ships in a single year, despite the opposition of two powerful Cabinet ministers, David Lloyd George (1863–1945) and Winston Churchill (1874–1965). This acceleration defeated Germany, which in 1912 effectively ended the naval race, shifting resources to the Army to meet the threat of Russia. This was a great naval victory. In the next two years Anglo-German relations improved, and the 'naval race' had no bearing on the outbreak of the First World War. However, the timing of the war was influenced by the Kiel Canal. This had been widened to permit Dreadnoughts to pass, and was only completed in the early summer of 1914. Without the canal Germany could not go to war.

'The Navy is the 1st, 2nd, 3rd, 4th . . . ad infinitum Line of Defence! If the Navy is not supreme, no Army, however large, is of the slightest use.'

Admiral Sir John Fisher

Between 1906 and 1914 the pace of naval technical development did not slacken. Fisher followed the *Dreadnought* with a new transitional warship, the battlecruiser. This was his ideal type, a ship combining the firepower of a battleship with the tactical and strategic speed of a cruiser. Such ships would solve the strategic problems of Britain's global empire, moving rapidly from one ocean to another. However, the British battlecruisers were also protected like cruisers, not battleships. Their thin armour would come back to haunt them. Battle ranges continued to increase, partly because new torpedoes fitted with gyroscopes and more powerful engines could reach out to 10,000 yards, and partly because the fire control instruments themselves had improved. In the late 1890s naval gunnery had suddenly moved ahead, with British reforms transforming the rate of hitting from 20 per cent to 90 per cent in a few years. Then improved range-finding instruments enabled opening shots to be fired at up to 15,000 yards with a small degree of error. However, the problem of firing heavy guns from one moving platform at another moving platform, when the platforms were moving at different speeds and on converging or diverging courses, remained. Naval gunners and engineers developed calculating equipment to solve the equations, and by 1914 the first mechanical analogue computers were ready for war. These generated information for a director system that ensured all heavy guns pointed at the same target. Only now could the theoretical range of heavy naval guns be exploited.

The guns themselves had also increased in size. *Dreadnought*'s 12-inch guns were replaced by 13.5-inch weapons in 1909, Japanese and American 14-inch guns in 1912, and then British 15-inch in 1914. Each increase in calibre had a significant impact on the size and striking energy of the shell, the 15-inch shell being twice as heavy as the 12-inch. Ships with 13.5-inch or larger guns were termed 'Super-Dreadnoughts'. They too were twice as big as the first of the type. Costs soared, making the ships an investment that had to be carefully guarded, rather than an instrument of war to be used in pursuit of victory. The loss of a capital ship became a matter of national significance, because there were relatively few of them and they took around two years to replace. In 1904 the Japanese had elected to sacrifice an army at Port Arthur, rather than take any risks with their fleet. Between 1914 and 1918 all the major powers would hoard their battleships, to a greater or lesser degree. This placed an added emphasis on other types.

One of these other types, the submarine, only became an effective weapon system around 1910 with the advent of diesel engines, improved torpedoes and wireless. Britain had more modern boats than any other power, but Germany made up a lot of ground after a late start, with excellent engineering. Destroyers had grown to around 1,000 tons, with oil-fired turbines capable of over 30 knots, torpedoes and 4-inch guns. A new light cruiser type of up to 5,000 tons, 28 knots and 6-inch guns led the scouting forces and supported destroyer flotillas. Germany pioneered rigid Zeppelin airships for strategic reconnaissance, while the British developed seaplanes.

By 1914 technology had transformed the strategic seascape. Capital ships no longer expected to venture into enemy coastal waters, for fear of mines, submarines and coastal artillery. Fisher had long expected that the North Sea would be deserted in an Anglo-German war, left to the submarines and destroyers while the heavy ships were held back for more important tasks. Even so, many statesmen and admirals on both sides expected an early and decisive battle on the lines of Trafalgar and Tsushima. If the war was going to be over by Christmas the fleets would have to come out and fight. In the event the war would surprise everyone.

THE FIRST WORLD WAR: INITIAL MOVES

The outbreak of war in August 1914 pitted Britain, France and Russia (the Entente) with Japan, against Germany and Austria-Hungary. The naval balance was wholly in favour of the Entente powers, who had almost a 50 per cent superiority in modern capital ships. The main question to be

British and German naval strengths, August 1914

	British		German	
	total	(home waters)	total	(home waters)
Dreadnoughts	20 + 17 under construction/ working up	(20)	13 + 7 under construction/ working up	(13)
Battlecruisers	8 +2 under construction/ working up	(4)	5 +3 under construction/ working up	(4)
Old battleships	40	(38)	22	(22)
Cruisers (heavy and light)	102	(48)	41	(32)
Destroyers/ torpedo boats	301	(270)	144	(144)
Submarines	78	(65)	30	(30)

answered in the war would be how to apply that superiority to achieve the political aim of defeating the enemy.

Rather than trying to deter war in 1914 through clear political statements and a movement of the fleet, the British government ignored the danger and allowed the First Lord of the Admiralty, Winston Churchill, to send the Grand Fleet – including all the Dreadnoughts under Admiral John Jellicoe (1859–1935) – to Scapa Flow in the Orkney Islands. From there it could have no effect on German decision-making. It was well placed, once war broke out, to intercept any German ships trying to enter or leave the North Sea, supported by the Second Fleet of older ships to close the Straits of Dover and escort the British Expeditionary Force (BEF) to France. A distant blockade of Germany had been established, at a range beyond that anticipated by Tirpitz. The German High Seas Fleet, a misnomer if ever there was one, took station at Kiel and Wilhelmshaven, linked by the Kiel Canal. It had no plans to seek out the British, rather lamely expecting them to come into German coastal waters, to be worn down by mines and torpedoes, until the Germans had the upper hand at sea. The only impact of the High Seas Fleet on the Schlieffen Plan was the railway timetable problem of integrating thousands of tons of coal moving from south to north with troop trains running from east to west; the German Army did not bother to include the fleet in their plan.

Outside Europe the long-anticipated cruiser war was soon over. British preparations were so thorough, and their cable communications so good, that the first 'British' shot of the war was fired by a harbour battery at Melbourne, Australia, to stop a German merchant ship leaving. German submarine cables were immediately cut, and German wireless codes were seized from merchant ships. The only German forces at large were the battlecruiser *Goeben* and the cruiser *Breslau* in the Mediterranean, a squadron in the Pacific under Vice-Admiral Maximilian Graf von Spee (1861–1914), and individual cruisers in the West Indies and East Africa. The *Goeben* escaped to Turkey after a catalogue of errors by superior British forces who were badly led, and not helped by poor staff work in London. The two isolated cruisers were soon dealt with. One blew up on her own, while the other was driven into an East African estuary. Admiral von Spee's squadron left the Caroline Islands and steamed across the Pacific to South America, where it was intercepted off Coronel in Chile by a smaller British force under Rear-Admiral Sir Christopher Cradock (1862–1914). Aware that the man who had failed to engage the *Goeben* had been court-martialled, Cradock engaged on 1 November, but both his heavy cruisers were sunk with all hands by their more powerful adversaries.

At this point Fisher, now seventy-four years old, was brought out of retirement to resume office as First Sea Lord under Winston Churchill. Fisher immediately sent two battlecruisers to intercept Spee, which they did as he approached the Falkland Islands in December 1914. Four of the five German ships were sunk and the only survivor was then hunted down. Spee had detached the *Emden* before crossing the Pacific, and she had a short but profitable career as a raider, before being intercepted by HMAS *Sydney* and destroyed off the Cocos Islands on 9 November 1914. The German base in China, Tsingtao, fell to the Japanese and other colonial possessions were taken by British, Australian, New Zealand and South African forces. The naval conflict outside Europe was the only war to be 'over by Christmas'.

In the North Sea the first major action occurred on 28 August, when a British submarine and cruiser sortie into the Heligoland Bight ran into stiff opposition from German cruisers. British battlecruisers under Vice-Admiral David Beatty (1871–1936) came up in support and sank three German cruisers before their heavy ships could arrive. The following month both sides scored their first submarine successes, and on 22 September *U-9* sank three old British heavy cruisers patrolling off the Dutch coast. One month later, on 27 October, the Dreadnought HMS *Audacious* sank after hitting a single mine off the Irish Coast. Two days after that, the First Sea Lord, Prince Louis of Battenberg, resigned following a vicious press attack on his German origins. Fisher returned, and immediately infused his ruthless energy and drive into a hitherto lethargic war effort. Even as he did so British and French warships in the Channel played a major part in stabilising the front line, using heavy bombardments to stall German offensives near Dunkirk.

However, this was not enough for Fisher. He knew that the Navy would only get one political chance to stage a major offensive, and he was determined that it should be aimed at the heart of German power. He would use naval superiority to take the war to Germany with an offensive into the Baltic, cutting German iron ore supplies. For this purpose he ordered a fantastic armada of specialist craft, ranging from five new battlecruisers, through anti-submarine and mine-sweeping types to landing craft and heavy gun monitors for coastal bombardment. He planned to advance up the Belgian coast to the Dutch frontier, cooperating with the BEF under his old colleague Sir John French (1852–1925). He would then use battlefleet superiority to push a powerful force, but not the Grand Fleet, into the Baltic. Here it would rely on Russian bases. If the Germans elected to give battle for the Baltic narrows, as he believed they would, they could be destroyed. If they did not, their bases and the Kiel Canal could be attacked and ruined. Pre-war planning at the Committee of Imperial Defence had concluded that iron ore supplies were vital to Germany, and that if the blockade could be tightened Germany would collapse.

'Damn the Dardanelles. They will be our grave.'

Sir John Fisher, 1915

GALLIPOLI

Unfortunately, while Fisher's plans for a sortie into the Baltic were being developed Churchill, who had already demonstrated a marked predilection for wild schemes by sending untrained naval reservists to Antwerp as infantrymen in 1914, pushed a scheme to attack the Dardanelles to force Turkey out of the war. This would also clear up the embarrassment of the *Goeben*. Initial long-range attacks in November 1914 had been surprisingly successful, the Turkish defences being antiquated and ill-prepared. However, the attacks warned the Turks and their German advisers, who rapidly reinforced the area. In January 1915 the War Cabinet adopted Churchill's plan. Fisher had never supported the scheme, rightly believing it to be a peripheral distraction that would not help to defeat Germany. Because he and Churchill worked at opposite ends of the day, Fisher in the morning and Churchill late at night, the subject was never discussed. Fisher knew the plan could not work without an army, but Churchill pressed on, wilfully misconstruing any evidence to support his plan.

Eventually an Anglo-French fleet of old battleships staged a grand attack on 18 March 1915 and, after initial success, lost three battleships on a single small minefield. The attack failed because the ships had no high-explosive ammunition; they were trying to demolish large earthworks with semi-armour-piercing shells, containing only about 12 pounds of black power. It was little wonder that they could only achieve results with direct hits on the enemy guns, for which they had to get in very close. (The same lack of high explosive led to the 'shell scandal' and the fall of the government in May 1915.) Until the forts were destroyed, as they could have been with proper ammunition, the mines could not be swept effectively and the attack was bound to fail. Attempts to pass integrated coast defence systems have to defeat one element in order to deal with the others. Within weeks the failure had been reinforced with a large-scale amphibious landing on the Gallipoli peninsula that once again proved to be a case of too little, too late. Fisher believed the Dardanelles was a distraction, and objected to the increasing demands it was making on his planning and resources. On 15 May he resigned when Churchill once again ignored him and sent reinforcements. Together with the 'shell scandal', Fisher's resignation brought down the government and forced Churchill out of the Admiralty. The cost of removing the dangerous and quixotic Churchill had been high. Fisher, the only British admiral of genius with ideas for carrying the war to Germany, could not be replaced. His successors, and Churchill's, were pedestrian men, lacking vision, drive and optimism. There would be no more big naval offensives in this war, wasting the Allies' greatest asset.

Anglo-French naval power in the Mediterranean played a key role in deterring Italy from joining her Triple Alliance partners. With her coast, communications, cities and industry all exposed to a superior fleet Italy simply could not go to war with Britain. Instead, she joined the Entente powers on 23 May 1915. For the rest of the war the Italian and Austrian fleets effectively neutralised one another in the Adriatic, with a little help from Britain and France. By contrast, Austrian and German U-boats operated in the Mediterranean, where they proved to be a serious menace.

WAR IN THE NORTH SEA

British strategy was finally decided by the unexpected success of the call for volunteers. With over 1 million men now under arms, and nowhere else to send them but France, Britain became a continental military power by default, and without ever making a conscious choice. The fact that her two allies, France and Russia, had effectively thrown away more than 1 million men in badly organised offensives in 1914 made the presence of large numbers of British troops essential. The cost was severe, for industry, exports and trade were decimated, allowing America and Japan to capture British markets, and forcing Britain to call in her overseas investments to fund the war. This war would cost Britain her economic pre-eminence, because it was not fought along traditional British lines. It has been argued that this 'Continental Commitment' was inevitable, but the records suggest there were alternatives, while the experience of fighting Napoleon demonstrated that asserting hegemony over the entire continent did not produce the benefits sought. A more dynamic use of sea power, and better planning, might have saved a great many British lives, much treasure, and a global position.

In the North Sea the British gained a priceless advantage from Signals Intelligence. Not only could they locate German wireless transmissions, but through a series of coups culminating in the Russian capture of a naval code book in the Baltic, they had broken into the German cypher. This provided an advantage that could be maintained throughout the war.

BRITAIN, HOME WATERS, NORTH SEA, CHANNEL AND GERMAN COAST, 1914–18

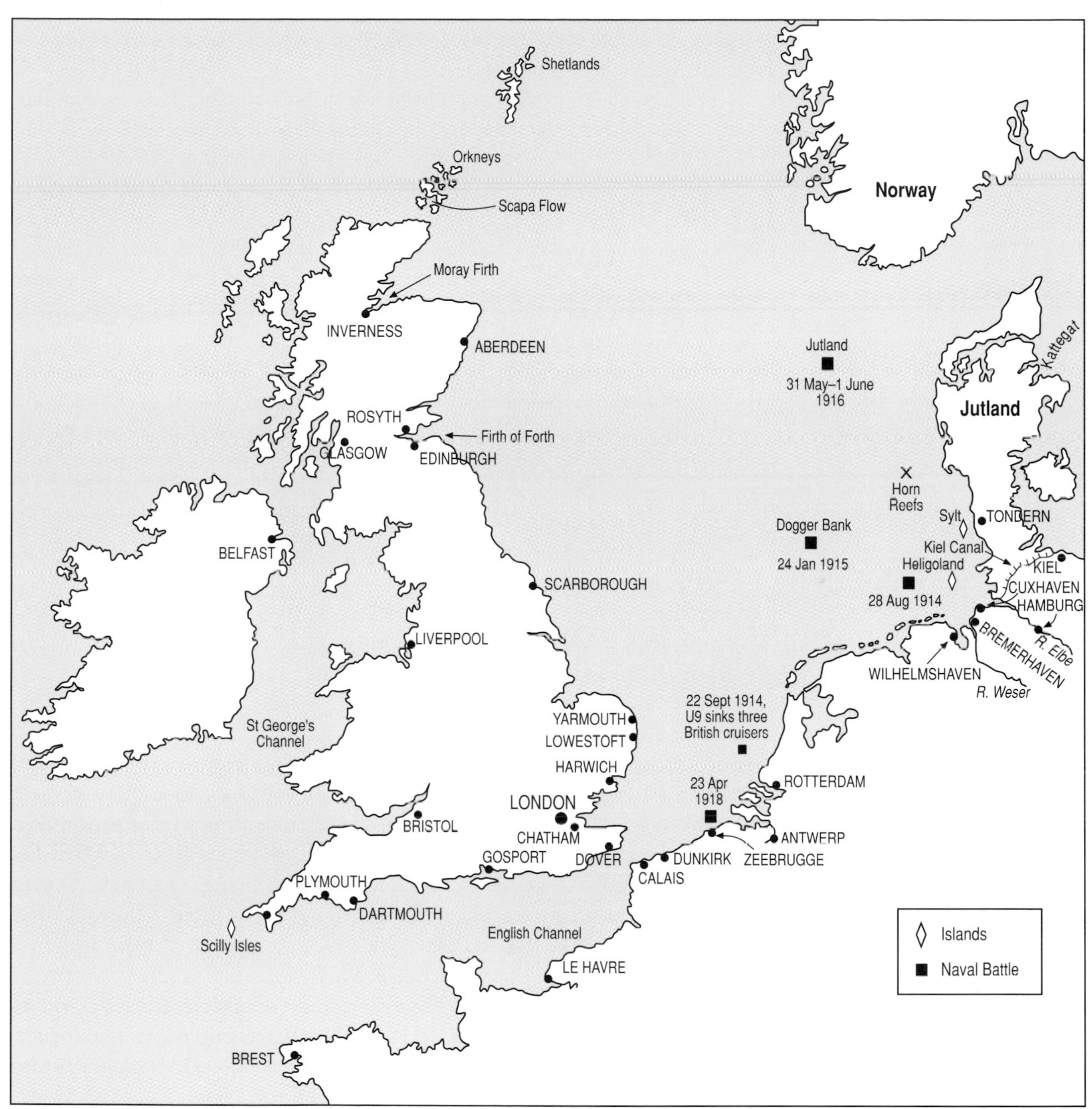

Room 40, the Signals Intelligence section, provided accurate and timely warning of almost all German naval activity. Unfortunately, this Intelligence was not always heeded or used with skill. The German battlecruisers under Admiral Franz von Hipper (1863–1932) had conducted coastal bombardments, hoping to draw a portion of the British fleet into action, without success. Quite what military targets they hoped to damage at Scarborough it is hard to imagine. However, when they sortied again in January 1915 the British set a trap. Beatty intercepted at daybreak on the

British and German strengths, Battle of Jutland, 31 May–1 June 1916

	British	German
Battleships	28	16
Battlecruisers	9	5
Battleships (pre-Dreadnoughts)	0	6
Armoured cruisers	8	0
Light cruisers	26	11
Destroyer leaders	5	0
Destroyers	73	61
Minelayers	1	0
Seaplane carriers	1	0

24th, with a more powerful force, and chased the Germans home, scoring a devastating hit on Hipper's flagship, the *Seydlitz*, which very nearly blew up after two magazines burnt out. Although the heavy cruiser *Blücher* was hit, stopped and sunk, poor British signalling and a lack of common sense among subordinates when Beatty's flagship dropped out allowed Hipper to escape with only one ship lost.

The German response was to begin Zeppelin bombing raids over Britain and to attack merchant shipping, the old strategy of despair for powers that had failed to secure command of the sea. Tirpitz hoped to cut British food supplies. The sinking of the 30,000-ton liner *Lusitania* off Southern Ireland by *U-20* on 7 May 1915, in which 1,201 people – among them 128 Americans – lost their lives, caused a protest from Washington that stopped the German campaign, and made clear the diplomatic limits of such action. Nor were the Americans prepared to tolerate British blockade policy, about which they protested with considerable effect. Only when the Americans joined the war would these issues be resolved. The German campaign continued under 'cruiser rules', which obliged them to give passengers and crew an opportunity to abandon ship. They continued to be successful, although British 'Q' ships (small ships with hidden guns that suddenly opened fire on unsuspecting submarines) forced them to be careful. Both sides went beyond what was considered acceptable before the war, but this was a total war, and all action that helped to advance the cause was tolerable.

Before accepting the logic of the U-boat war the Germans made one last attempt to whittle down the British fleet. In mid-1916 the Zeppelins and U-boats were recalled to link up with the fleet by the new commander, Admiral Reinhard Scheer (1863–1928). Scheer hoped to draw the British fleet over a submarine trap, keep contact with it through his Zeppelins, and when it was weakened engage and destroy a portion of the Grand Fleet. After a raid on Lowestoft and Great Yarmouth in April Scheer tried again in late May. In the interval Jellicoe had failed to draw him out with a seaplane raid, and now planned to sweep into the Kattegat to threaten the Baltic approaches. Forewarned of Scheer's moves by Room 40, Jellicoe and Beatty were at sea before the Germans, and the forces finally collided on the afternoon of 31 May off the coast of Jutland. Unaware that Scheer's entire fleet was out Jellicoe had not hurried south, allowing Beatty's battlecruisers to get too far ahead.

'There seems to be something wrong with our bloody ships today.'

Admiral David Beatty, 31 May 1916

Beatty met Hipper at 1530 hours and the two forces settled down to engage at about 16,000 yards at 1548 hours, heading south toward the High Seas Fleet. Superior initial range-finding, better light conditions and poor British fire distribution gave Hipper the edge. At 1602 hours HMS *Indefatigable*, Beatty's rearmost ship, blew up and sank with only two survivors. At 1626 hours HMS *Queen Mary*, his crack gunnery ship and next astern, also disappeared in a devastating explosion. Both ships had been destroyed by poor ammunition-handling procedures. Safety interlocks designed to stop any flash passing from the turret to the magazine had been deliberately removed in order to increase the rate of fire, and ammunition was also stacked in passageways. Beatty's flagship, HMS *Lion*, was also hit in one turret, but her safety interlocks had recently been replaced and she survived. At 1630 hours Beatty was reinforced by the four fast battleships of the 5th Battlesquadron, mounting 15 inch guns. These quickly turned the

JUTLAND, 31 MAY–1 JUNE 1916

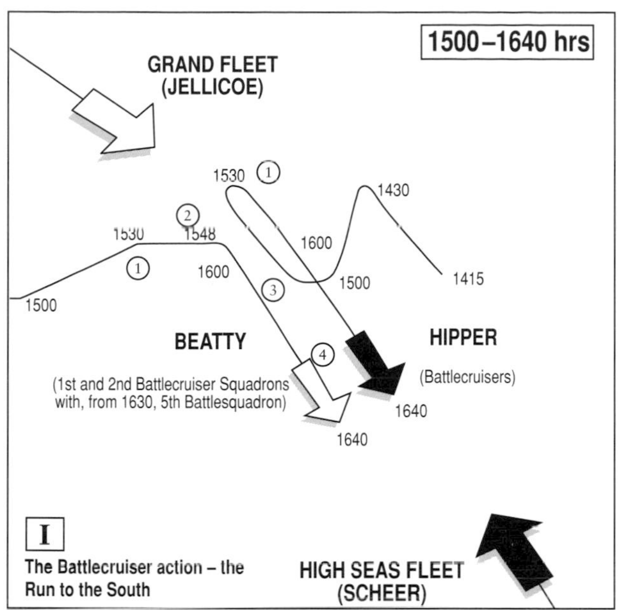

I
The Battlecruiser action – the Run to the South

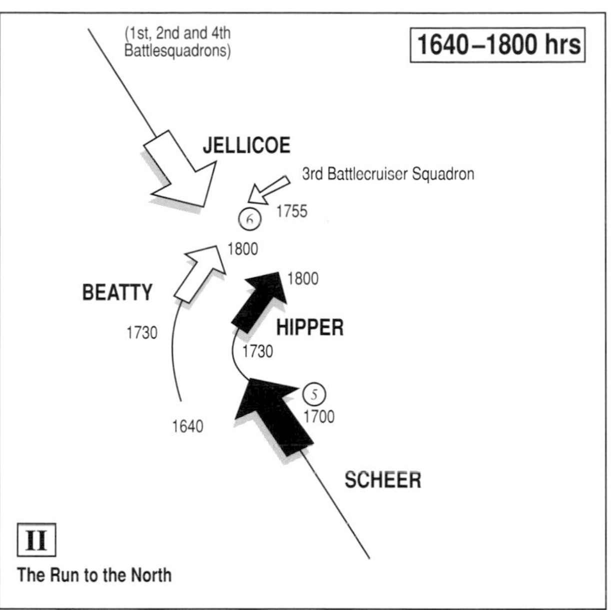

II
The Run to the North

1. Battlecruiser fleets sight one another, 1630 hours, 31 May
2. Engagement comences, 1548 hours
3. Battlecruiser HMS *Indefatigable* sunk, 1602 hours
4. Battlecruiser *Queen Mary* sunk, 1626 hours
5. High Seas Fleet opens fire, 1700 hours
6. 3rd Battlecruiser Squadron opens fire, 1755 hours

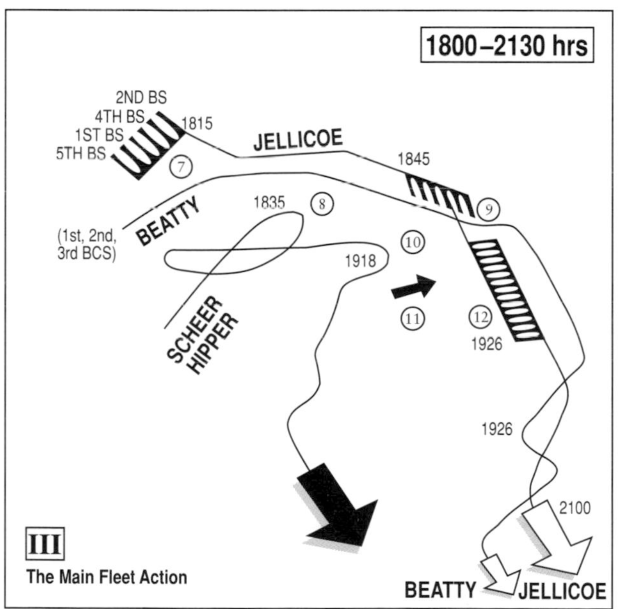

III
The Main Fleet Action

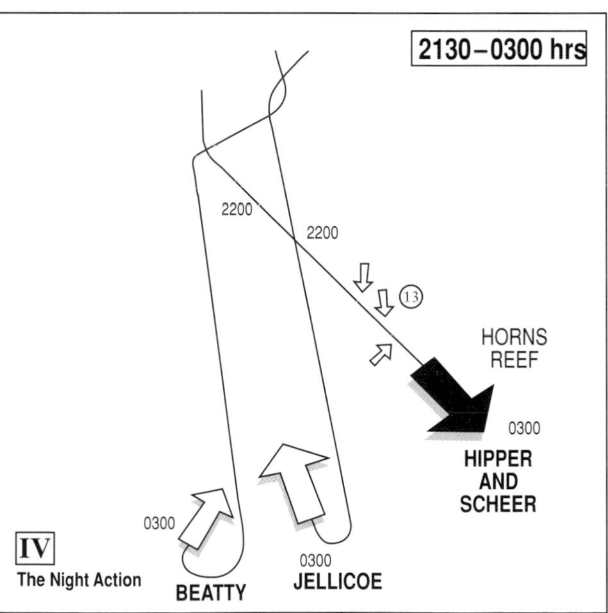

IV
The Night Action

7. Jellicoe's battle line deploys into column, 1815 hours
8. Jellicoe crosses Scheer's 'T', 1835 hours
9. Battlecruiser HMS *Invincible* sunk, 1835 hours
10. Jellicoe again crosses Scheer's 'T', 1910 hours
11. German torpedo boat attack, 1923 hours
12. Jellicoe turns away, 1926 hours
13. British destroyer attacks, 0100–0230 hours, 1 June

tables on the Germans, inflicting numerous hits which wrecked turrets and ruined the calm, undisturbed conditions which their sensitive fire control instruments required. German gunnery fell away just as the High Seas Fleet came into view to the south, and Beatty, recognising that his mission was to bring it under the guns of the Grand Fleet, turned north. This time the light favoured the British, who did more of the hitting.

Just before the British Grand Fleet appeared the 3rd Battlecruiser Squadron, which had been with Jellicoe, engaged Hipper's force, crippling his flagship *Lutzow* before HMS *Invincible* blew up like the other two battlecruisers. Jellicoe, despite poor reporting from most of his subordinates, was able to deploy his force of twenty-four Dreadnoughts in a single line, and cross the T of Scheer's sixteen Dreadnoughts and six pre-Dreadnoughts as he steamed north. At 1830 hours elements of Jellicoe's fleet opened fire on Hipper's battlecruisers and the leading German battleships, which were unable to see to reply effectively and were severely battered. Jellicoe's flagship, HMS *Iron Duke*, produced a devastating series of salvoes at ranges around 10,000 yards. At 1833 hours Scheer ordered his fleet to make an emergency turn away, all ships turning together. Jellicoe could not see this, and no one who could do so bothered to tell him. However, he continued south, and at 1855 hours Scheer tried again, colliding with Jellicoe at 1910 hours. This time Scheer had to throw in his battlecruisers and a destroyer torpedo attack to extricate his fleet with another emergency turn away at 1918 hours after further heavy damage.

Jellicoe responded to the torpedo attack by turning away, as he had always intended, thereby losing contact. The torpedoes were avoided, but the chance to follow the Germans and finish the battle was lost. This was important, because the High Seas Fleet had a number of damaged ships, and the pre-Dreadnoughts were 3 or 4 knots slower than the British fleet. A vigorous pursuit would have forced Scheer to fight or allow his fleet to be destroyed piecemeal. Jellicoe, more fearful of losing ships than anxious to secure victory, decided not to take the chance that evening. The visibility was very bad, well inside torpedo range, and he carried the whole war on his shoulders. Jellicoe knew that if he lost the fleet Britain was finished. Unwilling to fight at night, for which he had not trained his fleet, Jellicoe elected to cruise south, expecting to meet Scheer at daybreak off the Amrum bank, with the enemy still to his north, cut off from their bases. Unfortunately, Room 40 Intelligence that Scheer had called for a Zeppelin to be over the northern route (the Horns Reef passage) at daybreak, which would have told him where to be, was not passed on through a particularly inept piece of staff work.

'Jutland was as decisive as Trafalgar . . . The Germans had been driven home, and all thoughts about a renewed encounter with the Grand Fleet were equated with a suicide sortie.'

Holger Herwig, 'Luxury' Fleet: The Imperial German Navy 1888–1918 *(1980)*

To compound the error Scheer was able to push his fleet through the rear of the Grand Fleet during the night, after a series of close-range engagements in which German night-fighting skills were only matched by bold British destroyer work. Once again no one told Jellicoe what was happening and the next morning he was left to survey an empty sea, littered with wreckage, much of it British. Only then did he learn of Beatty's losses. By that time Scheer was almost home, the devastated battlecruiser *Lutzow* had been scuttled and several other ships were only just afloat. A deeply disappointed Jellicoe returned to Scapa. Within twenty-four hours he had twenty-four capital ships ready for action, Scheer had only ten. The German press release claimed victory, noting that they had sunk more British ships and killed more British sailors (6,094 to 2,551), but they ignored the loss of the *Lutzow*. The British communiqué was accurate and understated, leading many to believe that the Germans had won. However, when the truth came out it became clear that the Germans had lost. They had been driven from the field in confusion, and scuttled home unable to face another day.

At Jutland the British had won an expensive tactical victory, one that confirmed their strategic dominance of the war at sea. The British losses were primarily the three battlecruisers and three old heavy cruisers that blew up. All were avoidable; the heavy cruisers had no business being there, and the battlecruisers would probably have survived if their magazine safety systems had been in place.

While Scheer tried another U-boat ambush in August, sinking two cruisers, he recognised that Germany could not win the war at sea with her battlefleet. Jellicoe became more cautious, anxiously awaiting solutions to the various technical shortcomings revealed by the battle. In December he became First Sea Lord, and Beatty took over the Grand Fleet. While the Admiralty needed a new leader it is probable that Jellicoe, by now exhausted after three years commanding the Grand Fleet, was too tired for the new job, and did not bring to it the flexibility of mind and optimism needed to meet a new and more severe trial.

Jutland: the cost (vessels lost)

	British	German
Battleships (pre-Dreadnought)	0	1
Battlecruisers	3	1
Armoured cruisers	3	0
Light cruisers	0	4
Destroyers	8	5
Men killed	6,094	2,551
Men wounded	690	488

THE U-BOAT WAR

After Jutland, Scheer and other leaders of the German Navy recognised that the surface fleet could not win the war, and that the Navy had to do something to justify itself at a time when the Army was being bled white

The submarine U-35 uses its deck gun to sink a merchant vessel in the Mediterranean in 1917. Although the Germans inflicted heavy losses on Allied shipping, the adoption of unrestricted submarine warfare was an act of desperation and represented the failure of Germany's maritime strategy. (U-boot Archiv)

The introduction of convoys in April 1917 resulted in a substantial reduction in Allied losses to U-boat attack. Here, convoy HG 102 from Gibraltar to the east coast passes up the English Channel, 6 September 1918. (PRO ref: ADM 137/2771)

on the Western Front. Because the Army was temporarily unable to mount a significant offensive, the Army High Command adopted the Navy's plan to relaunch unrestricted U-boat warfare in December 1916, expecting to defeat Britain within six months by attacking her food supplies. With that the Entente would collapse. The danger of American intervention was dismissed, because the war would be over before the USA could do anything.

On 1 February 1917 Germany launched the campaign with 105 U-boats. The United States entered the war on 6 April, after further loss of American lives on merchant ships. By April the shipping losses had reached a peak of 860,334 tons per month. However, these figures simply could not be sustained, for there were not enough U-boats, and the British introduced convoy for the most dangerous routes from April. This removed the key German advantage, the ability to attack merchant shipping without fear of counter-attack. The most effective method of sinking U-boats remained mines, and it was gradually recognised that offensive mine-laying held the key to defeating the U-boat. Convoy would reduce losses, mines would wear down the U-boats. This was the reality of war at sea, a grim attritional struggle between small ships. British forces closed the Channel to submarines with minefields and nets by early 1918. A subsequent attempt to close the Northern Approaches with a 200-mile minefield between Scapa Flow and Norway was less effective. In the North Sea British mine-layers attempted to close the German passages, while German minesweepers struggled to keep them open. The cost was high. German casualties in minesweepers were higher than in U-boats. In November 1917 the British attempted to ambush the minesweepers in the Heligoland Bight, but botched the engagement.

Gradually the convoy system, using warships to escort the shipping, and often using a balloon or aircraft for observation in coastal waters, reduced the losses to manageable proportions. This was all the British had to do, for with the Americans in the war victory was inevitable if Britain and France could hold on until the middle of 1918. The massive movement of American troops and equipment to Europe in 1918 went ahead with very

Allied and neutral merchant shipping sunk by U-boats, 1914–18 (gross tons)

Year	Tons
1914	312,672
1915	1,307,996
1916	2,327,326
1917	6,235,878
1918	2,666,942
Total	12,850,814
(of which British)	(7,759,090)

little loss, and once the Ludendorff offensive had failed Allied victory was assured. Germany had gambled on a knock-out blow by U-boats, and the Royal Navy had countered the threat, not by defeating it, but by reducing it to an irritant. Anyone who had read their history would have known that this was the character of earlier attacks on commerce, those that Mahan had derided as indecisive. British morale received a timely boost on 23 April 1918, St George's Day, when a combined assault on the German-held port of Zeebrugge was carried through in heroic fashion. Although the results hardly justified the cost, the public relations aspect was nearly perfect. It provided a heroic leader in Rear-Admiral Roger Keyes (1872–1945), and some positive images of the war at sea. At the same time the blockade was tightened by America's entry into the war, leading to severe shortages of food and raw materials in Germany, with a disastrous impact on morale. Only Scandinavia remained as a source of supply, and this could not compensate for the loss of agricultural labour to the Army, and the chaos of Eastern Europe. Germany's will to continue the war was severely affected by the blockade.

U-boat losses, 1914–18

Total operational U-boats	351
Total sunk in combat	178
Other losses/decommissioned	39
Completed after Armistice	45
Transferred (surrendered) to Allies	179

THE END OF THE WAR

British naval offensives in 1918 were limited but portentous. HMS *Furious*, one of Fisher's Baltic battlecruisers, had been converted into an aircraft carrier, and she launched a raid that destroyed the Zeppelin sheds at Tondern on 19 July. Meanwhile, Beatty planned to build 121 torpedo bombers for a dawn attack on the High Seas Fleet at Wilhelmshaven in 1919. Modern coast defences would be out-ranged by changing the offensive weapon from a gun that fired a shell to an aircraft that dropped a bomb. The principle remained unchanged, only the method of delivering munitions had altered.

The large light cruiser/battlecruiser HMS Furious *was originally conceived as part of Fisher's strategic design to cut off Germany's iron ore supplies from Sweden by a sweep into the Baltic. However, before completion* Furious *was converted into a hybrid aircraft carrier, with a hangar for eight aircraft and a flight deck installed in place of the intended forward single 18-inch gun. Between the wars she was converted into an aircraft carrier carrying thirty-six aircraft.* Furious *had a distinguished record during the Second World War, and was finally broken up in 1948. This picture shows her during fitting out, July 1917. (PRO ref: ADM 176/283)*

At the outbreak of war in 1914 naval aviation was still embryonic, even more so than its land-based cousin. Although experimentation and development was taking place, there were many different attitudes to the future of maritime air power. Unsurprisingly, airships were favoured by Germany, and for a time by Britain, and indeed they seemed to have the features necessary for maritime operations – endurance and lifting/carrying capacity. Aeroplane development followed a number of routes, and in the early stages the debate centred on the relative advantages and failings of seaplanes and flying boats. The former were land planes with floats fitted to replace the undercarriage, while the latter had amphibious hulls and were purposely designed for operating from water. Seaplanes were smaller, handier and cheaper, while flying boats were longer-ranged but more expensive to construct and operate.

Although there were nascent maritime air forces in 1914 they had little in the way of considered doctrine. Airships at sea, as on land, suffered from operating difficulties and remained excessively expensive, eventually being replaced by cheaper and more versatile aeroplanes. Aircraft played only a limited role in fleet naval operations, but their real impact on the maritime war came in the U-boat campaign of 1917–18. Although the introduction of convoy for merchant ships was the key change, in conjunction with effective surface escorting, air power provided the seal on the U-boat's fate, for where aircraft escorted convoys, U-boats dared not close and attack. Aircraft could spot submarines and guide escorting surface vessels to attack them, and thus U-boats dived to avoid continued detection once located by an aeroplane. This meant a great reduction in speed and the U-boat lost touch with the convoy. The so-called 'scarecrow effect' resulted in no convoy losing a ship to submarine attack while escorted by aircraft. By the end of the war the basics of maritime air power were evident, but the aircraft had certainly not been able to convince conservative naval elements of its value, and the majority of the world's fleets continued to remain sceptical, at times healthily so, about the potential of air power well into the inter-war period.

The seaplane carrier HMS Ark Royal *launches a Short seaplane off the Greek island of Mudros, early 1916.* Ark Royal *later served as a depot ship and, during the Second World War, as a fighter catapult vessel. She was sold into mercantile service in 1946. (RMAS Collection)*

The scuttling of the High Seas Fleet at Scapa Flow. The battleship SMS Bayern *sinks by the stern, 1400 hours 21 June 1919. Ten of the eleven German battleships and all five German battlecruisers at Scapa Flow, together with several dozen smaller vessels, were sunk by their crews that day. (C.W. Burroughs/Stromness Museum)*

German frustration surfaced at the end of the war. With hostilities about to end the Naval High Command decided to launch one last sortie, to engage the British and go down fighting. This had more to do with preserving the Navy post-war than realistic strategy or diplomatic calculation. When the seamen heard rumours of this operation they refused to follow orders, and the fleet dissolved in mutiny, with the sailors going ashore to spread revolution through north Germany. The Kaiser's pride and joy had turned on its creator. After four years of boredom and poor officer–man relations the fleet fell to pieces.

Elsewhere the stalemate in the Adriatic had finally been broken by an Italian motor torpedo boat that sank one of the four Austrian Dreadnoughts on 10 July 1918. The Italians sank another at the end of the war with a three-man swimmer mission using limpet mines. They had also planned a large-scale assault on the main Austrian base at Pola, but ran out of time.

On 15 November the modern elements of the High Seas Fleet steamed to Scapa Flow to be interned. It was a great victory for the Royal Navy, and one that would be rendered complete the following year when the Germans scuttled their ships. This allowed the British to demand further German ships, leaving them with no warships from the Dreadnought era. Under the Treaty of Versailles Germany was not allowed battleships bigger than 10,000 tons, submarines or any new warships for some time. Germany was no longer a naval power. After four years of unremitting effort the Royal Navy had defeated every effort the enemy had made, and ground him

German naval losses, 1914–18

Battleship (pre-Dreadnought type)	1
Battlecruisers/heavy cruisers)	7
Light cruisers	18
Torpedo boats/destroyers	111
U-boats	199
Minesweepers	29
Gunboats	10
Auxiliary vessels	222

down until he could no longer resist. What the victory lacked in drama and immediacy was more than compensated for in effect. Without command of the sea the Entente powers would have been defeated, for it was the power to bring men, material and supplies from all corners of the globe that enabled them to survive, and eventually defeat Germany.

By contrast the United States had boosted her naval power. A spectacular fleet programme had been ordered in 1916 by President Woodrow Wilson (1856–1924) to coerce Britain. It included numerous battleships and battlecruisers far larger than existing British and German types, and was intended to make the United States Navy at least equal to the Royal Navy. When America entered the war much of the effort was redirected into anti-submarine craft, but a 1918 battleship programme was nevertheless announced, to ensure Britain did not underestimate American intentions at the peace conference. Almost the entire programme would be cancelled after the war, but not before it had alarmed Japan. The Japanese had used the war as an opportunity to expand into China, and meeting increasing American resistance, decided to build a large new fleet. The stage was set for another great arms race.

In Europe the German armistice allowed the British and French to extend the blockade into the Baltic. It also enabled the British to use a squadron to support the independence of the Baltic States against communist Russia. The highlight of these operations was a motor torpedo boat raid on the great Russian naval arsenal at Cronstadt, sinking two battleships. Naval forces were used elsewhere to support anti-communist forces, from the White and Black seas, through the Caspian to the Pacific. Naval power did much to help, but could not compensate for the failure of the White Russian forces on land.

Britain ended the First World War with a commanding lead in numbers of warships (although America and Japan had some impressive new battleships), and a wealth of experience in all forms of war at sea, from fleet action to anti-submarine screening. She led the world in carrier aviation, anti-submarine warfare, gunnery and almost all other aspects of war at sea. Her chain of global bases had been extended, her Middle Eastern oil supplies – for this fuel had now replaced coal – were secure and her empire had demonstrated a depth of commitment that augured well for the future. However, the price had been high, in men, money and material. Just how high would be made clear within two decades.

F I V E

WAR IN THE AIR, 1903–39

J O H N B U C K L E Y

The greatest impact of aircraft on modern war is usually associated with the era of the Second World War and after. Indeed, the widespread devastation of cities from the air in the closing stages of that war and post-1945 technological developments remain the enduring images of air power. However, the roots of modern air power lie in the period before 1939 and many of the facets of contemporary air warfare emerged long before the great campaigns of the Second World War. Moreover, features of air power peculiar to the period before 1939 mark out this earlier era as both critical and fascinating.

'On 17th December 1903, at Kill Devil Hill, Kitty Hawk, North Carolina, Orville Wright flew for twelve seconds, and thereby added a third dimension to war.'

J.F.C. Fuller

THE EARLY DEVELOPMENT OF AIR POWER

The birth of modern air power is usually dated to the first powered and controlled flights of the Wright brothers in the Kill Devil Hills, near Kittyhawk, North Carolina, in December 1903. However, significant as those achievements were, aerial thought and indeed aviation had been in existence for some time before the endeavours of Wilbur and Orville Wright. The first military use of aerial devices probably dates back to 300 BC China, where man-carrying kites were used for reconnaissance purposes, and up to the late nineteenth century military balloons, rockets and ultimately airships were developed and deployed. Notably, balloons were used by the Austrians to bomb Venice in 1849 and for observation by Union forces in the American Civil War (1861–5). The development of airships in the late nineteenth century, most famously associated with the German Count Ferdinand von Zeppelin (1838–1917), heralded powered flight, and by 1909 airships were being used commercially as well as by the military.

'When my brother and I built the first man-carrying flying machine we thought that we were introducing into the world an invention which would make future wars impossible.'

Orville Wright

However, the achievements of the Wright brothers radically altered the development of aviation, and with the emergence of true controlled powered flight the potential of military aircraft began to be recognised by those in power. With the arrival of Wilbur Wright and the 'Flyer' aircraft in Europe in 1908, the pace of aviation development accelerated dramatically as it became obvious that the Americans held a marked lead over their European rivals. Many in Europe, such as Henri Farman in France and the Short brothers in Britain, endeavoured to catch up, and interest in air power burgeoned. Some, for example Lord Northcliffe in the United Kingdom, noted the military potential and began lobbying for the creation of national air forces. Much of the pressure resulted from the growth of 'air mindedness', fuelled by interest in air power literature and fiction, of which the most famous example is H.G. Wells' novel, *The War in the Air* (1908).

War ministries had already begun investigations into the potential uses of aircraft. Contrary to popular perceptions, the authorities were not unduly conservative in their outlook, merely realistic about what was and was not possible. It should be noted that in the years leading up to 1914 there were many pressures on defence budgets, and whatever the potential of air power, the expansion of armies and navies had to remain the priority. Nevertheless, considerable progress was made. Many nations had army and navy departments devoted to aviation and aeroplanes, and investigations had been made into the use of aircraft for reconnaissance, observation and aerial bombing. Indeed, bombing was first used by the Italians in Africa (1911–12) and during the Balkan Wars (1912–13). France was the most sophisticated air power, though Germany had more aircraft (245 aeroplanes and 10 airships). Many of the minor powers (such as Austria-Hungary and Italy), or those with less advanced technological economies and industries (Imperial Russia) were struggling to cstablish themselves as air powers, and the First World War was to reveal such failings. Air power was already beginning to open up a divide between the most technologically advanced nations and the rest, a divide that would eventually see only a tiny handful of states able to maintain first-rate air power status.

H.G. WELLS (1866–1946)

Although H.G. Wells is more famous for his science-fiction works such as *The Time Machine* (1895) and *The War of the Worlds* (1898), his writing on warfare was equally, if not more, important. He was a keen wargamer and wrote on a number of aspects of war including armoured ground forces and air power. He had written on air power in *Anticipations* (1902), using terms such as 'command of the air', but his most important work in the pre-1914 era was *The War in the Air* (1908). Although others, including Jules Verne, had explored the power and potential of aircraft, Wells popularised, in the form of a novel, notions of an air war between the great powers such as Germany, Britain and even the United States. Cities, New York among them, were laid waste in the story by huge fleets of airships carrying aircraft. Although Wells misjudged some of the technical aspects of future air war, his vision of the world being ruled by destructive air forces touched a nerve with populations only just coming to terms with the achievements of the Wright brothers.

Before the Second World War Wells once again captured the mood with his book *The Shape of Things to Come* (1935), which was also released as a film (1936). In this work Wells built an apocalyptic vision of world civilisation coming to an end as the result of mass war, in particular aerial bombardment. Ultimately, the human race rebuilt itself, but for an inter-war audience already fearful of bombing and poison gas the images were particularly potent.

THE FIRST WORLD WAR

More than any other period in the history of air power, the First World War is seen as an era of fighter aces, chivalry and heroism. The reality, however, is radically different from this view, which largely evolved from wartime propaganda and post-war popular literature. More significantly, this image has concealed far more critical aspects of the development of air power in the 1914–18 war. In the space of four years the use of aircraft expanded and progressed markedly, laying the foundations for the growth of modern air power. By 1918 air forces were numbered in thousands of aircraft and tens of thousands of personnel. Between 1914 and 1918 the earliest air superiority campaigns and ground-attack operations were prosecuted, anti-U-boat air patrols undertaken and the first strategic bombing operations conducted. Nevertheless, the image of the air ace prevails and names such as the Germans Oswald Boelcke (1891–1916) and Manfred von Richthofen (the 'Red Baron') (1892–1918), the American Eddie Rickenbacker (1891–1973), and the Irishman Mick Mannock (1887–1918) occupy attention out of proportion to their importance in the air war. The age of the individual air ace was short-lived (a few months over the 1915–16 period) and was rapidly supplanted by large-scale attritional aerial campaigns, certainly by 1916–17. Moreover, the notion that the air war was in some way chivalrous and heroic is simply not supported by the evidence. The war in the air was as bloodthirsty as the war on the ground, inflicting appalling casualty rates, often caused by inadequate training. The great feats and achievements of the air aces have also been questioned: Richthofen preyed on slow reconnaissance aircraft, William Bishop probably invented the incident that earned him his Victoria Cross and Mick Mannock apparently enjoyed watching his German adversaries burn in the air.

Clearly, the air war of 1914–18 had wider and deeper implications than a study of the air aces would suggest. The impact of aerial bombing and

The industrial manufacture of aircraft was a decisive factor in explaining the Allies' success in the air war between 1914 and 1918. Although the Germans produced superior designs and shot down more aircraft than they themselves lost, they could not compete with the massive output from French and British factories. Here BE2c fuselages await completion on a British shop-floor. (JMB/GSL collection via P.G. Cooksley Collection)

Aircraft strengths, 1914–18

	August 1914	August 1918
Germany	180	2,592
France	136	2,820
Britain	68	1,644
Belgium	24	160
USA	(23)	270

(figures for aircraft deployed on the Western Front, except USA 1914)

combat profoundly altered perceptions of war, deepening the already marked move towards a more total form of industrial conflict. Air power, with its high wastage and attrition rates, was to prove a major drain on national resources and more importantly on particular areas of the economy – the most technologically based and consequently the most financially demanding. The wider and deeper aspects of the First World War in the air tell us a great deal more about the development of air power in this critical and formative period than do the much repeated tales of the air aces and their individual acts of unrealistically romantic heroism.

It is important to note that the respective belligerent powers adopted air strategies appropriate to national requirements. These were most clearly influenced by geo-strategy in that, for example, major continental powers such as France and Germany placed great emphasis on aerial observation and reconnaissance aeroplanes to support their armies, which were crucial to their national strategies. Conversely, the British developed maritime air power to support their navy, which was their defensive linchpin. In addition, as the war unfolded so air strategies evolved to meet the needs of the armed forces in general. For example, Germany adopted a defensive posture on the Western Front for long periods and its air force structure and doctrine mirrored this, with emphasis being placed on defending German airspace. In contrast, the French and British, with greater pressure from government for progress at the front, were far more aggressive with their air forces as they endeavoured to drive the Germans from the skies. However, German air power was used aggressively in support of national aims when necessary: for example, the first strategic bombing campaign was linked with the U-boat blockade in 1917 in an effort to knock Britain out of the war.

The first and most important role played by aircraft between 1914 and 1918 was reconnaissance and observation. For centuries armies had been effectively two dimensional in their Intelligence gathering, relying on scouting cavalry, fast-moving light infantry or espionage. The advent of air power, even in the relatively primitive form of balloons, added greatly to the ability of opposing forces to keep each other under observation, and the later introduction of aeroplanes dramatically increased this ability. Paradoxically, this new method of gathering information, highly effective as it was, became a severe hindering influence on offensive operations during the First World War. Military activity relies heavily on surprise and momentum, often gained by concealing intent until the moment of attack. In the age before air power this task was easier to accomplish: the arrival of the observation balloon and then the reconnaissance aircraft severely curtailed the ability of armies to catch their enemies unawares, especially on the constricted Western Front. Build-ups for major offensives were invariably kept under close observation from the air and the defenders were able to prepare in good time. For example, the Allied build-up

The Cacquot kite-balloon was the standard British observation balloon from mid-1916 onwards. It was 25 metres long, 8.2 metres in diameter, and used hydrogen gas to keep itself aloft. It operated at heights of up to 4,000 metres, and in winds of over 35 mph. (P.G. Cooksley Collection)

for the Somme offensive was already being noted in February 1916 by German aircraft, four and a half months before the attack began.

The second major impact of the reconnaissance and observation aircraft was its influence on the effectiveness of artillery. Balloons and then aeroplanes proved capable of directing and ranging artillery and thus dramatically increasing its importance, and it should be noted that artillery was the biggest killer on the battlefields of 1914–18. Aircraft, both balloons and aeroplanes, became commonplace directors of artillery fire and it was their observation and spotting activities that considerably improved the accuracy and effectiveness of shell-fire. The significance of this unglamorous role should not be underestimated, for artillery, when deployed properly, was key to preparing attacks and crucial in breaking them up. Paradoxically, therefore, air power contributed to the defensive nature of the war in two ways: by restricting the opportunities for surprise and increasing the lethality of artillery fire. As a result air power was important in precipitating the stalemate of the First World War, and although it was eventually to prove a factor in breaking the deadlock, during the 1914–17 period it was a smothering and constraining force.

'There can be no standing on the defensive . . . Survival in three-dimensional warfare depends on maintaining the offensive, whatever the odds or cost.'

General Hugh Trenchard, commander of the Royal Flying Corps, 22 September 1916

Beyond reconnaissance and artillery spotting, airborne duties either attempted to deny the use of aerial observation to the enemy or were peripheral to the outcome of the war. When the war became static in autumn 1914, the value of observation became clear and pre-war concerns over the combustibility of the hydrogen-filled balloon soon receded. Within weeks of the front settling down a string of observation balloons appeared over the lines, creating a sight peculiar to this period of military history, as by the middle stages of the war reconnaissance aircraft were beginning to replace the humble balloon. In some ways the balloon was superior to the aeroplane because it provided a more stable viewing platform and one with which ground communications were much easier. However, the vulnerability of the balloon and the increasing flexibility of the aeroplane eventually consigned the former to the history books.

Reconnaissance aeroplanes had already indicated their potential during the earliest stages of the war, when the battlefield was still fluid and mobile. Even when they were replaced in the west, albeit temporarily, by the balloon, on the Eastern Front aircraft continued to play an important role in reconnaissance duties because here the war remained, to a degree, one of manoeuvre. As the conflict on the Western Front unfolded, and aeroplane designs and the means of communicating with the ground became more sophisticated, so the value of reconnaissance and artillery observation aircraft increased. Aerial photography techniques improved dramatically and by the cessation of hostilities images of the ground could be taken from up to 15,000 feet. During the war the Germans apparently took enough photographs to cover the area of Germany six times over. Information from such sources was soon filtering down to army staffs and thence to front-line troops. It was becoming clear that the age of information and Intelligence-dominated operations had begun.

Although the first, and arguably most important, duty of aircraft in the First World War was reconnaissance and observation, the interception and destruction of other aircraft was to become a crucial factor. If enemy reconnaissance machines could be driven from the skies, then an important operational advantage would be obtained. However, in order to achieve such an advantage the means to destroy the enemy had to be developed and in 1915 innovation began in earnest. Even before the war broke out there had been contemplation of the nature of aerial combat and terms now familiar, such as air superiority and air supremacy, had been bandied about. In addition, the development of lightweight machine guns by Lewis and Hotchkiss offered a potential solution to the problem of how to shoot an aeroplane down from the air.

Nevertheless, in the early stages of the war aerial combat was sporadic. In any case the aircraft of 1914, with speeds of only 60mph and operational ceilings of 3,000 feet, were almost incapable of airborne interception and fighting. Moreover, many aircraft were designed with tractor engines, with the propeller at the front of the airframe pulling the aircraft through the air. This restricted the use of forward-firing machine guns because such weapons could not be discharged through the propeller. Other designs with two crewmen were slower and less manoeuvrable, and those with rear-mounted pusher engine/propeller arrangements were less efficient. The need for a fast and manoeuvrable single-seater aircraft with some means of carrying an accurate forward-firing machine gun was all too clear. The revolution in aerial combat came in 1915. The French pilot Roland Garros (after whom the French Open tennis stadium is named) had developed metal deflectors that encased part of his propeller blades and literally knocked bullets out of the way. This produced results of limited effectiveness and it was the development of a forward firing machine gun connected via interrupter gears to the engine, so that it did not fire when the propeller blade was in line with the gun barrel, that heralded the first true fighter aeroplane.

This breakthrough is usually attributed to Anthony Fokker (1890–1939), a Dutch aircraft designer, but there is evidence that the idea dates back to 1913 and a German engineer, Franz Schneider. The first fighter so equipped, the Fokker Eindekker, was introduced in 1915 and changed the face of air warfare. By the end of that year it was known as the 'Fokker Scourge' to the Allies, after losses to the new German fighter mounted alarmingly. The Germans launched the first concerted air superiority campaign over Verdun in 1916, with the aim of driving French aircraft from the skies over the contested area. These earliest confrontations demonstrated the importance both of properly organised air operations and of the vital role technology would play in determining success or failure in air warfare. The Allies reorganised and developed their own new fighters, and the technological battle swung to and fro over the remaining years of the war. Air groups expanded markedly and the nature of air warfare rapidly began to mirror that on the ground, being determined by strength in numbers and attritional methods. Ultimately, as in the Second World War, the Allies achieved superiority by mass producing high-quality aircraft more effectively than Germany and her allies.

'In the machines I flew previously a speedy retreat was the best means of defence against enemy airmen. Things are going to be different now.'

Max Immelmann, German ace, on delivery of the Fokker Eindekker, 1915

No other theatre of operations saw such a concerted effort to seize and then maintain air superiority as the Western Front, but paradoxically the value of total air supremacy was demonstrated most effectively elsewhere. Allied aerial ground support operations in Palestine showed what could be achieved, but the Turks had no real means of contesting air superiority, and for the Germans on the Western Front, merely challenging Allied air superiority was an effective use of resources. Denying air supremacy to the Allies was crucial, and the German air forces, heavily outnumbered as they were by 1918, especially in light of the ever-increasing flow of equipment and men from the USA, never totally lost control of their airspace.

The Fokker Eindekker took a devastating toll of French and British aircraft after it was introduced into service in the summer of 1915. It mounted one or more 7.92mm machine guns, synchronised to fire between the blades of the rotating propeller, but – like the British Sopwith Camel – its unforgiving flight characteristics caused many casualties among novice German pilots. By spring 1916 the Eindekker was obsolescent, although by the end of its service life it had nevertheless accounted for over 1,000 Allied aircraft. (P.G. Cooksley Collection)

From the first air superiority operations grew the opportunity for aircraft to intervene directly in the ground war. This later became known as battlefield air support or ground-attack operations. It soon became apparent that aircraft held a clear psychological advantage over ground troops, even when the land-based forces became used to air attacks and were able to develop countermeasures. The initial impact of concerted air attack on ground forces was notable for the panic created. The Allies developed the idea of ground-attack operations from their air superiority duties, for once they won control of German airspace, what might they do with it? Attacks on German ground forces and rear zones logically followed and Allied fighters began to be equipped with bombs. Almost immediately, battlefield air support operations divided into two distinct halves – close air support, directly attacking enemy front-line troops to gain advantages for friendly ground forces; and battlefield interdiction, disrupting enemy rear zones, supply lines and support units. The types of aircraft deployed on such operations also began to divide into two groups. Fighter aircraft equipped with bombs were often used, as they provided greater flexibility, being able to switch between air superiority and ground attack operations. However, dedicated ground-attack aircraft were also

The British Sopwith Camel entered front-line service in June 1917. Its exacting handling characteristics resulted in heavy losses among trainee pilots, but once mastered it was both a capable dogfighter and ground-attack aircraft. Almost 5,500 were produced, powered by several different engines and mounting a range of armaments. This is a replica aircraft, although one airworthy original remains in the USA. (Edward T. Maloney via P.G. Cooksley Collection)

THE FIRST AIR SUPERIORITY CAMPAIGN

The earliest air-to-air combats involved the use of revolvers, rifles and attempts to force the enemy out of the sky by aerial chicanery. The French pioneered greater aggression in the air by mounting machine guns in aeroplanes but the first true fighter aircraft with forward-firing synchronised machine guns was the German Fokker Eindekker of 1915. Such aircraft soon ended French bombing incursions into German airspace. Tactics developed rapidly, notably influenced by the Germans Oswald Boelcke and Max Immelmann (1890–1916), and formations of fighters were used at Verdun in 1916 in the first true air superiority campaign. Here, the Germans sought to drive the French from the skies while maintaining their own observation and reconnaissance operations. The French responded and increasing numbers of aircraft in larger units began to appear. The air war over Verdun degenerated into an attritional slog, but eventually the French markedly reduced German observation and spotting operations, causing a decrease in the potency of artillery fire. This was furthered when the French began a concerted campaign against German observation balloons.

Over the Somme, later in 1916, the Allies held an advantage in numbers of three-to-one and had also developed their own synchronised machine-gun-firing fighters. The Germans countered in 1917 by reorganising unit structures and introducing the excellent Albatros fighter; for the first half of the year they dominated the skies. Moreover, Manfred von Richthofen had risen to prominence, providing a boost to morale. However, by the autumn of 1917 the Allies had regained the initiative and did not relinquish it for the rest of the war.

developed, offering greater survivability against light anti-aircraft gunnery as well as heavier payload. Their critical failing was that they were easy prey for enemy fighters.

The air power strategies of the major belligerents dictated the type of ground-attack aircraft employed – the British in particular, with their more aggressive approach, utilised swing-role fighter-bombers, while the Germans, with more defensive and limited inclinations, developed rugged and ultimately purpose-designed types. The relative efficacy of these two approaches is difficult to gauge as Allied air strength in the latter stages of the war rendered the deployment of slower-moving dedicated ground-attack aircraft unduly dangerous. In 1917 and 1918 air power was employed aggressively in ground-support operations, despite the heavy loss rates of over 30 per cent. By the end of hostilities ground-support operations had become an integral part of the mix of modern forces required to conduct campaigns against first-class opponents. Indeed, many problems in utilising aircraft in these roles were being overcome, such as communications with ground troops, other aircraft, and close cooperation with mobile land forces, now including tanks in significant numbers. While air forces flinched from the heavy loss rates on close air support, the foundations had been laid for 'Blitzkrieg'.

STRATEGIC BOMBING IN THE FIRST WORLD WAR

'The idea was to equip from twelve to twenty Zeppelins and drill their crews to function as a coordinated task force. Each ship would carry about 300 fire bombs. They would attack simultaneously at night. Hence, as many as 6,000 bombs would be rained upon [London] at once . . . When asked for my technical opinion, morality, aside, I agreed it was definitely workable.'

Captain Ernst Lehman, German Army Zeppelin Service

Despite the impact of tactical air forces on the conduct of the First World War, the epitome of air power in time of conflict was the bomber, and some pre-war advocates, in spite of the state of prevailing technology in 1914, supported the creation of a massed bomber force to deliver great destructive blows against the enemy. Initially this was represented by the airship fleet of Germany, and Allied newspapers warned their readers of the threat of bombing raids as soon as the war broke out. This apocalyptic vision was of course wholly unrealistic. The majority of airmen were well aware of their aircrafts' limitations, but the enthusiasts had in the years before the war glossed over what was and was not possible. More than anything it was the prospect of demoralising the enemy with aerial bombing that sold the notion to politicians and military leaders, and the repeated outbreaks of 'Zeppelinitis' in newspapers increased the pressure on those in power still further.

Although some planning for early air raids had taken place, many difficulties were encountered in targeting, navigation and bomb aiming. Airships proved to be a profound disappointment, falling foul of north-west European weather. By 1916 they had been effectively replaced by long-range bomber aeroplanes. The most significant series of bombing raids came during the 'Gotha Summer' of 1917, so called because of the German Gotha bombers that spearheaded the campaign against Britain. In fact, the Germans used a number of heavy bomber models, including the Friedrichshafen GIII and the Zeppelin Staaken RVI as well as the more famous Gotha V. The campaign was part of a concerted effort by Germany to knock Britain out of the war via a U-boat blockade and a sustained bombing campaign of major cities, London in particular. For a time the bombing raids caused consternation in British government circles as fears over the levels of public panic rose. The initial inadequacies of British defences precipitated the drive for the creation of a single independent air arm and the Royal Air Force was formed in the spring of 1918 to deal with the threat posed by the air raids.

A German Army Schutte-Lanz airship. Unlike the more numerous Zeppelins, these airships had a wooden internal structure, rather than an aluminium one. This is SL 11, which was shot down over Hertfordshire on 3 September 1916 by Lieutenant W. Leefe Robinson. Among the crew, all of whom were killed, was the vessel's London-born captain, Wilhelm Schramm. (P.G. Cooksley Collection)

Although the German bombers enjoyed more success than the airships, they were still defeated by improvements in Britain's defences, the weather, and the difficulties inherent in mounting and maintaining a sustained strategic bombing campaign, particularly in terms of the resources required and the limitations of technology. The German bombers suffered from design flaws because of the rushed nature of their development and more Gothas were lost in flying accidents than in combat. Notably, a trend was established that came to be followed many times in other strategic bombing campaigns – daylight raids by airships in 1915–16 and heavy

One of the more unusual Riesenflugzeug *was this Steffen RI, seven of which were built by the Siemens-Schuckert Werke from 1915. All three of its engines were installed in the nose, from which power was transmitted to the two airscrews through a system of shafts and gears. (JMB/GSL Collection via P.G. Cooksley Collection)*

GOTHA SUMMER

By the autumn of 1916 it was clear to the Germans that the Zeppelin airship raids on Britain had failed and plans were developed for a new campaign in 1917 using heavy bomber aircraft. The new bombers were code-named G planes (*Grossflugzeug*), while later larger models were titled R planes (*Riesenflugzeug*). The bombers became known as Gothas, after one particular model, hence the phrase Gotha Summer, the epithet for the bombing campaign of 1917. The main target for the raids was the centre of London, notably the offices of government, such as Downing Street and the Admiralty. The intention was to deliver a psychological rather than physical blow and the German bombers were to operate in daylight, not only to improve accuracy, but also to demonstrate their invulnerability and superiority to the helpless Londoners. The ability to operate at 16,000 feet certainly gave the German bombers some protection from British fighters and the bombers' heavy defensive armament was intended to offer a still more effective defence. The first G plane raid took place on 25 May 1917, but the twenty-two bombers attacked Folkestone due to poor weather over London. Seventy-two people were killed and further raids followed with few bombers being lost. However, the British employed new and improved defences and August saw bomber loss-rates soar, at times up to 50 per cent per raid. The Germans switched to night raids in September.

The physical damage inflicted was negligible but the British government came under increasing pressure to respond to the German raids. Parliamentary debates commented upon the slump in morale and production, and Intelligence reports in Germany emphasised this unduly to an initially enthusiastic general staff. In reality, once the British had organised more effective defences the raids had few effects and the initial panic soon subsided. Indeed, one of the few tangible English losses to bombing during the war was the death, following a raid in 1915, of the cricketer W.G. Grace.

Nevertheless, the government attempted to act decisively and set up the Committee on Air Organisation and Home Defence Against Air Raids, chaired by Lieutenant-General Jan Smuts (1870–1950), which reported in August 1917, when the German bombers were already beginning to encounter difficulties. Ultimately this was to lead to the creation of the world's first independent air force, the RAF, in April 1918.

bombers in 1917–18 proved to be too dangerous and were replaced by night-time operations to keep losses down. This, however, seriously affected bombing accuracy, and ultimately did not provide the desired protection for the aircraft, eventually resulting in the abandonment of bombing operations.

Physical destruction in Britain from both airships and heavy bombers was minimal during the First World War, with total damage amounting to less than 1 per cent of that caused by rats. Around 300 tons of bombs were dropped on Britain and only some 1,400 people killed, a tiny fraction of the carnage of the Western Front. However, the psychological impact of bombing urban centres was to be far more profound and was to influence perceptions markedly in the post-war world. Importantly, the Allies were only just beginning to mount serious strategic bombing raids when the war came to an end, thus denying the nascent RAF the opportunity to encounter the realities of strategic air warfare. Indeed, although the RAF dropped some 543 tons of bombs on Germany, it was in the face of weakening opposition, and the bombing caused such little

On 19 October 1917, eleven German airships attempted to carry out a raid on British factories in the Midlands. However, very bad weather dispersed the force, and four airships subsequently crashed in France or, in one case, the Mediterranean. Only one Zeppelin was able to drop a total of seven bombs, one of which landed outside Swan and Edgar's shop in Piccadilly, London, killing or injuring twenty-five people. This is a photograph of the damage caused. (P.G. Cooksley Collection)

physical damage that post-war analysts, searching for something to acclaim, emphasised the effect of bombing on morale, even though this was difficult to quantify. However, the seeds of the RAF's inter-war *raison d'être* had been firmly planted.

The First World War proved many things about air power, but perhaps the most important lesson was air warfare's reliance on a firm and technologically advanced industrial base. Air power, with its high levels of attrition both of equipment and trained aircrew, wasted resources in a profligate manner, and demanded a great deal of the technologically based sectors of a nation's economy. The Allies adapted to this test more efficiently than the Central Powers, even Germany. The Germans made a number of errors of judgement, and in particular failed to adopt standardised procurement and production techniques until 1917, by which time it was too late. The British employed large amounts of unskilled, often female, labour under skilled direction to facilitate the expansion of their air industry and this allowed them to increase production dramatically. The French remained the leaders in the field, producing aero engines not only for their own aircraft but also for the British. It is worth noting that mass production, much feared by the Germans, did not result in lower quality. Indeed, although by the closing stages of the war the Germans had more advanced airframes to make good deficiencies in engine power, the overall technological balance of the air war had swung decisively in favour of the Allies by late 1917.

'I desire to point out that the maintenance of mastery of the air, which is essential, entails a constant and liberal supply of the most up-to-date machines, without which even the most skilful pilots cannot succeed.'

General Douglas Haig, 1916

THE INTER-WAR YEARS

The post-1918 world was scarred and shaken by the bloodletting of the First World War and the armed forces and strategic thinkers of the inter-war era were tasked with finding methods of fighting future conflicts without recourse to the remorseless slaughter of the trenches. A popular view began to emerge that air power held the key to rediscovering decisiveness in war. In particular, the employment of heavy bomber fleets to smash an enemy's resolve in a matter of days was cited by a number of theorists as the key to modern warfare. Although the damage and losses would be substantial from such air raids on urban centres, especially if, as some argued, poison gas was used, they would be much lower than the losses of a conflict on the scale of the First World War as a whole. Moreover, the war would be concluded rapidly, thus reducing the chance of economic and social collapse, which some predicted would follow any future major and long-lasting hostilities.

The roots of strategic bombing theory lay in the period before the First World War, and many of the terms and ideas later attributed to inter-war theorists actually began with lesser-known figures, such as Frederick Lanchester (1868–1946). The thesis of the strategic bombing advocates rested on the notion of the vulnerability of civilian populations to aerial bombardment. Many argued that the First World War had proven that morale would collapse during a sustained and heavy bombing campaign, forcing an enemy government to capitulate. The key to achieving this effect would be the creation of a massed heavy bomber fleet, larger and

The cost of the first air war, 1914–18 (aircrew losses)

Germany	6,840 killed
Britain	16,623 casualties (among them 6,166 killed)
France	7,200 casualties
USA	169 killed

Total air personnel casualties in the First World War amounted to over 50,000 men. Many fell in action, but losses during training and as a result of accidents were also high. Indeed, more British pilots were killed in training than in combat.

more potent than that of the enemy. It was considered that there was no realistic defence against a surprise bombing raid and therefore developing anything other than heavy bombers would be a waste of resources. Moreover, as such raids would bring the war to a halt in a matter of days, there was little point in investing in armies and navies as they would have little time to have an impact on the war. The most extreme air power advocates argued that almost all of a nation's defence budget should be spent on heavy bombers. Naturally, this brought them into conflict with the world's generals and admirals.

The most famous 'theorist' of air power was an Italian, General Guilio Douhet (1869–1930), who wrote a book entitled *The Command of the Air* in 1921 in which he set out some of the basic tenets of strategic air bombardment. In the United States, General Billy Mitchell (1879–1936) was also advocating much greater reliance on air power, and arguing that, for example, the big-gun battleship was impotent in the face of massed air attack. Mitchell and Douhet, although now acclaimed as great air power theorists, were in fact closer to being prophets or advocates. Mitchell's voice brought attention to the emergence of air power in the USA, but the Army and the Navy were already developing forces along such lines. Douhet was little read outside Italy and almost certainly had marginal, if any, impact on the progress of strategic bombing theory. The world's air forces were already investigating the potential of strategic bombing and many were oblivious to his writings.

In Britain the RAF, under the tutelage of its Chief of Air Staff, Sir Hugh Trenchard (1873–1956), was particularly taken with the notion of strategic bombing and the concept became the cornerstone of British air power in the inter-war years. The Americans also developed the idea of strategic aerial bombardment and by the time of their entry into the Second World War in 1941 had a carefully prepared plan for the deployment of a large heavy bomber fleet, albeit with a flawed doctrine. Other powers also studied strategic bombing, notably the Soviet Union, where by the mid-1930s the largest heavy bomber fleet in the world had been created, though it was later dismantled and allowed to crumble during the Red Army purges. The Luftwaffe in Germany also developed strategic bombing ideas, but was eventually drawn away by the needs of a more general operational level style of air warfare, designed to support land campaigns.

During the 1930s fear of aerial bombing grew markedly with a number of novels and films portraying the end of Europe or world civilisation as a result of the mass bombardment of cities. Such anxiety led governments to attempt to allay such fears by holding disarmament talks, but by the time of Hitler's ascent to power in 1933 hopes of success were already fading. Britain viewed Hitler's Germany as a direct threat and employed the strategy of using a bombing fleet as a deterrent to any future aggression. Germany also saw merit in using the bomber threat as a means of creating a defensive shield behind which she could rearm. Both countries were thus drawn into an arms race during the mid-1930s, with both making excessive claims over the respective sizes of their bombing fleets. Much of this was propaganda and bluff, but both governments recognised the importance of air power and the fear it elicited in urban populations.

'It is probable that future war will be conducted by a special class, the air force, as it was by the armoured knights of the Middle Ages.'

General William Mitchell, Winged Defence *(1924)*

Strategic bombing of Britain 1914–18

Method	Tons of bombs dropped	Casualties caused killed	Casualties caused wounded
Zeppelins	196	557	1,360
Bombers	73	860	2,060

'I think it is well for the man in the street to realise that there is no power on earth that can prevent him from being bombed.'

Stanley Baldwin, speech in the House of Commons, 1931

THE PROPHETS OF STRATEGIC AIR POWER

GENERAL GUILIO DOUHET (1869–1930)

Douhet is probably the most famous of the air power gurus and many of his ideas supposedly shaped the development of military air power, particularly before and during the Second World War. He was involved in the Italian air service as early as 1909 and organised the first ever bombing raid, carried out in Libya during the Italian-Turkish war (1911–12). Paradoxically, in his earliest writing Douhet did not consider aerial bombardment on a grand scale to be acceptable, though he was of course to change his mind. Though it is quite possible that he never learned to fly, Douhet became head of the Italian Army's air force in 1915, but was court-martialled soon afterwards for being overly critical of his superiors. He was recalled after the Battle of Caporetto (October–November 1917) and appointed to head the Central Aeronautical Bureau.

His most important contribution to the development of air power was his book of 1921, *The Command of the Air*. In this work he put forward the notion that the enemy's cities and civilians could be targeted by massed heavy bomber aircraft, possibly equipped with poison gas, the primary aim being to crush the enemy's morale. He was convinced that such brutal strategies would shorten future wars and thus avoid the long attritional slaughter of the First World War. Douhet argued that there was no defence against such an offensive and the only way to win was to bomb the enemy into surrender before he could do the same to you. He was briefly appointed by Mussolini, but although he continued to write, his importance waned until the Second World War, when his writing was used retrospectively to support the USAAF's bombing strategies. Since then his importance has been greatly exaggerated.

'A complete breakdown of the social structure cannot but take place in a country subjected to this kind of merciless pounding from the air. The time would soon come when, to put an end to the horror and suffering, the people themselves . . . would rise up and demand an end to the war – this before their army and navy had time to mobilise at all!'

Guilio Douhet, The Command of the Air *(1921)*

GENERAL WILLIAM MITCHELL (1879–1936)

Billy Mitchell is widely regarded, somewhat inaccurately, as one of the great visionaries of air power and a prime mover in establishing the aeroplane at the forefront of American military thinking. Mitchell, already commissioned in the Army, quickly recognised the potential of aircraft in the years leading up to the First World War, and became involved in the development of US air power, writing a number of articles on the subject. Indeed, in 1912, after being appointed to the Army General Staff in Washington, he compiled a report on the need for a strong US air arm. Following the entry of the USA into the war in April 1917, Mitchell was despatched to Europe, where he was almost certainly influenced by General Hugh Trenchard, one of the founding fathers of British air power. Mitchell began an abrasive and uncompromising campaign to expand America's capability in the air, which earned him resentment and hostility from fellow military leaders who did not share his vision. After the German surrender, he even expressed disappointment that the war had ended before American air power could prove its true worth.

In the post-war period Mitchell was appointed assistant chief of the US Army Air Service and pursued a long and bitter campaign to prove that aircraft were now more important to the defence of the USA than the US Navy. In 1921 he was allowed to initiate a series of tests to demonstrate the vulnerability of surface vessels to aerial bombers. Although the tests were superficial they did indicate that the Navy was not immune to the aeroplane. Realising that Mitchell was railing too hard against his fellows, his superiors attempted to keep him quiet, but to no avail. In 1925 he released a scathing report on the state of US air power, using phrases such as 'criminal and treasonable negligence', and was promptly court-martialled. He resigned from the Army in 1926 but continued his crusade almost until his death in 1936.

'A country should have the necessary air forces always ready at the outbreak of a war, because . . . it is upon a favourable air decision that the whole fate of the war may depend.'

William Mitchell, 1925

SIR HUGH TRENCHARD (1873–1956)

Hugh Trenchard was a crucial figure in the early development of British air power, though mainly as a shrewd political fighter rather than a theorist. He received his wings shortly before his fortieth birthday and was one of twenty pilots included in the Royal Flying Corps on its formation in 1912. During the First World War he rose to prominence and headed the RAF's strategic bombing efforts in that conflict. By 1918 he had become Chief of the Air Staff of the newly created RAF, a position to which he was reappointed in 1919, allowing him to guide the RAF through the difficulties of the 1920s. Trenchard believed that strategic bombing was the future of warfare, but recognised that in the fiscally stringent 1920s such thinking was not popular. He instead developed the policy of cost-effective aerial imperial policing to stave off efforts from the Army and the Navy to dismantle the RAF. When Trenchard retired in 1929 he had established the RAF as an institution, but had instilled somewhat skewed notions of strategic bombing at the heart of RAF philosophy, and little practical work and thought had been given to the realities of such operations. He continued to be an important figure in British air power, voicing his opinions in the House of Lords during the Second World War.

However, although the RAF's bomber barons believed that aerial bombardment could prove decisive in a matter of weeks, if the bomber fleet was properly prepared, neither the British nor German governments agreed; they saw the bomber fleet merely as a means of deterring enemy aggression. Even the Luftwaffe had reservations about aerial bombardment, in part confirmed by the experience of the Spanish Civil War (1936–9), the bombing of Guernica (April 1937) notwithstanding.

By 1937 it was clear to the British that their policy of deterrence was failing and they switched to air defence, founded on radar stations and new high-performance fighters such as the Hawker Hurricane and the Supermarine Spitfire. In many ways the advent of effective air defence undermined the notion that there could be no counter to a surprise heavy bomber raid. The dramatic increase in the performance of fighter aircraft in the mid- to late 1930s fused with early warning radar to render the lumbering heavy bomber highly vulnerable, and many of the failings of bombing campaigns in the Second World War resulted from such developments. The pressure of the arms race of the mid-1930s also inflicted considerable damage on the bomber forces of Britain and Germany. Both took delivery of obsolescent and inadequate aircraft merely to boost numbers, and the RAF certainly entered the war with ambitions far in excess of the capabilities of its aircraft and with poorly considered doctrine.

Aircraft technologies developed rapidly during the inter-war years. This is a German Heinkel 111B-1, a design that ostensibly originated to fulfil commercial requirements, but proved highly effective as a medium bomber during the early years of the Second World War. Not least, this was because of the lessons learned in the Spanish Civil War (1936–9) where this Heinkel served as part of the German effort to aid General Franco in his struggle against the Republican government. (P.G. Cooksley Collection)

Although strategic bombing became the most important influence on the development of air power in the inter-war period, progress was made in other fields, and air power was deployed on a number of duties. The RAF considered strategic bombing to be the key to the future of warfare, but in order to survive in the financially difficult environment of the 1920s the new arm employed its aircraft on a series of imperial policing duties. This proved to be much more effective and cheaper than using the Army or the Royal Navy, and thus endeared the RAF to the British government. For example, in suppressing a rising in Iraq in the early 1920s, the deployment of the RAF resulted in cutting costs by some two-thirds in the space of a year, saving some £16 million. The RAF was also used in operations in India, Africa and Palestine. The French employed aircraft effectively in defeating the rebellion of Abd al-Kharin in Morocco during the Rif War (1921–6) and the Italians also infamously employed air forces equipped with poison gas bombs against the Ethiopians during the 1935–6 invasion. In addition, the USA deployed air forces in imperial-style operations between 1927 and 1933 in supporting the Nicaraguan government during the Sandino War. The use of air power proved both militarily and cost effective in these circumstances and emphasised the growing divide between the military capability of the industrial and non-industrial worlds.

AIR POWER ON THE EVE OF WAR

On the outbreak of war in Europe in 1939, the German Luftwaffe was the most advanced air force in the world, with high-quality aircraft, good training and a considered air doctrine that supported national strategy. The Luftwaffe, however, had weak roots: the stress of war and poor leadership and management were to be its undoing. The British RAF was well prepared for aerial defence and had put in place a system for expanding its air force rapidly if necessary. The Soviet Union had a large air force (the *Voyenno-voznushnyye sily* – VVS) but it had been decapitated by Stalin's purges and was all but swept away in 1941 by the

Aircraft production of the major powers, 1932–9

	1932	1933	1934	1935	1936	1937	1938	1939
France	–	–	–	785	890	743	1,382	3,163
Germany	36	368	1,968	3,183	5,112	5,606	5,235	8,295
Japan	691	766	688	952	1,181	1,511	3,201	4,467
UK	445	633	740	1,140	1,877	2,153	2,827	7,940
USA	593	466	437	459	1,141	949	1,800	2,195
USSR	2,595	2,595	2,595	3,578	3,578	3,578	7,500	10,382

THE DEVELOPMENT OF AIRBORNE FORCES

For centuries before an assault from the skies was possible, military men yearned for a means by which to conduct airborne warfare to surprise the enemy, get behind his front line, and outmanoeuvre him. Indeed, soon after the Montgolfier brothers pioneered ballooning in France during the 1780s, the United States ambassador to France, Benjamin Franklin, wrote, 'Where is the prince who can afford to cover his country with troops for its defense that 10,000 men, descending from the clouds, might not, in many places, do an infinite amount of mischief before a force could be brought to repel them?' However, it was not until the Wright brothers' first manned flight in 1903, and then the first successful parachute jump from an aircraft nine years later, that airborne warfare became a practical proposition.

During the First World War there were numerous experiments with the parachute and the Italians, Russians and French all dropped a small number of agents behind enemy lines. There was even an American idea for a divisional-sized airborne drop to help the progress of US 1st Army, which was getting bogged down while trying to fight its way through the Argonne Valley in autumn 1918. Although the operation never went ahead owing to a lack of resources and the difficulties inherent in a plan years ahead of its time, the seeds of airborne warfare had been sown.

During the inter-war years it was in the more radical states of Germany, Italy and the Soviet Union that the greatest airborne developments took place. The British, Americans and French viewed airborne troops with a high degree of circumspection, and while they did experiment with the airborne concept, they could see no long-term future for such lightly armed troops. Generally, they considered them an expensive and unnecessary toy at a time of financial retrenchment.

Meanwhile, the Italians began parachute troop exercises in 1928 and by the outbreak of the Second World War could boast two airborne divisions. The Soviets formed their first parachute battalion in 1930 and by 1935 were dropping over 1,700 in a single wave with tankettes and light guns. Although many of the greatest proponents of airborne warfare were killed in Stalin's purges, the Soviets had 50,000 airborne troops by 1941. The Germans also poured resources into the development of an airborne warfare capability, thinking, as did the Soviets, about the role they could play in 'manoeuvre warfare'. To build up their airborne forces the Germans had to carefully side-step the military restrictions placed upon them by the Treaty of Versailles (1919). They did this by installing in key civil aviation positions men who did not forget the needs of the military and by exploiting secret contacts with the Soviet Union. By 1938, with Hitler firmly installed in power, Generalmajor Kurt Student (1890–1978), a former First World War fighter pilot, had created Germany's first airborne division. By the outbreak of the Second World War he had both a parachute and an airlanding division. Hitler had been excited by the airborne concept, and his elite troops did not have to wait long for their first action.

The Soviet air industry produced some excellent machines between the wars, one of the most famous of which was this Polikarpov I-16. During the late 1930s it was the best fighter type in the world, being fast, well armed and manoeuvrable. Hundreds served on the Republican side during the Spanish Civil War, where it proved superior both to the German Heinkel He 51 and Messerschmitt Bf 109B fighters. Around 7,000 were built, and in 1941 it formed the mainstay of the Soviet fighter fleet. Unfortunately, by this time new German designs had rendered it obsolescent, and losses among I-16s were very heavy indeed. (Real Photographs via P.G. Cooksley Collection)

Air strengths, September 1939

	First-line strength	Serviceable first-line aircraft	Reserves
Germany	3,609	2,893	900
Britain	1,911	1,600	2,200
France	1,792	n.a.	1,600
USSR	8,000 (est)	10,000 (est)	

German invasion. The French Air Force (l'Armée de la Air) was just emerging from a period of internecine bickering between the Army and the Air Force, and was not to be given enough time to pull itself together before war broke out and Germany invaded. The USA had an advanced and sophisticated aero industry with great productive potential, but like the other democracies was to be caught a little unawares in the early stages of the war. Conversely, Japan had a proficient front-line force, highly skilled and trained but with little to back it up or to facilitate expansion should the need arise.

By the late 1930s air power had developed significantly since the first flights of the Wright brothers. Concepts of strategic bombing were well established, aircraft were an integral part of the mix of forces necessary to conduct modern ground operations, and maritime air power was developing with the launch of dedicated aircraft carriers for many of the major world navies. Tactical air power had progressed only sluggishly in the inter-war era because of lack of investment, treaty restrictions and preoccupation with strategic bombing, but the technological foundations were laid in the years leading up to the Second World War. Air forces had clearly become an essential part of military power by the late 1930s and their influence on diplomacy and international politics was considerable indeed. Notably, President Roosevelt's ambassador in Paris reported after Hitler had met Chamberlain and Daladier at Munich, 'If you have enough airplanes, you don't have to go to Berchtesgaden.' The age of mass air power in which aircraft would be decisive and plentiful had arrived.

SIX

NEW IDEAS ABOUT LAND WARFARE, 1919–39

SIMON TREW

With some justification, the inter-war years are often seen as no more than a brief 'time out' during which the belligerents of 1914–18 licked their wounds and prepared to fight again. The First World War, far from being the 'War to end all wars', failed to resolve satisfactorily the problems that caused it, and the recasting of the global balance of power eventually brought new instabilities and tensions that led to renewed violence. From 1937 war erupted on an unprecedented scale, first in China, then in Europe and finally across the world. By September 1945 an estimated 60 million people had lost their lives in this conflict. This was at least three times the number that died during the First World War.

A NEW BALANCE OF POWER

As the guns fell silent on the Western Front in November 1918 it was hardly surprising that most people intended suffering of this kind should never happen again. Pacifism was an important inter-war force, and throughout the 1920s there were serious attempts to promote disarmament and collective security arrangements as means of ensuring peace. However, although few actively sought confrontation, for various reasons there remained (or developed) a widespread perception that violence was a legitimate way of pursuing political interests if the need arose. Coupled with developments in technology and other fields, which superficially indicated that future conflicts might be quick and decisive, this meant that by 1939 there was a reasonable degree of willingness to settle disputes through war. Unfortunately, as the next six years demonstrated, the very changes that were meant to avoid a repetition of the bloodletting of 1914–18 only made states more resilient and harder to defeat.

The basic cause of conflict in 1939 can be summed up in one word – ideology. The First World War shattered four of the world's great empires

'Do not let us now, in 1920, only look backwards to 1914. Let us think forwards to 1930, or we shall become pillars of salt in an arid and unproductive wilderness. . . . There is nothing too wonderful for science – we of the fighting services must grasp the wand of the magician and compel the future to obey us.'

J.F.C. Fuller, The Development of Sea Warfare on Land *(1920)*

(the German, Austro-Hungarian, Ottoman and Russian) and, although it was not immediately apparent, did terminal damage to another (the British). The United States had become a truly global player, and despite a temporary return to isolationism found it increasingly difficult to restrict its activities and interests to its traditional sphere of influence. In Eastern Europe, after a series of political upheavals and a bloody civil war, Tsarist Russia had been replaced by a Bolshevik regime dedicated to world revolution. Meanwhile, in other parts of Europe internecine struggles raged between supporters of the ideological left and right. Radicalised by the apparently harsh terms of the dictated peace settlements of 1919–21, and later by the effects of the Great Depression (1930–3), several powerful states drifted towards political extremism. In 1933 Adolf Hitler (1889–1945), leader of the National Socialist German Workers' Party (the 'Nazis'), came to power in Germany. He brought with him a virulent strain of extreme ethnic nationalism, coupled with a belief that only through violent struggle could any political entity prove its right to exist. Hitler was determined to overthrow the terms of the Treaty of Versailles (June 1919) by settling the age-old conflict with France, but even more important in his eyes was a crusade to the east. This was intended both to secure the resources necessary for the 'Thousand Year Reich' of which he dreamed, and to eradicate Bolshevism, which in Hitler's mind was inextricably linked with an alleged Jewish conspiracy to rule the world. For its part Britain

Rearmament began in earnest in the 1930s, most notably in Germany, where Hitler came to power in 1933. Here German heavy artillery, drawn by half-track tractors, passes a Nazi reviewing stand. (RMAS Collection)

remained grimly determined to retain a degree of imperial power, but found itself faced both in Europe and the Far East with powers seeking to undermine its influence. By 1939 there were huge differences between the ways that some of the most powerful states in the world believed that society, domestic and international, should be organised. This was a perfect recipe for generating the will to fight total war.

The 1920s and 1930s saw numerous developments that had a profound impact on the conduct of war. Mechanisation of industry accelerated rapidly, even in countries (like Japan) that had only felt the effects of the Industrial Revolution a few decades earlier. Mass-production techniques, pioneered by the Ford Motor Company before the First World War, spread equally quickly, increasing output and reducing costs. The exploitation of raw materials, construction of refineries and power plants, and increases in agricultural productivity lent new energy to the process of development, and supported an expansion in Europe's population from 401 million in 1920 to 543 million in 1940. Road, rail and other communications infrastructures grew, while despite the effects of the Depression, in all the advanced countries of the world standards of living rose. So did the quality of education, medical and other social services. Science also took leaps forward, especially in metallurgy, chemicals, propulsion systems and theoretical physics. In 1934 an Italian scientist, Enrico Fermi (1901–54), split the uranium atom, and in 1938 uranium fission was achieved. These developments opened the road towards the production of atomic weapons, changing the world forever.

Many of these advances were made for military purposes, or with military exploitation very much in mind. This was perhaps most true in the case of aviation, where metal alloy airframes and engines that were much more efficient than those available in 1918 transformed the

The dividing line between civilian and military technologies has often been blurred, and this was especially true during the inter war years. This is the Supermarine S.6 seaplane, which won the 1929 Schneider Trophy by achieving an average speed of over 328mph. The design was produced by Reginald Mitchell, who developed it into the Spitfire, one of the finest fighter aircraft of the Second World War. (Jonathan Falconer Collection)

Populations of the great powers 1920–40 (millions)

	1920	1940
USSR	126.6	194.0
USA	105.7	138.3
Japan	55.9	73.0
Germany	42.8	69.8
UK	44.4	48.2
Italy	37.7	45.0
France	39.0	42.0

Motor vehicle manufacture, 1938	
Germany (including Austria)	340,719
Italy	70,777
Japan	32,744
United States of America	2,489,085
Soviet Union	200,000
United Kingdom	447,561

capability to use aircraft to wage war. However, although this led to theories that saw air power as the decisive weapon in future conflict, other developments proved at least as significant. Improvements in the design and manufacture of the internal-combustion engine, and in suspension, gearbox and transmission systems, enhanced the performance of motor vehicles and made them more suited to the needs of armies. Cross-country capability was acquired by the development of multi-wheel drive systems and by the refinement of technologies (e.g. half-track designs) used during the First World War. For those countries with access to cheap oil and rubber, the prospect of using motorised transport to move and sustain their armies became very real during the inter-war years.

Similarly, armoured fighting vehicles (AFVs) developed dramatically from the lumbering and unreliable designs of 1918. There were significant changes in their protection, firepower and speed. Whereas even the fastest fully tracked vehicles in 1918 only managed 8 miles per hour, by 1939 tanks such as the German Panzer III travelled at 30. On the outbreak of the Second World War all tanks still carried machine guns, but these were now generally used as auxiliary weapons. Most vehicles relied on a high-velocity cannon – firing a range of ammunition types according to target, and mounted in a rotating turret – for their main armament. Admittedly, in tank design there was always some trade-off to make between armour, mobility and the power of the guns carried, and in 1939 the diversity of tank types in different armies bore testimony to this fact. However, in general terms of reliability, range, ergonomics and capacity to deliver sustained shock action, the capability of AFVs was substantially enhanced in the twenty years after 1918.

The ability to move large bodies of well-armed men quickly from one point to another by some means other than railways was a critical factor in the development of theories of warfighting. However, the increased pace of operations brought with it problems of command and control. Inter-war developments sought to address these too. Naturally, improvements in communications proved especially important. Even in 1918, most wireless sets were cumbersome, prone to breakdown and – because of their limited availability – were held mainly at higher levels of command. Soldiers in battle rarely had access to such forms of communication, which in any case was by morse code, not voice. During the 1920s, however, voice radio was introduced, while mass production and developments in the miniaturisation of components meant that by 1939 the armed forces of developed countries had large numbers of radio sets. In some armies, notably the German, the scale of issue became lavish. Each panzer, for example, carried at least a wireless receiver, and the possession of radios by supporting formations meant major improvements in all-arms cooperation. This increased the synergy with which the component parts of the warfighting machine could be used, and was greatly to benefit the Wehrmacht (Nazi Germany's armed forces) in the early part of the Second World War.

In 1918, though, all these developments lay in the future. With the 'Great War' over, most people turned their attention to reconstruction or domestic issues. Some, however, were already keenly examining the recent conflict to learn lessons about how the next war might be fought. This was true in most developed countries, but it was in Britain, Germany and the newly established Union of Soviet republics that the most important theoretical and practical work was done. The results of this work would be put to the test between 1939 and 1945.

BRITAIN LOSES ITS LEAD

Of all the major belligerents in the First World War, it was the British and Empire forces that emerged as the most skilled in warfighting. Other armies came up with specific innovations first, and the British made many mistakes, as disasters such as the first day on the Somme indicate. However, despite the appalling problems posed by trench deadlock, in the study and dissemination of lessons learned, in training, and in the use of combined arms, it was the British who eventually became the most professional. They were the first to identify the importance of truly operational thinking, and during the 'Hundred Days' offensive in the summer and autumn of 1918 achieved an inter-connected series of battlefield successes that broke the back of the German Army. These constitute some of the most impressive victories in British military history. The British were the principal pioneers of armoured forces during the First World War, and by 1918 had produced not only armoured cars for reconnaissance, heavy tanks for breakthrough and medium tanks for exploitation, but also a wide variety of specialist vehicles (e.g. radio, bridging and supply tanks). They also produced some of the most influential twentieth-century theorists of modern war.

John Frederick Charles Fuller (1878–1966). Fuller's interest in the occult and sympathy for the Nazis have contributed to his reputation as something of an oddball. Nevertheless he had a brilliant mind, and many of his works remain as readable and thought-provoking today as when they were first written.

One of these, Colonel J.F.C. 'Boney' Fuller (1878–1966), served as the Chief of Staff of the Tank Corps in France after it was established (initially as the Heavy Branch, Machine Gun Corps) in late 1916. A capable if eccentric officer, Fuller produced a number of plans for the use of tanks during the First World War. One of these, written in May 1918 and colloquially called 'Plan 1919' because Fuller hoped it would be used for an Allied offensive in that year, became particularly well known.

'Plan 1919' was based on the assumption that improvements in technology would allow the next generation of tanks to penetrate to a considerable depth beyond the tactical battle zone. In particular, Fuller emphasised the achievement of victory through an attack on the enemy's 'brain' (i.e. headquarters) instead of his 'muscle' (i.e. troops in the field). Imitating German storm-troop tactics, Fuller believed that concentrated AFVs could bypass centres of resistance and drive straight for divisional, corps, army, and even army group headquarters. Simultaneously, aircraft would bomb and strafe German supply lines, although signals communications would be left

'. . . the potential fighting strength of a body of men lies in its organization; consequently, if we can destroy this organization, we shall destroy its fighting strength and so have gained our object.

'There are two ways of destroying an object:

(i) By wearing it down (dissipating it)
(ii) By rendering it inoperative (unhinging it)

'In war the first comprises the killing, wounding, capturing and disarming of the enemy's soldiers – body warfare. The second, the rendering inoperative of his power of command – brain warfare.'

Major J.F.C. Fuller, memorandum of 24 May 1918 for 'Plan 1919'

intact to allow the bad news of the attack to spread. Once the enemy was gripped with panic, a combined arms assault on part of his front line would be launched, causing disintegration. Finally, a 'pursuing force' of medium tanks and lorry-borne infantry would be inserted to finish the Germans off. Although 'Plan 1919' was in many ways utterly unrealistic in the context of contemporary capabilities, its focus on defeating the enemy by dislocation rather than physical destruction was revolutionary.

For obvious reasons Fuller never had the opportunity to see 'Plan 1919' implemented. Ironically, for Fuller had fascist sympathies, some of the closest historical parallels to his proposal can be seen in the Soviet offensives of 1944–5. This was no accident, as the Red Army studied Fuller's ideas intensively throughout the 1920s and 1930s, and took much inspiration from them. The Germans also paid considerable attention to Fuller's literary output during the inter-war years, although they were less directly influenced by it.

Fuller was a prolific writer both before and after his retirement from the Army in 1933. He produced numerous books and essays, and lectured widely on his primary concern – the impact of new technologies on future war. Fuller was convinced that the internal-combustion engine, whether in land vehicles or aircraft, had revolutionised warfare by increasing its pace and the area over which it would be fought. No longer did mass armies need to grapple for months or years in bloody positional fighting. Instead, by mechanising themselves and using the speed, firepower and protection offered by tanks and aircraft, they could aim to surprise, dislocate and paralyse the enemy's command system. By attacking the opponent's ability to implement his plans, rather than engaging in pitched battles against his 'teeth arms', decisive victory could be achieved quickly and at minimum cost, even by relatively small numbers of men and machines.

In such a conflict, Fuller believed, conventional infantry would play a minor role. Because of their immobility, they would be unable to perform the operational-level functions – rapid movement over considerable distances to strike at the enemy's critical points – that AFVs could fulfil. Although infantry equipped with anti-tank guns would be used to defend the bases from which tank fleets would operate, and in complex terrain, in Fuller's vision of future conflict they would effectively be 'second-class' soldiers. Rather than the infantry–artillery nexus that had dominated the First World War, the bond between tank and air forces would now be decisive.

Fuller hoped that his ideas would be accepted and implemented in his own country, but in this he was disappointed. This was partly because of his abrasive personality, which alienated him from many of those in positions of influence, and partly because of the impractical nature of many of his suggestions. His tendency to dismiss their significance also won him few friends in the infantry, cavalry and artillery. However, the primary reason for Fuller's lack of success was that during the 1920s the British government's main overseas interest lay in running the Empire, and for such purposes the kinds of formations and equipment advocated by Fuller were perceived as an expensive and unnecessary luxury. Furthermore, in the early 1930s the effects of the Great Depression caused British defence expenditure to be cut drastically from its already low levels. With the Royal Navy and RAF taking priority in defence spending, Fuller's recommendations simply became unaffordable.

It would nevertheless be inaccurate to suggest that the British Army entirely rejected the reforms suggested by Fuller and others. Indeed, for a small army without any expectation of fighting another continental war, the British were surprisingly innovative. Successive Chiefs of the Imperial General Staff proved tolerant of new ideas, and in 1927 a brigade-sized 'Experimental Mechanical Force' (EMF) was established on Salisbury Plain. This is usually regarded as the world's first all-arms mechanised formation, and included light and medium tanks, motorised machine-gunners and motorised artillery and engineers. Several important and illuminating exercises were carried out using the EMF, and these were reported widely in the quality press, attracting worldwide attention. The British also designed some excellent tanks, notably the Vickers 16-tonner of 1929, and produced interesting doctrinal manuals for their use.

Sadly, the cutbacks of the 1930s had a severely detrimental effect on the British Army. Tank production programmes were cancelled, and such AFVs as were manufactured tended to be built 'on the cheap', with attendant problems of unreliability and underperformance. Exercises with mechanised forces also became more intermittent, with negative effects on the Army's ability to implement combined-arms operations. From 1935 prospects for mechanisation improved, but when they did so a number of problems came to light. Taken together, these were to leave the British Army in a state of some disarray in 1939.

First there was disagreement about the precise role of tanks. On the one hand a group of theorists led by Percy Hobart (1865–1957), an outspoken and radical Royal Tank Corps (RTC) officer, argued that tanks should play the primary role in future operations. Others, however, believed that tanks could only fulfil their potential if they acted as part of a combined-arms formation, supported by mechanised infantry, artillery and other services. This approach was most clearly articulated by George Lindsay (1880–1956), another RTC officer whose influence on British thought about armoured warfare during the 1920s has rarely received the credit it deserves. To compound the problem, some senior figures saw tanks as still having an important role to play in supporting infantry, as they had in the First World War. As the Germans demonstrated between 1939 and 1941, it was Lindsay's view that was most suited to the conditions prevailing at the time. However, in September 1934 Lindsay was deemed to have failed to prove his ideas in an exercise that some commentators have seen as deliberately fixed against him by his opponents. The result was that Lindsay's influence diminished, while that of others – especially Hobart – grew. Consequently, although Britain formed embryonic armoured divisions after 1938, these were 'tank heavy' and lacked the balance of personnel and equipment found in the German panzer divisions. Although (at least on paper) their strength in AFVs gave them a reasonable 'punch', they lacked the flexibility to deal with the range of tasks encountered in the early phase of the war.

The second problem related to the numbers and types of tanks purchased during the brief period of rearmament in the late 1930s. Because money remained short, relatively few tanks were bought by the

Army and Britain's tank-production infrastructure remained weak. Not only did the British enter the war with only two armoured divisions, but both were understrength. Furthermore, those tanks that the Army did possess were of very different types. This was partly because of the unresolved dispute about what tanks should do, and partly because of the underpowered engines available. Some AFVs were 'infantry' tanks (known as 'Matildas'), which were heavily armoured but slow. Others were 'cruisers', which were fast but poorly armoured. There were also a number of light tanks armed only with machine guns, in effect no more than reconnaissance vehicles. In the absence of quantities of 'gun' tanks, however, light tanks often found themselves used in battle, a role for which they were unsuited. Unlike the Germans and Soviets, the British had no general-purpose medium tanks in 1939.

In a sense, the third problem helped explain the other two. In simple terms, until just before the outbreak of the war British policy was to avoid sending a large expeditionary force to Europe. This was the result of a decision taken in 1934 and confirmed by Neville Chamberlain's government in 1937, to prioritise the rearmament of the RAF and Royal Navy at the expense of the Army, and to leave Western Europe to bear the burden of its own defence. In turn, this can partly be explained by a declining level of faith in armoured warfare, and a shift in favour of defensive land operations. Particularly important in this respect were the attitudes of the eminent British defence analyst, Basil Liddell Hart (1895–1970).

'. . . tanks are not an extra arm or a mere aid to infantry but the modern form of heavy cavalry and their true military use is obvious – to be concentrated and used in as large masses as possible for a decisive blow against the Achilles heel of the enemy army, the communications and command centres which form the nerve system.'

Basil Liddell Hart, 1925

Basil Liddell Hart served as an infantry officer during the First World War. However, during the early 1920s he was inspired by Fuller's writings, and became – as he himself acknowledged – a 'disciple'. In 1925, having left the Army to become military correspondent for the *Daily Telegraph*, he began a career as a journalist and commentator that was to last until the end of his life. During this period he produced many books and articles, which were widely read both at home and abroad, and which exercised considerable influence on his own government, as well as upon politicians and soldiers in several other countries. The originality of Liddell Hart's thought has become a subject of intense controversy, although phrases such as the 'expanding torrent' (basically, the principle of reinforcing success) and the 'indirect approach' (essentially, achieving victory by pitting strength against weakness) do seem to have been his own. On balance, however, it seems that his main role in the 1920s was to act as a powerful and public mouthpiece for others, especially George Lindsay. But regardless of the degree to which his writings reflected his own considerations, one important thing is clear – that after 1935 he became less and less convinced that armoured warfare could prevail against a powerful and prepared system of fortifications. Much the same was true of Fuller, who as early as 1932 began to lose his faith in tanks as weapons of decision in future conflict, and who turned his attention more to strategic bombing as the decisive instrument of war.

From the point of view of the supporters of mechanisation (and the Army generally), the problem was that in 1937 Liddell Hart had the ear of those in power. Having been appointed as private military assistant to Leslie Hore-Belisha (1893–1957), Secretary of State for War in Chamberlain's

THE LIDDELL HART CONTROVERSY

Captain (Rtd) B.H. Liddell Hart (1895–1970 – known as Sir Basil Liddell Hart after his knighthood in 1965), was a prominent and controversial figure throughout his life. Particularly in his later years, Liddell Hart was deeply concerned about his own place in history, and how future historians would assess his importance. In addition to his many books and other writings, he kept an extensive archive of his correspondence and other documents, and before his death took care that this would be properly preserved.

For most of his life, after brief service as an infantry officer in the First World War, Liddell Hart earned a living as a newspaper columnist and writer. His career demonstrates the extreme difficulty of associating military theory directly with military practice, and of identifying the influence of ideas on war. Liddell Hart was one of the very few military thinkers since Clausewitz who aspired to the heights of developing a genuine philosophy of war. He did not entirely succeed, but in the numerous revisions of his book *Strategy: The Indirect Approach* he came closer than anyone before or since. His own belief came to be that his military theories represented one aspect of a wider philosophical truth. Also like Clausewitz, Liddell Hart's ideas went in and out of favour with military practitioners, and have continued to do so after his death.

The first point of controversy surrounding Liddell Hart is his relationship with Major General J.F.C. Fuller (1878–1966), particularly in the development of ideas of deep penetration by armoured forces in the 1920s. Late in both their lives, Liddell Hart managed to persuade Fuller that although they had shared many ideas, the concept of deep penetration had been his rather than Fuller's. Such evidence as exists suggests that of the two Fuller was the real enthusiast for deep penetration in the 1920s; but such concepts long pre-date the existence of tanks capable of fulfilling such a role.

The second, and more serious, controversy associated with Liddell Hart is his influence on prominent German generals of the Second World War, notably Heinz Guderian and Erwin Rommel. As is recorded in his correspondence, after the war Liddell Hart helped a number of German commanders or their families find publishers for English-language editions of their memoirs. But in return he requested that passages should be added in which the generals paid tribute to the influence of Liddell Hart's theories on their conduct of operations. Liddell Hart's critics have taken this as evidence of his vanity and deceitfulness. His own view was that this was no more than a just recognition of his importance.

Evidence from the inter-war period shows that some of Fuller's writings were read by German staff officers, and also by Soviet officers developing their 'Deep Battle' concept. Liddell Hart's influence appears to have been more through digests of his writings for *The Times* and the *Daily Telegraph*, which circulated among European armies in this period. Liddell Hart and Fuller's portrayal of themselves as lone voices of British Army reform, ignored by incompetent and Blimpish generals, has also been shown to have been less than fair to senior officers who often welcomed their criticisms.

By the start of the Second World War Liddell Hart was out of favour in British military circles, partly because of his recent close association with the controversial Secretary of State for War, Leslie Hore-Belisha; but also because he had concluded that improvements in defence had provided an answer to deep penetration by tanks – something that he went to great lengths to conceal in later life. More fundamentally, as a believer in restraint and limitation, Liddell Hart opposed the very idea of fighting the Second World War by the same all-out industrialised means as the First. His befriending of German officers and their families after the war, although a reflection of the same beliefs, also made him an unpopular figure.

Liddell Hart's reputation enjoyed a revival very late in his life with the victory of the Israelis over their Arab neighbours in 1967. Liddell Hart claimed the Israelis, like the Germans, as the beneficiaries of his own 'indirect approach' ideas. Famously, his archive included a photograph from a prominent Israeli commander inscribed 'To the Captain who teaches generals'. As with the Germans, Liddell Hart's influence on Israeli military thinking certainly existed, but was less important than he maintained.

As is not unusual with prominent figures (especially those who leave extensive collections of letters), Liddell Hart's reputation came under sustained attack about a decade after his death from critics who argued that he had falsely exaggerated his own importance. By the end of the twentieth century he was seen as an ambiguous figure in the history of military thought: too important to ignore, but not yet having found his place. He remains one of a handful of military theorists (and the only Briton) with a genuine international reputation.

government, Liddell Hart advised that Britain should place a continental deployment very low on its list of priorities. Instead, reflecting increasing paranoia about the dangers of strategic bombing, he demanded efforts to provide Great Britain with improved air defences. This could only be done by diverting money from the ground forces. Liddell Hart's counsel prevailed.

The consequence was that in September 1939 the British Army went to war underprepared and, by virtue of its imperial defence commitments, overextended. Britain's attempt to deter Nazi aggression having failed, the Royal Navy intended to secure trade routes and institute an economic blockade of Germany, and the RAF hoped to use its bombers to strike at German industry, although all that it was actually allowed to target at this time was the enemy's navy. However, these were strategies of long-term attrition. Not until 1942 did the Western powers expect to go onto the offensive, and until then they would have to fight defensively, at least on land. Although the British did send an expeditionary force to the continent, it was small by comparison with the French Army. Despite the British Army's full motorisation (the result of its meagre size and Britain's access to cheap oil and rubber), it lacked a powerful armoured core, and those tank forces that it did possess were poorly equipped, inadequately trained in all-arms cooperation and badly structured. Neither was there any meaningful chance of effective cooperation with the RAF, which remained focused on strategic bombing and the air defence of the UK. From having had the world's most impressive mechanised formations and doctrine in the late 1920s, by 1939 the Army found itself ill-equipped to deal with the forces about to be unleashed against it. The effects would be fully felt in May 1940.

Hans von Seeckt (1886–1936). During a long and distinguished career Seeckt gave his services to the Austro-Hungarian, Turkish and Chinese Nationalist armies, as well as to Weimar Germany. However, his greatest achievement undoubtedly lay in helping the German armed forces to weather the storm caused by the Treaty of Versailles. A capable theorist as well as an excellent organiser, as early as 1921 Seeckt argued that the future belonged to 'mobile armies, relatively small but of high quality, supported by aircraft'. With good reason, he is widely regarded as the architect of Nazi Germany's military successes at the start of the Second World War. (RMAS Collection)

THE GERMAN REVIVAL

Contrary to popular impression and the beliefs of many of the German people, the German armed forces were decisively defeated by November 1918. That their tactical performance for most of the war had been superior to that of their opponents is irrelevant. Conflict on the scale and of the duration of the First World War was never likely to be resolved by a single battle. Rather, victory came from the successful coordination of resources at the strategic level, from the linking together of individual engagements into a coherent whole, and from the ability to win enough battles (not necessarily a majority) to create operational opportunities. Although the Germans achieved numerous tactical successes, it was their inability to understand how to employ their assets operationally and strategically that eventually led to their downfall.

When the war ended, therefore, it was hardly surprising that the Germans instituted a rigorous inquiry into the processes that had resulted in defeat. Barely a year after the Armistice, dozens of committees were already carrying out detailed analyses of various aspects of the conduct of the First World War, both on land and in the air. These committees were composed of regular staff-trained officers, under the energetic and capable direction of Colonel General Hans von Seeckt (1886–1936), Commander-in-Chief of the Army (Reichswehr).

Hans von Seeckt had one main aim – to preserve and rebuild his country's armed forces. Yet in June 1919 the Treaty of Versailles cut Germany's military might to the bone. From an army of over 4 million men in November 1918, the Germans were restricted to 96,000 NCOs and soldiers, and only 4,000 officers. A compulsory twelve-year period of military service was also imposed, with the aim of preventing the establishment of a large reserve, and of ensuring that the expertise of those personnel who were retained did not become too great. The General Staff was disbanded, the Army was not allowed any tanks, heavy artillery or poison gas, and an Allied control commission was stationed in Germany to monitor compliance. The Navy was slashed to a few pre-Dreadnought battleships and a small number of supporting craft, without any submarines, and the air arm completely disappeared. In essence, Germany was left without any ability to wage aggressive war.

These terms failed, however, to prevent the maintenance of a significant German military capability. Throughout the 1920s this existed in an intellectual form rather than a physical one. Even before Hitler's rise to power, however, the Germans were developing the ability to conduct rapid offensive campaigns of the kind apparently dictated by their central geographical position in a hostile Europe, which were similar to those of 1866, 1870, 1914 and 1918. These capabilities greatly increased after 1933, making the Wehrmacht strong enough to attack Poland in 1939 and to confront the combined forces of Western Europe the following year.

General von Seeckt's role in this process was immensely important. From the outset he sought to evade the terms of the Treaty of Versailles. First, he selected only the most capable officers for the Reichswehr. Second, he set them tasks fundamental to regenerating Germany's military strength. Finally, he helped to create the conceptual, moral and physical basis for Germany's success at the start of the Second World War by encouraging a vibrant debate about the conduct of future conflict.

Even in its emasculated form, the Reichswehr was a focus for well-informed discussion during the early 1920s. The General Staff had theoretically disappeared, but in reality it continued to exist within the Truppenamt (Troop Office), itself part of the Ministry of War. Virtually every important position within the Truppenamt and the Reichswehr was held by a member of the pre-1919 General Staff, whose officers represented an intellectual elite. Even a shadow air staff remained. Denied the physical ability to fight or train, their early work was theoretical, and took the form of analyses of the First World War and its implications for the future. These studies led to the first post-war German military doctrine, *Leadership and Battle with Combined Arms*, which was published between 1921 and 1923.

As its title suggests, the new doctrine articulated the need for a balanced, all-arms approach to warfighting. This was a conclusion partly based on the Germans' own experiences with stormtroopers and artillery in 1917–18. However, the doctrine also reflected analysis of the British and French use of AFVs, and contained several sections on the employment of tanks. In terms of the use of ground forces, it emphasised mobility and the avoidance of positional fighting, and incorporated a system of devolved command intended to facilitate the exploitation of

'Prerequisites for appointment to the General Staff were integrity of character and unimpeachable behaviour and way of life both on and off duty. Next came military competence; a man had to have proved himself at the front, had to have an understanding for tactical and technical matters, a talent for organization and powers of endurance both physical and mental; he had also to be industrious, of sober temperament and determined.'

Heinz Guderian,
Panzer Leader *(1952)*

'We believe that no leader who thinks or acts by stereotyped rules can ever do anything great because he is bound by rules . . . War is not normal . . . We do not want therefore any stereotyped solutions for battle but an understanding of the nature of war.'

Captain von Bechtolsheim, 1931, Reichswehr lecturer at the US Army Cavalry School, Fort Sill, Oklahoma

fleeting opportunities as the basis for seizing the initiative in battle. Although it only emerged in 1926, the air arm's own doctrine, *Directives for the Conduct of the Operational Air War*, was complementary. It advocated the aggressive use of air power to achieve air superiority, and to support ground operations by reconnaissance, artillery observation, close air support and deep interdiction of enemy mobilisation and deployment measures.

These publications are important, both because they established the basis for subsequent doctrine and the Wehrmacht's wartime operations, and because they show that from an early stage the Germans reached their own conclusions about the implications of technological change for future war. It is perfectly true that throughout the 1920s and 1930s the Germans paid very close attention to developments abroad. During this period their military journals carried numerous reviews of books by Fuller and Liddell Hart, as well as translations of articles by these and other British theorists. Reports of exercises by the EMF and its successor formations were published, and energy was devoted to securing and translating British doctrinal pamphlets on mechanised operations. Information was also collated about Soviet, French, Swedish and other countries' developments in armoured warfare, and about the foreign use of air power. However, although such research served as an important catalyst for discussion, the Reichswehr produced many of its own air and tank experts. Of the latter the most famous – Heinz Guderian (1888–1954) – was only one, and a relative latecomer to the debate at that.

During the 1920s the Germans made various attempts to circumvent the Treaty of Versailles. With few obvious friends, in April 1922 Germany took the unusual step of making a treaty with Bolshevik Russia, the other main European pariah state. Under the secret terms of this agreement, which lasted until 1933, the Soviets gave the Germans facilities for testing aircraft and training pilots, and for experiments in armoured warfare. In return the Germans provided the Soviets with technical expertise. In Germany itself, civil aviation was militarised by appointing officers to the Deutsche Lufthansa national airline, while the Germans also used civilian gliding clubs to train personnel in the basic principles of flying. In addition to wargaming, which had an established tradition in Germany, the Army came up with innovative means of training its troops, using motorised vehicles and dummy tanks and anti-tank guns in manoeuvres. It also despatched personnel abroad to witness other armies' exercises and report on their equipment. All of this took place with the encouragement of von Seeckt and his successors, and within a milieu that valued initiative and risk-taking, that saw technology as a force multiplier, and that sought efficiently to disseminate lessons learned.

In such circumstances it is unsurprising that the Germans made rapid strides in developing their ideas. Naturally, there was some disagreement within the armed forces regarding the likely form of future war. As in Britain, a number of officers believed that tanks had little value beyond infantry support, or thought that they would be as vulnerable to anti-tank weapons as infantry had been to machine guns after 1914. (Similarly, there was some support in Germany for strategic bombing of the kind advocated by Guilio Douhet in Italy or Hugh Trenchard in the UK.)

'Sport gliding' was used extensively by the Germans to train pilots during the inter-war years. As a noteworthy by-product, it also contributed to the creation of substantial airborne forces, who used gliderborne troops to great effect in the campaigns of 1940–1. (RMAS Collection)

Nevertheless, most senior commanders proved accommodating in their attitudes to technologically based modernisation, and to the sometimes radical suggestions that went with it.

It was Hitler's accession to power, however, that gave real impetus to the processes that led to the 'Blitzkrieg' (Lightning War) of 1939–41. The Nazi leader held out an enticing carrot to the armed forces by promising to restore German military strength and prestige, to recapture lost territories and to unite all Germans in a massive superstate. Although most officers were not ideologically pro-Nazi, many – especially the younger, more ambitious and doctrinally extreme ones – proved unable to resist Hitler's blandishments. When rearmament began in earnest in 1934 the German military 'conservatives', who supported a strategically

In the absence of a domestic tank industry and to evade the terms of the Treaty of Versailles, the Germans improvised a number of ways of developing their Panzer arm in the early 1930s. A secret training school was established in cooperation with the Soviets at Kazan, deep within the USSR, while in Germany itself exercises were carried out using civilian cars converted to look like tanks. This is a photo of one such vehicle. (Tank Museum)

'The officers of a panzer division must learn to think and act independently within the framework of the general plan and not wait until they receive orders.'

Erwin Rommel, The Rommel Papers *(1953)*

Organisation of a typical Panzer division, September 1939

- One panzer brigade, comprising two panzer regiments (each of two panzer battalions).
- One infantry brigade, comprising two motorised infantry battalions.
- One motorcycle battalion.
- One (motorised) reconnaissance battalion (armoured cars and motorcycles)
- One anti-tank battalion (motorised).
- One (motorised) artillery regiment, comprising one heavy and one light battalion.
- One (motorised) pioneer battalion (engineers)
- One (motorised) signals battalion.
- Medical, supply, administrative and military police troops.

defensive use of the new warfighting techniques, began a slow slide from power. To replace them arose a generation of what one writer has described as 'opportunistic technocrats'. These were officers who were more offensively inclined, and whose expertise in tactical and technical matters offered Hitler the prospect of fulfilling his political programme through short, decisive wars. This group was epitomised by Heinz Guderian.

The German armed forces experienced rapid growth from 1933. In 1934 the Air Force (Luftwaffe) was established as an independent service, and in October 1935 the first three panzer divisions were formed. These incorporated the first mass-produced German tank types. Although they went through several structural changes, in essence they reflected the combined arms approach articulated in 1923, which was reiterated a decade later in *Army Regulation 300, Troop Command*. This was the doctrine with which the German Army went to war in 1939. The panzer divisions contained a large armoured component – by 1939, over 300 tanks apiece. But they were also well-balanced fighting formations incorporating powerful mechanised and motorised infantry, artillery, anti-tank, anti-aircraft, reconnaissance, engineer and logistics units. They were tied together by the widespread provision of wireless sets, and were trained to act in a dynamic, flexible fashion to accomplish a range of tasks. By September 1939 there were six panzer divisions, and by May 1940, ten. The panzer divisions constituted an elite striking force within the Army, and were backed up by a Luftwaffe that in 1935 formally prioritised the support of ground operations through attacks on the enemy's armed forces, rather than his industry and civilian population.

The methods with which the Germans fought between 1939 and 1942 are commonly known as 'Blitzkrieg', and are sometimes claimed to have been revolutionary. However, the Germans hardly ever used this word, which was a journalistic term used to describe any short, sharp war or campaign, and it had absolutely no doctrinal meaning for them. This was not surprising, for the fighting methods used by the Wehrmacht were anything but new. Since the nineteenth century the Germans had sought to win wars by the encirclement and physical annihilation of their enemies in *Kesselschlachten*, or 'cauldron battles'. The German Army of 1939 did not dissent from these views; on the contrary, it endorsed them. Some officers did appreciate the potential of 'brain' – as opposed to 'muscle' – warfare. In practice, however, the Germans rarely sought to achieve decisive victory by dislocating enemy command and control facilities. Instead, their aim was to use the panzer divisions, supported by air power, to deliver overwhelming shock at the chosen point of attack, effect a rapid penetration and then drive deep to surround the enemy's armed forces. This would leave the latter with the choice of staying where they were, in which case their combat power would rapidly decline and they would be forced to surrender, or attempting to break out of the encirclement, in which case the superiority of defensively deployed firepower would destroy them. If enemy headquarters and communications were damaged by this type of operation, that was quite natural and a very useful side effect from the German point of view. But such disruption would be the by-product of success, not the means by which it was achieved. For the

HEINZ GUDERIAN (1888–1954)

Heinz Guderian was born on 17 June 1888 at Kulm (Chelmno), a small town in eastern Germany that later became infamous as a Nazi extermination centre. In 1907 he joined the Imperial German Army, training as a signaller, and during the First World War he served mainly in various headquarters on the Western Front. Appointed to the General Staff in 1918, Guderian was retained by the Reichswehr after the Treaty of Versailles. In the 1920s he became interested in the role of tanks in future war, and after serving as Chief of Staff in the Inspectorate of Motorised Troops, in 1935 he was put in charge of one of the first three Panzer divisions. He held important operational commands in the Polish, French and Russian campaigns (1939–41), and was Inspector General of Panzer Troops between March 1943 and July 1944. In July 1944 he was promoted to Army Chief of Staff, a position that he occupied until March 1945. Briefly imprisoned after the war, Guderian was released in 1948 and died six years later.

Heinz Guderian was a bold and capable commander of Panzer forces. According to Joseph Goebbels (Nazi propaganda minister), 'he was also an ardent and unquestioning disciple' of Hitler. However, as the war went on he increasingly clashed with the Fuhrer over strategic matters, and in March 1945 he was effectively sacked from his position of Army Chief of Staff. This photograph was taken during the 1940 campaign in France, when Guderian was commanding XIX Panzer Corps. (IWM)

Heinz Guderian became famous as the author of two important books. The first was a polemic/textbook on the use of armour published in 1937, titled *Achtung – Panzer!* The second was his memoirs, the English-language edition of which (*Panzer Leader*) appeared in 1952. In both he gave the impression that he should be regarded as the creator of the Panzer arm, a view that was confirmed by another famous German wartime commander, Erich von Manstein (1887–1973), and in numerous publications by foreign authors.

Guderian's role was important, but his contribution needs to be put in perspective. Until 1928 he wrote very little about tanks, and most of the early – but essential – theorising was done by men whose names are largely unknown in the West (e.g. Fritz Heigl and Ernst Volckheim). Neither did he have any significant input into German doctrinal publications. The 1933–4 regulations, for example, emphasised mobile operations and the use of combined arms, yet were written by Ludwig Beck (Chief of the General Staff 1933–8), who was later portrayed by Guderian as resistant to the latter's ideas. It was Beck (1880–1944) who also ordered the creation of the first three Panzer divisions. *Achtung – Panzer!* only appeared in 1937, more than half of it dealt with the use of tanks in the First World War, and the book contained suggestions about the deliberate targeting of the enemy's 'brain' that the Germans generally ignored in practice. Oswald Lutz, Guderian's superior in the Inspectorate of Motorised Troops when the first Panzer divisions were created, also received scant praise from Guderian, despite being a capable theorist in his own right.

On balance, it seems that Guderian's importance lay not so much in his intellectual contribution, as in the sheer energy and enthusiasm with which he advocated mechanisation in the German Army. Undoubtedly, Guderian was a very bright officer who understood how to use tanks as part of a combined arms package, and who wrote many influential articles on the subject. He was also a brilliant commander of Panzer forces, and his war memoirs are essential reading. But his main contribution was in articulating the need to concentrate tanks in powerful combined arms formations at a time when some officers were thinking of alternative uses for armour. In this sense his role in the creation and expansion of the Panzer forces was indeed instrumental, even if post-war writers have tended to exaggerate his overall importance.

Wehrmacht, the *Vernichtungsschlacht* – the annihilation of the enemy armed forces through a single, crushing blow – remained the epitome of warfighting, just as it had been for Helmuth von Moltke in 1870. The only significant difference in 1939 would be the means, and therefore the speed, with which the blow would be delivered.

In September 1939 Nazi Germany's air and ground forces were in several important respects the best in Europe. They were very well trained and their commanders were of generally excellent quality. They understood the importance of cooperation between land and air elements, and between the constituent components of the Army. They were also surprisingly experienced, having used the annexation of Austria (1938) and the occupation of Czechoslovakia (1938–9) to rehearse their units in rapid, long-distance moves (albeit unopposed ones). The Spanish Civil War (1936–9), in which German ground and air forces fought alongside Franco's Nationalists, also provided many useful lessons, especially in how to use the Luftwaffe to support land operations. Equally important, six years of Nazism had galvanised at least a proportion of the German people to overthrow the 1919 peace settlement and redraw the political map of Europe. As a result, the armed forces' morale – a critical factor in any war – was fairly high.

Types of division in the German Army, 1939

Panzer	6
Motorised Infantry	4
Light (partly armoured)	4
Infantry	86
Jaeger (light infantry)	2
Mountain	3
Airlanding	1
Other	1 cavalry brigade
(Total Army strength	3.74 million men)

Nevertheless, as many of its commanders recognised, the Wehrmacht had a number of weaknesses. In 1939 the German economy was still poorly organised for war. Competing demands from the Navy (Kriegsmarine), Army (Heer) and the Luftwaffe, and from the recently formed fighting units of the SS, could not be met simultaneously. Although Germany possessed the coal and steel needed for a highly developed railway network, she lacked the oil and rubber that was required for full motorisation. In 1937 there was one motor vehicle in Germany for every forty-seven people; the second worst ratio in Western Europe. Of 106 divisions in the Heer in September 1939, only 14 were fully motorised, and the rest relied mainly on 590,000 horses for their motive power. This created a two-tier army that possessed a small and highly mechanised elite, but the rest of which had changed little since 1918.

It is also doubtful whether the Germans had yet come to terms with the reasons for their defeat in the First World War. On the one hand it is difficult to think of soldiers who were better prepared for winning battles than the Germans in 1939. However, modern war has always been about much more than winning battles. By acquiescing in Hitler's demand that any war fought by Germany should be over quickly, in return for the glory and power that the Nazis offered them, the officer corps seemed to lose sight of this fact. Consequently, German forces lacked any genuine operational doctrine, as well as the logistics capability that would allow them to withstand sustained fighting. In essence, the Wehrmacht was a one-shot weapon, which would either achieve victory dramatically and rapidly, or – unless it could defeat its enemies in detail – would perish in an attritional, protracted struggle. From Hitler's point of view, of course, this was a gamble that he did not expect or intend to lose. But the question to be answered after 1939 was whether supremacy at the tactical level would prove sufficient to achieve his almost unlimited strategic goals.

SOVIET THEORIES OF 'DEEP BATTLE' AND 'DEEP OPERATIONS'

The Soviet Union expected and prepared for war almost from the moment that the Bolsheviks took power. The capitalist states attempted to destroy the new regime during the Russian Civil War (1917–21), and henceforth Soviet leaders were understandably reluctant to place their trust in negotiation. Instead, they aimed to acquire the strength to resist further aggression, which they regarded as an inevitable product of the tensions between capitalism and socialism. Given the issues at stake, they viewed future conflict as likely to be on a massive scale, with a coalition of powerful governments aligned against them. When it came, war would be total, requiring the full mobilisation of resources. Only if this was done could the Soviet Union hope to survive, and to spread its ideological beliefs.

Nevertheless, the USSR's military capability developed very slowly during the 1920s. The country was only semi-industrialised in 1914, and seven years of war left it in a debilitated condition. Infrastructure remained underdeveloped, and as late as 1928 there were barely 18,000 motor vehicles in the entire country. Not until 1929 was the first reasonably coherent plan for the expansion of the Soviet industrial base implemented, and even this was over-ambitious and poorly managed. However, it did result in a substantial enlargement of the USSR's armed forces. From 340 tanks in 1929, the Red Army's complement had risen to over 1,000 by 1932, and by 1935 this number had increased to 7,633. The quantity of artillery expanded equally dramatically from 999 guns in 1929 to 4,870 four years later, with a similar rate of growth occurring in the strength of the air force.

Soviet planning for war, however, was based on much more than the acquisition of large amounts of equipment. As in Germany, from the early 1920s the recent past was intensively studied to see what light it might throw on future conflict, and great efforts were made to understand the military implications of technological change. Radical intellectual communist officers, former tsarist personnel (*Voenspetsy*) and Russian Civil War commanders were all involved in this process. Foreign experience and the First World War on the Eastern Front were analysed, and inspired much of the initial theorising. Following the 'marriage of convenience' with Germany in 1922, a close relationship was also established with some of the best military minds in Europe. The result was a flood of literature and ideas that together formed the basis for a sophisticated approach to modern operations. This was generally described (if slightly inaccurately) as the doctrine of 'Deep Battle', and was enshrined in a series of Red Army manuals from 1928 onwards.

Among the elements of Soviet military thought, a number were especially important. First, the Soviets believed that under contemporary conditions the *Vernichtungsschlacht* was no longer achievable. As the First World War had shown, modern industrialised states were simply too powerful to be defeated in a single battle. Strategic victory in future war would come from an accumulation of operational successes, each flowing from the ability to link a number of battles to a common purpose. In

'The nature of modern weapons and battle is that it is an impossible matter to destroy the enemy's manpower in one blow in a single day. Battle in modern operations stretches out into a series of battles not only along the front but also in depth.'

Mikhail Tukhachevsky, 1926

The Soviets produced some very good armoured fighting vehicles during the 1930s. This photograph, taken in Bialystok in November 1939, shows one of them, the BT 5 tank. Designed primarily for long-range independent operations, the BT 5 was fast, reasonably reliable, and mounted a 45mm cannon as its main armament. This example has the word 'Stalin' painted on its turret, and is surrounded by BA-10 armoured cars and Stalinets caterpillar artillery tractors. (David King Collection)

Not all of the Red Army was truly 'modern', however. In 1941 a very large part of it continued to rely – as did the Germans – on animal transport. Here, horses pull machine gun teams in a military parade. (David King Collection)

particular, breakthrough attacks on the enemy's front – which was assumed to be continuous – would need to be exploited to cause significant damage to the enemy's ability to function effectively. Even then several blows, each creating the conditions for the next operation or for simultaneous strikes elsewhere, would be required before decisive victory was achieved. Each operation would also need to be planned carefully within the context of logistical viability.

In analysing the nature of modern warfare, the Soviets discerned that armies were essentially systems (in terms of thinking, planning and the fact that they were reliant upon communications and logistics). Their fighting units and rear services were interdependent, with neither being able to function without the support of the other. To achieve operational success, therefore, the enemy had to be prevented from coordinating his actions. The best way to do this was by attacking him simultaneously throughout a considerable depth, not just at the front line. By targeting the enemy's command and control, reserves, and ability to move, the Soviets believed that 'operational shock' could be inflicted, leading to paralysis, collapse and annihilation. Although tactical proficiency was desirable, what mattered most was being able to transform those battles that Soviet forces won into operationally significant successes. For an army composed mainly of poorly educated peasants who could not be expected to demonstrate great flexibility on the battlefield, this appeared to offer a solution to the problem of likely tactical inferiority.

Soviet doctrine did not emerge overnight, nor from a single source. Many theorists were involved, although three were especially important. These were Mikhail Tukhachevsky (1893–1937) (initially Chief of the General Staff, and later Deputy People's Commissar for Defence), Vladimir Triandafillov (1894–1931) (Deputy Chief of Staff of the Red Army) and K.B. Kalinovsky (commander of the first Soviet experimental mechanised force). Triandafillov and Kalinovsky were killed in an accident in 1931, but their ideas nevertheless proved highly influential. A significant role in the development of doctrine was also played by the Operations faculty of the Frunze Military Academy of the General Staff, which was set up in 1931.

During the late 1920s and early 1930s Soviet attention focused on the conduct of the 'Deep Battle'. This involved fixing and destroying the enemy throughout the depth of his tactical deployment (typically, 20 miles) using tanks, infantry, artillery and other arms, supported by air power. The Soviets envisaged heavy concentration of force at their chosen points of attack, but also sought to engage the enemy across a broad front, thus concealing their own intentions and preventing defensive redeployments. The aim was to punch holes through the enemy's tactical zone within twenty-four hours, thus facilitating his encirclement and annihilation. Emphasis was placed on hitting as many targets as possible at the same time, and on deliberate attacks on enemy headquarters and lines of communication. This would cause maximum disruption and create the conditions for a rapid breakthrough. The principles of 'Deep Battle' were first incorporated in the 1929 *Polevoi Ustav* (*Field Regulations*), and were refined in *PU-36*, the last completed *Field Regulations* before the outbreak of the Second World War.

'The setting up of a deep battle – that is the simultaneous disruption of the enemy's tactical layout over its entire depth – requires two things of tanks. On the one hand they must help the infantry forward and accompany it; on the other they must penetrate into the enemy's rear, both to disorganize him and to isolate his main forces from the reserves at his disposal. This deep penetration by tanks must create in the enemy's rear an obstacle for him, on to which he must be forced back and on which his main forces must be destroyed.'

Mikhail Tukhachevsky, 1932

'The art of the attacker is to unleash the entire mass of forces quickly enough to break out to the flank and rear area of the enemy forces to cut his withdrawal routes and disrupt any new grouping of forces the enemy is preparing.'

V.K. Triandafillov, The Nature of the Operations of Modern Armies *(1929)*

From 1931, however, considerable attention was given to how to capitalise upon the success achieved in the 'Deep Battle'. As the Soviets appreciated, only by exploiting their advantage could they gain genuinely overwhelming victories. For this purpose the capture or destruction of higher headquarters, supply depots, airfields, road and rail junctions, river crossings, unmanned defence lines and other targets behind the enemy's tactical zone would be required. Some of these objectives were likely to be over 100 miles away, and only if they were attacked quickly could enemy countermeasures be pre-empted. Nevertheless, if this could be done there would be several positive results. First, the enemy's ability to organise his assets across a large area would be disrupted, while those of his units still fighting in the tactical zone would be more easily destroyed. Second, the establishment of new lines of defence would be prevented, allowing an advance to a considerable depth (200 miles or more). Last, by securing important lines of communication, Soviet fighting and support formations could move forward quickly, allowing a rapid build-up for the next offensive.

This phase was known to the Soviets as the 'Deep Operation', and its most articulate expression came in the *Osnoy Glubokoy Operatsii* (*Fundamentals of the Deep Operation*), a series of lectures published by the Frunze Academy in 1933. At first this served as an unofficial handbook on operational matters, but in 1936 it was used as an approved text by the newly established General Staff Academy. However, although the doctrine was an essential ingredient in the recipe for success, other things were needed too. In particular armoured, mechanised and motorised units needed to be created, and guidelines drawn up for their use. Educated, mentally agile commanders were also required if the doctrine was to be implemented in a flexible and constructive fashion.

The Soviets tried hard to improve the quality of their armed forces during the mid-1930s. Thousands of tanks were produced for supporting infantry and cavalry in the 'Deep Battle', or for independent action in the 'Deep Operation'. Many of these vehicles used technology obtained from foreign sources, for example the fast, well-armed BT series, which used the revolutionary American Christie suspension system. This later formed the basis for the Soviet T-34, the best medium tank of the Second World War. The motorisation of the Red Army improved after 1931, when the Ford Motor Company established a factory at Gorki, while the Air Force also received new equipment. Many of its aircraft were of outstanding quality, and although all types were manufactured, from strategic bombers to short-range interceptors, particular emphasis was placed on using the Air Force in direct support of the land battle.

New formations were also established to make the most of the improved equipment. The Soviets believed that troops who had just achieved a breakthrough would be too disorganised to carry out immediate exploitation, and recognised that the composition of the 'shock armies' used in the 'Deep Battle' generally made them unsuited for such a role. Several mechanised corps were therefore created, each incorporating up to 1,000 tanks, as well as supporting arms. Together with cavalry and motorised units, these were to act as a second echelon, waiting for the shock armies to blast gaps in the enemy's defences before launching their own offensive into his rear. Powerful airborne forces were also set up to facilitate the pre-emption of defence lines and to prevent the timely arrival of enemy reserves during the 'Deep Operation'. Wargames and exercises were held to improve cooperative techniques and test doctrine, and numerous schools and academies were opened for the training of officers. Special attention was paid within these establishments to the study of combined arms and the understanding of new technologies.

By 1936 the Red Army was a capable instrument of war, although it had some weaknesses. At the tactical level, for example, the Soviets still relied mainly on drills and massive physical force to compensate for the inferior quality of their personnel. Neither was much attention paid to how to conduct large-scale defensive actions of the kind that the Red Army needed to fight in 1941. However, Soviet forces were at least as well equipped as those of Western European countries, and possessed more tanks than the rest of the world's armies put together. They were also further advanced doctrinally than any of their potential enemies.

Between 1936 and the end of 1938, however, the Red Army suffered a catastrophe. For various reasons – not least, his personal paranoia – the Soviet leader Josef Stalin (1879–1953) became convinced that his officer corps was plotting against him. In July 1936 he therefore ordered a campaign of terror to remove this perceived threat. Eventually, over 35,000 officers were executed, among them Mikhail Tukhachevsky and many of those who had been responsible for creating the Red Army's doctrine. Although some senior personnel survived, and a few became highly successful wartime commanders, the short-term effects were disastrous. The Red Army was effectively decapitated, and the vast literature produced by its foremost figures was removed from view. Over-promoted junior officers found themselves without the means to address their new responsibilities, and were often too terrified to demonstrate any personal initiative. Political commissars – who were ideologically reliable, but who usually knew little about military matters – were also given considerable influence over command decisions.

In the turmoil following Stalin's purges the Red Army also underwent major structural changes. In November 1939 the mechanised corps were disbanded, and although this decision was later reversed, the Soviet forces were still being reorganised when the Nazis invaded in June 1941. Similarly, although some impressive new equipment entered service, there was little opportunity to integrate it properly with existing arms. Overall, there was a massive reduction in the Red Army's fighting ability, something which was clearly demonstrated by its inept performance in the war against Finland (November 1939–March 1940). Rather like their future allies the British (if for different reasons), in a few years the Soviets had gone from a position of great strength to one of considerable weakness. In 1941 they would pay an appalling price for this deterioration.

The inter-war years were tremendously important in terms of their impact upon the future of war. Not only did they see the emergence of powerful ideologies that could apparently overcome one another only by using massive violence, but they also witnessed a rapid development in the tools with which belligerents would fight. Intellectually too, the ideas of people like Fuller and Tukhachevsky provided the basis for some of the

Stalin's purges: senior officers executed, 1936–8

	Number in army	Number executed
Marshals	5	3
Army commissars (1st class)	2	2
Army commanders (1st class)	4	2
Army commanders (2nd class)	12	12
Commissars (2nd class)	15	15
Corps commanders	67	60
Corps commissars	28	25
Divisional commanders	199	136
Brigade commanders	397	221
Brigade commissars	36	34

KHALKHIN-GOL (NOMONHAN), AUGUST 1939

In late August 1939, after several skirmishes between Japanese and Soviet troops along the disputed border of the Mongolian People's Republic (which was under Soviet control), a major clash took place on the River Khalkhin-Gol. Soviet-Mongolian forces amounted to 57,000 men with 498 tanks, 385 other armoured vehicles, 542 guns and mortars and 515 aircraft. They were under the control of Corps Commander Lieutenant-General Georgi Zhukov, and were opposed by powerful elements of the Japanese Kwantung Army, who, however, lacked large quantities of tanks or anti-tank weapons. The battle commenced with a Soviet attack on 20 August 1939, and resulted in the encirclement and destruction of most of the Japanese 23rd Division. With Japan's forces ejected from Mongolia, an armistice was signed on 16 September.

Zhukov's conduct of operations at Khalkhin-Gol demonstrated many of the features of 1930s Soviet doctrine. Skilful deception and concealment measures ('Maskirovka') helped to disguise the build-up of Red Army forces, who then unleashed a concentrated assault on the flanks of the Japanese deployment. All-arms cooperation between infantry, artillery and infantry-support tanks facilitated a relatively rapid breakthrough, while fixing attacks on the centre of the Japanese line prevented the enemy from withdrawing his forces intact. Meanwhile, Red Army mechanised and motorised units avoided pitched battles wherever possible, and struck deep to encircle Japanese troops who were cut off from reinforcement by Soviet air power. Red Army logistics also performed well, leading to a brief but violent campaign that resulted in a decisive Soviet victory.

The Battle of Khalkin-Gol was hardly reported in the West, where attention focused on the Nazi invasion of Poland. However, it demonstrated that despite Stalin's purges, the Red Army was still capable, when well led, of achieving impressive military successes based on the principles of 'Deep Battle'. It also enhanced the profile of Georgi Zhukov, who would become one of the most successful, and certainly the best known, of Stalin's marshals during the Second World War.

most spectacular operations carried out between 1939 and 1945, as well as for doctrinal developments that can be traced to the present day. In particular, in trying to discover alternatives to the deadlock of the Western Front, concepts of 'manoeuvre warfare' emerged, offering quick and decisive victories that not surprisingly proved highly attractive to politicians and military leaders alike. Nevertheless, the Second World War would prove that at the strategic level, warfare remained as attritional as it had been between 1914 and 1918. As the Soviets recognised, when modern industrial states with huge populations went to war, decisive results would take a long time and enormous effort to achieve. Tragically, it would take the deaths of tens of millions of people and the destruction of property on an unprecedented scale to demonstrate this brutal fact.

SEVEN

LAND WARFARE IN EUROPE, 1939–42

STEPHEN WALSH

Between September 1939 and October 1941 the German armed forces (the Wehrmacht) carried all before them, delivering a series of shattering blows against one European state after another. But was it German brilliance that led to these triumphs, or could the Nazis' success be better explained by their opponents' errors? Furthermore, did the Army's great strength – its tactical skill in pursuit of the decisive battle of annihilation – disguise a fundamental misunderstanding of how land warfare in the middle part of the twentieth century was best waged? Why, in late 1941, were the limits of German power finally revealed? Only by answering these questions can one show why a war that started so well for the Nazis ended in such catastrophic and complete defeat.

'BLITZKRIEG' IN POLAND

As earlier chapters have indicated, the German Army's understanding of strategy was rooted in the nineteenth-century concept of the *Vernichtungsschlacht*, or integral battle of annihilation. The Germans believed that destruction of the enemy's forces through tactical excellence in fighting would bring about strategic military success and the achievement of a war's political aim. In 1914 this belief had proven unsustainable. However, rather than attribute the failure of the Schlieffen Plan to its impracticability, the Germans put the blame on flaws in execution by their own field commanders. During the inter-war years they remained obsessed by the idea of destroying their enemies in vast cauldron battles, or *Kesselschlachten*. Relying on shock action by armoured and air forces to seize the initiative, and on tactical creativity, boldness and flexibility to hold it, the Wehrmacht sought to strike deep into the enemy's rear to surround and annihilate him. This, in essence, was what 'Blitzkrieg' as a warfighting technique was all about.

The opposing forces, Poland 1939 (not including reserves)

	German	Polish
Infantry divisions	28	17+3 brigades
Motorised infantry divisions	7	–
Panzer divisions	5	–
Others	–	6 cavalry brigades

The Polish Campaign: German and Polish losses

	German	Polish
Killed	8,082	c. 70,000
Wounded	27,278	c. 130,000
Missing	5,029	–
Prisoners	–	c. 400,000
Escaped to neutral states	–	c. 90,000

By summer 1939, as part of his plans to dominate Europe, Hitler was determined to crush Poland. Relieved of the danger of war on two fronts by the Nazi–Soviet Pact (August 1939), in September he set out to do this. The German plan ('Fall Weiss' or 'Case White') reflected the traditional inclination towards enveloping and destroying the enemy army. It was encouraged by the fact that Germany's occupation of Czechoslovakia in March 1939 had effectively encircled Poland. Taking advantage of this, the Army High Command (*Oberkommando des Heeres* or OKH) planned to surround and wipe out Polish forces west of Warsaw and the River Vistula. The main blow was to be delivered by Army Group South (8th, 10th and 14th armies), advancing north-east from Silesia and Slovakia, while Army Group North (3rd and 4th armies) was to strike south-east from Pomerania and East Prussia. Splintered and surrounded, the Poles would be destroyed in a series of tactical *Kesselschlachten* within a wider encirclement. To this end most of the panzer and motorised divisions were concentrated on the flanks, in Pomerania and Silesia. At no stage was the Polish capital Warsaw a specific objective.

The Germans' opponents were brave and tenacious. However, they were also badly outnumbered. Against 2,100 panzers (of which 1,300 were armed with cannon as well as machine guns) the Polish Army could only deploy 887 tanks and tankettes (of which barely 200 were 'modern' by any stretch of the imagination). In terms of artillery, mobility and communications they were equally outclassed. Encircled to north and south, yet with their most valuable industrial regions and population centres in the west, the Poles were compelled to disperse their armies along the country's borders. This reduced the depth of their defences and increased the chances of the breakthrough they sought to prevent. Although the Poles hoped to ensnare the Germans in a positional struggle while defending their territory, only an Allied offensive in the west promised to save them from defeat. And, as Hitler appreciated, in the face of Franco-British unpreparedness such an offensive was unlikely.

The Nazi attack began on 1 September 1939. Within three days the Luftwaffe won control of the skies, allowing the full weight of German air power to support the ground invasion. Meanwhile, Army Group North overran the Polish Corridor between East Prussia and Pomerania, and Army Group South struck east towards Łódź and Kraków. 10th Army, containing many motorised units, drove deep to create the southern prong of the encirclement. Even so, in the face of a fighting withdrawal by the enemy, OKH was compelled to order German forces to perform a second pincer movement east of the Vistula towards the River Bug. By 16 September this outer encirclement was complete. The Germans then turned to destroy Polish units trapped between the two rivers.

West of Warsaw, however, the Nazis faced increasingly dogged opposition. Polish forces coalescing on the River Bzura created a substantial concentration of combat power that dealt the over-extended 8th Army several stinging blows. This forced the Germans on to the defensive, but once reinforcements from 10th Army arrived it was possible to begin the liquidation of the Bzura pocket. On 16 September alone 820 Luftwaffe aircraft dropped over 700,000 pounds of bombs on the encircled enemy, breaking their morale. Two days later resistance

POLISH CAMPAIGN, SEPTEMBER–OCTOBER 1939

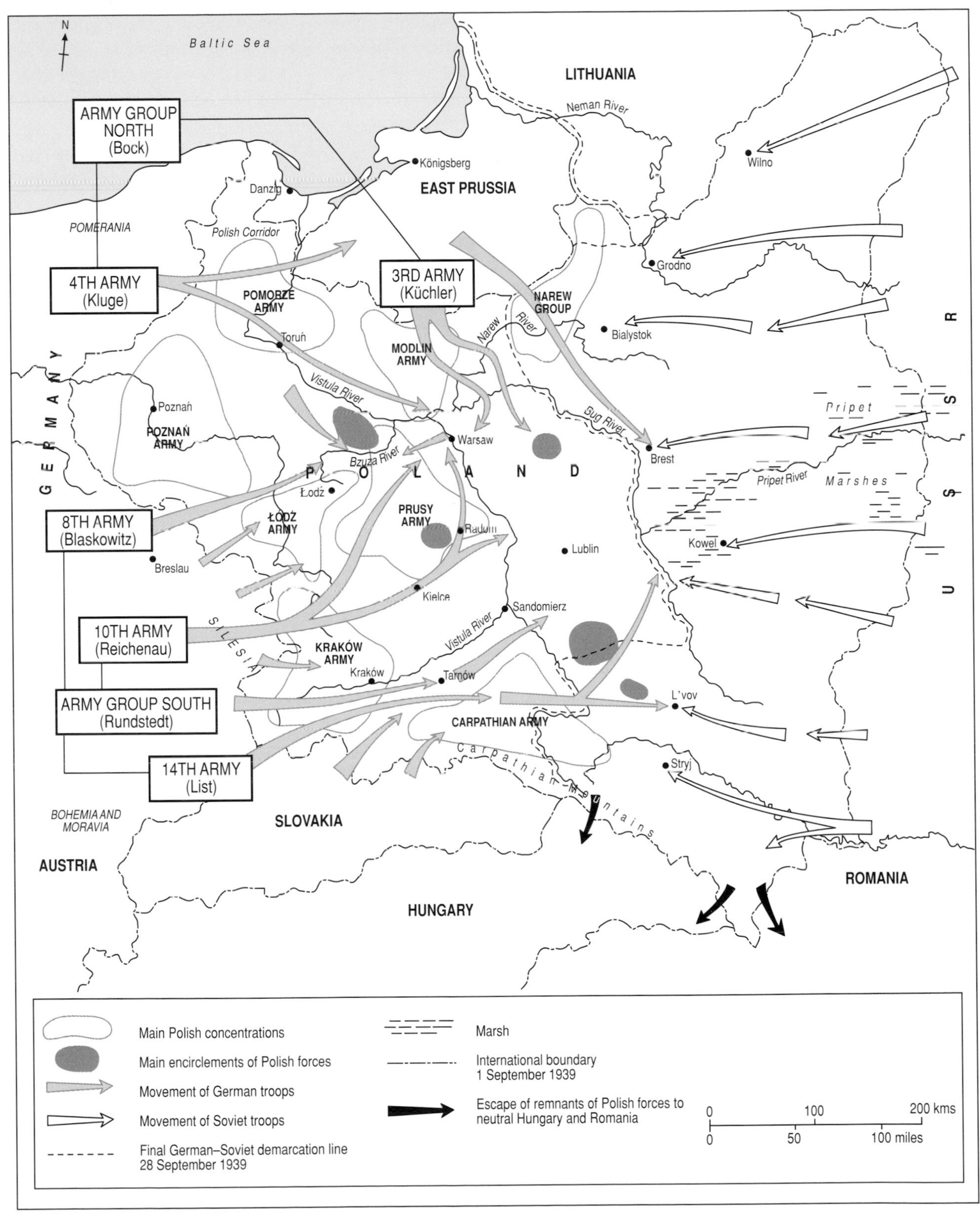

collapsed. Roughly a quarter of the Polish Army – 120,000 men – went into German captivity.

By this point it was clear that the Nazis were on the verge of achieving a decisive victory. *Kesselschlachten* around L'vov accounted for much of the rest of the Polish forces, and although over 100,000 troops remained to defend Warsaw, in the face of an air and artillery bombardment that threatened massive civilian suffering they were quickly compelled to surrender. To add insult to injury, from 17 September Red Army units moved west to claim Stalin's share of Poland. Caught between two powerful enemies, the last Polish soldiers capitulated on 6 October 1939.

The Polish campaign revealed the Germans' continuing attachment to the tactical idea of the *Kesselschlacht* and the strategic concept of the *Vernichtungsschlacht*. Although the pace of advance was slowed by the inclusion of panzer divisions in infantry armies, by exploiting the advantages of armour, motorisation and air power the Polish Army was destroyed with impressive skill and speed. Irrespective of their impossible strategic position, like Germany's subsequent victims the Poles were incapable of waging a modern war of the kind to which they were exposed. Their commitment to linear and positional warfare, and their inadequate communications, had ensured that troops in forward positions were quickly encircled and destroyed. For all their bravery, the result was disaster.

HITLER TURNS WEST

After conquering Poland Hitler wanted to attack France as quickly as possible. For various reasons the assault was delayed until May 1940, but when it finally came it was devastatingly successful. In a landmark campaign the Wehrmacht overran France, Belgium, the Netherlands and Luxembourg in only six weeks, crushing their armed forces and causing a precipitate withdrawal by the British Expeditionary Force (BEF). This was one of the most complete military victories in history, and superficially justified the concept of decisive strategic success in one campaign. Furthermore, it was achieved against an enemy who in several respects appeared superior, yet who succumbed to German tactical flair and boldness with remarkable rapidity. It was in many ways the perfect 'Blitzkrieg' campaign.

A well-known image of 'Blitzkrieg', with German tanks and infantry advancing unopposed across open country in summer 1940. Intimate armour-infantry cooperation of this kind was criticised by commanders like Heinz Guderian for wasting the primary attributes of the Panzers, and it tended to be rare in the early part of the war. The tank in the foreground is a Czech-manufactured Panzer 35t, 118 of which were used by 6 Panzer division in 1940. (RMAS Collection)

Nevertheless, it is important to recognise that the French High Command's approach to warfare contributed significantly to Germany's triumph. Unlike their opponents, the main lesson that the French drew from the First World War was that victory resulted from cumulative attrition. They believed that the enemy would be defeated through a combination of fortification and firepower, with attacks canalised into prepared killing zones. In its offensive component, their doctrine was redolent of the step-by-step approach of

ARMOUR IN 1940

Contrary to popular perception, the Germans did not have any notable superiority in armoured fighting vehicles (AFVs) in 1940. The French alone had more tanks than their enemy, and together with British AFVs the Western powers actually had a clear numerical advantage. Furthermore, some of the French tanks – especially the Somua S 35 and Char B – were powerful fighting machines at least as good as anything the Germans could deploy. Both sides fielded large numbers of obsolescent AFVs, and less than 1,000 of the Wehrmacht's 2,581 Panzers could genuinely be considered modern.

These figures, however, disguise the Germans' superiority in several crucial areas. Unlike French and British vehicles, the Panzers were lavishly equipped with wireless sets. This allowed maximum flexibility in the use of German armoured sub units, and facilitated cooperation with other arms of service. Because they regularly worked together, the components of the Panzer divisions operated as an efficient team, whereas all-arms training in Western units was poor. Although the French were grouping some of their tanks in armoured divisions by 1940, they still had only six such formations to the Germans' ten Panzer divisions. Many French tanks were 'penny packeted' in individual battalions attached to infantry units, and this stood in stark contrast to the concentrated Panzer Corps and Gruppes with which the Germans operated in 1940. Furthermore, the Panzer divisions were much better balanced in terms of infantry, artillery, engineers and other supporting services than their opponents' equivalents. When employed by capable commanders who exercised initiative and applied strength against weakness, it is hardly surprising that the Germans made so much of their armoured assets in 1940. Together with the Luftwaffe, they provided a lethal instrument of war to which their enemies had no effective response.

The French Char B1 bis was probably the best tank in service in May 1940. It mounted a 47mm anti-tank gun in the turret and a 75mm howitzer in the hull. The Char B provided the main striking force of the four divisions cuirassée established by the French in 1940, and 403 were built before the Allied collapse. (Tank Museum)

1918, with set-piece assaults to limited objectives. Although they had more tanks and artillery than the Germans, they placed little emphasis upon speed of communications, a high tempo of operations or initiative among junior commanders. This was very different to the attitude adopted by their enemy.

The perceived advantages to the French of fighting defensively, and the strategy of the 'continuous front', were most clearly manifested in the Maginot Line. This was a system of fortresses constructed in the early 1930s that guarded the border with Germany. As a defensive position it was impressive, but it fostered a passive mentality. Unfortunately, at a time when the Nazis were busy in Poland, the system protected Germany better than France. Neither did the Maginot Line cover the Franco-Belgian border. The resulting 'Belgian Gap' distracted the attention of the French High Command in 1940, to the extent that it could not conceive of a major attack elsewhere. This was not least because it was through the same area that the Germans had invaded in 1914.

To their cost, the Western powers relied heavily on positional, linear defences in the campaign of 1940. This was most obviously true of the French, who spent billions of francs constructing the Maginot Line in the 1930s. However, other European states adopted a similar strategy, as these Belgian fortress guns illustrate. (IWM MH24417)

In an irony of history, the original Nazi plan for the invasion of Western Europe ('Fall Gelb' or 'Case Yellow') did envisage northern Belgium as the point of main effort. However, its implementation was prevented by a series of delays and then by the hand of fate. On 10 January 1940 a German aircraft crashed near Mechelen, on the Dutch–Belgian border. On board was a copy of the Luftwaffe's plans for supporting the ground invasion through the Low Countries. Nevertheless, when the French Commander-in-Chief, General Maurice Gamelin (1872–1958) learned of the incident, he saw it as a deliberate attempt by the enemy to persuade him to alter his strategy in expectation of the Nazis changing theirs. Having anticipated the main attack in Belgium, he became convinced that this was where the blow would fall. Consequently, he not only remained committed to sending the best French troops and BEF into Belgium, but also reinforced these units to allow an advance into Holland. This was not a strategy of manoeuvre. Rather, it was a plan to move the 'continuous line' to a static position further north-east, so as to fight alongside the Dutch and Belgians and avoid damage to northern France. Tragically for France, the Mechelen Incident did not represent a deliberate plant. The German plan had in fact been compromised. But for Hitler this was to prove a blessing in disguise.

In February 1940 Generalmajor Erich von Manstein (1887–1973), Chief of Staff of the German Army Group A, proposed that the *Schwerpunkt* (main effort) of the attack be shifted away from Army Group B in northern Belgium, to the Ardennes. This was an upland area in southern Belgium and Luxembourg. It was fairly heavily wooded, lacked major roads and was dissected by numerous streams and rivers. For these reasons it had been dismissed by the French as a likely invasion route. However, its apparent drawbacks made it attractive to Manstein. He believed that a concentrated blow here would overwhelm the opponent's defences and carry the mobile divisions of Army Group A across the River Meuse into northern France, where the terrain was ideal for manoeuvre warfare. Meanwhile, a diminished but still powerful Army Group B would attack the Low Countries, defeat the Dutch and Belgians and fix the best French and British troops away from the decisive area. Further south, Army Group C would carry out a deception role opposite the Maginot Line with the aim of tying down further enemy forces. In March Hitler accepted Manstein's ideas.

Erich von Manstein (1887–1973) is widely regarded as the Wehrmacht's finest field commander. His plan to seize the initiative in 1940 succeeded even beyond his expectations, and his operational record on the Eastern Front was also highly impressive. However, his aristocratic values and outspokenness alienated him from Hitler, and he was permanently retired from the Army in April 1944.

It is important to understand the new German plan for what it was. Manstein did not propose any encirclement of the enemy. And although it was remarkably bold, his scheme was not a complete operational plan designed to annihilate the numerically superior Western powers in one campaign. Instead, it represented an attempt to smash the enemy's

'continuous line' at its weakest point, thus avoiding a linear, attritional contest. Its limited scope is confirmed by General der Panzertruppen Heinz Guderian, commander of XIX Panzer Corps in 1940, who admitted that he never received prior orders as to what to do once a bridgehead over the Meuse was captured. This would tend to confirm the view that even if the campaign was later regarded by the Germans as a validation of the *Vernichtungsschlacht*, it was not planned in detail as such.

A German Panzer II halts before a blown bridge on the River Meuse at Monthermé, France, May 1940. The flag on the engine deck was designed to facilitate recognition from the air, but was in fact far too small to fulfil this purpose. (Tank Museum)

THE GERMANS STRIKE

On 10 May 1940 'Case Yellow' began. Once again the Luftwaffe played a pivotal role, exploiting its superior numbers of modern aircraft to gain air superiority at several critical points. Airborne forces attacked bridges over the Lek, Waal and Maas rivers, cutting the Netherlands in two, shattering their opponent's cohesion and contributing to a Dutch capitulation four days later. German glider troops also assaulted the Belgian fortress of Eben Emael, at the junction of the Albert Canal and River Meuse. This was the linchpin of Belgium's defences, and its spectacular capture conferred immediate credibility on Army Group B's apparent status as the Nazis'

'Soldiers of the Western Front, your hour has come. The fight which begins today will determine Germany's destiny for a thousand years.'

Adolf Hitler, 10 May 1940

'CASE YELLOW' – THE OPENING STAGES

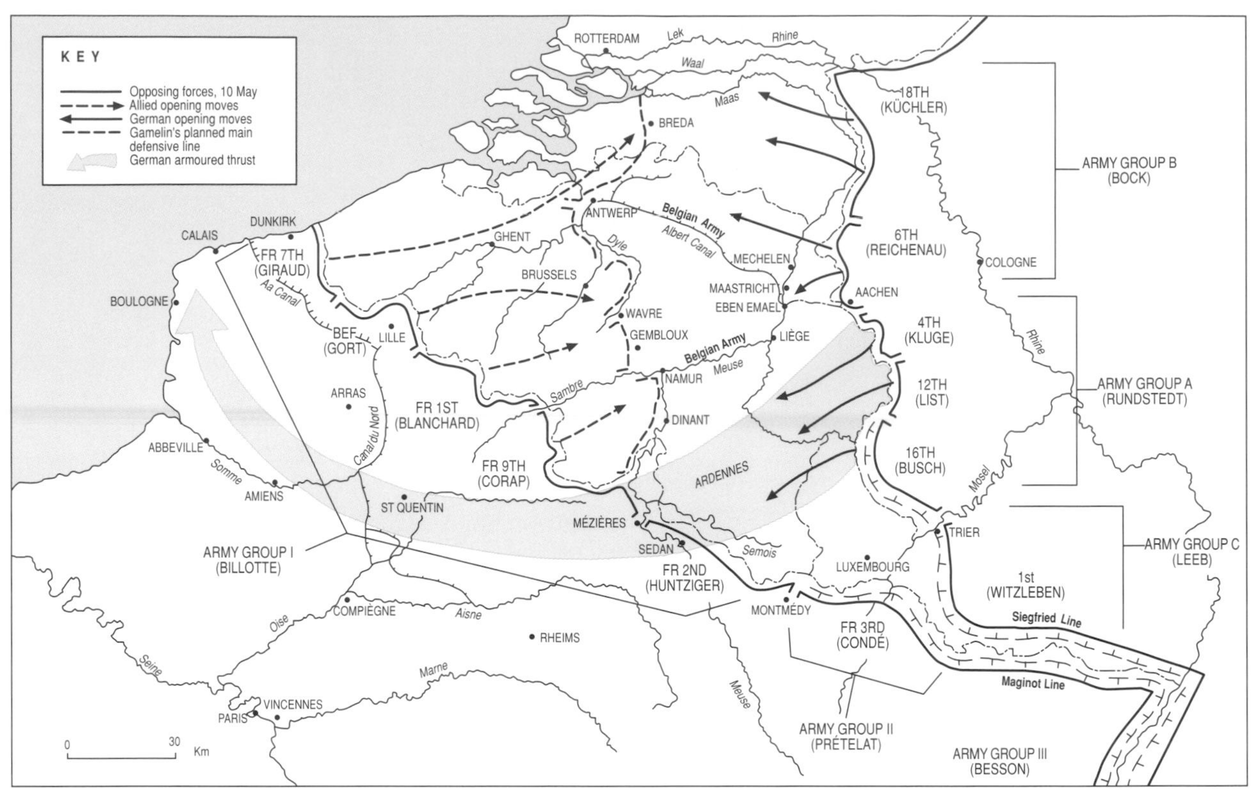

The opposing forces, Western Europe 1940 (including reserves)	German	Western Powers
Infantry divisions	125	86 French 22 Belgian 10 British 8 Dutch
Panzer/ armoured divisions	10	6 French (plus 2 British armoured regiments)
Motorised infantry divisions	7	7 French
Cavalry divisions	–	5 French

main fighting formation. It also delivered a profound moral blow at the start of the campaign from which the Belgians never recovered.

As French and British troops moved into Belgium, further south the armoured spearhead of Army Group A, Panzergruppe Kleist, spent the first few days of the campaign penetrating the Ardennes. Benefiting from fighter cover provided by the Luftwaffe, initially its advance went largely unnoticed. As a result it was able to brush aside the weak resistance offered by Belgian and French screening forces. By the evening of 12 May seven panzer divisions (of ten in the Wehrmacht) were approaching the east bank of the Meuse, trailed closely by a stream of motorised and infantry formations. In a devastating attack the following day several of the panzer divisions crossed the Meuse and established firm bridgeheads. By 16 May German troops were flooding into northern France and heading towards the English Channel.

The physical and psychological effects of the blow were immense. In the face of flexible, dynamic and aggressive German leadership at all levels, the cumbersome command structures of the Western powers proved woefully inadequate. Inefficient communications and poor liaison between the British, French and Belgians compounded their problems. Although the French High Command finally ordered reserves to the Meuse, none arrived in time to resist the initial assault. Forced to move under heavy air attack along roads clogged with refugees, several formations disintegrated

THE BATTLES ON THE MEUSE

The penetration of seven Panzer divisions to the Meuse within three days of the start of the campaign demonstrates the skill with which the Germans had planned and carried out their move through the Ardennes. Nevertheless, the river provided a major obstacle to a further advance, and its west bank was defended by troops from the French 9th and 2nd armies. Admittedly, these were generally low-quality units (reflecting the insignificance attributed to the Ardennes in French planning), but powerful reserves were already *en route* to bolster the line. If they arrived before the Germans crossed the river in force, Manstein's plan might yet fail.

Speed, therefore, was of the essence if the Germans were to maintain the initiative. Fortunately for them, although the French had blown the Meuse bridges, a weir had been left intact near Dinant for fear that otherwise the river would become fordable. However, the French had failed adequately to protect this crossing, and when troops from 7 Panzer Division stumbled upon it they were quick to seize the opportunity to establish a bridgehead. By the morning of 13 May the Germans already had a foothold on the west bank of the Meuse.

The critical sector, however, lay further to the south, at Sedan. This was the hinge of the French 'continuous line', and a successful attack here threatened to split the Western armies in two. The Germans knew this, and consequently devoted enormous resources to ensuring victory at this point. Not only was the entire XIX Panzer Corps (three divisions plus the elite *Grossdeutschland* infantry regiment) used against the enemy defences here on a narrow front, but 910 aircraft (roughly a third of the Luftwaffe's strength) were also allocated to support the assault. The effects on the single French reserve division opposing them were lethal.

The attack at Sedan began on the afternoon of 13 May. After an intense artillery and air bombardment, the Panzer divisions' infantry and combat engineers crossed the river in rubber boats. Shocked by the concentrated, all-arms nature of the assault, which was delivered by well-trained and energetically led soldiers, the French were unable to stop the attackers, and by nightfall their defences had crumbled. Within a few hours the Germans constructed pontoon bridges and ferries to reinforce the assault troops with tanks and other heavy equipment. By 14 May considerable forces were assembling south of the river, ready for a breakout to the west.

The all-arms nature of the Panzer divisions allowed them to cope with a range of obstacles on their own. Here, a 37mm anti-tank gun covers an assault crossing by infantry in rubber boats near Dinant on the River Meuse. (Ullstein Bilderdienst, Berlin)

The French were shocked by this setback. Having assumed that no assault crossing could take place for at least another three days, they were now compelled to react to the presence of powerful enemy formations on the west bank of the Meuse. Sadly, muddled staff work and poor communications meant that although reinforcements were beginning to arrive in strength, none were committed to the kind of concentrated counterblow that might still have pushed the Germans back across the river. Instead, in the small hours of 15 May General André Corap (1878–1953), commander of the 9th Army, ordered that a general withdrawal from the Meuse take place with the aim of re-establishing the 'continuous line' further to the west.

Corap's decision confirmed the defeat of the French forces on the Meuse. Deficient in motor transport and fuel, units attempting to retreat found themselves rapidly encircled and destroyed by fast-moving German spearheads. Meanwhile, along a 50-mile section of the Meuse, German Panzer and infantry divisions crossed the river unopposed. By the morning of 16 May some 2,000 tanks and well over 150,000 men were in a position to begin the drive to the Channel.

The battles on the River Meuse between 13 and 15 May constitute the decisive engagements of the 1940 campaign. Had the French line held, the advantages achieved by the Germans from their surprise blow through the Ardennes would have been lost, and a difficult attritional contest – the outcome of which was uncertain – would have ensued. Yet in only three days the French front was exploded wide open, allowing an avalanche of German armoured and infantry units to drive deep into their opponent's rear. The result was the encirclement and destruction of the best forces available to the Western powers in 1940, and the collapse of their war effort.

even before they engaged the enemy. Many soldiers panicked and fled, exacerbating the chaos and sense of shock. Others, unable to cast aside their defensive mindset, allowed themselves to be bypassed or launched ponderous counter-attacks that were repulsed with relative ease. In all important respects the Germans proved themselves superior at the decisive moment. Not only had they knocked their enemies off balance by surprising them, but they also appeared capable of maintaining their momentum.

Yet all was not as well with the Germans as it seemed. Almost as much as the French, they had been astonished by the success of the attack through the Ardennes. Although the French assumed that the panzers would head towards Paris or move south-east behind the Maginot Line, OKH actually lacked any plans for exploiting its initial success. In the middle of the campaign the Germans argued about the surest way to secure a decisive *Kesselschlacht*. Superficially, disagreements focused on whether or not the panzer divisions should be allowed to operate freely in advance of the relatively slow-moving infantry units. The latter, after all, were required to protect the 'Panzer Corridor' across northern France against possible flank attacks. However, the real issue was how to make a tactical concept work at the operational level with an army that was not fully mobile. As in Poland, there was no existing operational or campaign plan to link together the various tactical successes of the German Army to achieve a strategic victory. In 1939 and 1940 this problem would be swept under the carpet by continued tactical excellence and the mortal wounds inflicted on an inferior enemy during the opening phase of operations. It was nevertheless a fundamental weakness in the German approach to warfighting, and it would become acute in Russia the following year.

'I never received any further orders as to what I was to do once the bridgehead over the Meuse was captured. All my decisions until I reached the Atlantic seaboard at Abbeville were taken by me and me alone.'

Heinz Guderian,
Panzer Leader *(1952)*

Having thrown the Western powers into disarray at the start of the campaign, the Germans spent the subsequent weeks reaping the rewards of their achievement. Despite arguments among senior commanders which threatened to slow its advance, by 19 May Panzergruppe Kleist's spearheads were in open country, and the next day they reached the Channel. Marching hard to keep up, German infantry divisions made the encirclement watertight and secured the main thrust against attacks from the flanks. Weak counterblows were in fact delivered by the French from the south on 19 May and by the British from the north two days later, but these merely dented the German lines. Nevertheless, Hitler continued to worry that the enemy might rally, and these incidents contributed to his decision to halt the panzers on the Aa Canal on 24 May. Assisted by gallant resistance from the French 1st Army, the BEF had time to organise an evacuation via the port of Dunkirk, although its heavy equipment had to be abandoned. Meanwhile, caught in a trap between Army Group B on the one side, and the coast on the other, on 28 May the Belgian Army finally capitulated after heavy fighting. Within days they were joined in captivity by the shattered remnants of France's finest fighting units.

After a short pause to reorganise, on 5 June the Germans launched 'Fall Rot' ('Case Red'), the final phase of the campaign in Western Europe. As with their actions after crossing the Meuse, this was an entirely improvised operation. Indeed, despite an excellent road infrastructure, good weather and effective air transport, the Germans found themselves facing an unforeseen supply crisis that might have cost them dear against a less badly injured foe. Furthermore, although their best formations had been destroyed, the French were determined to salvage something from the catastrophe. For several days, using a 'chequerboard' defence of mutually supporting positions instead of a linear deployment, they fought hard to prevent a breakthrough on the River Somme. Initially they achieved some success. However, in the face of a numerically superior, mobile, well-led enemy, the French could only hold for a short period. By 9 June their front had ruptured almost everywhere, and when deep thrusts by panzer units encircled the Maginot Line from the north, the French government's will to continue the war collapsed. On 22 June 1940, amid bitter recriminations, the armistice document was signed. As a final humiliation the ceremony took place at Compiègne, where Marshal Foch had received the German surrender in 1918.

As in Poland, the campaign in Western Europe appeared to confirm that decisive victory could be achieved through a rapid, almost seamless offensive effort. In just over a month, at a cost of 45,000 killed, the Germans defeated enemy forces of 3½ million. In the process they demonstrated the value of rigorous training, dynamic leadership and good communications. They also proved the importance of inter-service and all-arms cooperation, and showed a remarkable ability to improvise. Nevertheless, there were several cracks in the façade of German military excellence. Astonishingly, the Germans went to war without any real plan for achieving victory. They were also prone to disagreements about how best to conduct operations; in this respect, Hitler's interference was a particularly worrying sign of things to come. Despite their tactical skill, against well-prepared opposition the Germans had experienced numerous local setbacks. Finally, with their economy still mobilising for war, they

'Therefore the doctrines of the "Blitzkrieg" should not be considered as novelties, but as the new application of the simple classic theories of military science . . . The secret of the "Blitzkrieg" lies not in German material superiority, but mainly in the Allies' technical inferiority.'

F.O. Miksche, Blitzkrieg (1941)

'This colossal empire in the east is ripe for dissolution. We are chosen by Destiny to be the witnesses of a catastrophe which will afford the strongest confirmation of the nationalist theory of race.'

Adolf Hitler, Mein Kampf

had shown themselves logistically unprepared for anything beyond a very short campaign. They had achieved an overwhelming victory against an operationally incompetent enemy. But the question was whether they could do so against more serious opposition.

THE INVASION OF THE SOVIET UNION

At 0315 hours on Sunday 22 June 1941 the Germans launched Operation 'Barbarossa'. With it began a racial war of annihilation, carried out by the Nazis in pursuit of *Lebensraum* (living space) for the German people. Simultaneously, Hitler set out to destroy the 'Jewish-Bolshevik' political system, which he regarded as an abomination, and to secure resources to protect Germany against blockade. Equally, he hoped that by robbing Britain of her last potential European ally, he would induce her government to make peace and acknowledge Germany's pre-eminence on the continent. Yet despite stunning successes during the summer and autumn of 1941 the Germans did not defeat the Soviet Union in a single campaign. So why did methods that worked in 1940 fail in the following year?

An invasion of the Soviet Union posed problems on a scale not confronted in earlier operations. Geography, distance and time dominated calculations and influenced the entire campaign. In France the panzers had only needed to travel 200 miles to get from the Meuse to the Channel. Yet it was 1,000 miles from Warsaw to Moscow, and 1,200 from Leningrad to Rostov. Furthermore, the Russian climate limited mobile operations to between May and November. This made timing a critical factor, not least because the Germans were determined to win in a single campaign. Soviet roads were poor and their railways used a wider gauge than those of the Germans. This made rapid resupply problematical beyond a limited distance. The Germans recognised that, unlike in 1940, a single encirclement would not deliver a mortal blow. Nevertheless, it was still assumed that the Red Army could be annihilated in a series of *Kesselschlachten*. Whether the Germans could in fact achieve this without suffering unsustainable attrition was debatable. In essence, however, the Germans treated 'Barbarossa' as just another campaign. In it a *Vernichtungsschlacht* would be achieved by similar methods to those used previously.

Operation 'Barbarossa' evolved from a plan drawn up in summer 1940 by the Chief of Staff of 18th Army, Generalmajor Erich Marcks (1891–1944). He believed that victory could be achieved in a single campaign by destroying the Red Army in two phases. First, Soviet forces would be smashed in cauldron battles throughout European Russia. This was an important industrial and agricultural region, and Marcks calculated that the enemy would stand and fight for it. This would render him vulnerable to encirclement by German mobile groups. After this, remaining Red Army units would be annihilated in a decisive battle for Moscow. Together with a second massive military reverse, the loss of the Soviet capital would achieve victory in a single campaign taking around ten weeks. However, because the Germans lacked the strength to attack everywhere at once, Marcks emphasised that the main effort must be in the centre, towards Moscow.

Although amended slightly by OKH, this was a sensible proposal that stood some chance of success. Admittedly, it relied on the Soviets not withdrawing behind the Dvina and Dnieper rivers, but this was a sound assumption. Unfortunately for the Germans, in December 1940 Hitler himself changed the plan. Combining over-ambition with timidity, the Nazi leader rejected the idea that his forces should go all-out for the Soviet capital. Instead, he ordered that they capture targets throughout the western part of the Soviet Union. In particular, he stressed that Russian forces in the Baltic region must be destroyed, and Leningrad captured, before the final drive on Moscow commenced. His instructions were summarised in Führer Directive 21, issued on 18 December 1940.

Directive 21 was not a detailed campaign plan. Rather, it laid out objectives for the first phase of operations, in which three army groups (North, Centre and South) totalling 3½ million men would drive east to surround and destroy enemy forces. Each army group would have at least one powerful Panzergruppe (Army Group Centre had two). These contained the vast majority of the 3,350 tanks available to the Germans. Their role was to spearhead the offensive on narrow axes, smash the enemy's linear defences and thrust deep to create huge *Kesselschlachten*. These pockets would be destroyed by infantry armies following in the wake of the panzers. However, although Directive 21 was vague on the subject, the Germans would have to stop after 300 miles because logistics would become a problem as the campaign developed. This would allow railways behind the front lines to be converted to Western European gauge, reducing the burden on the Army's inadequate truck fleet and facilitating resupply of the fighting units. Only after this was done, and once the alleged threat to Army Group Centre's northern flank was removed, would the offensive recommence. Against minimal opposition it was anticipated that a line from the Volga mouth (in the south) to Archangel (in the north) could be reached before winter. The result would be the eradication of the Soviet threat and the fulfilment of Hitler's political aims.

It is essential to understand that everything was predicated on a short campaign. The

THE BALKANS, OCTOBER 1940–MAY 1941

In October 1940 Benito Mussolini (1883–1945), Italy's fascist dictator, sought to assert the prestige of Italian arms by launching an invasion of Greece. This move was undertaken with the approval of his ally, Adolf Hitler, and the campaign was expected to end quickly. However, in the face of fierce Greek resistance the Italians were driven back into Albania, and only with difficulty did they stabilise the front. Thereafter, indecisive fighting dominated by terrain and weather continued until February 1941.

Italian failure raised the prospect of a prolonged Balkan conflict, with British intervention on behalf of the Greeks. On the eve of the invasion of the Soviet Union this severely threatened Nazi interests in the region. Hitler therefore decided to support Mussolini by ordering a German attack on Greece via Bulgaria, and by pressuring neighbouring Yugoslavia into joining the Axis powers. However, although Yugoslavia's government signed the Tripartite Pact on 25 March 1941, two days later the government was overthrown in a *coup d'état*. Suspecting a British plot, an enraged Hitler vowed to teach the Yugoslavs a lesson while conquering Greece in a 'Blitzkrieg' campaign.

Operation 'Punishment' began with a massive air strike on Belgrade on 6 April 1941. Yugoslav ground forces were then crushed by a series of hammer blows, leading to the country's unconditional surrender eleven days later. Simultaneously the German 12th Army invaded eastern Greece (Operation 'Marita'), isolating enemy troops in this area before moving west to trap the bulk of the Greek Army between themselves and the Italians in Albania. Overwhelmed with the same speed and ferocity as the Poles, French and Yugoslavs, the Greeks surrendered on 24 April. To add insult to injury, the Germans also drove a British-led expeditionary force, sent from Egypt to help the Greeks, into humiliating withdrawal. Once again the tactical excellence of German ground and air forces had held the key to victory. At a cost of fewer than 6,000 casualties, the Nazis defeated armed forces of over 1 million in less than a month. When Crete was captured by airborne assault in May, the Germans were able to launch Operation 'Barbarossa' with a completely secure Balkan flank.

'Three army groups, each of approximately the same strength, were to attack with diverging objectives. No single clear operational objective seemed to be envisaged. Looking at it from a professional point of view this did not appear at all promising.'

Heinz Guderian,
Panzer Leader *(1952)*

The opposing forces, 'Barbarossa' 1941 (Western USSR only)

	German	Soviet
Military personnel	3,150,000 (plus 500,000 allies, mainly Finns and Romanians)	3,000,000
Tanks	3,350	c. 20,000
Aircraft	2,775	c. 10,000

Wehrmacht's tactical superiority was to ensure victory before any serious difficulties arose. There were no contingency plans if the war dragged on. However, in a country as large and powerful as the Soviet Union, success required a carefully calculated use of means in pursuit of precise military aims. Otherwise resources could be wasted in fighting which made no decisive contribution to defeating the enemy, even if the results were superficially spectacular. The Germans needed a plan that linked separate battles into a coherent operational whole, the objective of which would be to render the enemy incapable of effective resistance, and not necessarily to annihilate him. Yet Directive 21 repeated many of the errors of the Schlieffen Plan, that other statement of disastrously misplaced strategic faith. As in 1914, only if the enemy fought in a suicidal fashion was victory likely to result.

Paradoxically, the successful method of 1940 – the *Kesselschlacht* – actually undermined German chances of defeating the Soviets in one campaign. In Western Europe the decisive encirclement had resulted from an advance in good weather over a limited distance, using excellent roads. This made the gap between the panzers and the follow-on infantry very short in time and space. Consequently, enemy forces had few chances to escape. Given the geography of the region, a break-out attempt would also have taken place on predictable axes against elite formations that were not required elsewhere. None of this was true in the Soviet Union. Here many pockets, some of them immense, would need to be destroyed. The panzers would also have to advance rapidly to prevent Red Army troops not caught by the initial blow from withdrawing behind the Dvina–Dnieper line. As only 34 of the 145 German divisions used in 'Barbarossa' were fully motorised, this meant leaving the *Kesselschlachten* to the infantry. Their ability to create watertight perimeters and speedily destroy the surrounded enemy was doubtful. So was their ability to keep up with the panzers on dirt roads at the height of summer. In simple terms, forward momentum and the rapid annihilation of the pockets were fundamental to success. Yet with an army that was divided in two – a minority riding on wheels or tracks and a majority moving on foot – they were incompatible. In such circumstances the achievements of the mobile units were likely to be the critical factor. If they failed, and the campaign settled down into a positional, attritional struggle, the Germans would be in deep trouble.

That the Nazis came so close to winning can best be explained by the behaviour of their enemy, not the worthiness of the 'Barbarossa' plan. Despite having a standing strength of about 5 million, in 1941 the Red Army was in dire straits. Stalin's purges had decapitated the officer corps, destroying in the process much of the sophisticated doctrine developed in the 1930s. Political commissars dominated military decision-making, leading to clumsy inefficiency in combat. This was clearly demonstrated in the Winter War against Finland between November 1939 and March 1940. In this conflict the Soviets suffered over 200,000 casualties and overcame their opponent only by sheer weight of numbers. Although some reforms were instituted after this debacle and as a result of witnessing German success in France, at the time of 'Barbarossa' the Red Army was still in disarray.

Even worse, in 1941 Stalin compelled his forces to adopt a strategy of forward defence. At no point did he permit the Red Army to trade space for time by withdrawing before the German blow. Like the Poles and French before them, the Soviets relied on linear deployments which put them in an ideal position to be encircled. Only by manoeuvre could they avoid this, and with initiative neither encouraged nor tolerated, paralysis and confusion were more likely. Although the Red Army had 20,000 tanks, only 1,800 of them were modern KV-1s and T-34s. Even these tended to be 'penny packeted', rather than concentrated in large units. Radios were conspicuous by their absence and crew training was poor. Much the same was true of Soviet artillery, which was ubiquitous but badly integrated with other arms. More positively, the Red Army soldier was tenacious and rugged. Together with the enormous manpower reserves available to Stalin, this was to be a vital factor in accounting for Soviet survival and the gradual attrition suffered by the Germans. But the cost was to be appalling.

STALIN'S PRE-EMPTIVE WAR, MAY 1941

In the 1990s a considerable controversy arose about Soviet intentions in spring 1941. According to some commentators, the Red Army at this time was planning a pre-emptive strike against Germany, which would have rendered 'Barbarossa' irrelevant. The evidence lies in a document first revealed by a Soviet defector, Viktor Rezun, which showed that in May 1941 a senior Soviet commander, General Georgi Zhukov (1896–1974), proposed an offensive against the Germans. However, although such a suggestion was certainly made, this does not mean that there was a clear decision to attack. Zhukov's proposal was one among many, and was made at a time when war was seen as imminent. Red Army troops were indeed deploying in large numbers along the border, but their aim was to defend the Soviet Union, not to attack. Furthermore, senior German officers – among them the Military Attaché to the USSR, General der Kavallerie Ernst Köstring (1876–1953) – were aware of these deployments, yet saw in them no prospect of a Soviet attack. Stalin's desperate attempts to avoid provoking the Nazis also suggest that he wished to avoid war in 1941. Even if he had wanted to launch an offensive, the Red Army was incapable of conducting it. Stalin knew the weaknesses of his forces. Nobody had done more to create them.

'BARBAROSSA' BEGINS

'Barbarossa' began on 22 June 1941. The Nazi offensive achieved a high degree of surprise, and Soviet frontier defences were smashed or bypassed within hours. Driving deep into the enemy's rear, Army Group Centre's 2nd and 3rd Panzergruppes met near Minsk within a week, creating a vast encirclement to the west. Behind them, attacks by the German 4th and 9th armies formed another pocket near Bialystok, leaving over 400,000 Soviet troops to be killed or captured in subsequent *Kesselschlachten*. 2nd and 3rd Panzergruppes then pressed on towards Smolensk, which they reached on 16 July. Meanwhile, Army Group North's 4th Panzergruppe crossed the River Dvina on 26 June, shattering the enemy's North-western Front (Army Group) and advancing towards Leningrad. Only in the south did the Germans encounter effective resistance. Here the Soviets were driven back, but their line only buckled. As early as 27 June Army Group South's orders were revised to envisage a less ambitious encirclement. Although the subsequent Uman *Kesselschlacht* tore a gaping hole in the South-western Front, by August the Germans had still not crossed the River Dnieper. Hitler's concerns about this situation would exercise a vital influence upon the campaign.

'The whole structure is rotten. One kick and we can bring the building down.'

Adolf Hitler, 1940

On 1 August Smolensk fell after heavy fighting. The Germans were only 250 miles from Moscow and 2 million soldiers had been removed from the enemy order of battle. Decisive Soviet defeat appeared to be only a matter of time. Yet even at this stage the Germans were encountering problems. For one thing, the enemy appeared to have much larger forces than had been anticipated. Despite being encircled, many Red Army units fought with great determination, if not skill. This made the *Kesselschlachten* time consuming and resource intensive. In turn, this placed heavy demands on German logistics, which rapidly became stretched. Extreme weather exacerbated supply problems. Heavy rains in July turned roads into quagmires, and intense heat thereafter caused dust clouds that led to numerous breakdowns. By late July almost 40 per cent of the Wehrmacht's lorries were unserviceable. panzer losses were even higher. Spare-part provision became a major issue, not least because the Germans were using many vehicles captured in 1940. Yet in an effort to motorise a larger proportion of the armed forces, spares production had been cut back in favour of vehicle manufacture months before 'Barbarossa' began. Neither was it easy to use the railways to push men and material forward. Track conversion was simple enough, but infrastructure repair and development was far more complicated. Although personnel were allocated to these tasks, they simply lacked the equipment and time to put more than a small proportion of the rail network into effective use. Within six weeks of the invasion the Germans were already encountering supply crises. The situation in subsequent months was to get much worse.

The summer of 1941 also saw significant disagreements within the German High Command about how to continue the campaign.

Contrary to popular perception, the Wehrmacht made massive use of horses throughout the Second World War (one author has commented that the German war effort 'ran on oats as much as gasoline'). Over 600,000 horses accompanied the Germans into the Soviet Union, where hundreds of thousands perished in the next four years. Even so, in February 1945 the Wehrmacht possessed almost 1.2 million horses, and German infantry divisions, with an authorised strength of 3,057 horses apiece, relied almost entirely on the animals for their transport needs. (Military Features & Photos)

Generaloberst Franz Halder (1884–1972), Chief of Staff of OKH, believed that after a three-week pause to regroup, the Germans should focus their efforts on Moscow. He believed that doing this would force the Soviets to defend their capital in a manner that would allow them to be encircled and destroyed. Hitler, however, remained obsessed with Leningrad and the supposed risk of a Soviet counterblow from the north. He was also worried about the presence of Red Army forces south of the Pripet Marshes. Contrary to Directive 21 these had not yet been destroyed. Indeed, they appeared to be in a position to attack the southern flank of any offensive mounted by Army Group Centre. As early as 19 July Hitler therefore issued another directive, diverting 2nd Panzergruppe south to break into the rear of Soviet forces around Kiev. Simultaneously, 3rd Panzergruppe was to move north to help capture Leningrad. In doing this, Hitler rejected Halder's plea to make a battle for Moscow the catalyst for a decisive *Vernichtungsschlacht* in August 1941.

'It is becoming more and more obvious that the Russian colossus has been under-estimated. We calculated around 200 enemy divisions at the beginning of the war. Now we know of at least 360 . . . And when we destroy a dozen of them, the Russians put another dozen in their place.'

Colonel-General Franz Halder, Chief of the German General Staff, diary entry for 11 August 1941

This decision caused a furious row at a time when the enemy was on his knees. Once again it illustrated the consequences of not having an operational campaign plan to achieve decisive victory. What the Germans needed to do was plan the timing and location of their cauldron battles in order to husband strength for the engagements that really mattered. However well they fought, they lacked the resources to conduct simultaneous *Kesselschlachten* across the entire front. Furthermore, by oscillating between the destruction of the Red Army or the capture of Leningrad and Ukraine as his number one priority, Hitler compounded the Wehrmacht's problems. On the one hand he was endorsing objectives (agricultural and industrial resources) to help Germany fight a long war, while on the other demanding victory in a single, lightning campaign. The two positions were irreconcilable.

Probably more than anything else, the argument between Hitler and his generals saved the Soviet Union from defeat. Had the Germans been able to launch a concentrated attack towards Moscow in late August they would almost certainly have seized the city. Whether they had the logistics capacity to carry out such an attack is open to intense debate. However, a successful offensive would not only have destroyed much of the Red Army before further reserves could be mobilised, but would also have paralysed the Soviet rail system. This would have left Soviet units to the north and south of Moscow unable to move, and these could then have been mopped up at the Germans' leisure. Despite its flaws, 'Barbarossa' would have succeeded in 1941.

However, after a month of inaction Hitler finally got his way, and 2nd Panzergruppe moved south on 21 August. The results were certainly impressive. Despite requests from his commanders to evacuate Kiev before the trap sprang shut, Stalin refused to allow any withdrawal. Consequently, when on 16 September 2nd Panzergruppe met Army Group South's spearheads at Lokhvytsya, 750,000 Soviet soldiers were encircled. This was the largest single *Kesselschlacht* created in 1941, and although over 100,000 troops eventually fought their way out, it left the Red Army in Ukraine temporarily shattered. It also allowed German attention to be refocused towards Moscow. Indeed, even before Soviet forces near Kiev had been destroyed, Hitler issued orders for Army Group Centre to be

Soviet casualties (prisoners), 22 June–13 August 1941

Baltic region	150,000
Bialystok–Minsk encirclements	324,000
L'vov area	150,000
Uman encirclement	103,000
Dnieper area	144,000
Smolensk encirclement	310,000
Roslavl area	38,000
West of Kiev	18,000
Total	1,237,000

reinforced for a renewed advance east. The offensive was code-named 'Typhoon'.

THE DRIVE ON MOSCOW

Soviet losses, Vyaz'ma–Bryansk area, 2–17 October 1941	
Captured	673,098
Tanks captured or destroyed	1,277
Artillery pieces captured or destroyed	4,378
Anti-aircraft and anti-tank guns captured or destroyed	1,009

Operation 'Typhoon' began on 30 September, nine weeks after Smolensk fell. In a classic envelopment the Soviet Western and Reserve Fronts were annihilated at Vyaz'ma within days. Meanwhile, 150 miles to the south 2nd Panzergruppe and other German units surrounded Bryansk Front and accelerated their advance to encircle Moscow from the rear. This was the supreme crisis for the Red Army. Its linear defences had again been fragmented and there was panic in Moscow. However, a week into October it started to rain. For German supply and combat units this caused major problems, and the speed of their pursuit immediately slackened in the autumn mud. In turn, this gave the Soviets precious time to organise the defence of their capital. Had the Germans not diverted their energies two months earlier, they would never have had the chance.

During 'Barbarossa' the Red Army had been unable to combine linear and deep defences. However, around Moscow Soviet commanders were helped by several factors. Significantly, the terrain here was broken up by forests, marshes and numerous rivers. These canalised German attacks along predictable axes, and together with the worsening weather this prevented the fluid manoeuvre operations which had characterised the earlier part of the campaign. The obvious nature of the objective also made surprise difficult to achieve and Intelligence easier to acquire. Consequently, the Soviets were able to concentrate their diminished resources in depth at the critical points – for example, 50th Army's positions around Tula and 16th Army's defences north of Moscow. These deployments forced the Germans into frontal assaults against strong opposition, enabling the Red Army to fight on something like equal terms for the first time in the war.

The Soviets were also assisted by a timely transfer of forces from other parts of the country. Although Soviet manpower reserves did much to ensure survival in 1941, the inefficiency with which they were used meant that by late autumn Red Army strength on the Eastern Front had fallen to 2.3 million. However, when Soviet spies indicated that Japan's eyes were on the Pacific and not the Soviet Union, Stalin ordered fifteen divisions to be sent to the capital from the interior. Moscow's pivotal position in the rail system was instrumental in this redeployment, and also provided a major advantage in terms of tactical mobility. Under the effective direction of General Georgi Zhukov, who had earlier organised the defence of Leningrad, by November Soviet strength in the decisive area had grown appreciably.

'We have severely underestimated the Russians, the extent of the country and the treachery of the climate. This is the revenge of reality.'

Heinz Guderian, Commander of 2nd Panzergruppe, 1941

By contrast, the Germans found themselves rapidly approaching the end of their tether. Although personnel numbers were still reasonably high, few motor vehicles remained serviceable, and the tank strength of the panzer divisions had shrunk by almost 90 per cent. In freezing weather German locomotive boilers began to burst with alarming frequency, cutting the flow of supplies to a trickle. Nevertheless, as the ground hardened they

decided to make a final attempt to seize the Soviet capital, and on 15 November this began. Aiming to break through north and south of Moscow while fixing Soviet troops to the west, the Germans ground their way forward in bitter attritional fighting – the very antithesis of 'Blitzkrieg'. However, they failed to capture Tula, and although a few weak units penetrated into the north-west suburbs of the capital, Soviet reserves soon stabilised the front. After a fortnight the attackers were exhausted, and on 4 December they came to a complete halt in temperatures of minus 35°C. As in 1914, the Germans had lost the critical battle of the campaign. Then, as they contemplated failure, the Soviets stunned them by launching a counter-offensive.

The Soviet T-34 came as a thoroughly nasty surprise to the Germans in 1941. However, 'penny-packeting' of this powerful asset (the Germans rarely encountered it in groups of more than half a dozen vehicles) meant that its full effect was not felt until later in the war, when hundreds of T-34s were concentrated in tank and mechanised corps and armies. This is a T-34/76D, an improved model that appeared in the spring of 1942. (Tank Museum)

The arrival of Soviet divisions from Siberia and elsewhere had not only prevented a German breakthrough, but also enabled an overnight transition from defence to attack. Nevertheless, it is important to remember that both sides were extremely tired, and the Red Army was still a long way from the efficient military machine that it would become by 1945. Its experience in offensive manoeuvre warfare was limited and mistakes in execution were frequent. Stalin also showed a pronounced tendency to emulate Hitler, demanding that his commanders carry out impossible tasks with inadequate resources. Consequently, although the Germans were pushed back over 100 miles on a wide front, Army Group

German casualties on the Eastern Front, 22 June–30 November 1941

743,112 men killed, wounded or missing (not including sick)

'BARBAROSSA'/'TYPHOON', JUNE–DECEMBER 1941

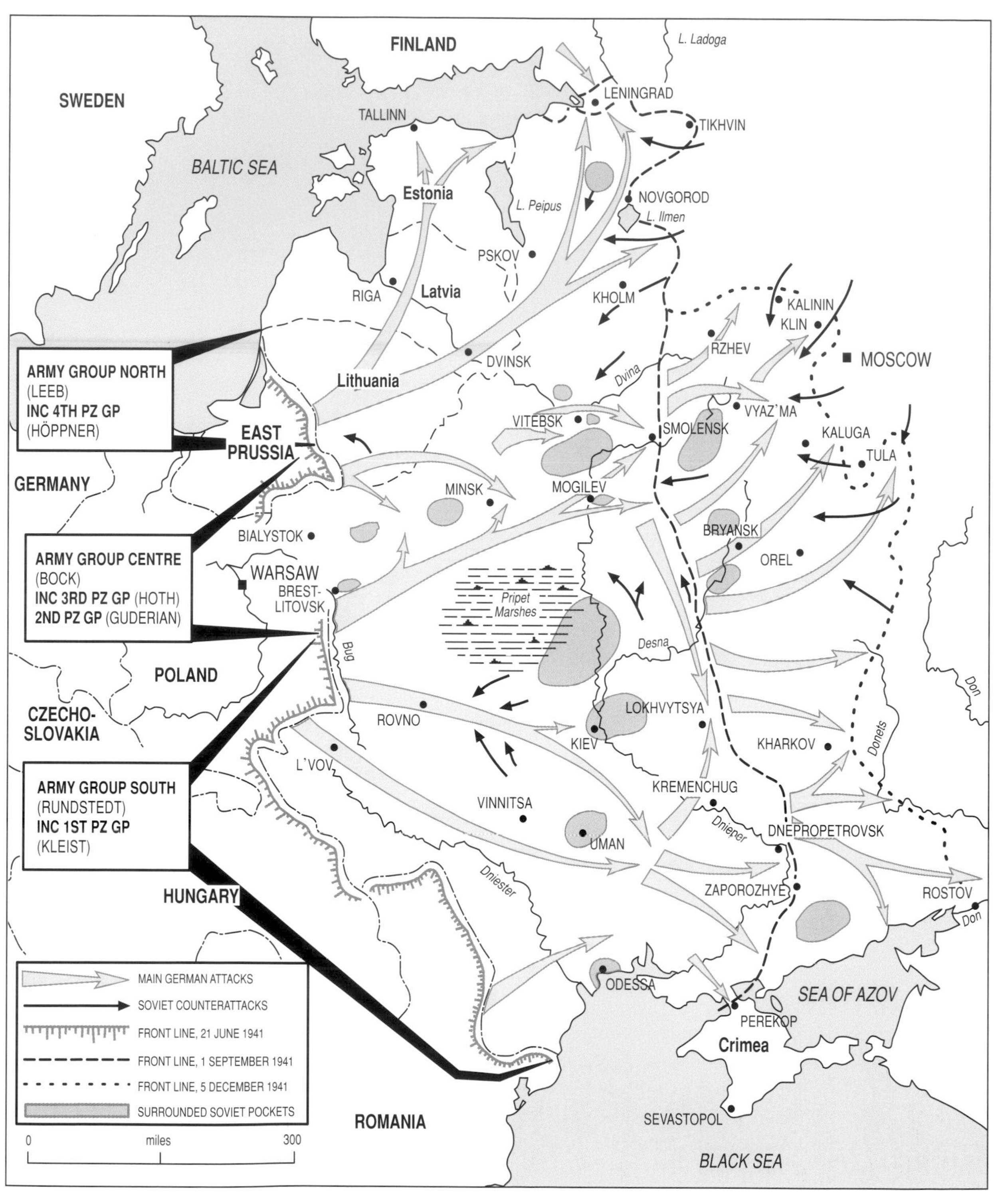

Centre was not encircled and German forces did not disintegrate. Instead, they held their new positions and waited for the Soviet offensive to burn itself out, which it did in early 1942. By April of that year, as the spring thaw arrived, operations on the Eastern Front were brought to a temporary halt.

Between September 1939 and October 1941 the Germans waged war with a quality of execution that can only be admired. In two years they conquered much of Europe and came within an ace of defeating the Soviet Union. In the process they appeared to justify the continued relevance of the *Vernichtungsschlacht*, applying the traditional tactical concept of the cauldron battle with a speed and violence that their opponents could not match. It is easy to understand why they should have found this method so attractive. After all, if it worked, they could reasonably hope to revenge themselves for the humiliation of 1919 without contemplating a prolonged attritional war that they could not win. Nevertheless, while their tactical brilliance could take them part of the way down the route towards decisive success, it could not secure victory in 1941. The first two months of 'Barbarossa' could hardly have been more successful. Yet the subsequent disaster only underscores the failure to appreciate that unless it acted suicidally, a modern state like the Soviet Union could not be defeated in one campaign purely through accumulated tactical success. The Germans' traditional beliefs and the achievements of 1939 and 1940 had made it impossible for them fully to comprehend the importance of the operational level of war. The *Vernichtungsschlacht* might have been relevant to the Soviet Union, but this was a different campaign, requiring an operational rather than a tactical approach. In this sense, the German Army's conduct of land warfare in the period September 1939 to March 1942 represents a landmark in more than one way, defining as it did the limits of tactical excellence and the emergence of the operational level of war.

'The German Army in fighting Russia is like an elephant attacking a host of ants. The elephant will kill thousands, perhaps even millions, of ants, but in the end their numbers will overcome him, and he will be eaten to the bone.'

Colonel Bernd von Kleist, 1941

E I G H T

LAND WARFARE IN EUROPE, 1942–5

STEPHEN HART

Following their failure to defeat the Soviet Union in 1941, and after America's entry into the war, the Germans found themselves on the strategic defensive. In 1942 they would once again seize the operational initiative, pushing back the Red Army and causing a degree of panic among its leaders. But within months the Wehrmacht suffered a disastrous defeat at Stalingrad, beginning a process that was to culminate in the collapse of the Nazi regime in May 1945. During this period the war on the ground raged across several fronts, from the deserts of North Africa to the mountains of Italy, and from the icy wastes of northern Norway to the sands of the French riviera. But actions on the Eastern Front and in north-west Europe shed the greatest light on the pursuit of decisive victory by the major belligerents. Consequently, it is upon these theatres that this chapter will focus.

FALL 'BLAU'

By March 1942 the German Army in the east (the Ostheer) was a shadow of its former self. Of the 3½ million men who had invaded Russia the previous June almost a third had become casualties. A total of only 140 operational tanks remained in the panzer divisions that had spearheaded 'Barbarossa', while one-sixth of the Army's truck fleet had also disappeared, with most of the rest unserviceable. Replacements were arriving, and the Red Army was itself in no condition to continue its attacks, but the prospects for a renewed German offensive designed to achieve decisive victory through a single, crushing blow were poor. Even Adolf Hitler, who had taken over as Commander-in-Chief of the Army in December 1941, appears implicitly to have recognised this.

This did not mean, however, that the Germans were willing to allow their opponents to dictate the future course of operations. Hoping to capitalise on the arrival of new equipment and personnel from the Reich, and on the increasing commitment of resources by Germany's allies to the war in the east, Hitler and his generals were determined at least to lay the foundations for a successful war of attrition. They therefore intended to

As with the great Steppes of the southern USSR, the open terrain of North Africa made it an ideal theatre for mobile operations. This was made clear first by the British, who in Operation 'Compass' (December 1940–February 1941) made a daring thrust to out-manoeuvre and destroy a large Italian army, and later by the ambitious, long-range mechanised offensives undertaken by Erwin Rommel's (1891–1944) Afrika Korps. However, neither the Germans nor their opponents succeeded in transforming any of their attacks into an immediately decisive victory, and in retrospect the see-saw advances of their respective offensives demonstrated the overwhelming influence that logistics exerted on sustained mobile operations. This was a lesson that the Allies proved quicker at assimilating than did the Wehrmacht.

The arrival of Erwin Rommel's forces in the Western Desert in early 1941 transformed the war in North Africa and led to a series of German-Italian victories. Here a British soldier, enjoying a rare moment of success, inspects a knocked out Afrika Korps Panzer IV. (Illustrated London News)

The most important battle of the North African campaign occurred near the small railway halt of El Alamein between 23 October and 4 November 1942. In this clash Lieutenant-General Bernard Law Montgomery's (1887–1976) 8th Army defeated Rommel's Panzerarmee Afrika at the gateway to the Nile Delta, thus stalling one of the pincers of Hitler's strategic design for autumn 1942. Equally important, the battle represented a turning point in the fortunes of the British Army during the 1939–45 war in Europe. Prior to El Alamein the British had mainly experienced defeats; after it there would be few serious setbacks.

'It was only in the desert that the principles of armoured warfare as they were taught in theory before the war could be fully applied and thoroughly developed. It was only in the desert that real tank battles were fought by large-scale formations.'

Erwin Rommel

In early August 1942 Montgomery had taken command of a dispirited army that had been pushed east almost as far as the Suez Canal. In the following two months he built up large force strengths and rekindled troop morale. However, only at the end of October, once his forces were fully prepared, did he launch his counter-offensive.

The Battle of El Alamein comprised three phases. In the first, two British corps broke into the Axis defences with help from concentrated artillery, but proved incapable of breaking through. This forced Montgomery to undertake a series of limited blows (the second phase) to crumble the German–Italian defences, and once this was accomplished he launched the third phase, a breakout attempt code-named 'Supercharge'. In this, after the New Zealand Division punched a hole through the northern German defences 8th Army's armour moved through, exploiting deep into the enemy rear and causing the collapse of his front. However, although Rommel had been decisively defeated, Montgomery pursued the retreating Axis forces so cautiously that he failed to destroy them. Not until May 1943, when Tunis fell, was the Axis presence in North Africa finally eradicated.

The success of El Alamein nevertheless imprinted itself on Montgomery's mind, and the techniques he used there became the basis of his operational methods. For the rest of the war the hallmarks of his generalship would be massive force strengths, concentrated artillery and tactical air power, the cautious and methodical conduct of a set-piece battle, and overly timid exploitation of any success achieved.

Stalingrad chronology, 1942	
28 June	4th Panzer Army launches attack towards Veronezh.
6 July	Stalin orders retreat towards Volga.
11 July	Hitler orders bulk of 11th Army to Leningrad.
12 July	Soviet Stalingrad Front formed.
13 July	Hitler diverts 4th Panzer Army away from advance towards Volga, south to secure Don crossings.
23 July	Hitler orders capture of Stalingrad and Baku.
29 July	Hitler orders 4th Panzer Army to resume advance towards Volga.
24 Aug	German units reach Volga north of Stalingrad.
2 Sept	Soviets abandon outer defence line around Stalingrad.
18 Nov	German 6th Army stops offensive in Stalingrad.
19 Nov	Soviet counteroffensive (Operation 'Uranus') begins.
21 Nov	Stalingrad encircled by Soviet forces.
12–24 Dec	Failed German attempt (Operation 'Wintergewitter') to relieve 6th Army.

carry out another major offensive as soon as the weather improved. This would aim not only to destroy Soviet troop formations, but also to wreck the USSR's long-term economic ability to continue the war. The Germans aimed first to cut off the principal routes from the Caucasus region, the source of 90 per cent of Soviet oil, to the enemy's industrial centres further north. Army Group South would then drive south-east through the Caucasus mountains, capture the oilfields and thus solve Germany's own dire fuel shortage. More ambitiously, Hitler hoped that his forces might press on to the Middle East to meet the north-easterly advance of Rommel's Afrika Korps from Egypt. The operation was code-named 'Fall Blau' ('Case Blue') and was confirmed on 5 April 1942 in Führer Directive 41.

'Fall Blau' was undeniably ambitious. By late June, when the offensive began, Army Group South could field just ten panzer divisions with 1,495 tanks. Not only was this less than half the number used in 'Barbarossa', but the concentration was obtained by denuding the rest of the Eastern Front, across which the Germans assumed a defensive posture. However, their opponents were also in a difficult position. Although in 1941 the Soviets had moved over 1,000 factories east, out of range of the Nazis, few of these were fully back in production. Furthermore, an ineptly conducted operation near Kharkov in May cost the Red Army many of its remaining tanks, as well as 277,000 men. With aid from the United States still to arrive in significant quantities, and a system of command and control that continued to stifle initiative, the Soviets could not confidently resist even a limited German offensive. 'Fall Blau' had a reasonable chance of success, so long as it was conducted skilfully. Even if it could not guarantee the Nazis decisive victory, it could none the less significantly improve their strategic position.

On 28 June 4th Panzer Army advanced towards Voronezh, a Soviet-held city on the left wing of the front held by Army Group South. This attack was important, for Stalin was convinced that by capturing Moscow the enemy could still win the war, and to him the German assault looked (as it was intended to) like an attempt to outflank and seize the Soviet capital from the south. Substantial Red Army reserves were immediately committed around Voronezh, leaving Soviet forces further south weak and overstretched. This meant that when 'Fall Blau's' main effort shifted to this area in early July the Red Army could do little to stop the German advance.

Although Army Group South's offensive made good progress between the Don and Donets rivers in July, it is clear that many of the problems encountered by the Germans in 1941 were reasserting themselves. In particular, Hitler's interference in operational matters served increasingly to dissipate his forces' efforts. Barely had 'Blau' begun before mobile formations vital to maintaining momentum were detached and sent elsewhere. Similarly, having cleared the Crimea, rather than being directed into the Caucasus the bulk of the German 11th Army was despatched to Leningrad, over 1,000 miles away. Even more important, Hitler allowed his opponents time to construct a defensive screen in front of the city of Stalingrad by deciding in mid-July to divert 4th Panzer Army away from its advance towards the River Volga. As events would prove, these were developments of vital significance.

In May 1942 the Red Army launched an offensive to recapture Kharkov, a significant communications centre and the fifth largest city in the USSR. However, the operation met with disaster, and the attackers lost around a thousand tanks, 5,000 guns and mortars and over a quarter of a million men. Here Soviet prisoners wait to begin the long march west. (David King Collection)

The main reason for the Germans' inability to select and maintain an aim during summer 1942 was that unlike a year earlier, Stalin did not insist on a strategy of forward defence. On 6 July, after taking advice from his senior commanders, he ordered Soviet units facing Army Group South to retreat towards the Volga. By the time that German troops arrived at their tactical objectives their opponents had therefore usually escaped, and frequent changes of plan resulted. After several weeks of chasing phantom formations across the Steppes, Hitler and his commanders began to believe that their enemy might indeed have collapsed. The result was increased confidence and a substantial expansion of 'Blau's' initial aims. Having split Army Group South into two, on 23 July Hitler ordered the new Army Group A (1st Panzer, 17th, 3rd Romanian and 8th Italian armies) to advance through the Caucasus mountains to the oilfields at Baku. Meanwhile, Army Group B (4th Panzer, 2nd, 6th, and 2nd Hungarian armies) was instructed not only to interdict the River Volga near Stalingrad – as originally intended – but also to capture the city itself.

In early August elements of 1st Panzer Army reached Maikop, an important oil centre in the Caucasus foothills, but were disappointed to find its facilities destroyed by the enemy. Further north, on 23 August General der Panzertruppen Friedrich Paulus's (1890–1957) German 6th Army broke through Soviet defences on the east bank of the River Don and headed towards the Volga north of Stalingrad. Despite bitter resistance, in the following fortnight they pushed forward on a wide front, reached the river and linked up with troops from 4th Panzer Army –

THE GERMAN OFFENSIVE, SUMMER 1942

which had reversed its detour towards the Caucasus – on the southern outskirts of Stalingrad. By mid-September, in a city that had already been reduced to rubble by the Luftwaffe, intense fighting began against the Soviet 62nd Army.

Although the Germans had advanced over 600 miles by autumn 1942, 'Fall Blau' actually eroded their strategic position in the east by massively extending their front. The supply lines of Army Groups A and B were overstretched, and the Germans increasingly relied on poor-quality satellite troops (Romanians, Hungarians and Italians) to hold large sectors of the

line. German units in the Caucasus found themselves ill-equipped for clearing mountainous terrain, and proved incapable of opening the routes to Baku. Similarly, in Stalingrad close-quarter urban combat negated the Wehrmacht's advantages in tactical mobility and air power, leaving the Germans unable to clear pockets of stubborn resistance. Although reinforcements were poured into Stalingrad, a month after the Germans arrived there Hitler's orders to capture the city had still not been fulfilled.

By contrast, the Red Army's position as winter approached had improved considerably. By conducting a delaying withdrawal during the summer and fighting only on ground of their own choosing, Soviet forces had preserved their strength. Although much territory had been lost and there were moments when retreat threatened to turn into rout, through a combination of strict discipline and patriotic appeals to defend 'Mother Russia' the cohesion of the Red Army had been preserved. Stopping the German advance in the Caucasus had secured the major oilfields and high rates of attrition were being imposed on the enemy in Stalingrad. When Stalin finally acknowledged that the main enemy effort was not in fact against Moscow, but towards the south-east, substantial Red Army forces were redirected to the Stalingrad area. Here, as 6th Army was fought to an exhausted standstill, the Soviets concentrated for a counter-blow.

The Battle of Stalingrad is seen by some historians as the turning point of the Second World War, although others believe the German failure to capture Moscow in 1941 was even more important. Whatever the case, the annihilation of 6th Army was a catastrophe for the Wehrmacht. Here nervous German infantry, deprived of the Panzer and air support that had led them to earlier victories, engage the defenders of Stalingrad. (David King Collection)

Soviet soldiers, equipped with American M3L light tanks, machine guns and clothing, pose for the photographer. The contribution of US (and, to a lesser extent, British) aid to the Red Army's success has only recently become clear. In addition to supplying most of the Soviets' needs in motor transport, aviation fuel, locomotives and railway wagons, the Western Allies provided vast quantities of machine tools, raw materials and military equipment. Among the latter were 14,430 tanks, most of which were used in the infantry support or training roles. These M3s were less than popular with their crews because of their petrol engines, which tended to burn furiously if the tank was hit. (US National Archives)

THE SOVIET COUNTER-OFFENSIVE

On 19 November 1942 the Red Army launched Operation 'Uranus', a two-prong offensive north-west and south of Stalingrad that quickly overran weak Romanian opposition. However, although the attack was not unexpected, its violence and ambition came as a great surprise to the Germans. This was partly because the latter's attention was fixed far to the north, in the region west of Moscow. Here the Germans knew that their enemy was about to launch Operation 'Mars', a massive but (for the Soviets) disastrous attempt to destroy Army Group Centre. In the Stalingrad area effective Soviet *Maskirovka* (a term incorporating the use of camouflage, deception and disinformation to disguise the scale, timing and direction of an attack) also caused German Intelligence badly to underestimate the nature of the forthcoming blow, which was to be launched by over a million men, supported by 13,540 guns and 894 tanks. When the attack began Axis forces were ill prepared to meet it.

A Soviet commissar speaks to his soldiers. Before October 1942 such officers had considerable status in the Red Army, and – despite their lack of military knowledge – played an important role in tactical decision-making, often with disastrous consequences. From 1943, however, the number of commissars in the Red Army was slashed, and their role became focused on the political indoctrination of troops. They also fulfilled a disciplinary function and played a part in the treatment of psychological casualties. (RMAS Collection)

Using a concentrated mixture of infantry, artillery and armour to smash the Romanian lines, and highly mobile tank, mechanised and cavalry corps to exploit in depth, within four days the Soviet pincers met at Kalach on the River Don. In the process the Red Army achieved what no one else had in the war to date – the encirclement of a German field army. 'Uranus' constituted a classic double envelopment in pursuit of limited (80-mile) objectives. More importantly, it demonstrated that the Soviets were learning from their previous failures, and that despite the purges the sophisticated doctrine of the inter-war years could be regenerated. Indeed, on 9 October Stalin agreed that in the future military decisions should be made solely by field commanders, not in conjunction with their political commissars. Although he would continue to meddle in operational affairs, at a time when Hitler was involving himself more and more in the details of operations, Stalin was showing signs of leaving such things to the experts. The positive effects for his armed forces were significant.

The only hope for the encircled 6th Army at Stalingrad was to break out immediately, before the Soviets consolidated their encirclement. But Hitler forbade the abandonment of the city, which because of its name ('Stalin's City') had taken on enormous symbolic significance, and ordered an offensive to relieve the trapped Axis forces. However, Operation 'Wintergewitter', launched in mid-December, failed to cut its way through to Stalingrad, and Luftwaffe attempts to supply 6th Army by air met with failure. Meanwhile, from 16 December the Soviets advanced quickly towards Rostov in Operation 'Saturn', threatening Army Group A's escape route from the Caucasus. Forced to focus on preventing a new disaster on an even greater scale, the Germans abandoned 6th Army to its fate. The Soviets began the annihilation of the pocket on 10 January 1943, and amid desperate scenes on 31 January Paulus (whom Hitler had made a Generalfeldmarschall two days earlier) surrendered to a Russian lieutenant. On 2 February all German resistance ceased: 91,000 men, the starving survivors of an army a third of a million strong, stumbled into captivity.

The Stalingrad defeat was a catastrophe for Germany. The aura of invincibility that had surrounded the Wehrmacht was shattered. In Germany three days of national mourning were declared and a deep (though rarely acknowledged) foreboding of defeat permeated both armed forces and people. For the Soviets, Stalingrad represented the moment that they stopped losing. Soviet will and operational planning had proven superior to that of the Ostheer. The fear of defeat was banished and replaced by a calm surety that victory, although it would not be easy, would come. The fact that it would not come easily was demonstrated in the offensives launched by the Red Army to capitalise upon the victory at Stalingrad.

Following the defeat of 6th Army the Soviets' intention was to transform operational success into strategic victory by trapping Army Group A in the

'We have borrowed from the Russians their earlier system of rigidly laying down the law on virtually everything and going into the tiniest details, and therein lies the blame for our defeats. . . . Thus, we have forfeited one of the fundamental requirements of a successful and versatile military command. We have become benumbed and are incapable of strategic action.'

General Reinhard Gehlen, 1942 (Head of Foreign Armies East, the German Intelligence organisation dealing with the Eastern Front)

THE SIEGE OF LENINGRAD, 1941–4

One important reason for the Germans' inability to achieve decisive success on the Eastern Front after 1941 was their distorted interpretation of the notion (in itself, fundamentally correct) that war constituted a clash of moral forces. This distortion arose from their misplaced confidence in the superior racial will of the 'Aryan' Germans – a view that the 900-day siege of Leningrad proved to be false.

The siege began on 8 September 1941, when German forces cut the last land route from Leningrad to the rest of the USSR, trapping 2.4 million Soviet citizens, most of whom were subsequently mobilised for the city's war effort. German strategy sought to besiege the city into surrender through starvation, and initially it looked as though this approach would succeed. Daily food rations for non-workers were cut to just two slices of 'bread' (containing supposedly edible cellulose extracted from sawdust), and although ice roads carved across the frozen Lake Ladoga for delivering supplies saved thousands of lives, 178,000 Leningraders died of starvation in December 1941 and January 1942. Emaciated and hunger-wracked, civilians ate their pets, consumed wallpaper (for the flour in the paste) and even resorted to cannibalism. Yet the will to resist survived and the city held out. Although in mid-1943 the Soviets re-established a tenuous land-link with Leningrad, not until January 1944 was the city freed from its virtual encirclement. During this time 1.2 million Soviet civilians and 300,000 Red Army troops died in the Leningrad area.

The Nazis had expected their invasion of the Soviet Union to deliver a swift victory on the grounds that the allegedly backward, semi-literate, Asiatic Soviet people could not resist the onslaught of the technologically advanced, racially superior Germans. In this ruthless ideological clash of wills the Nazis believed that Soviet determination to survive could not match the German will to conquer. The siege demonstrated how wrong the Nazis were in their estimation of this balance of wills. In microcosm it represented the determination of the Soviets to repel – and thus survive – the brutal war of racial annihilation unleashed upon them by Nazi Germany. Notwithstanding the Wehrmacht's undoubted tactical skills, when gross misappreciation of this balance of wills was combined with faulty strategic and operational conduct of the campaign, with an inability to learn the right lessons, and with Hitler's interference, it is easier to understand how the war in the east ultimately destroyed Nazi Germany.

OPERATIONS IN THE SOUTHERN SOVIET UNION, NOVEMBER 1942–MARCH 1943

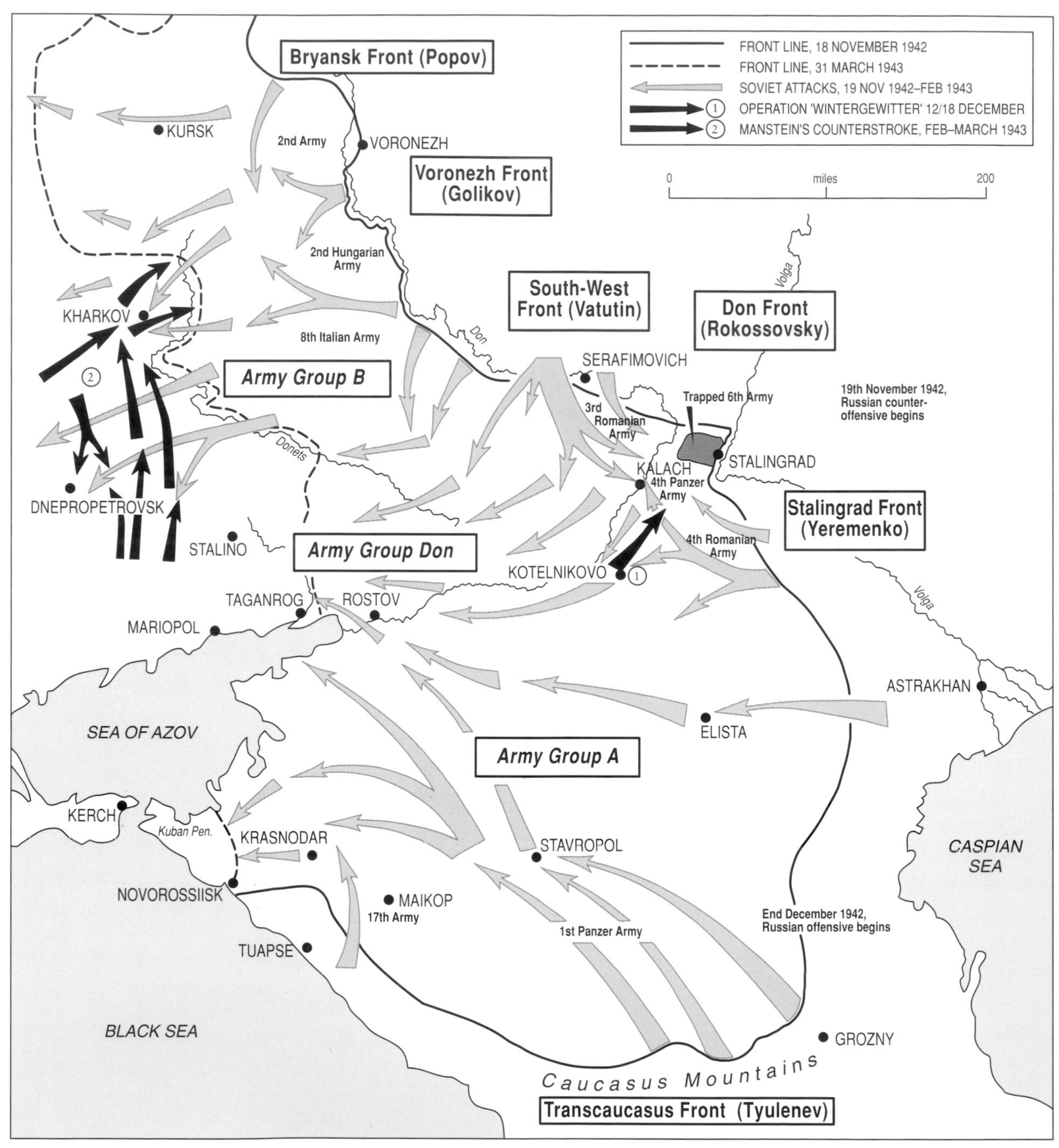

Caucasus, thus completing the destruction of what had been Army Group South in its entirety prior to July 1942. This would involve a general offensive to conquer eastern Ukraine around Kharkov and above all to recapture Rostov, the gateway to (and exit from) the Caucasus.

These plans were risky, in that there was little time for preparation. Nevertheless the gamble was considered worthwhile, and in the early stages of the offensive it seemed that the Soviets' plans would succeed beyond their own hopes. Having destroyed the 2nd Hungarian and 8th Italian armies, on 29 January 1943 the Soviets launched Operation 'Gallop', with the aim of clearing the Donbas region and driving the Germans back across the River Dnieper. On 2 February (the day that the remnants of 6th Army surrendered) they followed it with Operation 'Star', which was intended to seize Kharkov. Both operations enjoyed immediate success, with Kursk being taken on 8 February as part of the more northerly 'Star' offensive. Kharkov was liberated eight days later.

The Germans fought with a tenacity born of desperation, and in a series of skilful defensive encounters kept open a corridor from the Caucasus through which the majority of Army Group A escaped. On 13 February Army Groups A and B were dissolved and reconstituted as Army Group South under Generalfeldmarschall Erich von Manstein. Instead of holding Kharkov Manstein deliberately conceded it to the Soviets (despite specific orders to the contrary). This decision was based upon the belief that having come so far so quickly, the Soviets were stretching their supply lines to the limit, and that by allowing them this apparently easy prize they would be encouraged to push their advance further than was sustainable. Once they had done so Manstein planned to counter using reserves such as the SS Panzer Corps.

On 19 February 1943 Manstein launched his counter-stroke. Stalled at the end of their logistics chain, and exhausted by having launched a blow into thin air, the Soviet armoured spearheads were attacked on their northern flank by the SS Panzer Corps, and on their southern flank by 1st Panzer and 4th Panzer armies. The operation was remarkably successful; within days the two wings of the German attack met up, mauling three Soviet armies in the process. The city of Kharkov was retaken on 15 March, and only the spring thaw and Army Group Centre's unwillingness to send forces south prevented the Soviets from suffering further defeats. The Eastern Front temporarily ceased to be mobile, and stabilised along a line similar to that of June 1942. However, unlike in the previous summer, in March 1943 a large salient jutted into the German lines, centred on the city of Kursk.

Although the battles in February and March offered the Germans a revenge of sorts, their operational success could not compensate for the crushing strategic defeat suffered at the hands of the Red Army since November 1942. In five months the situation on the Eastern Front had been transformed from a position where the Germans looked forward to victory over the Soviet Union to one where they had only narrowly averted the complete destruction of their forces in the south. Well over a million Axis personnel had been killed, wounded or captured since 'Blau' began, and the territory that they failed to recover through Manstein's counter-stroke was lost permanently. It would soon become clear in the two-front war of attrition which followed that Germany's defeat was all but inevitable.

KURSK AND THE SOVIET ADVANCE WEST

In the aftermath of Paulus' surrender, and having stabilised the Eastern Front, the Germans strove to rebuild their shattered forces. Aided by improved industrial production, they even managed by June 1943 to

Soviet mobile formations, organisation 1942–4

A vital part of the Soviets' ability to carry out increasingly successful mobile offensives from 1942 onwards lay in the re-organisation of their mechanised and tank forces. In particular, the development of tank and mechanised corps provided the Red Army with a powerful exploitation aim. Typical compositions of such forces at different stages of the war were as follows:

Tank Corps	July 1942	July 1943	Dec 1944
Personnel	7,800	10,977	12,010
Tanks	168 (70 T-70 light tanks, 98 T-34 medium tanks)	209 (T-34 or T-34/85)	207 (T-34/85)
Self-propelled guns	–	21 Su-76	63 Su-76/122/152
Guns/mortars	98	160	182
Rocket launchers	8	8	8

Mechanised Corps	Sept 1942	Dec 1943	Dec 1944
Personnel	13,559	16,369	16,442
Tanks	175	197 (T-34 or T-34/85)	183 (T-34/85)
Self-propelled guns	–	49 Su-76/85	63 Su-76/85/152
Guns/mortars	90	252	234
Rocket launchers	8	8	8

create an impressive armoured reserve, including small numbers of the new Panther and Tiger tanks. The question, however, was how to employ these assets during the summer campaigning season – almost certainly the last opportunity for the Nazis to gain a favourable outcome (i.e. a stalemate) to the war in the east.

One option was to amass German armour in reserve, allow the Soviets to attack, wait for them to run out of steam and then commit the panzers to another counter-stroke. However, the Germans remained wedded to their fixation with offensive action and continued to view the achievement of *Kesselschlachten* as the best route to military success. Furthermore, Hitler was aware of the damage done to his allies' morale in early 1943, and was desperate to avoid any further retrograde steps that might result in them deserting him entirely. In April, therefore, he decided to commit his reserves to another offensive, code-named 'Citadel', that would seek to destroy Soviet forces in the Kursk salient through a double envelopment. Although the temptations of the *Vernichtungsschlacht* lingered, the Wehrmacht now at least recognised the spatial problems of such a strategy. Rather than attempting the complete destruction of the Red Army in a single campaign, the Germans focused on the relatively limited objective of annihilating a million Soviet troops in a geographical area just 130 by 90 miles.

'This offensive is of decisive significance. It must end in a quick and decisive success . . . The victory at Kursk must have the effect of a beacon seen around the world.'

Adolf Hitler

'Citadel', however, represented a further degradation of German offensive art. The attack started even later in the year than 'Blau', itself later than a delayed 'Barbarossa'. Hitler repeatedly postponed the offensive so that new 'wonder' weapons could be delivered. The German plan also represented a fundamental misuse of the regenerated panzer arm, since it engaged an enemy entrenched in a deep web of mutually supporting positions that together constituted the strongest defences yet constructed in the war. Even though the Germans assembled a formidable force with 2,387 tanks along the shoulders of the salient, the Soviets counter-concentrated even greater strength.

In retrospect, Hitler relied too heavily on the new Panther and Tiger tanks to generate success. His repeated postponement of the offensive to gain a few newly produced panzers, and successes achieved by the Soviet Intelligence services, cost the Wehrmacht the element of surprise and permitted the Red Army to strengthen its positions. Moreover, the Germans played down available information concerning the strength of enemy defences, preferring to believe that the more forces were deployed in the salient, the more would be destroyed. In this respect the ideologically driven Nazi underestimation of the Soviets, prevalent since before June 1941, persisted into 1943. This was despite recent evidence indicating that the Red Army was becoming superior to the Germans in the conduct of operations.

'Citadel' commenced on 5 July 1943 without the benefit of operational surprise. Soviet Intelligence had discerned the precise start time, and three hours before the attack began heavy artillery fire hit the German assembly areas. Quickly, 'Citadel' degenerated into a bitter attritional battle devoid of much manoeuvre. This was a struggle that the Germans could ill afford, and that commanders like Heinz Guderian (now Inspector General of Armoured Forces) had hoped to avoid. Although the Germans advanced slowly from the northern shoulder of the salient, after seven days they

The opposing forces, Operation 'Citadel', July 1943

German
9th Army, 4th Panzer Army and Army Detachment Kempf; total 2,700 tanks and assault guns, 4,895 pieces of artillery, over 500,000 men.

Soviet
Central Front, Voronezh Front and (in reserve) Steppe Front; total 4,000 tanks and assault guns, 20,000 pieces of artillery, over 1 million men.

General of the Army Konstantin Rokossovsky, commander of the Soviet Central Front (Army Group) at Kursk, inspects a knocked out Ferdinand assault gun in the aftermath of the battle. The Ferdinand was one of the 'wonder weapons' with which Hitler hoped to turn the tide on the Eastern Front. Massively armoured and mounting a powerful 88mm gun, ninety Ferdinands (the entire production run) were used on the northern shoulder of the Kursk salient, where this example was disabled. Rokossovsky is in the centre of the photograph, standing on the ground in front of the German vehicle. (David King Collection)

were still only a fifth of the way towards their objective. Indeed, in the face of heavy counter-attacks they were forced to go on to the defensive.

The southern German pincer initially achieved greater success and managed to penetrate several belts of Soviet defences. However, the pace of advance was sluggish, and by the time the panzers finally shook themselves free of the main defensive zone, the Red Army had had ample opportunity to deploy powerful reserves. On 12 July, near the village of Prokhorovka, the SS Panzer Corps was hit head on by 800 tanks from Lieutenant-General Pavel Rotmistrov's (1901–82) 5th Guards Tank Army. Tactically, the engagement proved inconclusive since both sides suffered heavy losses, but operationally it confirmed the Germans' failure and indicated that the initiative had shifted in favour of their opponents. From 18 July the southern German forces began fighting withdrawals in the face of Soviet counter-attacks.

Throughout the first week of 'Citadel', moreover, STAVKA (the Soviet high command) had husbanded considerable reserves behind the Kursk salient. After 12 July, having waited for the enemy to tire themselves, the Red Army launched a counter-offensive along the north-eastern edge of the northern shoulder. This hit the Germans – still fixed by the contact battle in the salient – in the flank and caught them off balance. Within three weeks the Soviets staved in the salient's northern shoulder. In the

ITALY 1943–5

Metaphor for the Italian campaign. A typical German demolition of a mountain road, November 1943. (RMAS Collection)

As 'Citadel' raged, and after a protracted battle that delivered local Allied air superiority, on 10 July 1943 Anglo-American forces initiated Operation 'Husky', an amphibious and airborne invasion of Sicily that began the Italian campaign. Given the low morale of the Italian defenders and the meagre German presence, the Allies expected a swift victory. But the methodical style with which Montgomery managed operations allowed the enemy to conduct a successful fighting withdrawal, and although more audacious attacks by US troops under General George Patton (1885–1945) led to the capture of Messina, the taking of the island did not demonstrate much skill on the part of the Allies. Worse, in the time that it took to capture Sicily the Germans were able substantially to reinforce their presence on the Italian peninsula.

With Sicily secured, the Allies invaded mainland Italy in September 1943. Although the Italians surrendered immediately, the Germans were able to create a front south of Rome, and from November the Allied advance slowed to a crawl. The campaign came to represent a strategic dead end, with the Allied objective henceforward being primarily to tie down enemy forces that might otherwise have been committed in the east or in France.

However, the Italian campaign did provide further opportunities for the Allies to refine the fighting methods developed in North Africa. They improved their artillery tactics, learned to secure air superiority before initiating the land battle, developed ground–air liaison, and began to emphasise infantry–tank cooperation in the face of a growing threat posed by German troops equipped with hollow-charge weapons (*Panzerfausts*). This gradual learning curve stood the Allies in good stead for their forthcoming invasion of north-west Europe. Yet despite these improvements, Allied progress in Italy until 1945 was characterised by slow advances through often poorly coordinated, firepower-laden, set-piece battles in the face of effective German defensive actions.

south, after a pause for reorganisation, the forces involved in stemming the original German onslaught also went on to the attack, erasing the German penetration and eventually recapturing Kharkov. On 13 July, with his offensive stalled and on learning that a second front in Europe had opened as a result of Anglo-American landings in Sicily, Hitler called off 'Citadel'. It had been an abject failure, resulting from the Germans' faulty operational art, their poor Intelligence, a lack of surprise, the disappointing performance of their new tanks, and unwarranted over-optimism, together with Soviet skill and numbers. In a battle of futile attrition for which Nazi Germany was ill-suited the Ostheer had squandered its last chance to alter the course of the war in the east.

After Kursk the strategic initiative in the east passed firmly to the Soviets. Now, as the Red Army advanced, the Ostheer proved incapable of undertaking the economical mobile defence that had worked so well at Kharkov. Alternating Soviet offensives on different sectors of the front forced the Germans to rush their overstretched panzer divisions from one crisis to another. Although they could still accomplish tactical successes, they could no longer achieve a decisive, operational-level blow to stem the Soviet onslaught.

Recognising its declining mobility and obeying Hitler's prohibition on tactical withdrawals, during the Soviet advance to the River Dnieper in autumn 1943 the Ostheer resorted to fortified positional defence. Nevertheless, during winter 1943–4 increasingly sophisticated and powerful Soviet attacks smashed the German line, drove deep into Ukraine and encircled enemy forces at Cherkassy. The Ostheer's favoured doctrinal response to such encirclements, as at Kamenets-Podolsk in March 1944, was to attempt a break-in from outside the pocket combined with a break-out from within. Yet notwithstanding minor German successes, by the time the Soviets temporarily halted in April 1944 they had penetrated to within sight of the Carpathian mountains.

The Soviet advance into Ukraine, however, merely represented one of ten staggered offensives coordinated in time and space undertaken by the Red Army in pursuit of its strategy of successive operations. The summer

By 1944 the Red Army's senior officer corps was more than a match for its opponents. Soviet operations were generally well planned and efficiently executed, rendering the Germans' tactical superiority increasingly irrelevant to the outcome of the war. Here Georgi Zhukov (seated left) and Konstantin Rokossovsky (front right) plan the demise of the German Army. The officer using the telephone is Colonel General Pavel Batov, one of Rokossovsky's army commanders. (David King Collection)

'We must not replace crushing strikes with pinpricks . . . It is necessary to prepare an operation which will be like an earthquake.'

Marshal Georgi K. Zhukov, 12 May 1944

1944 offensive in Belorussia (Operation 'Bagration') not only constituted the most successful of these operations, but also demonstrated that a large-scale attack could be sustained long and deep enough to produce a decisive, operational level victory against the Germans. Between 21 June and late August 1944 the four (later five) Soviet Fronts (army groups) involved in 'Bagration' and its associated operations destroyed the German Army Group Centre, and advanced almost 300 miles along a 300-mile front to the River Vistula in Poland. The effects on the German war effort were devastating.

During spring 1944 Stalin and his STAVKA contemplated where they should undertake their next strategic offensive. The obvious area to attack was in Ukraine, where the front already ran west into the Axis line, since a successful advance into the Balkans would force Germany's allies out of the war. But the Soviets rightly rejected this option as too obvious. Indeed, the Germans had anticipated such a move and, having learned from their mistakes at Kursk, concentrated their armour in the south for a counter-stroke. Instead, it was decided that the Red Army should attack in Belorussia, where a German salient jutted east into Soviet territory, along the most direct route to Berlin. However, as the Soviets recognised, the Reich capital itself remained several offensives away.

The Soviets had to plan 'Bagration' carefully because – contrary to popular perception – in 1944 they still lacked the resources to achieve overwhelming superiority across the entire front. On 21 June, when the offensive began, the Red Army possessed an overall manpower advantage

Jewish Partisans played an important part in guerrilla operations behind enemy lines in the USSR. Over a million Jews were murdered by the Nazis in the Soviet Union, but thousands took up arms in the struggle for survival. These are some of them. (David King Collection)

of just 1.5 to 1, although (partly thanks to American aid) equipment superiorities were greater. This inauspicious personnel ratio was partly offset because most German forces were concentrated in the front line, leaving few reserves. But to augment their chances of success, and to permit impressive concentration of force on the main offensive axes, the Soviets undertook sophisticated *Maskirovka*. They took measures to reinforce enemy preconceptions that any attack would come in Ukraine, concealed their assembly of troops in Belorussia, and constructed routes across swamps to attack the Germans from an unexpected direction. These moves ensured that the Soviets enjoyed local manpower superiorities of ten to one in the chosen assault sectors.

The STAVKA plan envisaged two shallow (40-mile) tactical encirclements at the northern (Vitebsk) and southern (Bobruisk) apexes of the salient to crumble its corners while simultaneous attacks isolated Orsha and Mogilev. Soviet understanding of German static defensive techniques led them to select these four communications centres as objectives. From recent experience, the Soviets anticipated that Hitler would declare these cities 'fortresses' and forbid their defenders from withdrawing. Therefore the Red Army could bypass and encircle these places, secure in the knowledge that their garrisons would be fixed by Hitler's order. While Soviet forces surrounded these towns, mechanised units would simultaneously strike deep into the German rear to create another pocket east of Minsk. At the same time the Red Army was to launch flank protection attacks north and south of the main blow. The latter (the L'vov–Sandomierz Operation) subsequently became a major expansion of 'Bagration'.

During the night of 19/20 June 1944 Soviet partisans operating behind enemy lines attacked 1,800 transportation targets to hinder German reactions, and the next day Soviet reconnaissance troops assaulted the opponent's front line to discover its weak spots. On 22 June the main attacks began, backed up by intensive tactical air support. Shattering the defenders' cohesion, just six days later the Red Army completed the encirclement of Bobruisk and Vitebsk, trapping some 120,000 Germans fixed by Hitler's prohibition on withdrawals. By 3 July the Soviet pincers closed west of Minsk, encircling large enemy forces to the east. During this first, stunningly successful fortnight of 'Bagration', the Soviets destroyed 25 German divisions and inflicted 300,000 casualties. Without pausing to regroup the Red Army ruthlessly exploited its victory through several follow-up operations that took its forces 200 miles deeper into the enemy rear.

In mid-July, as the thrust against Army Group Centre began to tire, the Soviets commenced their subsidiary L'vov–Sandomierz Operation. This attack, spearheaded by several elite tank armies (each with hundreds of tanks and tens of thousands of men), sucked the Germans' meagre reserves away from the area of 'Bagration'. By late August, when these offensives finally stalled, the Red Army had established three key bridgeheads over the River Vistula in Poland, and had reached the Baltic coast to cut off the German Army Group North. Overall, in sixty-five days the Soviets inflicted 900,000 casualties on the Germans, although in the process they suffered 771,000 killed, wounded and missing (31 per cent of the forces

Organisation of a typical Soviet tank army, 1943–4

- Two tank corps
- One mechanised corps
- One anti-aircraft division
- Two heavy mortar regiments
- Two self-propelled artillery regiments
- Two anti tank regiments
- Two assault-gun brigades
- One towed artillery regiment
- One motorcycle regiment
- Engineer, chemical, aviation, signals, transport and repair services

OPERATION 'BAGRATION' AND L'VOV–SANDOMIERZ OPERATION

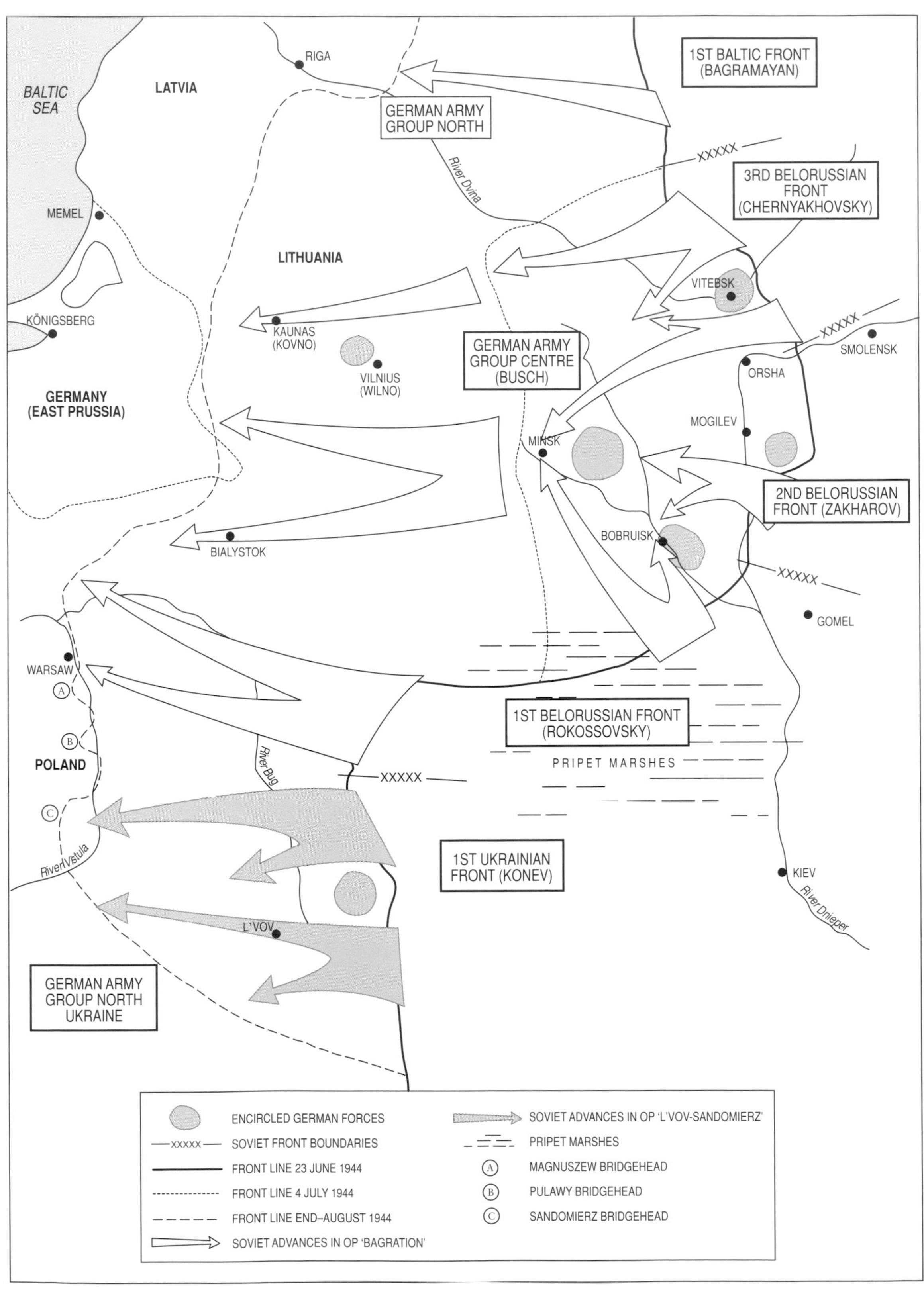

committed). From late August a new Soviet offensive in Ukraine advanced rapidly into the Balkans, caused Romania's and Bulgaria's defection from the Axis alliance, and forced the Germans to abandon Greece, Albania and much of Yugoslavia. From October the Soviets drove forward into central Hungary, but their thoughts had already turned to plans for a major offensive from the Vistula early in 1945.

NORTH-WEST EUROPE, 1944–5

If the Eastern Front constituted the centre of gravity of the Second World War in Europe, then north-west Europe represented the critical theatre for the Western Allies. Yet in this campaign the latter pursued an approach to land warfare that rejected both the German strategy of the *Vernichtungsschlacht* and the Soviet strategy of successive operations. Instead, the Western Allies developed warfighting methods based on a cautious, attritional, firepower-reliant operational technique. This approach was epitomised by the operations carried out by Field Marshal Montgomery's 21st Army Group and was termed 'Colossal Cracks' by its commander. Tracing its immediate origins back to the October 1942 clash at El Alamein, it involved meticulously planned set-piece battles employing a heavy concentration of force, massive artillery and strategic aerial firepower, and the integrated use of tactical air support. Montgomery conducted these battles carefully and methodically, with close regard to the logistical situation, and with a firm grip maintained according to a previously prepared 'master plan'.

'The commander must decide how he will fight the battle before it begins. He must then decide how he will use the military effort at his disposal to force the battle to swing the way he wishes it to go; he must make the enemy dance to his tune from the beginning and never vice versa.'

Field Marshal Bernard Montgomery, Memoirs *(1958)*

This is not to say that the Western Allies ignored the role of mobile operations as the chief instrument of decisive military victory. Despite the problems of tactical movement caused by the effects of massed firepower on the battlefield, the Allies – particularly the Americans – still believed that it was through mobile operations that they would complete the defeat of the German Army in the west (the Westheer). But given their opponent's tactical prowess and Allied concerns over both their own forces' morale and the level of casualties, a more attritional approach was necessary first to grind down German combat power. Once this had been achieved, sustained mobile offensives could be undertaken without grave risk of enemy counter-strokes. It was through such eventual mobile operations that the Allies planned to exploit battlefield advantage and achieve decisive success. Hence, the German, Soviet and Western Allied approaches to war were united by the belief that ultimately it was mobile operations that would translate any operational-level potential into the reality of decisive victory.

The adoption of a firepower-laden approach owed much to British concerns regarding casualty levels and troop morale. By summer 1944 Britain had a chronic shortage of trained military manpower, and it was clear that the Anglo-Canadian 21st Army Group would be unable to replace all the casualties it would suffer in helping to liberate Europe. This formation represented Britain's most important field army, and if it was lost the British contribution to any eventual Allied success would be seriously diminished. From D-Day onwards, therefore, Montgomery had to avoid sustaining heavy casualties. Furthermore, the manpower shortage placed a premium on boosting troop morale to get the best out of the

British artillery was among the best in the world by 1944, and Montgomery used it on a large scale in most of his battles. Here a 5.5-inch medium gun, surrounded by ammunition, supports the attack on the Odon Valley, 16 July 1944. (RMAS Collection)

relatively meagre personnel resources available. Although the morale of many of Britain's conscript soldiers remained more fragile than that of the resilient Westheer, Montgomery believed that if his soldiers had the support of copious materiel, and were not subjected to massive losses, their fighting spirit could be preserved. If 21st Army Group combined high morale with sheer weight of materiel, Montgomery asserted, it could defeat even the cream of the enemy's forces.

Anglo-Canadian operational methods in the west also represented an appropriate way of achieving British war aims given the capabilities of their troops compared with those of the Wehrmacht. These objectives did not seek simply to extinguish the Nazi canker, but rather to defeat the enemy with tolerable casualties, although with a high military profile within a larger Allied effort. This in turn would ensure Britain considerable political influence in post-war Europe. To accomplish such aims, Montgomery sought to husband his resources through a sustained display of adequate combat performance that would help to crush the enemy through an attritional war of materiel until mobile operations could secure decisive victory. Any attempt tactically to out-perform the Westheer was unnecessary. Instead, it was essential to do what in 1944 the British Army did best: rely on materiel, sustain morale by evading defeats, avoid excessive casualties, and grind down the enemy by attrition based on massive firepower.

THE BATTLE OF NORMANDY

The Allied D-Day invasion on 6 June 1944 caught the enemy by surprise, and the latter's lethargy – exacerbated by a confused and contradictory

Part of the Allied D-Day invasion armada heads for Normandy. The tank is a Sherman of 13th/18th Royal Hussars, who landed on Sword Beach on the morning of 6 June. (RMAS Collection)

command structure – let slip their best opportunity to fulfil Rommel's intent of swiftly driving the attackers back into the sea. While the Allies strove to extend their lodgement, German strategy sought to fix the invaders in a narrow beachhead until reinforcements could be rushed to the area. In late June the Germans deployed the II SS Panzer Corps to Normandy with the aim of carrying out a counter-attack to throw the Allies into the Channel. Forewarned by 'Ultra' Intelligence, Montgomery resumed his offensive to suck the SS armour into the line and thus prevent it concentrating for an attack. On 25 June he launched Operation 'Epsom', an offensive by British VIII Corps that failed to outflank the city of Caen from the west but none the less pinned down the newly arrived German forces.

After the demise of the Westheer's counter-attack, German strategy aimed to contain the Allies in a small area, denying them the space and terrain required for mobile operations. In July the Germans strengthened their defences south-east of Caen along the vital Bourguébus ridge, against which Montgomery launched his 'Goodwood' offensive on 18 July. The operation involved an attack spearheaded by three British armoured

The sinews of war. Despite the widespread provision of wireless sets, all armies continued to rely extensively on field telephones for communications during the Second World War. Here a Royal Signals linesman lays cable as infantry from 7 Armoured Division move up to the front in Normandy, 11 June 1944. (RMAS Collection)

divisions from the restricted bridgehead east of the River Orne, and sought to break through enemy positions south of Caen. To what extent Allied commanders hoped that 'Goodwood' would achieve decisive success remains controversial. Certainly, Montgomery exaggerated his aims to win strategic bomber support for the offensive, and together with a heavy artillery bombardment the effects of Anglo-American air attacks upon the forward enemy defences were indeed shattering. However, although British armour initially advanced rapidly, the deeper German positions remained largely intact. By nightfall, in the face of enemy counter-attacks British momentum had been halted. Amid bitter recriminations, the offensive was called off forty-eight hours later.

Nevertheless, 'Goodwood' served another purpose within Montgomery's theatre strategy – to draw German forces away from western Normandy to facilitate Operation 'Cobra', the break-out offensive by General Omar Bradley's (1893–1981) 1st US Army, which up to then had been grinding its way slowly southwards. On 25 July 'Cobra' began with

THE FAILURE OF GERMAN LOGISTICS IN NORMANDY

Although historians have long recognised that supply problems contributed to the Nazis' defeat in Normandy, it is only recently that they have demonstrated precisely how German logistic deficiencies facilitated the Allied breakout. Given earlier British and American setbacks in the face of effective German resistance, the sudden success of 'Cobra' appears surprising. Yet this can now be explained by the collapse of German logistics.

Contrary to popular perception, the German Army of 1939–45 remained predominantly horse-drawn outside its elite Panzer divisions. Indeed, by 1944 massive motor vehicle losses had significantly reduced its motorised capabilities. Hence, when the Germans expanded the previously neglected Westheer during 1943 they were unable to increase its logistics capacity proportionately. Given its inadequate truck fleet, the Westheer had to rely on French railways when the Allies invaded to move reinforcements to the front and to supply those forces already there.

During spring 1944 Allied air power smashed the French rail network so comprehensively that on 5 June 1,700 military trains were delayed *en route*. This caused the Germans significant problems: although their 7th Army in Normandy had stockpiled munitions and fuel reserves sufficient for three weeks' combat, its trucking capacity could not meet even half its minimum daily combat resupply requirements, and it relied on rail deliveries to make up the shortfall. Thus, after D-Day 7th Army had to choose between moving reinforcements to the front or attempting to resupply those already there, since it could not accomplish both. In a decision typical of the extemporised German approach to war, which seldom accorded sufficient consideration to logistics, the Westheer chose to get troops to the front and then worry about resupplying them.

Allied air power played a decisive role in the Battle of Normandy. Benefiting from complete air supremacy, and in many cases operating from forward airfields in the beachhead, British and American aircraft ranged at will over the battle area, spotting for artillery, attacking ground targets and interdicting German movement. Strategic and medium bombers also did much to assist the Allied ground forces by isolating Normandy from rapid reinforcement and resupply. As shown here, the effects on the French railway network were especially destructive. (RMAS Collection)

Up to mid-June 7th Army's use of its available trucks to move troops to the front prevented it from replenishing more than 15 per cent of its daily munitions expenditure. This forced it to devour forward reserve stocks, which fell so low that continuation of a viable defence in July seemed unlikely. The Westheer's continued effective resistance owed much to its concentration of all engineering efforts on reopening (and then keeping open) just two rail routes into Normandy. Between 19 and 23 June the Germans reopened the routes west from Paris to Serdon and north from Tours to Alençon. Consequently, despite Allied air attacks, the Germans were able marginally to improve their supply situation by the start of July, at least in their eastern sector.

By now the Germans had split their forces – 7th Army in the west facing the Americans, while Panzer Group West opposed the Anglo-Canadians in the east. During July 7th Army's poor logistical situation declined further because the Tours–Alençon railway remained constrained by the limited capacity of the damaged Loire River bridge at Tours. Although this line was able to bring in one-third of the total supplies that reached 7th Army, on 15 July Allied air attacks again closed the Loire crossing. Thereafter, with its only rail resupply route cut 7th Army grew increasingly short of supplies, a deficiency exacerbated by the British 'Goodwood' offensive on 18 July. This sucked Panzer Group West into a desperate defence that prevented its own truck columns from moving supplies – as planned – from the eastern rail link to 7th Army.

Although the Tours bridge was repaired on 23 July, this gave 7th Army insufficient time to remedy its supply shortages before 'Cobra' began. Consequently, by the evening of 26 July LXXXIV Corps had exhausted its stock of 88mm anti-tank rounds. Moreover, 2 SS Panzer Division was unable to stop the rapid American advance, despite then being rated the most effective German formation in Normandy. Logistics problems account for this failure, since on 27 July the division had to abandon two Panther tank companies because it had no fuel for them. Such shortages prevented the Germans from replicating the mobile counter-attack tactics that had halted 'Goodwood'. For the first time in Normandy the German resistance to an Allied offensive was ineffective; but this failure lay more in logistics deficiencies than in superior Allied strength or innovative American tactics.

This example clearly illustrates an essential lesson that emerged from land warfare in Europe between 1939 and 1945: however impressive an army's tactical abilities, effective combat performance required an adequate logistical base. It was the Allies, not the Germans, who recognised clearly the constraining impact that logistics increasingly exerted on land operations, as the failure of the German December 1944 Ardennes counter-offensive and the success of the Soviet January 1945 Vistula–Oder Operation both demonstrated.

massive strategic bomber strikes that smashed the German positions. During the next two days the Americans broke through these defences, despite reasonable enemy troop densities, and advanced south. This rapid American breakthrough owed less to effective US tactics or low German force levels, however, than to the collapsing German logistics system.

On 30 July the Americans captured Avranches, at the foot of the Cotentin peninsula, which enabled them to break out in all directions into the interior of France. The stunning success now achieved by US forces, which rapidly fanned out east towards Paris, south to the River Loire and west into Brittany, highlighted the main weakness in Montgomery's approach. For although 'Colossal Cracks' remained essential to open the way for subsequent mobile warfare, the cautious operational culture that this method encouraged made it difficult for most Anglo-Canadian commanders to adapt quickly to the speed of action required for successful mobile operations.

During early August, as American armour raced deep into the German rear, Hitler rejected the only sensible strategy in the circumstances – a

Operation 'Goodwood'. Tanks of 23rd Hussars – part of 11 Armoured Division – move past Ranville Church on the morning of 18 July. The regiment lost twenty-six of its fifty-nine Shermans on this day, providing further evidence of the inability of Allied armour to cope with German anti-tank defences. Nevertheless, 'Goodwood' convinced the German C-in-C West, Field Marshal Kluge, of the inevitability of the Westheer's defeat, a view that he relayed to Hitler on 21 July. Kluge committed suicide a month later. (IWM B7524)

general withdrawal to the River Seine. Instead, he ordered his forces to launch Operation 'Lüttich', an armoured thrust from Mortain towards Avranches which was intended to cut off the dozen US divisions that had broken out to the south. Somehow, the Germans scraped together a weak mechanised force and even managed to supply it with enough fuel for several days' sustained action, albeit only by denuding supplies to the rest of the front. Predictably, however, after some initial success 'Lüttich' stalled in the face of the arrival of American reserves.

This failure simply pushed German armour west, deeper into an Allied encirclement then forming between Mortain and Argentan. As US forces advanced east behind the German positions, they threatened to surround the remains of twenty-five enemy divisions around the town of Falaise. To complete the encirclement Anglo-Canadian troops drove south from Caen to meet the Americans. By 20 August the Allies had sealed the pocket, although 25,000 Germans subsequently fought their way out. But having lost its heavy weapons, all the shattered Westheer could do was retreat beyond the Seine in the face of an unstoppable Allied advance. Meanwhile, American forces that landed in southern France on 15 August raced north to meet the armies breaking out from Normandy. During early September the Allies advanced deep into France, linking up and pushing into Belgium and southern Holland. The Allies had not only decisively won the Battle of Normandy, but also the struggle for France.

'MARKET GARDEN' AND THE BATTLE OF THE BULGE

If logistics weakness had played a crucial role in the Westheer's downfall, autumn 1944 revealed that it could also hamper the development of Allied strategy. Because of German demolitions and mining, few of the ports captured by the Allies during their breakout could quickly be used for resupply purposes. Bypassed enemy garrisons also held on to several important coastal towns, denying the Allies access to their facilities, in some cases until the end of the war. With supply lines stretching all the

As the strained expressions on the faces of Lieutenant-General Omar Bradley (left), General Montgomery (centre) and Lieutenant-General Miles Dempsey (commander of British 2nd Army, right) indicate, relations between the Western Allies were often difficult. This had a significant impact on the campaign in North-west Europe, and – by implication – on the political map of post-war Europe. This photograph was taken in Normandy on 10 June 1944. (RMAS Collection)

way back to the Normandy beaches, by mid-September the Allied advance ground to a halt. Grateful for the opportunity to reorganise and reinforce their units, the Germans quickly created a new defensive line.

To regenerate momentum Montgomery decided to launch Operation 'Market Garden', an uncharacteristically bold scheme intended to 'bounce' the River Rhine before the Germans recovered their cohesion. The main motivation behind this strange operation, however, lay in inter-Allied frictions. September 1944 offered the British the chance of defeating the Westheer before American numerical might dominated the Western Alliance. By getting to the Rhine first Montgomery could win logistical priority from Dwight D. Eisenhower, the Supreme Allied Commander, at the expense of the two American army groups (Bradley's 12th and Devers' 6th), thus facilitating a triumphant British advance to Berlin. In 'Market Garden' Montgomery ordered General Brian Horrocks' XXX Corps to advance north through Holland to link up with Allied airborne forces dropped at key locations along the way, among them the British 1st Airborne Division at Arnhem. However, a desperate defence by improvised German forces slowed Horrocks' advance and eventually crushed British resistance at Arnhem bridge. With this success the Westheer managed to stall the momentum of the Allied offensive in the north. Montgomery's atypical display of audacity resulted in the nearest thing to a British defeat since before El Alamein.

Flushed with the victory at Arnhem and the repulse of an American attempt to penetrate German frontier defences east of Luxembourg, Hitler promptly stunned his senior generals by ordering them to plan a major counter-offensive. By striking through the Ardennes, crossing the River Meuse south of Liège and advancing to Antwerp, this blow would wrest back the initiative in the west. Ideally, Montgomery's 21st Army Group and large US forces would be encircled and destroyed, and the Western Allies might even be compelled to make a compromise peace. In turn, this would allow the Germans to move units east to stabilise the front against the Soviets.

Hitler wanted the offensive to secure a strategic victory, not just a tactical one, and insisted the attack advance 100 miles to seize the port of Antwerp and cut off Montgomery's divisions from the Americans to the south. However, although the panzers had penetrated the Ardennes with relative ease in 1940, the situation in 1944 was different. US troops in the area were thinly spread, but they were still considerably stronger than the Belgian and French screening forces that had defended the Ardennes four and half years earlier. Weather conditions were poor – although this at least temporarily negated the Allies' overwhelming strength in air power – and the road infrastructure remained underdeveloped. German units were of very mixed quality, with many of their personnel drawn from the Kriegsmarine or Luftwaffe, or from the youngest and eldest age groups. Worst of all, German logistics were hopelessly inadequate to the task. Deficient in ammunition, fuel, cross-country vehicles and heavy engineering equipment, the attackers were almost entirely reliant on the shock of their initial blow to carry them to Antwerp. As their field commanders fully realised, any loss of momentum in the early stages of the offensive would be disastrous.

On 16 December Army Group B's 6th Panzer, 5th Panzer and 7th armies thrust towards the River Meuse. However, although the Americans were surprised, and some German units succeeded in infiltrating their front, stubborn resistance soon revealed the fragility of Hitler's plan. With important roads blocked at St Vith and Bastogne, and near the Elsenborn Ridge in the north, the Germans were unable to gain room to manoeuvre in strength. Furthermore, the Allies' reaction was remarkably swift, and the arrival of powerful American reserves meant that any chances of achieving the decisive success that Hitler envisaged rapidly evaporated. Although weak German spearheads penetrated to within a few miles of the Meuse, a lack of petrol and the effects of Allied air attacks from clearing skies proved devastating. By Christmas Day the offensive had been halted, and in bitter fighting the Germans were then driven back to their start line. In retrospect, the Ardennes offensive proved to be a futile and ultimately disastrous gamble that threw away Germany's last, precious, armoured reserves. The road to the Rhine and to final Allied victory was now open.

'I had merely to cross a river, capture Brussels and then go on and take the port of Antwerp. And all this in the worst months of the year, December, January, February, through the countryside where snow was waist-deep and there wasn't enough room to deploy four tanks abreast, let alone six armoured divisions; when it didn't get light until eight in the morning and was dark again at four in the afternoon, with divisions that had just been reformed and contained chiefly raw, untried recruits, and at Christmas time.'

General Josef 'Sepp' Dietrich, commander of 6th Panzer Army, December 1944

THE END OF THE WAR IN EUROPE

The Vistula–Oder operation, 12 January–2 February 1945: the opposing forces

German
520,000 men
800 tanks
4,100 artillery pieces

Soviet
2.2 million men
6,464 tanks and self-propelled guns
33,500 artillery pieces

As the Western Allies advanced slowly into Germany, in early 1945 the Soviets released a devastating blow of their own. This offensive took its name from the rivers where it began and ended – the Vistula and the Oder respectively – and represented the culmination of the Red Army's long learning curve towards the effective implementation of Deep Operations within the strategy of successive operations. At its end the Soviets stood only 40 miles from Berlin.

In September 1944 the Red Army's exploitation of 'Bagration' established three bridgeheads over the River Vistula in Poland, from which they launched their new offensive on 12 January 1945. In the north Marshal Georgi Zhukov's First Belorussian Front (Army Group) attacked from Magnuszew and Pulawy towards Poznan and Berlin, while in the south Marshal Ivan Konev's (1897–1973) First Ukrainian Front advanced from Sandomierz towards Breslau. By the start of the offensive the Soviets had established a five to one numerical superiority both in personnel and equipment, but this was achieved by Soviet *Maskirovka* and German errors, rather than simply being the product of vast Soviet resources. In reality the Red Army was running short of manpower, and during the offensive this led it not just to seek decisive success, but to achieve success with tolerable casualties. The Wehrmacht remained maldeployed in the east because Hitler's insistence kept too many of his divisions in East Prussia and Hungary, where Soviet fixing attacks were under way. In addition, the Red Army implemented extreme economy of force by massively thinning its forces between the three bridgeheads to concentrate overwhelming strength in its assault sectors.

The Soviets' execution of the offensive involved sophisticated techniques made possible by overwhelming numerical advantages, and reflected the enormous intellectual energy that the Red Army had devoted to absorbing the lessons of war since 1941. Once the offensive commenced the Soviets wished to penetrate the German tactical defences rapidly, and then quickly to exploit deep into the German rear to 'bounce' a series of as yet unmanned defence lines. One way of maintaining their momentum after the initial breakthrough was to use three echelons of forces, operating to a depth of over 80 miles. The first echelon, which fielded forward detachments (all-arms mobile brigade groups with a powerful armoured core), was to fight a deep operational battle, racing ahead of the main Soviet forces to seize key locations. By taking these points the forward detachments would prevent the Germans from moving reinforcements or supplies to the front. Thus these units sought to paralyse the Germans' ability to react systemically to the unfolding offensive, in part by separating the contact battle from the depth battle. The Soviet second echelon, consisting of their spearhead tank armies, advanced behind the forward detachments, while behind the tank armies came the Soviet combined arms ('rifle') formations, mopping up and consolidating as they went.

Using these techniques the Soviets raced through Poland, entered eastern Germany and consolidated bridgeheads over the Oder in early February. In the process the German Army Group A was smashed. However, despite their success the Soviets decided not to risk their achievement with a last-

gasp thrust to Berlin, fearing that if they did so they might encounter German counter-strokes. Moreover, by this time Soviet forces were exhausted, and despite herculean efforts their supply lines had become over-extended. This problem reinforced the lesson that logistics constituted the principal constraint on the continuation of large mobile offensives. The decision not to risk a thrust to Berlin guaranteed the success already achieved, and was representative of the way that the Red Army conducted its offensives during the last twelve months of the war. The operation had carried 2.2 million Soviet troops 280 miles across a 300-mile front and had inflicted 320,000 casualties for the relatively modest cost of 195,000 men. This was an unprecedentedly favourable casualty exchange rate for an attack on this scale, and helps to identify the Vistula–Oder Operation as one of the most successful offensives of the 1939–45 war in Europe. Yet this operation constituted just one element in a coordinated series of Soviet offensives that drove the Germans back into the Reich during spring 1945. During late April these drives linked up with Western Allied forces that had crossed the Rhine in March, encircled and destroyed the German armies in the Ruhr and then advanced rapidly into the heart of the Reich. Finally, with Hitler dead and Berlin in Soviet hands, on 7 May 1945 Nazi Germany surrendered unconditionally to the Allies.

Soviet T-34s at the Brandenburg Gate, Berlin. The Berlin Operation, which began on 16 April 1945, involved over 2 million Soviet and 800,000 German soldiers. Despite desperate resistance, within three days of the start of the battle Soviet forces shattered the German defences on the rivers Oder and Neisse, and in late April penetrated into the heart of the Reich capital. Hitler committed suicide on 30 April, and fighting in the city came to an end on 3 May. (Central Armed Forces Museum)

The cost of the Second World War (all figures estimates)

	Mobilised (millions)	Military dead (millions)	Military wounded (millions)	Civilian dead (millions)	Economic and financial cost $ billion)
Principal Allies					
USSR	20.00	7.50	14.01	15.00	200
China	10.00	1.00	2.00	1.00	?
USA	14.90	0.29	0.57	(less than 10,000)	350
Britain	6.20	0.39	0.47	0.06	150
France	6.00	0.21	0.40	0.10	100
Main Axis Powers					
Germany	12.50	2.85	7.25	0.50	300
Japan	7.40	1.50	0.50	0.30	100
Italy	4.50	0.08	0.12	0.10	50

'The nation has proved itself weak, and the future belongs solely to the stronger Eastern nation. Besides, those who remain after the battle are of little value; for the good have fallen.'

Adolf Hitler

During the period 1942–5 the main belligerents in Europe developed different military strategies and operational techniques in pursuit of decisive battlefield success. The Red Army, through the experience gained in protracted and bitter combat on its own soil, gradually relearned its pre-war doctrine of Deep Operations, until by 1944 it could enact impressive 'manoeuvre' offensives which fully embraced the significance of logistics. By contrast, the German Army's attempts to implement its own brand of high-tempo mechanised warfare (colloquially known as 'Blitzkrieg') degenerated in the face of worsening battlefield odds and a failure to recognise adequately the growing impact of logistics on the art of war. For their part the Western Allies developed a more cautious, firepower-laden approach based on casualty conservation and set-piece battles, which nevertheless looked to eventual mobile exploitation as the instrument to achieve decisive operational success. Like the Soviet method, this approach paid proper attention to the importance of logistics. The result for the Nazis was ultimately cataclysmic.

N I N E

NAVAL WARFARE IN THE WEST, 1919–45

T I M B E A N

The period between 1919 and 1945 saw the balance of world naval power undergo a number of dramatic changes. From 1919 a series of arms control treaties prevented a repeat of the pre-1914 naval race, bringing a degree of stability to international affairs. Unfortunately, this success proved short-lived, and the rise of expansionist fascist regimes in Germany, Italy and Japan led to the collapse of naval arms limitation in the late 1930s. When war broke out in Europe in 1939, nearly all the major powers were engaged in, or commencing, massive naval construction programmes. The new 'naval race' and the violent struggle at sea from 1939 to 1945 dramatically reshaped the balance of world naval power. At the end of the war the Japanese, German and Italian navies had been crushed, and Britain had lost her position of global naval supremacy to the United States – the first time in history that mastery of the sea passed uncontested between two nations.

THE INTER-WAR YEARS

In 1921 and 1922 representatives of the five great powers – the United States, Britain, Japan, France and Italy – met in Washington to discuss proposals for arms limitation. The motivation for what became the first mutual arms control treaties stemmed from moral revulsion at the First World War, and the belief that the pre-1914 naval race had contributed to its outbreak. The lead taken by the United States in proposing limitations on naval forces was unique, given that President Wilson's 1916 'Big Navy Act' would have given her global naval supremacy in the 1920s. There have been few occasions in history when a state has passed up the chance of military supremacy over its rivals.

The 1922 Washington Naval Treaty was the first in a series between 1922 and 1936 that limited world naval power. It brought in a range of measures which restricted the size and armament of certain classes of

The belief that aircraft carriers might have value in naval warfare led to a rush to construct them in the years immediately before the Second World War. This photograph shows HMS Indomitable *(laid down November 1937) and HMS* Victorious *(laid down May 1937). It was taken in August 1942, during an attempt to run a convoy to the island of Malta, at that time under heavy attack from Axis air forces. The Hawker Hurricane in the foreground sits on a much older British carrier, HMS* Eagle *(launched in 1918). Despite the impression of calm, within days HMS* Eagle *would lie at the bottom of the Mediterranean, a victim of the German submarine U-73. HMS* Indomitable *was badly damaged and HMS* Victorious *less severely during the same operation, in both cases by land-based aircraft. (IWM A15961)*

warship. Battleships could not exceed 35,000 tons or have a main armament of guns larger than 16 inches. Cruisers and aircraft carriers were restricted to 10,000 and 27,000 tons respectively. Complex controls on the number of capital ships (battleships and battlecruisers) that signatories could build or modernise were also included, although British attempts to ban or restrict submarine warfare were rejected. The most important part of the treaty was the fixing of naval tonnage ratios. Britain and the USA were given parity at 500,000 tons each, Japan was to have 300,000 tons, and France and Italy each accepted 175,000 tons. Subsequent conferences over the next decade at Geneva (1927) and London (1930 and 1935) attempted to extend and refine the treaty, but the so called 5:5:3:1.75:1.75 ratios remained the central pillar of future negotiations on naval arms control until the system collapsed in the mid-1930s.

The Washington Treaty proved popular with politicians and the public, but the reaction of senior naval officers was less unanimous. Britain and Japan fared best out of all the signatories. Although Britain emerged from the First World War with her maritime supremacy intact, economic and financial problems meant she could not afford to maintain such large forces. The restriction of rival navies – especially the US Navy (USN) – resolved the dilemma of imperial security at low cost. However, despite similar security afforded to Japan, many officers of the Imperial Japanese Navy (IJN) vehemently opposed the imposition of restrictions and did their utmost to undermine and then destroy the treaty system. The Imperial Navy responded aggressively to the Washington Treaty by building up to its tonnage limits and enhancing the capabilities of individual warships and weapons as a means of circumventing restrictions. These actions prompted other navies to take a similar course, creating a sense of mistrust that slowly undermined confidence in arms control. Japan's withdrawal from the treaty system in 1936, prompted by extremist naval officers, led to its collapse, beginning a massive naval race that the world had sought to avoid.

Despite – or perhaps because of – the emphasis on naval arms control in the inter-war years, the period between 1919 and 1939 saw the refinement of numerous existing technologies, as well as the creation of new ones. Radar, increasing gun accuracy and range, and stronger, lighter armour improved the combat power of warships. Conversion from coal to oil fuel systems, and the adoption of superheated steam turbines, led to faster vessels with longer range and greater tonnage. Representative of the strides made in surface ship design were the Japanese 'super battleships' *Yamato* and *Musashi*. Built after the treaty period, these leviathans displaced 69,000 tons and had a top speed of 27.7 knots. Their main armament comprised nine 18.1-inch guns housed in three turrets – each turret being heavier than a single destroyer. Yet despite the power and grandeur of these vessels, they fell victim to the single most important revolution in sea warfare during this period: air power.

Historically, inter-war navies have been portrayed as hostile to the potential of air power, especially aircraft carriers. This was not altogether surprising, for shortcomings in the range, durability and armament of aircraft throughout much of the period made it unlikely that carriers would be given the primary role in combat. However, although British, Japanese, Italian and American doctrinal publications emphasised battleships and long-range gunfire as the decisive factors in combat, they did not exclude maritime air power from their plans. Throughout the 1920s all navies invested, with varying consistency, in aircraft carrier design and construction. Indeed, at the outbreak of war in 1939 the British, American and Japanese possessed significant numbers of carriers, equipped with new aircraft of greater range and bomb load. Japanese carrier formations were the best organised and trained in the world, and in the opening months of the Pacific War they demonstrated the full potential of naval aviation, transforming it from a support role to the principal measure of sea power. But even then, it still required much trial and error to overcome the many, largely unforeseen, problems of operating carriers and their airgroups.

The argument between the carrier and battleship advocates was part of a series of complex debates within navies about the future conduct of war at sea. The role of technology was only one part of a much wider discussion about the intellectual basis for conducting operations. In the light of the First World War most navies paid considerable attention to the Battle of Jutland. They did not necessarily intend to repeat that action; rather, they wished to solve the problems that had denied the British the decisive victory which many – not least the Royal Navy – believed should have been theirs. At the same time their First World War experience had re-taught navies the lesson that it was rare, if not impossible, to overwhelm enemy naval power in a single engagement. The size of modern navies, the enormous resources that created and supported them, coupled with the vastness of the sea and the inability to impose any physical control over the enemy meant that the decisive battle of annihilation was effectively impossible. An enemy fleet could withdraw to port, repair and sail again at a later date to contest control of the sea. War at sea would be attritional, consisting of a search for numerical and material superiority through a series of engagements over time that either exhausted one side, causing its eventual collapse, or created the conditions for a final crushing blow.

British and American concepts of the decisive battle largely addressed the issue of tactical victory in an engagement with the enemy. They were not blind to the fact that strategic victory might require a number of such engagements, and that battle was just one of a variety of tasks which navies had to perform in securing command of the sea. Although both the Royal Navy and US Navy can be accused of overstressing training for general battle at the expense of other techniques, particularly amphibious and anti-submarine warfare, this stemmed from budgetary constraints as much as institutional factors. The Allies possessed a relatively flexible and balanced approach to sea power that they refined during the course of the war to secure victory.

By contrast, the German and Japanese navies went to war without adequate resources or suitable strategies to secure sea power. Consequently, despite considerable professionalism and tactical skill they were unable to achieve strategic victory. Maritime power rested upon the ability to sustain the mobilisation and organisation of a wide range of national resources: financial, economic, human, technical and military. The failure, conscious or unconscious, of Germany and Japan to establish a basis for maritime power is crucial to the explanation of their defeat at sea. At the same time the Kriegsmarine's and Imperial Japanese Navy's misconceptions of sea power and the role of battle represented their own institutional failure.

'We never really understood the sea. Not one of us.'

Vice-Admiral Wolfgang Wegener, 1929, referring to the First World War

This failure was all the more surprising, given that after the First World War the German Kriegsmarine had devoted much time to analysing the reasons for its defeat and seeking solutions. In particular, Vice-Admiral Wolfgang Wegener (1875–1956) wrote an influential critique of German naval strategy in the First World War, highlighting the impotence of the High Seas Fleet in the face of British geographical and numerical advantages. Sensible though these points were, however, Wegener's solution to Germany's dilemma was as inherently flawed as Tirpitz's. His idea that establishing bases in Denmark and Norway would compromise the Royal Navy's blockade, giving access to the Atlantic, was optimistic at best, but the concept of using French ports, without any explanation of how they were to be secured, was even more so. That events transpired during the war in a manner that seemed to justify Wegener's strategic ideas should not obscure the fact that they did not form a logical basis for pre-war naval planning.

Through a perverse logic Wegener's ideas about geographic lines of communication led the German Naval Staff (Oberkommando der Marine – OKM) to conclude that command of the sea consisted solely of economic warfare. In line with this precept they advocated a doctrine of 'tonnage warfare', which stated that sinking 750,000 tons of British merchant shipping a month for a year would defeat Britain. By seeing war in purely economic terms, and making tonnage sunk the sole aim and measure of sea power, the Kriegsmarine rejected battle with enemy naval forces, seeing it as unnecessary and likely to divert forces from key economic targets. Rejection of battle and the need to dominate specific vital lines of communications (in preference to sea denial) demonstrates the OKM's failure to understand the nature of command of the sea. Command is about the ability to use the sea for one's own purposes in wartime and to deny such advantages to the enemy. Battle, involving the destruction of enemy naval forces, exposes an opponent's sea communications to attack or blockade, conferring the ability to control movement at sea. By rejecting battle, the Kriegsmarine denied itself the ability to achieve control over key sea lanes. During the war it pursued its tonnage quotas, lashing out against Allied shipping at many points, inflicting heavy loss and disruption. Yet, it could not close the sea lanes to Allied shipping. For all its tactical successes the OKM lacked the ability to translate them into strategic victory.

By contrast, the Imperial Japanese Navy's distorted view of sea power made the concept of the decisive battle the central and unquestionable article of faith. Not surprisingly, its planning in the 1920s focused upon the problems of war with the United States. Aware of their inability to engage in a protracted struggle with the USA, the Japanese devised the concept of the 'Interceptive Operation' to achieve a swift victory. This originated from plans drawn up after the Battle of Tsushima in 1905, which emphasised annihilation of the enemy in a single engagement off the Japanese coast. Throughout the inter-war years technological advances in torpedoes, long-range gunnery and air power led to revisions of the operational concept, and the gradual movement of the battle's location eastwards to the Mariana Islands. In its final form the 'Interceptive Operation' envisaged that as the US Fleet advanced across the Pacific, submarine and air attacks would deplete it by 30 per cent. Further attacks by surface units at night using long-range torpedoes would blind and disorganise the US Fleet, before it was overwhelmed by long-range fire from battleships.

The viability of this concept was questionable on several counts, not least that for reasons of secrecy it had never been tested in manoeuvres; it was a true 'war on paper'. The Japanese also assumed that their opponent would conform to the role assigned to him in the plan, thus committing the cardinal error of underestimating the enemy. But the greatest flaw was the erroneous assumption that war at sea was purely about the decisive battle. During the Second World War the tendency to husband main fleet units for the decisive battle saw other elements of the IJN exposed to defeat, and regular failure to exploit advantages gained in action for fear of incurring losses. The lack of a balanced approach to sea power also meant that the IJN lacked the ships and doctrine for trade defence, with the result that the Japanese merchant marine was effectively annihilated, bringing Japan to her knees.

THE SECOND WORLD WAR IN THE WEST, 1939–45

The struggle for the world's oceans between 1939 and 1945 was concerned with securing command of the sea to exploit maritime communications for economic and military purposes. In carrying out this traditional role of sea power, Allied navies played an important part in the defeat of Germany and Italy. Command of the sea gave the Allies access to

'For the Western Allies, sea power remained as ever the midwife of victory on land.'

Correlli Barnett, Engage the Enemy More Closely: the Royal Navy in the Second World War *(1991)*

The economic and industrial foundations of Allied victory were exemplified by the 'Liberty' ship, nine of which are shown here during fitting out. The problems of building merchant vessels quickly, using a largely unskilled workforce and a restricted number of berths, were solved by the application of mass production techniques. US shipbuilders created a standardised, workmanlike vessel 420 feet long and capable of carrying 10,000 tons of cargo. Construction time was drastically cut from 355 days to an average of 41, although one ship was launched only 4 days and 15.5 hours after its keel was laid. A total of 2,710 Liberty ships were built during the Second World War. (US National Archives)

raw materials that were essential in a war dominated by economic production, and the ability to transport men and materiel to the battle fronts of Europe. The inability to wrest command of the sea from the Allies represented the failure of the German Kriegsmarine and the Italian Regia Marina.

In the Mediterranean, Italian and British forces made repeated attempts to cut each other's supply lines to the ground forces fighting in North Africa. The Royal Navy's successes made a vital contribution to Allied victory in North Africa and Italy's surrender in September 1943. However, the most important naval campaign in the west was the long and bitter struggle waged by the Kriegsmarine against Allied shipping. The German aim was to destroy Britain's vital Atlantic 'life line' and starve her into surrender. To this end, in the course of six years of bitter struggle the Kriegsmarine sank 5,150 merchant ships totalling 21,570,720 tons. Of these losses, 68 per cent were caused by U-boats. However, these impressive figures obscure the more fundamental point that the German Navy was comprehensively defeated by the Allies. The Battle of the Atlantic was a competition to organise economic, technical and military resources which, in fact, the Allies won decisively.

THE FIRST PHASE: SEPTEMBER 1939–DECEMBER 1941

At the outbreak of war the Commander-in-Chief of the Kriegsmarine, Gross-Admiral Erich Raeder (1876–1960), commanded a small but balanced navy. Assured by Hitler that there would be no major war until the mid-1940s, Raeder's plan for a large fleet (enshrined in the January 1939 'Z' construction programme) was not scheduled for completion until 1944. Consequently, with only two battleships, three armoured and two heavy cruisers, a number of supporting light cruisers and destroyers, and fifty-seven U-boats, Raeder planned to attack enemy merchant shipping and avoid battle against his superior forces. Kriegsmarine operations would be supplemented by mining British waters and support from the Luftwaffe.

The restriction of German forces to bases in the North Sea made access to the Atlantic risky in the face of Allied air and naval strength. In order to use its limited surface forces to maximum effect against unfavourable odds the OKM therefore adopted Commodore Helmuth Heye's (1895–1970) concept of 'cruiser warfare'. Heye argued that German warships, augmented by armed merchant ships, could individually slip through the Allied blockade to attack and disrupt enemy shipping across the world. To hunt down these raiders, the Allies would have to disperse their warships, and this might expose them to attack from German vessels exploiting strategic mobility to concentrate superior numbers against the enemy. Over time this strategy of attrition would reduce German naval inferiority, although it was not expected to destroy Allied naval superiority.

'It must not be forgotten that defeat of the U-boats carries with it the sovereignty of all the oceans of the world.'

Winston Churchill, November 1939

However, the loss of the pocket battleship *Admiral Graf Spee* in December 1939, after it had sunk a mere 57,000 tons of Allied shipping, was an early warning that cruiser warfare would be difficult to implement in the face of Allied naval strength and strategic mobility. In early 1941 a sortie by the heavy cruisers *Scharnhorst* and *Gneisenau* sank another 110,000 tons and disrupted convoy sailings in the Atlantic, but the Royal Navy responded quickly to counter them. Increasing OKM fears about the viability of surface operations in the face of the Royal Navy, especially against increasingly effective British land- and carrier-based aviation, were confirmed in May 1941 with the loss of the battleship *Bismarck*, and after this Kriegsmarine surface operations were severely curtailed. The subsequent withdrawal of surface forces from French Atlantic ports (captured in June 1940) to Norway in January 1942 ended their role in the Battle of the Atlantic, although they continued to pose a serious threat to Allied convoys to Russia until late 1944. Attacks by armed merchantmen persisted, with declining results, until October 1943. Total sinkings by raiders were just 1.3 million tons.

The potency of mines was similarly short-lived. In the opening few months of the war German mines accounted for the impressive total of 262,000 tons of Allied shipping. Impressive returns were also scored in the first six months of 1940, but from then on British countermeasures reduced losses to manageable levels. Although mines came close to closing the port of London, their main effect throughout the war was occasional disruption to shipping routes.

U-boat operations opened dramatically with the sinking of the British battleship *Royal Oak* inside the Royal Navy's main fleet anchorage at Scapa Flow on 14 October 1939. However, results against merchant shipping were less spectacular. Average monthly

THE 'PQ' CONVOYS

During the war, Allied sea power played a critical role in supplying the Soviet Union with substantial quantities of equipment and raw materials. Half of the supplies came in neutral ships across the Pacific, and a quarter through Persia. The remainder had to cross the inhospitable Arctic Ocean to the northern ports of Murmansk and Archangel. The Arctic convoys (codenamed 'PQ') began in August 1941, and despite brief suspensions continued to the end of the war. Attacks from U-boats and aircraft inflicted heavy losses on several occasions, most famously when convoy PQ 17 lost two-thirds of its ships in July 1942. The threat of attack from powerful German surface ships based in Norway was also a constant worry, until they were destroyed by Allied attacks or decommissioned on Hitler's orders in 1944.

Rear Admiral Karl Doenitz (1891–1980), shown here seated, commanded German U-boat forces throughout the Second World War. A gifted tactician who did much to raise the standards of the Kriegsmarine's submarine arm, Doenitz refused to accept the potential of aircraft as U-boat killers, leading to the neglect of radar for his forces until late in the war. Although Doenitz was sentenced in 1946 to ten years imprisonment for war crimes, the available evidence does not support claims that he implemented Hitler's demands that the crews of torpedoed ships be killed. Nevertheless, like most Kriegsmarine officers Doenitz was deeply loyal to Hitler, who appointed him as his successor in April 1945. (U-boot Archiv)

sinkings from September 1939 to March 1940 totalled only 110,000 tons. This was far short of OKM's target, and was easily absorbed by the British. This mediocre performance resulted from the early British introduction of convoy and the small number of U-boats capable of operating in the Atlantic from distant North Sea bases, and was compounded by the diversion of submarines to support the invasion of Norway in April 1940. Although successful, the Norwegian campaign cost the Kriegsmarine half its destroyers and a heavy cruiser sunk, with several other ships damaged. This drastic reduction in forces caused Raeder strongly to oppose the invasion of Britain (Operation 'Sea Lion') because of inadequate protection for the landing forces. To his relief the attack was cancelled after the Luftwaffe's failure to secure air superiority over the English Channel in autumn 1940.

The fall of France in June 1940 saw the U-boats return to the attack on British shipping. From June to November 1940 they sank 1.6 million tons: U-boat crews nicknamed this 'the fortunate time'. This impressive performance stemmed from several factors, in particular the ability of German naval Intelligence (*B-Dienst*) to read British communications, which enabled the commander of the U-boat service, Rear Admiral Karl Doenitz (1891–1980), to direct his limited number of boats accurately against enemy shipping. The capture of new bases in western France also gave U-boats direct access to the Atlantic, increasing their time on patrol, and significant support was now available from the Luftwaffe. Despite problems of inter-service rivalry and the need to develop air–naval cooperation from scratch, the Luftwaffe made a valuable contribution to the Atlantic campaign, attacking shipping and locating convoys for the U-boats. However, much of this valuable support was lost when numerous Luftwaffe aircraft were withdrawn for the invasion of Russia in June 1941.

German success in 1940 occurred at a time when British defences were vulnerable. The Admiralty lacked sufficient forces to counter German attacks, especially because large numbers of escorts were tied up on anti-invasion duties. Many ships were obsolete, or, like the new *Hunt* destroyer class, lacked the range and handling capabilities for deep-ocean operations. RAF Coastal Command experienced similar problems. In particular, a lack of very long range (VLR) aircraft restricted its ability to patrol out into the eastern Atlantic. Nevertheless, the home waters situation improved in late 1940 with the release of escorts and aircraft from anti-invasion duties for convoy protection. Furthermore, in August changes in British signal codes ended Doenitz's ability to target shipping accurately. This combined with the exhaustion of U-boat crews after a period of intensive operations, and there was a decline in their effectiveness.

Problems with the availability of operational U-boats affected Doenitz's ability to implement a sustained war of attrition against British shipping throughout the war. The need to repair, refit and resupply boats, and to rest crews, meant that the number of submarines at sea fluctuated. These periods of respite allowed the Allies to regroup and re-organise their defences. Raeder's attempt to increase U-boat strength to 300 by cancelling the 'Z' plan and redirecting resources from surface vessels to submarines in September 1939 was only marginally successful, and took time to bear fruit. Indeed, at the end of 1940 Doenitz's operational strength was only half that at the outbreak of war. Although the situation had improved by the end of 1941, when eighty U-boats were in service, this was matched by rising numbers of British escorts. The inferior ratio of U-boats to Allied escort strength was a constant problem for the OKM, and throughout the war the Kriegsmarine was at least two years behind in its U-boat requirements. Raeder's 300 U-boats might have secured victory in 1939 or 1940, but by 1943 the figure was too low.

After a period of relative quiet, the months between March and July 1941 saw the U-boats regain the initiative, beginning another period of heavy British losses. This was partly achieved by conducting operations further out into the Atlantic, beyond the range of British air and escort cover. Valuable contributions were made by the skill of individual U-boat commanders and Doenitz's widespread introduction of 'Wolf Pack' tactics. Despite this, success was again short-lived. In mid-1941 the extension of escort cover in the Atlantic, through the introduction of a complex system which used four escort groups to protect a convoy at different stages of its voyage, closed the mid-ocean 'gap'. The arrival of significant numbers of Canadian warships and the start of air operations based in Newfoundland and Iceland also increased protection. But by far the most important development by late 1941 was the British ability to

Allied merchant tonnage sunk by U-boats in the Atlantic, July–Dec 1940 (gross tonnage)

July–Sept	756,307
Oct–Dec	796,442

'If Holland and Belgium are successfully occupied, and if France is also defeated, the fundamental conditions for a successful war against England have been secured. England can then be blockaded from western France by the air force; the navy with its U-boats can extend the range of the blockade. England will not be able to fight on the continent . . . Time will not be on England's side. Germany will not bleed to death on land. Such a strategy has been shown to be necessary by the First World War.'

Adolf Hitler, 23 May 1939

Allied merchant tonnage sunk by U-boats in the Atlantic Jan–Dec 1941 (gross tons)

Jan–March	613,691
April–June	979,774
July–Sept	392,118
Oct–Dec	328,690

read German signal codes. This Intelligence (code-named 'Ultra') enabled the British to divert convoys away from U-boat patrol lines. The contribution of code-breakers stationed at Bletchley Park ultimately proved vital to winning the Battle of the Atlantic. Taken as a whole, these countermeasures reduced losses in the second half of 1941 to an average of 268,000 tons a month.

A number of other factors were also responsible for Britain's survival in the first twenty-eight months of the war. Of particular importance was the depth of her economic resources and her skilfully organised war effort, which allowed her to absorb the heavy losses inflicted on shipping. The Kriegsmarine's failure to take these factors into consideration was a serious error in its 'tonnage warfare' calculations. In 1938 Britain required 60 million tons of imports carried in 22 million tons of shipping. However, prioritisation of imports, rationing, increased domestic food production and re-organisation of government transport and shipping departments, meant that by 1944 Britain could survive on 27 million tons of imports. Furthermore, up to December 1941, British losses (to all causes) of 9 million merchant tons, were alleviated by new construction and by the acquisition of neutral shipping totalling 7 million tons. With hindsight, the conclusion to be drawn from these figures is that the Kriegsmarine's tonnage warfare concept was inherently flawed.

WOLF PACKS

The 'Wolf Pack' concept was developed by Rear Admiral Karl Doenitz in the inter-war years. An experienced submariner with a distinguished record in the First World War, Doenitz believed that to locate and overwhelm convoys U-boats had to operate in large groups, not individually, as they had done in 1917–18. U-boats were deployed in groups of three stationed across probable, or known, convoy routes. When a U-boat made contact it relayed the convoy's position so that higher head-quarters could concentrate other groups of submarines. These would subject the convoy to successive large-scale attacks, inflicting heavy loss. Although these tactics did prove effective on numerous occasions, the popular image of successive convoys being ripped to pieces by Wolf Packs is erroneous. During the war 98 per cent of all inbound ships in convoy reached Britain untouched.

The British also received invaluable assistance from the neutral United States. In November 1940 President Franklin Roosevelt (1882–1945) introduced Lend-Lease, which was designed to furnish the British with weapons and materiel they could not produce, or afford to purchase. In early 1941 this programme was extended to include the transfer of American escorts and oil tankers to the British, and the repair of Royal Navy warships in US shipyards. Indirect military assistance was provided in February 1941 when American naval forces began patrolling the waters off Greenland and Iceland. This increasingly unneutral American stance was extended in April, when waters west of twenty-six degrees were included in the US 'defence zone'. In July American warships began escorting any ships that requested it from Iceland, and in September cover was extended to British convoys in the western Atlantic. US actions closed the central and western Atlantic to the U-boats at a time when British anti-submarine warfare (ASW) measures increasingly restricted operations in the eastern Atlantic.

The victory scored by the British over the U-boats between 1939 and 1941 was an impressive achievement, but it was not decisive. Strategically, the need to concentrate available shipping to supply Britain's war effort had forced withdrawal from many profitable export trades. The resulting loss of revenue raised serious questions about Britain's ability to wage a

The escort carrier HMS Avenger, *like most such ships, was converted by an American shipyard from a merchant vessel and given to the Royal Navy under the terms of Lend-Lease aid. She carried fifteen aircraft and displaced 15,000 tons fully loaded. Although available in large numbers by late 1942, the need to support amphibious landings in North Africa (Operation 'Torch', November 1942) and to refine training and operational techniques, meant that it was only the following year that such vessels began to have a major impact on the Battle of the Atlantic. By the end of the war escort carriers had accounted for thirty-nine U-boats on their own, and for another twelve in cooperation with other vessels.* Avenger *herself, however, was sunk by a U-boat in November 1942. (IWM FL1268)*

protracted war. Tactically, ineffective depth charges, unsuitable tactics, poor performance of the ASDIC underwater detection system, lack of air and surface radar and untrained personnel prevented decisive offensive action against the U-boats. Only forty-nine had been sunk since the start of the war, and although this represented a large portion of Doenitz's existing strength, the expansion of U-boat numbers would enable the Germans to mount even more destructive attacks on shipping in the near future. Only through sustained offensive operations could the British retain their tentative grasp on command of the sea. Acknowledging this, the Royal Navy and RAF Coastal Command initiated a series of training, construction and research programmes to equip them with forces capable of defeating the U-boats. However, considerable time was required to create, refine and then deploy these new forces on a sufficient scale to win the Battle of the Atlantic. Considering the poor state of British ASW defences in the first years of the war, it is interesting to speculate that if the U-boats had sought battle with the escorts, they might have defeated them. Without protection the convoys might well have been overwhelmed, as Doenitz intended.

THE ATLANTIC: JANUARY 1942–APRIL 1943

The entry of the United States into the war in December 1941 appeared to offer Doenitz the opportunity to regain the initiative by opening up the lightly protected western Atlantic to intensive U-boat attack. Previously, Hitler had refused permission to operate in US-defended areas for fear of drawing the Americans into the war. Now, with restrictions lifted, Doenitz mounted Operation 'Paukenschlag' ('Drumbeat') against the US Atlantic coast, savaging inadequately defended coastal shipping. This new phase in the Battle of the Atlantic was reminiscent of the campaign of 1939–41.

Allied merchant tonnage sunk by U-boats in the Atlantic Jan–Dec 1942 (gross tons)

Jan–March	1,124,000
April–June	1,466,000
July–Sept	1,141,000
Oct–Dec	1,396,000

However, initial German success against weak defences gradually declined as Allied countermeasures were introduced.

The US commander of the Eastern Sea Frontier, Rear Admiral Adolphus Andrews (1879–1948), possessed a motley collection of small, obsolescent ships and aircraft, inadequately equipped and poorly trained for ASW operations. Inter-service wrangling over the most effective method to employ aircraft against submarines exacerbated his problems. Furthermore, support from USN destroyers failed to appear in the opening months of 1942 because they were employed in protecting convoys of troops to Britain. That these convoys suffered no losses was a notable success for the USN, although of little comfort to merchant seamen. Compounding these dire circumstances was the refusal of Admiral Ernest King (1878–1956) (US naval Commander-in-Chief) to permit the formation of convoys, believing that no convoys at all were better than badly protected ones. This combination of weak, ill-directed defences, the high density of shipping and an immensely long and exposed coastline, led to heavy losses. The U-boat crews called it 'the second fortunate time'.

Yet the continuing lack of operational boats meant that the blow inflicted was not as great as it might have been. Diversion of U-boats to other theatres, and the Type VII's lack of range, meant that only twenty-two out of a total strength of ninety-one boats were available for operations in January 1942. Their effectiveness was reduced by operating at great distance from their bases, and by increased wear and tear. Attempts to extend time spent on patrol with special resupply U-boats (nicknamed 'milk cows') were only marginally successful.

The favourable circumstances off the US coast did not last long. Although over a quarter of all Allied losses occurred off America between 1942 and 1945, the introduction of countermeasures in March 1942 reduced sinkings off the US coast to 260,000 tons that month. This was achieved primarily as a result of King granting permission to introduce a number of interlocking daylight coastal convoys. These were assisted by an increase in ASW forces, which by April rendered the US east coast even less profitable for the U-boats. Sinkings in this area remained high throughout much of the year as US forces struggled to acquire the weapons and skill needed to engage and defeat the enemy, but like the British in the Atlantic in 1941 they had reduced the problem to manageable proportions.

Declining fortunes off the American coast led Doenitz to switch his main attack to target the lightly defended Gulf of Mexico and the Caribbean. Once again, initial successes were scored, but as the Allies deployed ASW forces into the area the effectiveness of German operations declined. This tendency to switch the point of attack against weakly defended sea areas was a characteristic feature of the U-boat command's direction of the Battle of the Atlantic.

U-BOATS

At the start of the war the Kriegsmarine had two main types of U-boat in service: the Type VII and Type IX. The Type IX was not as cramped as the Type VII, and with nearly twice the range (11,000 nautical miles) and torpedoes (twenty-two) was better suited for long-distance operations. Although both types were upgraded during the war – in particular by the addition of anti-aircraft guns and *Naxos* radar to counter enemy aircraft – they were gradually outpaced by improvements in Allied escort and weapon design. The Kriegsmarine did belatedly try to restore its fortunes with the Type XXI 'electro-boat'. Its fast speed underwater, ability to dive deeper and – by means of a *schnorkel* breathing apparatus – remain submerged for a long time, were intended to allow it to out-fight the escorts. In reality, the Type XXIs were too late and too few in number. They also suffered from serious technical flaws, including a weak hull and a tendency for the *schnorkel* to asphyxiate the crew. The Type XXI was not the war-winning weapon that Doenitz desired.

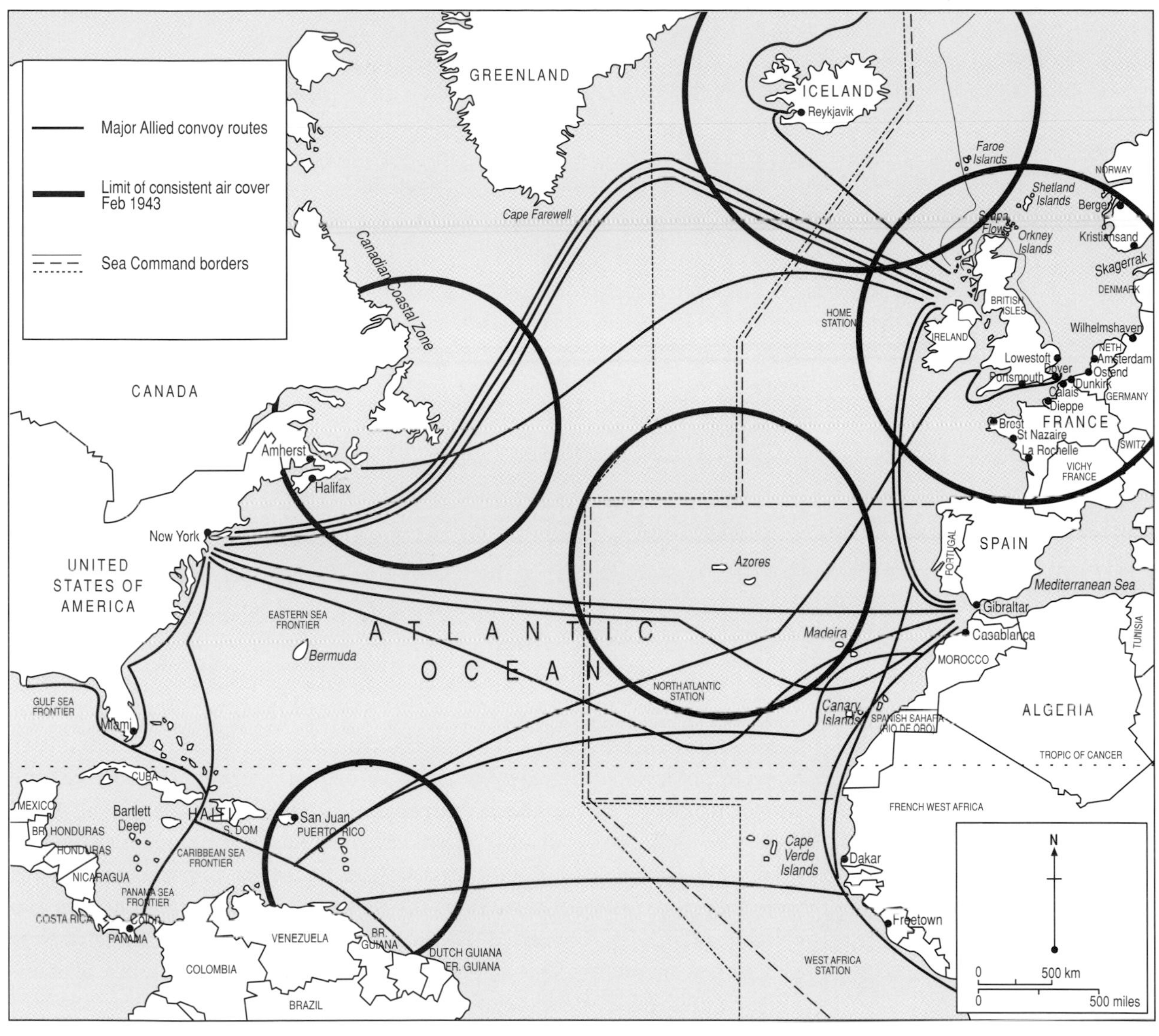

Doenitz and his staff believed that total tonnage sunk was the key determinant of victory, not where it was sunk. A ship lost in the Caribbean would eventually mean one fewer for the decisive North Atlantic theatre. This strategy, however, was deeply flawed. To prevent Allied shipping using the north Atlantic route, it was necessary to engage forces in battle in order to secure command of the area. Heavy losses in secondary theatres such as the Caribbean, or in African waters, might cause consternation to the Allies, but could not break the Atlantic 'lifeline'. Additionally, as the Allies widened escort and air cover to the main sea lanes U-boats were forced into peripheral theatres where targets were fewer and less valuable.

The start of July 1942 saw attacks recommence in the central Atlantic as the Germans again probed for weak spots. This area was beyond the range of land-based Allied air cover, and with no carriers available because

Death of a merchant vessel. The munitions ship Mary Luckenbach, *part of the Arctic convoy PQ 18, blows up after being torpedoed by a German aircraft off Spitzbergen, 14 September 1942. (IWM A12275)*

of pressures in the Pacific and Mediterranean, the U-boat commanders hoped to operate with greater freedom. With a strength of 121 U-boats the situation looked favourable for operating a number of 'Wolf Packs' to deliver crushing blows against Allied convoys. However, actual results – at a monthly average of 400,000 tons – were far below expectations. There were several reasons for this. First, the inexperience of many U-boat crews affected tactical performance. Second, overextended patrol lines made it easy to detect convoys, but difficult to concentrate U-boats to attack them. Third, Allied ASW forces were increasingly better organised, trained and experienced. At the end of 1942 the British had 384 operational escorts, while Canadian and American numbers were steadily rising. Fourth, in the autumn of 1942 the Allies reacquired the ability to read U-boat 'Enigma' signals traffic (lost at the start of the year), allowing them again to bypass enemy patrol lines.

Dramatically, apparent Allied superiority was thrown into doubt by losses in the first three months of 1943, as U-boats mounted a series of well-coordinated and ferocious attacks against shipping in the north Atlantic. Although only 1.6 million tons were sunk, the loss of forty ships in well-defended convoys in March 1943 caused consternation. The Admiralty's subsequent observation that 'the Germans never came so near to disrupting communications between the New World and the Old' was a chilling admission. It raised serious questions about the continued validity of convoy, and with no alternative tactic, defeat seemed a real possibility. Fears that U-boat strength would reach over 600 by the end of the year, and the impending loss of signals Intelligence, heightened Allied worries.

Allied merchant tonnage sunk by U-boats in the Atlantic Jan–Dec 1943 (gross tons)

Jan–March	1,061,172
April–June	526,544
July–Sept	210,939
Oct–Dec	131,578

In reality, the events of March 1943 were an exception in a downward trend in U-boat effectiveness which had begun in late 1942. This was recognised at the time by the March 'Monthly Anti-Submarine Report', which observed that 'Considering the weight of attacks developed, the convoys came through for the most part remarkably well.' German losses also ran high at sixty-six U-boats in the first three months of 1943. Equally important, 60 per cent of German submarine patrols were ineffective. Furthermore, Allied worries about a dramatic increase in the number of U-boats were ill-founded. At the close of 1943 Doenitz had 413, of which only 168 were operational. Last, the ability to read German signals was lost for only ten days in March, and as a result throughout 1943 the Allies received a steady flow of information about U-boat operations. March 1943 was actually part of a longer phase in the struggle at sea that laid the foundations for a series of spectacular Allied victories from May onwards.

'The defeat of the U-boat is the prelude to all effective aggressive operations.'

Winston Churchill, 11 February 1943

THE FINAL PHASE: MAY 1943–MAY 1945

From late 1942 to April 1943 the Allies had gradually deployed new ASW forces, and these had started to curtail the effectiveness of German attacks. Of course, the U-boats had been contained by Allied countermeasures on several other occasions, only for them to retake the initiative at a later date. The difference in 1943 was that Allied ASW forces were now capable of undertaking offensive operations to hunt down and destroy U-boats in large numbers. The first major blows came in May when forty-one U-boats were sunk without inflicting significant loss on convoys. The severity of this defeat was acknowledged by Doenitz's temporary withdrawal of his forces from the Atlantic.

Allied success rested upon a number of developments. The effectiveness of escorts and aircraft was enhanced by new technology. In 1942 mid-sea refuelling of escorts extended their range and operational effectiveness, and by summer 1943 over 300 vessels were fitted with this capability. Similarly,

'Our losses have reached an intolerable level. The enemy air force played a decisive role in inflicting these high losses.'

Admiral Karl Doenitz, calling off attacks on North Atlantic convoys, 1943

Death of a U-boat. U-625, a Type VIIC submarine, sinks 450 miles west of Ireland following a depth charge attack by a Canadian Sunderland flying boat, 10 March 1944. Despite taking to their dinghies the entire crew perished, as did 28,000 other U-boat crewmen during the war. (US Navy)

Allied merchant tonnage sunk by U-boats in the Atlantic Jan–Dec 1944 (gross tons)

Jan-March	84,675
April–June	103,596
July–Sept	111,817
Oct–Dec	66,905

The U-boat War, 1939–45

	U-boats		
	Built	Sunk	At sea in Atlantic (average)
1939 (Oct–Dec)	7	9	14
1940	48	22	14
1941	198	34	26
1942	243	86	72
1943	264	237	90
1944	237	261	53
1945 (Jan–March)	79	68	47

from March 1943 greater numbers of VLR aircraft extended air cover over the Atlantic. Introduction of Type 147 Holding ASDIC and 'Huff Duff' (High Frequency Direction Finding) devices on escorts, and centimetric radar on ships and aircraft, meant that U-boats could be accurately detected when surfaced or submerged. They could then be attacked with more powerful and different types of depth charges using new tactical firing patterns.

Technical innovations were complemented by improvements in training and tactics. As early as 1940 an ASW training school had been established at Tobermory on the Scottish coast, but it was not until late 1942 that ships could be trained to cooperate to maximum effect in escort groups. By mid-1943, possession of 490 escorts allowed the British and Canadians to introduce routine training for escort groups every 100 days. This facilitated regular dissemination of new tactics developed for the Navy by the Western Approaches Tactical Unit, and for the RAF by its Operational Research Section. This ended the pattern of blindly probing for U-boats, and of uncoordinated attacks. In particular, Coastal Command's effectiveness was dramatically increased. As the RAF moved forces sideways into the battle in the spring of 1943, for the first time in the war sinkings of U-boats by aircraft surpassed victories by surface forces: 130 compared to 51 between March and December 1943.

In late 1942 convoy protection increased for a variety of reasons. It was found that enlarging convoys from twenty-six to fifty-four ships enhanced protection by concentrating escorts, and decreased the chances of being detected. Over the next two years convoys were increased to a peak of 120 ships. This was also complemented by an expansion in total escort numbers, and the introduction of five 'Hunter Killer' groups. Each centred around an escort carrier, the 'Hunter Killer' groups closed the mid-Atlantic 'air gap', provided reconnaissance for convoy escorts, reinforced convoys under attack, and hunted down U-boats located by Intelligence. Delays in their deployment in 1942 had been caused by lack of training, and diversion to support landings in North Africa in November.

Significant as ASW developments were, the blow delivered to the U-boats in May was not a decisive strategic victory. The nature of war at sea excludes victory through a single decisive engagement. Instead, the Allies had to inflict a series of blows against the U-boats, wearing them down in a war of attrition in order to retain command of the sea.

Doenitz recommitted his forces in August, confident that retraining and reorganisation would overcome Allied defences. This proved overly optimistic. A change in Allied naval codes hindered the U-boats, although this was ameliorated by the ability to read merchant signals until the end of 1943. 'Ultra' Intelligence enabled the Allies to keep diverting convoys away from U-boats, but more significantly 'Hunter Killer' and 'Mid Ocean Escort' groups could mount offensive operations to destroy them. RAF Coastal Command attacks against U-boats crossing the Bay of Biscay to the Atlantic inflicted further losses. German attempts to fight U-boats across the Bay, first by equipping them with anti-aircraft guns, and then by convoying them with surface forces and air cover, were less than successful. Changes in 'Wolf Pack' tactics and use of homing torpedoes could not reverse German fortunes, as the Allies quickly evolved counter-measures. Critically, Doenitz's refusal, despite strong circumstantial evidence, to accept that the Allies had developed effective air-to-surface radar and broken German naval codes, led him to continue to throw his forces against strong Allied defences in a suicidal manner. Between September and December 1943 forty-nine U-boats were sunk in the north Atlantic alone, for just fourteen Allied ships.

For the rest of the war German production managed to keep pace with U-boat losses, permitting continued operations which tied down large

THE MEDITERRANEAN, 1940–5

Italy's belated declaration of war on 10 June 1940 began a protracted and costly struggle between the Royal Navy and the Italian Regia Marina, the latter assisted by German air and naval forces, for control of the Mediterranean. Hostilities opened bizarrely with a Royal Navy victory over the French fleet at Mers El Kebir and Dakar. This 'unnatural and painful' attack, as Winston Churchill described it, was carried out because of British fears that in the wake of France's defeat her fleet might be seized by Germany. Shortly afterwards British and Italian naval forces, covering convoys, clashed inconclusively at Punta Stilo on 9 July 1940. This pattern of engagements fought over British convoys to Malta, and Axis ones to North Africa, dominated the struggle in the Mediterranean, with neither side able to achieve decisive results. The Italian Navy laboured under the problems of poor gunnery, inadequate radar and increasing restrictions on operations caused by fuel shortages. In addition, obsolescent aircraft and inter-service clashes meant that the Regia Aeronautica failed to provide adequate support to the fleet throughout the war.

The British managed to keep the edge over the Italians by exploiting signals Intelligence and through skilful coordination of the western Mediterranean forces at Gibraltar, with those in the east at Alexandria. Their advantage in aircraft carriers was also vital in the face of Italian and German air power. In numerous engagements carrier aviation blinded enemy aerial reconnaissance, protected convoys and harried enemy vessels. Its most impressive success was the crippling of three Italian battleships in Taranto harbour on the night of 11 November 1940. The effects of the raid were short-lived, but it was an immeasurable contribution to the Royal Navy's growing psychological superiority over the Regia Marina. Another heavy blow was delivered by Admiral Andrew Cunningham's (1883–1963) forces off Cape Matapan in May 1941. This gradual process of attrition, combined with British and American victories in North Africa in late 1942, broke the Italian Navy as a fighting force.

British victory was not cheaply bought. The enemy air siege of Malta in 1941 came close to starving the island into submission. Malta convoys such as 'Halbard' (September 1941) and 'Pedestal' (August 1942) suffered heavy losses from German and Italian air and submarine attacks, as they attempted to bring vital supplies to the island. The carriers *Ark Royal* and *Eagle* were sunk and the *Illustrious* and *Furious* were badly damaged. Heavy losses were sustained in the evacuation of British forces from Crete in May and June 1941. A daring attack by Italian frogmen in Alexandria harbour also crippled the battleships *Queen Elizabeth* and *Valiant* in December 1941.

Allied naval losses in the Mediterranean, 1940–5 (vessels sunk)

Aircraft carriers	2
Battleships	1
Cruisers	17
Destroyers	56
Submarines	35

Despite these losses the Allies were able to conduct a series of major amphibious landings between November 1942 and August 1943. Operations 'Torch' (North Africa), 'Husky' (Sicily) and 'Avalanche' (Italy) secured Allied control of much of the Mediterranean and precipitated Italy's surrender in September 1943. Subsequent amphibious operations in Italy in early 1944 ('Shingle') and southern France in August ('Anvil-Dragoon'), demonstrated the scale of Allied victory at sea in the western and central Mediterranean. Nevertheless, in the east German air power in Greece and adjacent islands contained minor Allied offensives. The failure of Allied naval forces to inflict any notable losses during the German withdrawal from Crete and the Aegean Islands in autumn 1944 was a missed opportunity, but it came at the end of a war that had already been won.

'The battle of the Atlantic was the dominating factor all through the war. Never for one moment could we forget that everything happening elsewhere . . . depended ultimately on its outcome.'

Winston Churchill, Closing the Ring *(1951)*

numbers of Allied forces. But the Kriegsmarine's inability to match advances in escort technology with improved U-boats meant that the Allies were able to retain their command of the sea. Widening attacks against Indian Ocean and South Atlantic shipping achieved desultory returns. Only 770,000 tons of shipping were sunk in 1944. After heavy losses in March 1944 most U-boats were withdrawn for anti-invasion duties. When the Allies mounted the invasion of France in June (Operation 'Neptune') only negligible results were achieved. Doenitz's last act of the war, as Hitler's successor as head of state, was to order the surrender of Germany in May 1945.

During the Second World War the Kriegsmarine inflicted 21 million tons of losses on Allied merchant shipping. Yet this was more than offset by total Allied construction of 42 million tons. Overall, the U-boats were too few in number to take real advantage of what proved to be only passing Allied weaknesses. The Battle of the Atlantic was a technical and economic race in which the Germans failed to compete with vast and skilfully organised Allied resources. In part this was the result of the demands of fighting a major land war, but not wholly so. In the course of five and a half years, out of 830 U-boats that saw service 784 were lost, 696 by Allied action.

TEN

NAVAL WARFARE IN THE PACIFIC, 1941–5

TIM BEAN

Between December 1941 and September 1945 Japan and the United States fought one of the largest, most destructive and swiftest naval wars in history. During this conflict the Japanese obsession with the single decisive battle, coupled with a misplaced faith in their seamen's fighting spirit, proved a poor basis for conducting a war against the overwhelming resources of the United States. Despite demonstrating a high degree of tactical skill, the Imperial Japanese Navy (IJN) was gradually crushed by the US Navy (USN) in a series of engagements between 1942 and 1944.

INITIAL CONQUESTS: DECEMBER 1941–APRIL 1942

Ostensibly, Japan's decision to go to war with the United States in December 1941 was motivated by the need to acquire the raw materials of South-East Asia to sustain the conflict she had begun against China in 1937. The imposition of a US embargo on exports to Japan and the future expansion of the US Navy were viewed in Tokyo as confirmation of the inevitability of war with the USA. Confronted by economic collapse, future loss of naval supremacy and perceived American aggression, Japanese leaders decided to seize the resources of South-East Asia before time and events overwhelmed them. However, the apparent logic of a pre-emptive strike to exploit Japan's advantages in position and military force missed the fundamental point that regardless of the strategic option selected, action would probably end in her defeat. The unique feature of 1941 was that Japan's leaders consciously adopted a policy that not only made defeat inevitable, but assured that it would be overwhelming. By going to war with the world's most populous state (China), its largest empire (Britain) and its greatest economic power (the United States), Japan ranged against her a combination of enemies so strong that she was guaranteed to suffer the very catastrophe she sought to avoid through war.

'In the first six to twelve months of a war with the United States and Great Britain I will run wild and win victory upon victory. But then, if the war continues after that I have no expectation of success.'

Admiral Isoroku Yamamoto, commander-in-chief, Japanese Combined Fleet

Japanese operations commenced at 0025 hours on 8 December 1941 with landings at Kota Bharu on the Malayan peninsula. Around 80 minutes later, across the international date line on 7 December, carrier aircraft attacked the US Pacific Fleet at Pearl Harbor in the Hawaiian islands. Over the next four months the Japanese overwhelmed Allied positions in the central Pacific, the Philippines, Malaya, Burma and the East Indies. The speed of the Japanese advance was the result of excellent planning and a conduct of operations characterised by economy of effort, concentration of force, offensive spirit and maximum exploitation of surprise. Allied forces were handicapped to varying degrees by numerical, materiel, geographic and higher command deficiencies, and proved powerless to stop the onslaught.

At the start of the war the Japanese undertook a number of secondary operations to secure the rear and flanks of their main thrust into the Philippines–Malaya–East Indies triangle. The seizure of Hong Kong and the central and western Pacific islands of Guam, Wake and Makin consolidated Japan's outer defensive perimeter, while the destruction of the US Pacific Fleet at its Hawaiian anchorage on the outbreak of war was intended to render the Allies totally unable to oppose Japanese advances. It was also hoped that the attack would deliver a shattering, possibly war-winning, blow to American morale.

'Yesterday, December 7th 1941, a date which will live in infamy, the United States of America was suddenly and deliberately attacked by the naval and air forces of the Empire of Japan . . . No matter how long it may take us to overcome this premeditated invasion, the American people in their righteous might will win through to absolute victory.'

President Franklin Delano Roosevelt, 8 December 1941

The raid on the Hawaiian islands commenced at 0749 hours on Sunday 7 December with attacks by over 350 aircraft from Vice-Admiral Chuichi Nagumo's (1887–1944) First Carrier Striking Group. The audacity of conceiving and executing the raid was confirmation of the IJN's skill in carrier operations. For the loss of twenty-nine aircraft the Japanese sank or crippled eighteen warships, among them five battleships. In reality, however, the blow delivered to the US Pacific Fleet was not mortal. It was also possibly unnecessary, and it was definitely counter-productive. The aircraft carriers *Enterprise* and *Lexington* were not in Pearl Harbor when the attack occurred (a fact known to the Japanese), and even if they had been, their loss would still have left the Americans with five carriers. The Japanese failed to target minor warships and destroy dry docks, machinery, storehouses and oil storage tanks, and the USN was still capable of conducting limited offensive operations. In fact, prior to the raid numerical, qualitative and logistic weaknesses probably meant that this was all that the Pacific Fleet was capable of. These points are eclipsed by the fact that politically the operation was a disaster because it stirred up intense anger in the American population: a far more lethal force than five obsolescent battleships.

'A military man can scarcely pride himself on having "smitten a sleeping enemy"; it is more a matter of shame, simply, for the one smitten.'

Admiral Isoroku Yamamato, commander-in-chief, Japanese Combined Fleet, 9 January 1942

As their flank and rear were secured Japanese army and naval forces opened a series of attacks against Allied positions in South-East Asia and the Philippines. With the bulk of their carrier forces committed to the Pearl Harbor operation, Japanese advances were tied to the range of land-based aircraft. This forced them to undertake successive attacks in which advance air bases were secured, from which aircraft could support the next phase of operations; a sort of aerial 'leap frogging'.

In the Philippines pre-emptive air attacks from bases in Formosa effectively destroyed US air power on the northern island of Luzon on 8 and 9 December 1941. The simultaneous seizure of airfields on islands

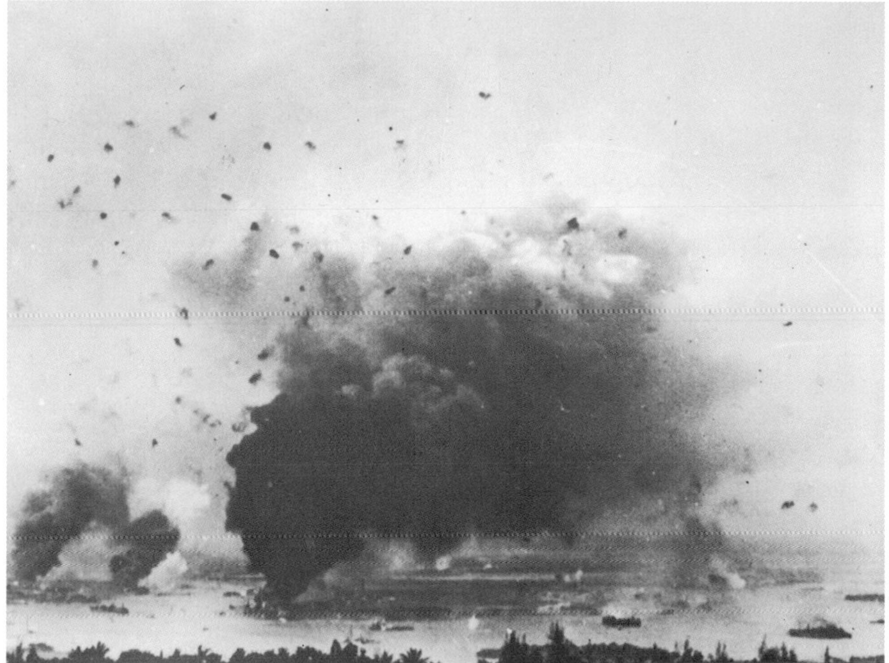

'A dastardly and unprovoked attack' (President Franklin Roosevelt). Pearl Harbor under attack, 7 December 1941. This view from the north shows Ford Island in the centre. The mass of smoke to its left is from 'Battleship Row', where seven US battleships were moored. Over 2,400 Americans were killed in the raid (1,200 of them in the battleship Arizona, *which blew up) and another 1,178 wounded. The Japanese attacks also accounted for 205 US aircraft destroyed or damaged, almost all of them on the ground. (IWM MH6014)*

The aftermath. The damaged battleship Maryland *towers over the upturned hull of the battleship* Oklahoma. *The* Oklahoma *was hit by four torpedoes on her port side, and with no time to close hatches or internal doors, she capsized. Rescuers, seen here on the vessel's bottom, saved thirty-two sailors by cutting holes in the hull, but the ship herself was unsalvageable. (US National Archives)*

Dates. Numbered from left to right in ascending order

a. 30 May 1942 Indo-Burmese border reached
b. 28 April 1942 Burma secured
c. 8–9 March 1942 Burma invaded
d. 8 Dec 1941 landings on Kra Isthmus
e. 15 Feb 1942 Singapore surrenders
f. 16 Feb 1942 Palambang and Bangka Is secured
g. 5 March 1942 landings on western Java
h. 29 Jan 1942 landing in south west Borneo
i. 15 Dec 1941 landing in British Borneo
j. 10 Jan 1942 landing at Tarakan
k. 24 Jan 1942 landing at Balikpapan
l. 20 Feb 1942 landing at Banjarmasin
m. 1 March 1942 landing in eastern Java
n. 19 Feb 1942 landing on Bali.
o. 25 Dec 1941 fall of Hong Kong.
p. 10 Dec 1941 landings at Aparri and Vigan
q. 24 Dec 1941 landings in Lingayen Gulf
r. 19 Dec 1941 landings at Davao
s. 11 Jan 1942 landings at Manado
t. 24 Jan 1942 landings at Kendari
u. 8 Feb 1942 landings at Makassar
v. 20 Feb 1942 landings on Timor
w. 19 April 1942 landings at Hollandia
x. 10 Dec 1941 landings on Guam
y. 23 Jan 1942 landings at Rabaul.
z. 9 Feb–8 March 1942 landings on New Guinea
aa. 31 March 1942 landings on Bougainville
bb. 3 May 1942 landings on Tulagi and Guadalcanal
cc. 2 Dec 1941 Nagumo's Carrier Striking Group sails from Hitokappu Bay
dd. 13/21 June 1942 landings on Aleutian Is
ee. 11 Dec 1941 first attempt to take Wake Is repulsed
ff. 23 Dec 1941 second, successful attempt to take Wake Is
gg. 10 Dec 1941 landings on Makin and Tarawa
hh. 7 Dec 1941 attack on Pearl Harbor by Nagumo's Carrier group

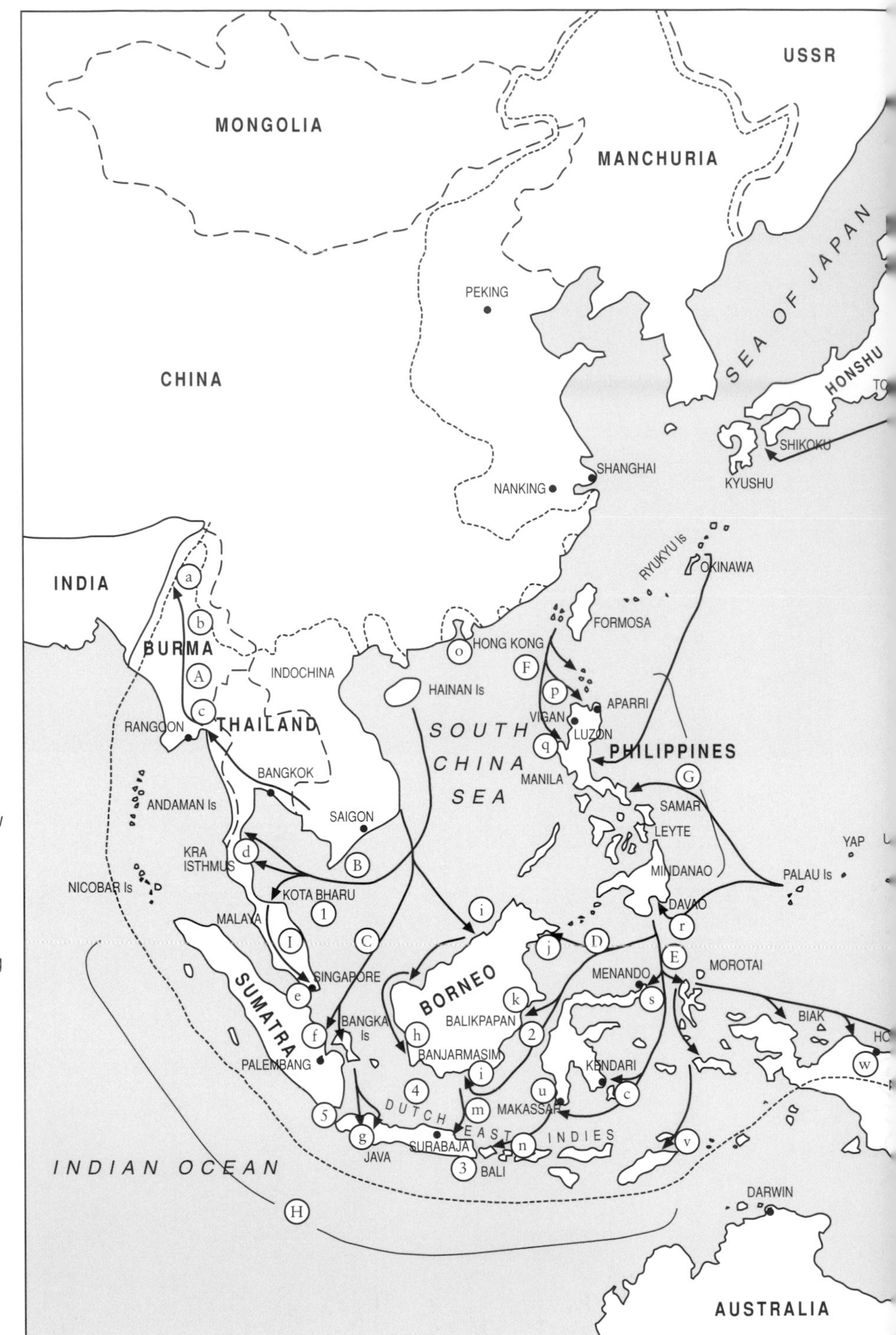

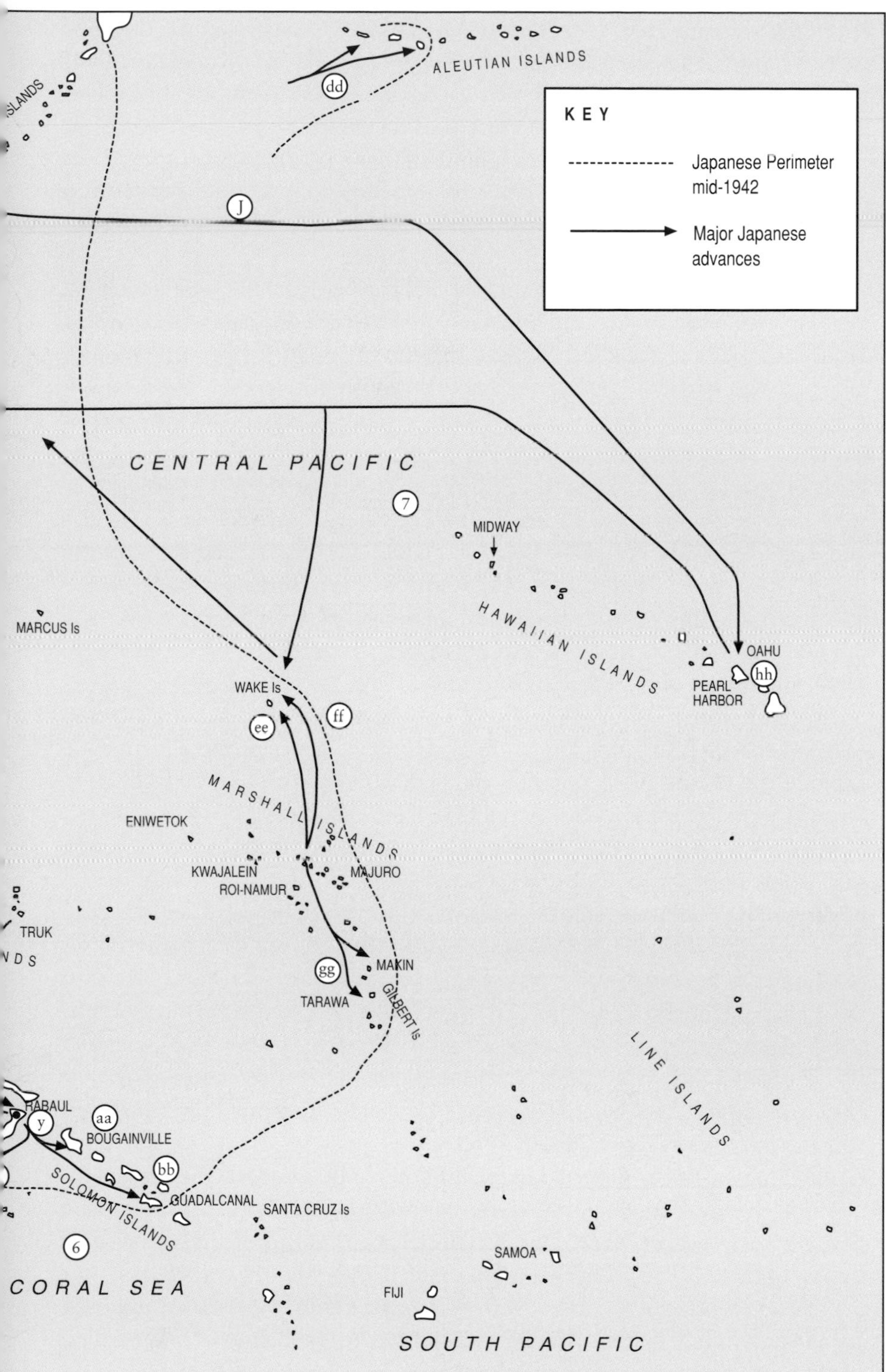

Formations conducting Operations (commanding officer's names in brackets)

A. 15 Army (Ioda)
B. 25 Army (Yamashita) and Main Body 2 Fleet (Kondo)
C. Western Force (Ozawa)
D. Central Force (Hirose)
E. Eastern Force (Takahashi)
F. 14 Army (Homma)
G. USAFFE (MacArthur)
H. ABDA (Wavell), from 10 Jan 1942–25 Feb 1942
I. Malaya Command (Percival)
J. Carrier Striking Force 'Kido Butai' (Nagumo)

Naval Engagements

1. Sinking of *Prince of Wales* and *Repulse* (10 Dec 1941)
2. Balikpapan (23–4 Jan 1942)
3. Lombok Straits (18–19 Feb 1942)
4. Java Sea (27–8 Feb 1942)
5. Sunda Strait (28 Feb 1942)
6. Coral Sea (4–8 May 1942)
7. Midway (4 June 1942)

to the north, and at Aparri and Vigan in northern Luzon, allowed the transfer of elements of the 23rd Air Fleet from Formosa, extending Japanese air cover over the north and centre of the Philippines. In the south the seaplane base at Davao on Mindanao was destroyed by the light carrier *Ryujo*. The overall effect of these operations was threefold. First, they secured the main amphibious forces from American air and naval attack, and the subsequent landings on Luzon (23 December) forced an American retreat to the Bataan peninsula (where they surrendered on 9 April 1942). Second, they isolated the Philippines, thus preventing American reinforcement. Third, they provided flank protection and staging areas for the advance into the East Indies.

US and Japanese fleets, December 1941

	USA	Japan
Battleships	17	10
Aircraft carriers	7	10
Cruisers	37	36
Destroyers	171	113
Submarines	111	63

Concurrently with operations in the Philippines, attacks were launched against Thailand, Burma and Malaya. Operating from bases in occupied French Indo-China, the 22nd (Naval) Air Flotilla provided cover for landings along the Kra Isthmus. Naval forces were deployed in dispersed task groups – a typical feature of IJN operations. Direct support was provided by light forces of the Second Fleet, covered by a screen of submarines to the south. Heavier surface units under Vice-Admiral Nobutake Kondo (1886–1953) were in distant support. The sortie of the British capital ships *Prince of Wales* and *Repulse* briefly brought Kondo steaming south until aircraft sank the British ships on 10 December 1941. With their sea communications secure and having achieved air supremacy, Japanese ground forces ruthlessly destroyed British resistance on land. Singapore surrendered on 15 February 1942, and Burma was secured by late April.

As Philippine and Malayan operations progressed Vice-Admiral Kondo redeployed his naval forces into three groups to overrun the East Indies, encircle the main Allied position on Java and break the Malay Barrier. Accordingly, from 7 January 1942 Vice-Admiral Ibo Takahashi's (1888–1947) Eastern Force, forming the right-hand pincer, moved through the Molucca Sea, seizing airfields on Celebes at Menado, Kendari and Makassar by 8 February. In tandem, Rear Admiral Hirose's Central Force drove through the Makassar Strait, securing Balikpapan and Banjarmasin in south-east Borneo a week later. This completed the right-hand pincer of the encirclement, bringing the 21st Air Flotilla in range of Java. The left-hand pincer, under Vice-Admiral Jisaburo Ozawa (1886–1966), secured Bangka Island and Palembang (Sumatra) at the same time. The isolation of Java was completed when Nagumo's carriers obliterated the northern Australian port of Darwin on 19 February.

Allied naval forces proved remarkably, yet understandably, ineffective at opposing Japanese moves in the southern seas. Japanese air superiority made daylight surface operations risky. Confused night engagements occurred at Balikpapan (24 February) and off eastern Bali (18–19 February), but inexperience prevented Allied vessels inflicting heavy losses on exposed Japanese landing forces. Attempts to solve the problems of inter-Allied cooperation saw the creation of a Joint Striking Force under the Dutch Vice-Admiral Karel Van Doorman (1889–1942), and after several abortive sorties Doorman engaged Japanese units on 27–8 February in the Battle of the Java Sea. However, in a running clash repeated attempts to outflank the Japanese and engage their transports cost the Allies half their force. Defeat stemmed from a lack of common doctrine, poor command and signal arrangements, the obsolescence of many Allied warships and superb Japanese tactics. The surviving Allied vessels escaped or were lost in the subsequent engagement off the Sunda Strait. The final attack saw Japanese troops invade Java on 1 March; Allied resistance there ended a week later.

THE ROAD TO MIDWAY

As the first phase of operations drew to a close in March 1942 Japanese leaders had to confront a new situation. Although Japan had secured vital raw materials, in reality she had simply solved one strategic problem by replacing it with another. This was brought home to the Japanese in February, when US carriers launched raids against positions along the Japanese perimeter in the Pacific. These had perturbing implications for Tokyo. First, they demonstrated that the knock-out blow had failed, and that America and her Allies were not inclined to make a compromise peace. Second, they proved the vulnerability of the Japanese defensive perimeter to attack, and third, they showed that the US Pacific Fleet was still a threat. Individually, these factors were ominous, but taken together they led to a chilling conclusion: that Japanese plans for conducting the war were tactically, operationally and strategically flawed.

Although not fully comprehending this dire situation, Admiral Osami Nagano (1880–1947), Chief of the Naval Staff, and Admiral Isoroku Yamamoto, Commander-in-Chief of the Combined Fleet, were acutely aware of the need to force the war swiftly to a conclusion. Consequently, they abandoned a lengthy defensive strategy centred around the interceptive operation. But the two men were divided over where to attack. After bitter wrangling, a compromise was reached that seemed to satisfy the naval staff's preference for an attack in the south-west Pacific (Operation 'Mo') and the Combined Fleet's proposal to provoke a decisive battle with the US fleet by invading the Hawaiian island of Midway (Operation 'Mi'). The reality was that by going for several objectives the Imperial Navy undermined either operation's chance of success and presented the Americans with an opportunity to strike several counter-blows.

Staged in the south-west Pacific, Operation 'Mo' involved an amphibious attack against the Allied base at Port Moresby in southern New Guinea. Because two US carriers had been active in the area in March, the *Shokaku* and *Zuikaku* of the 5th Carrier Division were deployed to provide distant cover to the landing forces, with the light carrier *Shoho* in direct support. These forces gave the Japanese no margin of superiority, unnecessarily allowing the Americans to fight on equal terms. Aware of Japanese strength and intentions from Intelligence decrypts, Admiral Chester Nimitz (1885–1966), Commander-in-Chief of the Pacific Fleet and Pacific Ocean Areas, despatched Admiral Jack Fletcher's (1885–1973) Task Force 17, with the carriers *Lexington* and *Yorktown*, to intercept the Japanese. The subsequent Battle of the Coral Sea (5–8 May) was confused, being marked by mistakes and losses on both sides. However, although the Japanese won a tactical victory, sinking the heavy carrier *Lexington* and damaging the *Yorktown* for the loss of the *Shoho*, the mauling of the *Shokaku* and the carrier air groups confirmed the need to abandon Operation 'Mo' for lack of air cover. Of greater significance was the fact that the loss of the 5th Carrier Division critically weakened Japanese strength for the Midway operation.

Brushing aside the reverse at the Coral Sea, Yamamoto pressed on with operation 'Mi', which was expected to unfold in a series of predetermined phases. First, an attack against the Aleutian islands (Operation 'Al') was to divert American attention away from Midway. Second, the defences of Midway would be neutralised on 4 June by Nagumo's First Carrier Striking Group, and the island would be invaded two days later by forces from the south under Kondo. This would compel the US fleet to give battle, allowing it to be annihilated by superior Japanese strength.

The simplicity of the 'Mi' concept hides its myriad defects, of which three were critical. The idea that the Americans would uncover their key Hawaiian bases to defend the Aleutians was unrealistic, but to expect them to sacrifice their entire fleet for Midway was ludicrous. In addition, the whole plan expected the Americans to conform to Japanese expectations; there was no consideration that they might try to seize the initiative. Finally, dispersal of naval forces in separate task groups, in particular three light carriers, meant that Nagumo's vanguard was weak and exposed. The First Carrier Striking Group comprised just 4 carriers with 229 aircraft. Facing it, Nimitz had 3 carriers with 234 aircraft, to add to the 110 aircraft on Midway. The failure to concentrate his superior resources at the point of contact was Yamamoto's final and fatal error.

The battle of 4 June was decided in the first six hours. In this time the Japanese mounted one attack against Midway but were subjected to eight American air attacks, the last of which proved mortal. In 5 minutes the carriers *Kaga*, *Akagi* and *Soryu* were destroyed. Subsequent US attacks sank the last carrier *Hiryu* in the evening, although in return the *Yorktown* was crippled and later sunk. This crushing Japanese defeat is generally blamed on Nagumo's hesitant and contradictory orders, but this ignores the real issues. Yamamoto's plan left Nagumo without the strength simultaneously to conduct reconnaissance, neutralise Midway and effectively guard against US attack. The Japanese could deal with one of these tasks, not all, but American refusal to play by Yamamoto's timetable demanded that they do so. Nimitz's forces were able to exploit superior reconnaissance, a general

The Japanese carrier Kaga *was originally designed as a battlecruiser, but was converted after the Washington Treaty of 1922.* Kaga *took part in the Pearl Harbor operation, but was sunk at Midway on 4 June 1942. Her loss resulted from a combination of flawed design and circumstance. Hit by four 1000lb bombs, her lack of structural defences, damage control personnel and fire fighting equipment meant that fires spread quickly through hangars full of ordnance and fuel lines. She finally sank when her aviation fuel tanks exploded. (RMAS Collection)*

idea of the enemy's location and the advantages of position and surprise, all of which were assisted by luck. At Midway the Japanese paid the price for ignoring the two eternal characteristics of war: chance and friction.

Our forces suffered a defeat so decisive and so grave that the details were kept . . . [a] guarded secret . . . Even after the war, few among high-ranking officers were familiar with the details of the Midway operation.'

Admiral Nobutake Kondo

STALEMATE: THE SOUTH-WEST PACIFIC, AUGUST 1942–SEPTEMBER 1943

The US victory at Midway was not the decisive turning point of the Pacific war. Despite its losses, the Japanese Navy still possessed a formidable array of warships, as well as highly trained personnel (over half the aircrew involved survived Midway). By contrast, the US Navy remained weak. Rather, the critical period of the war occurred in attritional fighting in the south-west Pacific between August 1942 and November 1943. In this period US naval and air force units established a growing quantitative and qualitative superiority that laid the foundations for a series of dramatic victories in 1944 and for the defeat of Japan the following year.

In mid-1942 lack of resources led both sides to settle upon a series of limited offensives in the south-west Pacific. American landings on Tulagi and Guadalcanal on 6–7 August and the establishment of an airbase at Henderson Field began a bitter struggle for control of the southern Solomons. The critical period of this campaign lasted from August to late November 1942, although the Japanese did not acknowledge defeat by evacuating their forces until February 1943. Mid-1943 then saw the Americans consolidate their positions in the lower Solomons, developing an effective logistic infrastructure for subsequent advances into the central and northern islands in the group. From July to September 1943 Allied forces gradually pushed northwards, seizing forward airbases on the Russell Islands, New Georgia, Vella Lavella and the Treasurys. Allied commanders bypassed the most heavily defended Japanese positions whenever possible, isolating them with air and naval forces and leaving them to 'wither on the vine'. This technique unhinged Japanese plans to hold the Americans in a series of costly attritional battles. The establishment of airstrips at Empress Augusta Bay (on Bougainville) in November 1943 signalled the start of the final neutralisation of Japanese air and naval forces at Rabaul.

The success of Allied operations in the Solomons obscures the narrow margin between defeat and victory in the initial operations around Guadalcanal. Until October 1942 inadequate logistic infrastructure in the south-west Pacific, as well as shipping shortages and a paucity of combat units, threatened Operation 'Watchtower' with defeat. The failure of Imperial General Headquarters to concentrate its superior forces to exploit American vulnerability was also a major strategic blunder. Three factors help to explain this state of affairs. First, poor Intelligence led the Japanese to believe that this was only a minor operation. This linked with the second factor, which was a belief that the Americans could not mount a major offensive until late 1943 and that forces had to be preserved until then for a decisive battle. Third, the south-west Pacific was not considered to be the location for the anticipated decisive battle. This meant that local forces were left to deal with the situation until late 1942. The 18th Army at Rabaul

Admiral Isoroku Yamamoto (1884–1943). Yamamoto was a fervent supporter of naval aviation who believed that the days of the battleship were over. Rightly pessimistic about Japan's chances in any prolonged war with the USA, he tried to deal a knockout blow by planning and executing an attack on the American naval base at Pearl Harbor, Hawaii. Although the raid was a tactical success, it failed to achieve its strategic objectives, and by the late summer of 1942 Japanese forces were on the defensive. Yamamoto himself was killed on 18 April 1943 when the aeroplane in which he was travelling was shot down by US fighters in the Solomons. (US National Archives)

OPERATIONS IN THE SOUTH-WEST PACIFIC, AUGUST 1942–APRIL 1943

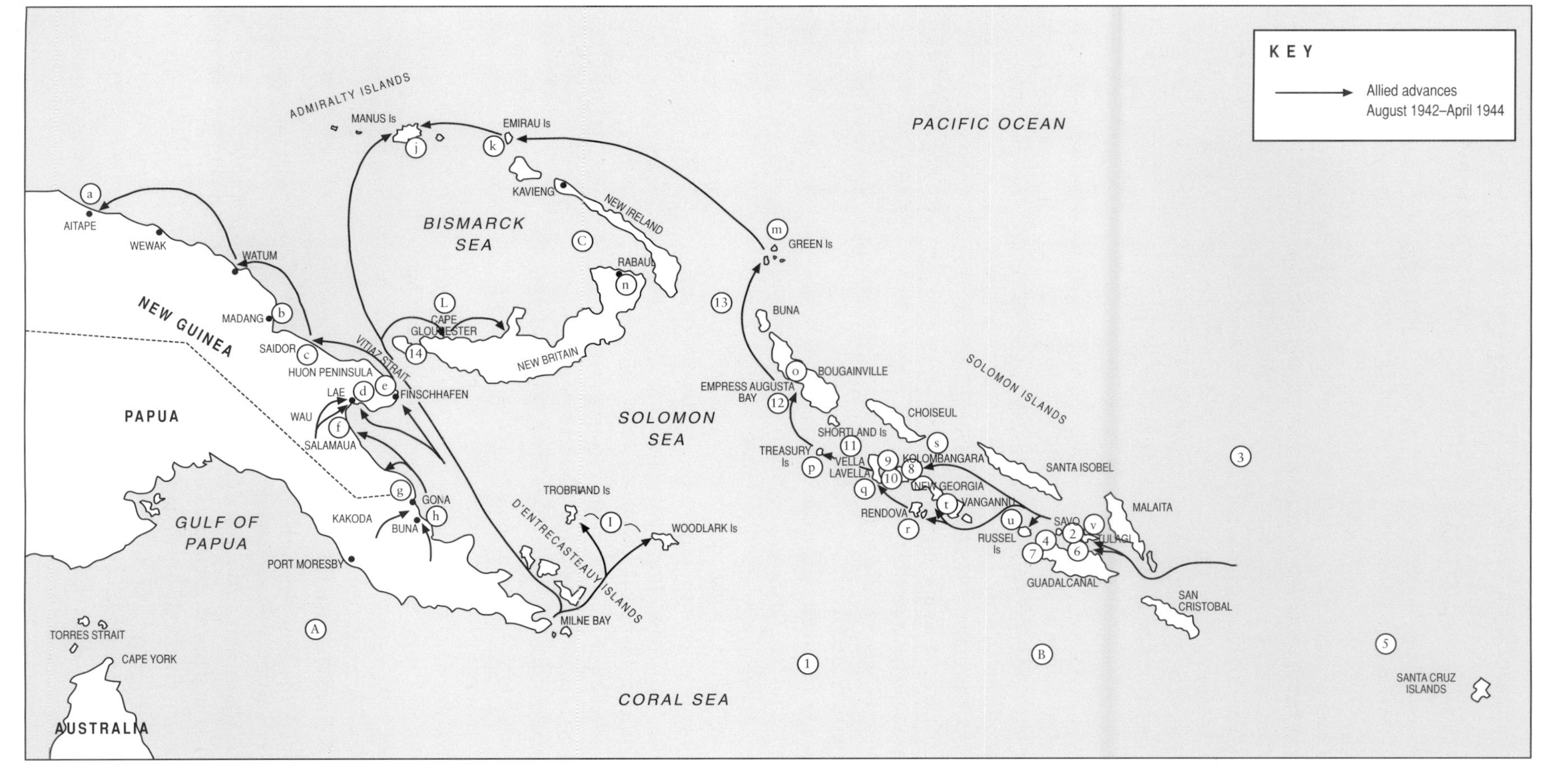

Dates generally numbered from left to right in ascending order.

a. 22 April 1944, US landings at Aitape
b. 25 April 1944, Australian forces secure Madang
c. 2 Jan 1944, US landings at Saidor
d. 16 Sept 1943, Allied forces secure Lae
e. 22 Sept 1943, Australian forces land at Finschhaffen. Secured by 2 Oct 1943
f. 12 Sept 1943, US forces secure Salamaua
g. 9 Dec 1942, Australian forces secure Gona
h. 2 Jan 1943, US forces capture Buna
i. 23 June 1943, US forces secure Woodlark and Trobriand Is
j. 29 Feb 1944, US landings at Los Negros, Manus secured by 25 March 1944
k. 20 March 1944, US forces occupy Emirau
l. 26 Dec 1943, US forces land at Cape Gloucester
m. 15/20 Feb 1944, New Zealand forces secure Green Islands
n. March 1944–Sept 1945, Rabaul besieged
o. 1 Nov 1943, US landings at Empress Augusta Bay on Bougainville. The island was never fully secured
p. 27 Oct 1943, Allied landings in the Treasury Islands
q. 15 Aug 1943, US landings on Vella Lavella
r. 30 June 1943, US landings on Rendova
s. 4/5 July 1943, US and Japanese landings at Kula Gulf (New Georgia)
t. 21 June 1943, US landings on New Georgia
u. 21 Feb 1943, US forces secure Russell Islands
v. 7 Aug 1942, US landings on Tulagi and Guadalcanal

Formations (including commanding officers' names in brackets)

A. South-West Pacific Area (MacArthur)
B. South Pacific Area (Ghormley, later Halsey)
C. Eighth Japanese Area Army (Imamura)

Naval Engagements

1. Coral Sea (4–8 May 1942)
2. Savo Island (Aug 1942)
3. Eastern Solomons (22–25 Aug 1942)
4. Cape Esperance (11/12 Oct 1942)
5. Santa Cruz (25–6 Oct 1942)
6. First and Second Guadalcanal (12/13, 14/15 Nov 1942)
7. Cape Tassafaronga (30/31 Nov 1942)
8. Kula Gulf (6 July 1943)
9. Kolombangara (13 July 1943)
10. First Vella Gulf (6/7 Aug 1943)
11. Second Vella Gulf (6/7 Oct 1943)
12. Empress Augusta Bay (1/2 Nov 1943)
13. Cape St George (25 Nov 1943)
14. Bismarck Sea (2–4 March 1943)

reacted swiftly to Allied advances in August, but a tendency to commit forces in a piecemeal manner saw a series of poorly conducted offensives in August, September and late October fail to retake Guadalcanal. Not until November did Imperial General Headquarters recognise that the battle for Guadalcanal was a decisive one, and by this time American military strength had reached a level that guaranteed US victory. The defeat of a last-minute attempt to land 30,000 Japanese troops on Guadalcanal only confirmed growing American superiority in the lower Solomons.

Also critical to the issue of victory or defeat around Guadalcanal and the Solomons was the ability of each side to move troops and supplies by ship, something which arose from a series of struggles for control of the air and sea. The inability of the Japanese to secure air superiority stemmed mainly from the fact that their aircraft from Rabaul had to operate at the extreme limit of their range. This reduced the number of missions flown and led to piecemeal and uncoordinated attacks. Failure to construct large mutually supporting air bases throughout the Solomons exacerbated these problems in the early stages of fighting around Guadalcanal. Consequently, Allied air power on Guadalcanal interdicted Japanese shipping, restricting them to night runs using fast destroyers. The so-called 'Tokyo Express' proved incapable of supplying Japanese forces and many troops died from disease and starvation. Desperate attempts to neutralise Henderson airfield with naval bombardments illustrate the failure of Japanese air power. In the course of these operations the IJN suffered defeat at the Battle of Cape Esperance (11–12 October).

In 1943 newly completed bases in the central and northern Solomons proved too small and exposed to frustrate Allied operations. Japanese air offensives in April and July, supported by disembarked carrier aircraft at Rabaul, failed to regain command of the air, and the heavy losses suffered among experienced aircrew led to a steady decline in Japanese combat effectiveness.

At sea a series of naval engagements fought in 1942 and 1943 saw the Japanese Navy fail to establish command of the waters around the Solomons. Despite possessing overwhelming qualitative and quantitative superiority, belief in the need to preserve strength for a future decisive battle led to IJN forces being committed piecemeal. Naval operations were also characterised by poor strategic direction and lack of inter-service cooperation. At Savo Island (9 August 1942) the Japanese Navy inflicted a heavy defeat on Allied forces, but failed to follow up this success by destroying the exposed transports off Tulagi. In the Battle of the Eastern Solomons (22–5 August) Yamamoto's dispersal of forces in isolated task groups, and orders simultaneously to protect the transports and destroy the

THE ASSASSINATION OF ADMIRAL ISOROKU YAMAMOTO

In early 1943 Admiral Isoroku Yamamoto, Commander-in-Chief of the Combined Fleet, decided to undertake a personal inspection of forward positions in the northern Solomons. Admiral Nimitz learned of his rival's intentions from Intelligence decrypts and ordered long-range P-38 'Lightning' fighters of the 339th Fighter Squadron from Guadalcanal to shoot Yamamoto's aircraft down. On 18 April the Americans intercepted the two G4M 'Betty' bombers carrying the admiral and his staff as they prepared to land on Bougainville. Yamamoto was killed. The impact of his death on the course of the Pacific war, however, is generally overstated. His conduct of operations in 1942 and 1943 revealed the same errors of judgement that typified his successors, raising doubts about subsequent claims that he was one of the great naval commanders of history.

'There is no question that Japan's doom was sealed with the closing of the struggle for Guadalcanal.'

Vice-Admiral Raizo Tanaka, Imperial Japanese Navy, Struggle for Guadalcanal *(1956)*

US fleet resulted in a draw. The carriers *Enterprise* (USN) and *Shokaku* (IJN) were damaged while the Japanese light carrier *Ryujo* was sunk. Yamamoto's reluctance to commit his superior battlefleet to the two Guadalcanal cruiser-battleship night actions of 12/13 and 14/15 November also missed an opportunity to inflict a decisive blow against US naval forces, while lack of inter-service cooperation further frustrated operations.

Rather than directly supporting the Army's attempt to retake Guadalcanal in October, the Japanese Combined Fleet sought to engage the US fleet in a decisive battle. Santa Cruz (25–6 October), however, was a brutal mêlée in which both sides lunged at each other in a series of piecemeal and poorly coordinated assaults. The Americans damaged two Japanese carriers, but had one of their own badly hit and another sunk. This time lack of fuel prevented the Japanese exploiting their narrow success. Tactically the Japanese did hold their own against the Americans, scoring a series of victories over the US Navy in 1942 off Cape Tassafaronga (30–1 November) and in 1943 at Kula Gulf (6 July) and Second Vella Gulf (6–7 October). At Kolombangara (13 July) they managed to grab a draw after an initial reverse. However, defeats at First Vella Gulf (6–7 August), Empress Augusta Bay (2 November) and Cape St George (25 November) meant that the Japanese never seriously disrupted the US advance in the central and northern Solomons.

In August 1942 the need to concentrate forces at Guadalcanal forced the Japanese in New Guinea to abandon an overland advance on Port Moresby. In September, with the enemy on the back foot, Allied forces began a series of offensives northwards that culminated with the capture of Buna in January 1943. Aircraft operating from Buna and other new bases then defeated Japanese troopships at the Battle of the Bismarck Sea (2–4 March 1943), emphasising Allied air superiority and isolating Japanese forces in central New Guinea from outside reinforcement. After a period of re-organisation and reinforcement the Allied advance on Rabaul recommenced in late 1943. Operations were characterised by initial attacks from the Fifth Air Force to neutralise Japanese air power, followed by American and Australian ground forces seizing forward airbases from which the next advance would be staged. In August and September, Lae and Wau were taken by converging attacks inland and by landings by the VII Amphibious Corps. Finschaffen fell in October, and subsequent advances along the Huon peninsula neutralised Japanese forces in central New Guinea. Seizure of positions at Cape Gloucester in December 1943 and the Admiralty Islands in March 1944 completed the encirclement of Rabaul from the west. On 12 March 1944, however, Allied commanders cancelled the attack on Rabaul, preferring to neutralise Japanese forces there and on neighbouring New Ireland. These garrisons remained besieged until their surrender at the end of the war in September 1945.

A NEW STRATEGIC BALANCE, 1943–4

In 1943, before the ring closed around Rabaul, the Japanese officially ended operations to consolidate their perimeter in the Pacific, and shifted to the strategic defensive. Superficially, this decision seemed sound. After two years of war the Allies had made only minor inroads against Japanese outposts in the south-west Pacific, and had yet to engage the principal line of defence along the New Guinea–Rabaul–Marshall Islands axis. Imperial General Headquarters was confident in its ability to wear down Allied forces in a war of attrition along this line. Central to Japanese strategy was the belief that Allied advances would continue to be protracted and localised, giving them time to reinforce a threatened sector. Furthermore, although Japanese losses in 1942–3 had been heavy, they were not exorbitant and in time could be replaced. Critical to defending the Japanese perimeter was the fact that the Combined Fleet remained a powerful and balanced force. Its new commander, Admiral Mineichi Koga (1885–1944), was confident of defeating the US fleet in a decisive battle.

In reality, the growing impact of US industrial and technical resources meant that the strategic situation in the Pacific in 1943 was radically different to the way in which it was perceived by the Japanese High Command. By late 1943 American resources were sufficient to mount simultaneous offensives in the south-west and central Pacific, yet the Japanese did not have the ability to counter either of these, let alone both. The Americans also possessed the capability to descend on any part of the Japanese perimeter and overwhelm local defences before the Japanese could react. This situation was exacerbated by the decline in the Combined Fleet's combat power, which was caused by block obsolescence among its destroyer units and carrier-borne aircraft. Similar problems threatened elements of the battle line in the near future. Yet Japan lacked the industrial resources to replace her wartime ship losses, let alone to undertake a large-scale fleet modernisation. When this was set alongside US naval and aircraft production, the IJN's fate was sealed. While the Japanese struggled to regain their pre-war strength in fleet and light carriers, by the end of 1943 American strength had increased threefold, despite war losses, with more on the way. By the time the Imperial Navy's desire for decisive battle was finally realised in June and October 1944, the balance had shifted significantly in favour of the US Navy.

US and Japanese naval construction, 1942–5 (ships built)

	USA	Japan
Battleships	10	2
Aircraft carriers	137	13
Cruisers	48	5
Destroyers	349	55
Submarines	203	121

THE ADVANCE TO THE PHILIPPINES, NOVEMBER 1943–OCTOBER 1944

US operations in the central Pacific began on 20 November 1943 with landings on Makin and Tarawa in the Gilbert Islands. Operation 'Galvanic' was a success and set the pattern for future American advances across the islands of the central Pacific in 1944. In the weeks prior to the landings land- and carrier-based aircraft bombarded the islands, isolating them from reinforcement, neutralising local Japanese air power and softening up ground defences. Although Tarawa saw bitter fighting, pre-war US Marine Corps amphibious assault doctrine was largely vindicated. Lessons learned at Tarawa were successfully applied in January and February 1944 against the Marshall Islands of Kwajalein, Roi-Namur and Majuro (Operation 'Flintlock'), and Eniwetok (Operation 'Catchpole'). Japanese garrisons on the neighbouring islands of Wotje, Maloelap, Mili and Jaluit were neutralised by local US air and naval forces.

AMPHIBIOUS OPERATIONS

The success of US amphibious operations in the Pacific war stemmed from techniques developed by the United States Marine Corps (USMC) during the inter-war years. Difficulties experienced during the First World War in conducting large amphibious assault landings created a widespread belief that they were no longer viable in modern war. The USMC, needing to justify its continued existence in a period of financial stringency and believing that a future war in the Pacific would hinge on the ability to secure advanced island bases, worked to resolve the problems of opposed beach landings. In the 1920s and 1930s officers such as Lieutenant-Colonel Earl H. Ellis (1880–1923) carried out theoretical and practical exercises to develop a coherent doctrine for amphibious operations. The result was the 1934 *Tentative Landing Operations Manual*, which in 1938 became *FTP-167, Landings Operations, US Navy*. The marines identified, and tried to provide solutions to, six primary problems: command arrangements, naval gunfire support, close air support, ship-to-shore movement, securing a viable beachhead and logistical matters. The solutions put forward were largely vindicated during the war. In matters such as combat loading of supplies the USMC was startlingly original, although in the area of close air support it fell short because of the limits of existing technology. Subject to minor revisions in 1940 and after Tarawa in 1943, these documents served as the basis for American and Allied landing operations in all theatres throughout the Second World War.

US forces land on Iwo Jima during Operation 'Detachment', 19 February 1945. This photograph illustrates the importance of careful planning and coordination of the various elements of the attacking force, as several waves of assault vehicles approach the beach under close cover from two destroyers. At Iwo Jima 9,000 US Marines were landed on the island in just 45 minutes. (US Navy)

The speed of the US advance caught the Japanese by surprise, throwing them off balance and exposing the weaknesses of the interceptive operation. The string of islands along the Japanese perimeter lacked individual strength, and were not mutually supporting or arranged in depth. In short, the perimeter consisted of a series of disconnected and easily isolated strongpoints; it was a series of holes, not a barrier. The Combined Fleet could offer no support because its carriers had not replaced their losses at Rabaul. When US carrier groups raided the main base at Truk in the Carolines in early February 1944 (Operation 'Hailstone') Koga's forces beat a hasty retreat westwards to the Palau Islands.

The last surviving pre-war US carrier, USS Enterprise *(far right), cuts a solitary figure among the new Essex class carriers and fast battleships (and, in foreground, an escort carrier) of the Pacific Fleet. The awesome scale of American naval power portrayed in this photograph goes a long way to explaining the IJN's defeat in the Pacific War. (IWM NYF22732)*

Logistics and firepower were the sinews of American military strength in the Pacific War. Here a US landing craft unloads an M3 half-track armed with a 105 mm gun and several machine guns. As the war progressed US engineers developed techniques that allowed them to bring transport vessels right up to the beach to land troops and supplies, facilitating the rapid concentration of force necessary to achieve their objectives and conserving shipping resources, which otherwise threatened to become overstretched. (via Tank Museum)

US fast carrier attacks against Japanese positions in the Pacific intensified throughout 1943–4 as more carriers, improved tactics and better logistics increased the power and scope of US operations. Grouping carriers together for mutual support in task groups, rather than operating them individually, greatly improved their offensive and defensive capabilities. Tactically, US commanders saturated enemy defences with attacking aircraft, proving that, 'the more you use, the less you use'. Between 1 November 1943 and 30 April 1944 fast carrier groups attacked twenty-five major targets over an area of approximately 3½ million square miles. During the Marshalls landings, in 24 days they conducted something in the region of 11,000 sorties, against 10 major targets spread over 168,000 square miles, losing just over 90 aircraft (half in combat). The damage that these raids inflicted is difficult to assess accurately, but at Truk in twenty-four hours (17–18 February), they destroyed around 250 aircraft and sank approximately 200,000 tons of merchant shipping for negligible loss.

The ability to conduct operations of such scale and intensity across the vast Pacific ocean with only a few major bases was the product of innovative logistic measures. US engineers developed techniques for building forward bases quickly on new positions. The advanced mobile bases were staging posts for supplies and materiel needed in the combat zone. Construction of floating dry docks facilitated repair of shipping near the front. When new positions were seized, the mobile bases were brought forward to establish new supply lines. At sea the carriers relied upon a fleet train consisting of tankers, cargo, hospital and repair ships, and escort carriers which provided replacement aircraft. After January 1944 the fast carrier groups did not return to Pearl Harbor until the war ended.

The neutralisation of Truk and the Caroline Islands by aircraft based in the Marshalls, coupled with their isolation from the south by Allied advances in New Guinea, led to the decision to bypass them altogether. In June US forces struck at Saipan, Tinian and Guam (Operation 'Forager') in the Marianas to establish forward bases for the invasion of the Philippines or Formosa. US submarines and long-range B-29 Superfortress aircraft based in these islands would make a major contribution to the defeat of Japan.

The American landings brought them into contact with the main Japanese defence line of Halamhera–Biak–Palau–Mariana. The establishment of yet another 'main line' along which to fight the decisive battle reflected a Japanese strategy for conduct of the war that might best be described as progressively unrealistic. Since mid-1943 the Japanese High Command had delineated numerous points where the decisive battle would be fought, and successively abandoned each. In May 1944 the Combined Fleet intended to fight in the area of Palau or the Western Carolines, where it could be supported by land-based air power. Yet typically, the hesitant reaction of the Navy to an American attack against Biak, followed by the attack in the Marianas, undermined Japanese plans.

The strategic significance of the Marianas in relation to the Philippines and Japan's maritime communications to South-East Asia meant that the Imperial Navy had to offer battle. Vice-Admiral Jisaburo Ozawa's First Mobile Fleet had 9 carriers with a complement of 450 aircraft to confront Admiral Raymond Spruance's (1886–1969) Fifth Fleet of 15 carriers and

900 aircraft. Ozawa intended to use the longer range of his lighter carrier aircraft to engage the Americans before their aircraft were in range. Once the US carriers were defeated, heavy surface units would attack the amphibious forces. The initial attack was to be made in cooperation with land-based aircraft in the Marianas, thereby engaging the Americans on both flanks and restricting their ability to manoeuvre and counter-attack.

Ozawa's operational concept fell apart for several reasons. US carrier forces had already neutralised local land-based air power, leaving the Fifth Fleet free to manoeuvre and in possession of numerical superiority. Japanese forces needed surprise in order to locate the enemy and deliver the first blow before the US carriers could close the range. However, Spruance was aware of Ozawa's approach and general location from signals Intelligence and submarine reports. Divided between engaging the Japanese fleet and protecting the transports, and aware of the Japanese predilection for using decoys to hide a final attack by concealed units, Spruance retired eastwards rather than close with Ozawa on 18 June. Critics have argued that this was a mistake because it surrendered the initiative to the Japanese, allowing them to mount a long-range first strike on 19 June before US scout planes had relocated them. The validity of these comments is debatable, especially in light of US defensive superiority based on radar, massive anti-aircraft firepower, aircraft numbers and pilot quality. In the resulting battle inexperienced and outnumbered Japanese pilots were overwhelmed by technically and qualitatively superior US air power. The Battle of the Philippine Sea (19–21 June) was one of the most one-sided naval engagements in history. Although only two Japanese carriers were lost and three damaged by US counter attacks on 20–1 June, the near total annihilation of Japanese naval aviation was a blow from which the Imperial Navy never recovered.

'Hell is on us.'

Mamoru Shigemitsu, Japanese Foreign Minister, following the Battle of the Marianas

THE INVASION OF THE PHILIPPINES AND THE BATTLE OF LEYTE GULF, 23–8 OCTOBER 1944

In July 1944 the American High Command debated whether to invade Formosa or the Philippines in order to sever Japanese shipping routes to the vital raw materials of the East Indies. The problems inherent in landings on Formosa and US leaders' feelings of a moral duty to liberate the Philippines, led to the decision to invade the southern island of Mindanao on 15 November 1944.

Preliminary operations in September saw landings on Morotai (to provide forward airbases near New Guinea) and the Palau Islands (to secure the right flank of Philippine operations). In late August and early September attacks by Admiral William Halsey's (1882–1959) Third Fleet on the Visayan Islands in the central Philippines revealed the weakness of Japanese defences in this area. Consequently, the invasion of the Philippines was brought forward to 20 October and switched to the central island of Leyte. Although this decision made the Palau operation unnecessary, Nimitz's insistence that it take place resulted in heavy American losses. It was his only strategic error of the war.

The landings at Leyte Gulf on 20 October involved troops despatched from bases as distant as Hollandia (1,250 miles) and Manus (1,500 miles).

'I will break into Leyte Gulf and fight to the last man . . . would it not be shameful to have the fleet remaining intact while our nation perishes.'

Admiral Takeo Kurita

Leyte Gulf: the cost (vessels lost)

	USA	Japan
Fleet carriers	–	4
Escort carriers	2	–
Battleships	–	3
Heavy cruisers	–	6
Light cruisers	1	4
Destroyers	3	11

To cope with an accelerated timetable and to support it, this converging armada required a vast logistical effort, which was understandably not without its problems. Covering the invasion were the Third and Seventh Fleets with a combined strength of 35 fleet, light and escort carriers operating over 1,500 aircraft, supported by 12 battleships and over 140 cruisers and destroyers.

The threat posed to Japanese communications with the East Indies by US occupation of the Philippines forced the Imperial Navy to give battle. Realising the vast disparity in forces, Japanese commanders had no expectations of winning a decisive battle, and at best hoped to break up the landings in Leyte Gulf. To achieve this, Ozawa's decoy force of four carriers (operating just 116 aircraft) was to lure the American fleet northwards, thereby uncovering the approaches to Leyte Gulf for powerful surface units. Passing north of Leyte via the San Bernando Strait, Admiral Takeo Kurita's (1889–1977) First Attack Force was to unite with Vice-Admiral Shoji Nishimura's (1889–1944) Central Force. Vice-Admiral Kiyohide Shima's Second Attack Force was to come via Surigao Strait in the south to destroy the lightly protected transports in Leyte Gulf. The 'Sho' (victory) plan involved the majority of the Japanese Navy's remaining forces – in total 9 battleships, 20 cruisers and 35 destroyers. Even the superbattleships *Yamato* and *Musashi*, which had spent most of the war at anchor awaiting the decisive battle, were committed to what was essentially a mass suicide mission.

The Battle of Leyte Gulf (23–8 October 1944) was the largest naval engagement in history, fought over 178,000 square miles and lasting over six days. It witnessed the end of the Imperial Japanese Navy as an effective fighting force. In the face of overwhelming US naval and air power the Japanese were doomed to failure; that they came close to partial success stemmed more from the poor judgement of Admiral Halsey than from Japanese abilities.

During the battle the Japanese were unable to ensure the careful integration of all the elements of their plan and this was essential if there was to be even the remotest chance of success. Ozawa's Decoy Force initially failed to divert the Third Fleet's carriers northwards away from Leyte. Destruction of land-based Japanese aircraft in the days prior to the battle denied Kurita any protection against the American planes. Consequently, US submarines and carrier aircraft located Kurita's Central Force and subjected it to heavy attacks during 23 and 24 October. The high rate of attrition inflicted on the Central Force compelled it to make a temporary withdrawal westwards. It was only late on 24 October that Halsey's scouts located Ozawa's Decoy Force, and only when he was confident that the threat from Kurita had been neutralised did he rush his carriers northwards. The ensuing engagement off Cape Engano on 25 October was totally one-sided with Ozawa losing all his carriers, while the rest of his ships escaped destruction only because a crisis to the south forced Halsey to abandon the pursuit.

Initial operations in the south went favourably for the Americans. On 24–5 October, off Surigao Strait, in a fierce night action Nishimura and Kiyohide Shima's forces – advancing separately and unable to manoeuvre in the narrow strait – were overwhelmed by Admiral Thomas Kincaid's (1888–1972) Seventh Fleet. Although this secured the forces in Leyte Gulf against an attack from the south, Halsey's failure to station covering forces off San Bernando Strait allowed Kurita to double back during the night of 24–5 October and attempt to enter Leyte Gulf. That Halsey did not pay severely for his negligence was due to the outstanding fight put up by US escort carrier groups off Samar. During several hours of fighting these carriers and their escorting destroyers, under direct fire from Japanese naval guns, repeatedly attacked Kurita's forces, disrupting and diverting his advance on Leyte. The weight of the American onslaught, lack of information about who and what he was engaging, and heavy casualties convinced Kurita to break off the action and retire. Considering the nature of his orders, and the general resolve with which Japanese forces pressed home suicide attacks throughout the war, Kurita's withdrawal to conserve his strength appears ironic. It was also pointless. There was nothing to be gained by saving the ships of a beaten navy to fight another day.

Explaining Halsey's error in leaving the San Bernando Strait unprotected is problematic. Although Halsey's orders instructed him to make the destruction of Japanese naval forces his main aim, this did not absolve him from other missions, particularly his instructions that 'Forces of Pacific Ocean Areas will cover and support forces of the South West Pacific'. Accommodating these diverging demands required Halsey to execute careful judgement in deploying his forces. His failure to do so deserves censure, especially in light of the fact that there were more than adequate resources to accomplish both tasks. This raises the possibility that Halsey's mistakes stemmed from the fact that the scale of operations at Leyte was beyond his capabilities as a commander to manage.

'In case opportunity for destruction of a major portion of the enemy fleet is offered, or can be created, such destruction becomes the primary task.'

Admiral Nimitz's orders to Admiral Halsey before the Battle of Leyte Gulf

THE BLOCKADE AND DEFEAT OF JAPAN

The loss of 4 carriers, 3 battleships, 10 cruisers and supporting vessels, totalling 320,000 tons, at Leyte Gulf effectively destroyed the Imperial Navy as a fighting force. For the remainder of the war its ships were able to conduct only minor operations outside the reach of US naval forces. At the same time, Leyte's significance should be judged not only in terms of the crippling blow delivered during the battle, but with reference to the destruction of naval and merchant shipping around the Philippines that preceded and followed it. In the month after the battle the Imperial Navy suffered a further 129,000 tons of losses. In October and November 1944 US carrier and submarine forces sank 424,156 tons of merchant shipping in theatre. Total shipping losses in the entire Pacific for this period amounted to over 893,000 tons. When considered alongside Japanese shipping resources of just 3 million tons and basic import requirements of over 2 million tons, the loss in sixty-one days of just under 30 per cent of its shipping was a devastating blow to Japan's already parlous strategic position.

The maritime blockade of Japan was an important factor in her eventual defeat, and stands as one of the few successful commerce wars in history. Like Britain in the Second World War, as an island nation Japan was totally dependent upon overseas imports of food and raw materials, and acquiring these had been a key motive behind the decision to go to

The blockade of Japan

Number of Japanese merchant ships sunk by US submarines	1,178
Merchant tonnage sunk	5,053,491 tons
Number of Japanese naval vessels sunk by US submarines	214
Naval tonnage sunk	577,626 tons

Dates numbered from left to right in ascending order

a. Dec 1944, start of British 14th Army offensive to liberate Burma
b. 3 May 1945 British liberate Rangoon
c. 9 Aug 1945, Soviet Forces invade Manchuria
d. 1 July 1945, Australian forces land in British North Borneo
e. 1 May 1945, Australian forces land at Tarakan
f. 10 June 1945, Australian forces land at Balikpapan
g. 19 Aug 1945, farthest advances of Soviet forces by the end of hostilities
h. 9 Jan 1945, US landings in Lingayen Gulf
i. 6 Feb 1945 Manila declared secure/3 March 1945 Manila actually secured
j. 1 April 1945, US forces land on Okinawa ('Iceberg')
k. 20 Oct 1944, US landings on Leyte
l. 15 Sept 1944, US landings on Morotai
m. 19 Feb 1945, US landings on Iwo Jima
n. 15 June 1944, US landings on Saipan
o. 27 July 1944, US landings on Tinian
p. 21 July 1944, US landings on Guam
q. 22 Sept 1944, US landings on Ulithi
r. 15 Sept 1944, US landings on Palau
s. 15 Sept 1944, US landings on Morotai
t. 27 May 1944, US landings on Biak
u. 22 April 1944, US landings at Aitape and Hollandia
v. 29 Feb 1944, US landings on Manus
w. 1 Nov 1943, US landings on Bougainville
x. Feb–Oct 1943, general Allied advances in the Solomons
y. 6–7 Aug 1942, US landings on Tulagi and Guadalcanal.
z. 17 Feb 1944, US landings on Eniwetok
aa. 1 Feb 1944, US landings on Kwajalein atoll
bb. 31 Jan 1944, US landings on Majuro
cc. 20 Nov 1943, US landings on Makin and Tarawa
dd. 18–20 Aug 1945, Soviet invasion of south Sakhalin Island and the Kurile Islands
ee. 11 May and 15 Aug 1943, US landings on Attu and Kiska
ff. 1 Nov 1945, projected invasion of Kyushu, 'Operation Olympic'
gg. March 1946, projected landings on Honshu, 'Operation Coronet'

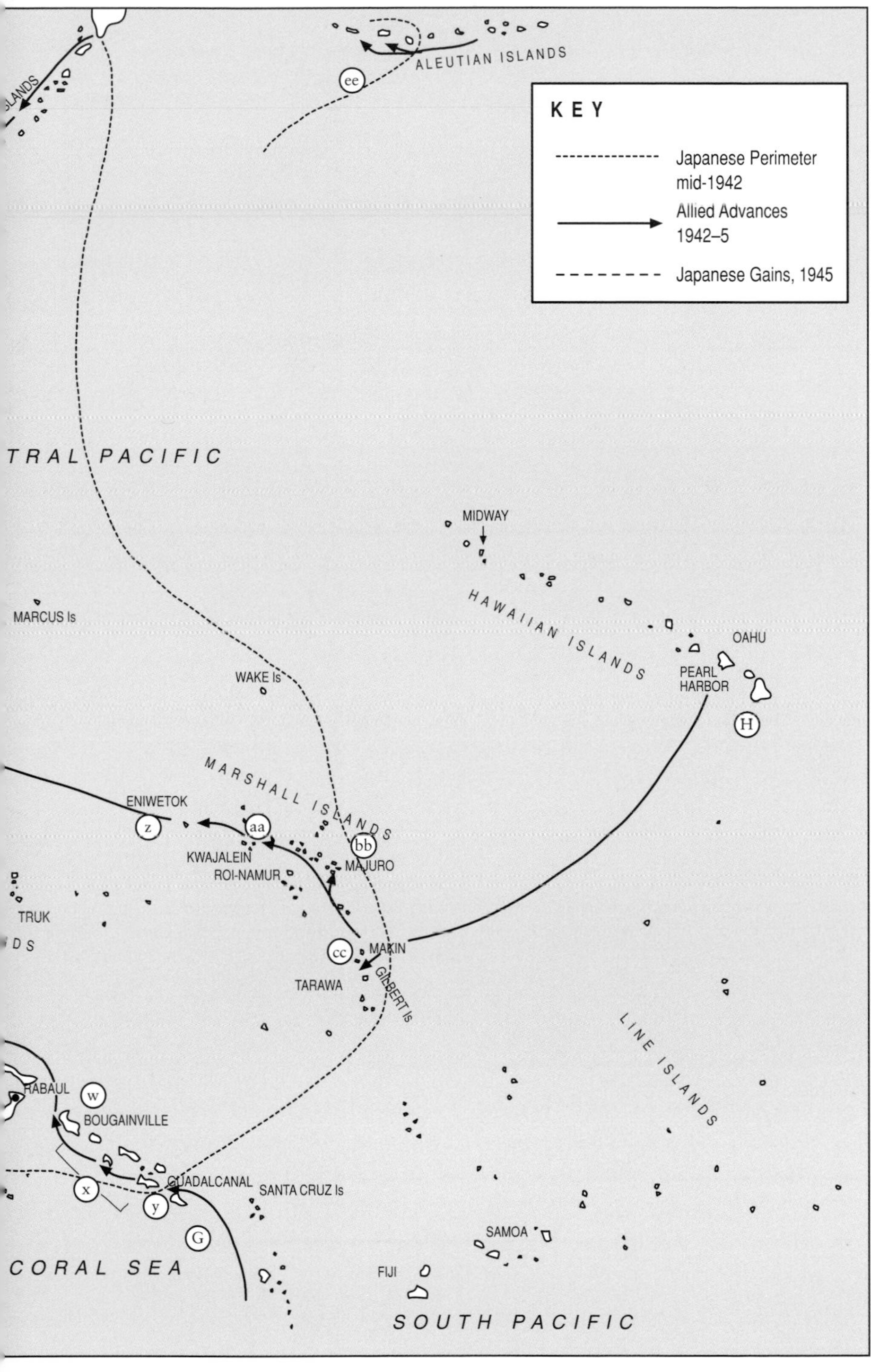

Formations conducting operations (commander's names in brackets)

A. British Imperial 14th Army (Slim)
B. Japanese Burma Area Army (Kawabe)
C. Soviet Far Eastern Command (Vasilevsky)
D. Japanese Kwantung Army (Yamada)
E. Japanese 'Chinese Expeditionary Force'
F. South-west Pacific Area (MacArthur)
G. South Pacific Area (Ghormley then Halsey)
H. Three separate commands – Pacific Ocean Areas (Nimitz) Pacific Fleet (Nimitz) Army Forces Pacific (Richardson)

Major Engagements

1. 19–21 June 1944 Philippine Sea
2. 23–8 Oct 1944, Leyte Gulf. This engagement consisted of three distinct actions. These are 3) Cape Engano, 25 Oct; 4) Samar, 25 Oct; 5) Surigao Strait, 25 Oct
6. 25 July 1945, Battle of the Inland Sea

'I pay my respects to the greatness of American mass production. I think that . . . this war will be decided by production power.'

Lieutenant-General Kuribayashi, Japanese commander on Iwo Jima

From early in the war it was clear that the Japanese had barely enough shipping to supply domestic needs and support their forces across the huge areas conquered in 1941–2. When merchant vessel losses began to accelerate in 1943 their problems became insurmountable. This series of photographs shows the sinking of the large troopship Teiko Maru *by the US submarine* Puffer *in February 1944. (US National Archives)*

war in 1941. Yet, from the outbreak of hostilities Japanese shipping resources of just under 7 million tons were inadequate to the dual demands of supplying her vast area of conquests and the Home Islands. In the early years of the war a steady rate of loss was inflicted by American forces, but although this put strain on Japanese shipping commitments (one of the reasons for the withdrawal from Guadalcanal had been the loss of over 100,000 tons of shipping) the burden did not prove crippling. Even so, over time these losses, compounded by inadequate shipbuilding and repair facilities, meant that only 5 million tons of shipping were operational in late 1943.

After November 1943 shipping losses rose rapidly, and by mid-1944 over 1 million additional tons had been lost. This escalation was a result of the US advance into the central Pacific, which brought its land and carrier aviation within range of previously secure Japanese maritime communications. Complementing these operations was an increasingly effective submarine campaign. Capture of forward bases at Kwajalein, the Marianas and Ulithi brought US submarines closer to the Japanese shipping lanes in the western Pacific, Philippines and the vital South China Sea and increased their time on combat patrols. In mid-1945 US land-based aircraft also began operating from newly secured bases close to Japan on Okinawa and Iwo Jima, and a substantial mining campaign in Japanese home waters added a further dimension to the tightening blockade of Japan. The combination of surface ships, carriers, submarines, land-based aircraft and mines presented the Japanese with a multifaceted attack which they lacked the resources to counter. This situation was made worse by the Imperial Navy's lack of convoy doctrine and specialised anti-submarine warfare ships, aircraft and tactics. Belated attempts at remedying the situation by establishing convoys in 1943 foundered because of lack of resources and the willingness of US submarine forces to engage the escorts in battle. In prosecuting a strategy for securing command of the sea, as opposed to the German or Japanese concepts of sea denial, the Americans crippled Japanese trade defence measures and overwhelmed the exposed convoys.

The scale of American naval superiority by January 1945 enabled the Fast Carrier Force of the Third Fleet to enter the South China Sea, striking at enemy airfields and shipping. This dominance was further illustrated in April when airfields in the Home Islands were attacked. The inability of the Japanese to prevent US naval forces operating off Japan and in the neighbouring seas demonstrated the overpowering nature of the defeat inflicted on naval and air forces. In a desperate attempt to halt the American onslaught the Japanese resorted to suicide (kamikaze) attacks.

Although Japanese aircraft had frequently carried out kamikaze attacks throughout the war, these had been on an individual basis and were not systematic. In October 1944 for the first time the Japanese High Command deliberately organised large-scale attacks against American forces off the Philippines, sinking six warships and extensively damaging another forty-three vessels. Similar, smaller-scale operations were conducted against the landings on Iwo Jima (Operation 'Detachment') in February 1945. The invasion of Okinawa (Operation 'Iceberg', April 1945) witnessed the first massed kamikaze attacks. These severely tested American defences and inflicted heavy losses, but ultimately failed to prevent the fall of the island.

To counter the kamikazes, in November 1944 the Americans re-organised the Fast Carrier Force, concentrating ships together in order to maximise defensive firepower. Destroyers were employed as radar pickets to detect approaching aircraft as early as possible, while carrier air groups were increased from 40 per cent fighters to 80 per cent by late 1945. This reduced the carrier forces' offensive power, but did allow sustained combat air patrols and sweeps over Japanese bases to restrict Japanese air operations.

Okinawa also saw the last sortie of major Japanese naval forces when the superbattleship *Yamato* was sent on a one-way suicide mission against US landing ships. Located by carrier aircraft, however, she was attacked and sunk before she could fulfil her mission. The final blows came in July 1945 when British and American carriers raided dockyards in the Inland Sea, sinking or damaging the Imperial Navy's few remaining ships.

By late July 1945 Japan was sliding over the edge into military, economic and social collapse, with the very real threat that the latter would

Kamikaze sorties, by month

October 1944	55
November	143
December	232
January 1945	230
February	196
March	37
April	1,162
May	596
June	210
July	20
August	59

Although the burden of the war at sea against Japan was overwhelmingly borne by the United States Navy, the ships of other Allied powers also participated in the conflict. Australian, New Zealand, Dutch and British vessels served alongside US naval forces in the first year of the war and continued to carry out important tasks in secondary theatres until September 1945. The largest Allied contribution to the Pacific war came in early 1945 when the newly formed British Pacific Fleet, under the operational command of Vice-Admiral Sir Bernard Rawlings, arrived to take part in the invasion of Okinawa. Designated Task Force 57 (TF 57), the British fleet of four aircraft carriers provided cover to the left flank of US forces operating off Okinawa, mounting strikes against Japanese air bases and installations on Formosa (modern-day Taiwan). In July 1945 TF 57 took part in Admiral Halsey's destruction of the remnants of the Imperial Navy in Japanese coastal waters. American attempts to deny the Royal Navy any claim to having participated in the destruction of Japanese naval power resulted in TF 57 being relegated to attacks on secondary targets. However, the British did in fact sink the escort carrier *Shimane Maru* off Takamatsu on 24 July. Subsequently the fleet flagship *Duke of York*, with supporting units, formed part of the Allied naval force present in Tokyo Bay on 2 September for the formal Japanese surrender. Admiral Sir Bruce Fraser, Commander-in-Chief British Pacific Fleet, signed the instrument of surrender on behalf of Great Britain.

The performance of the British Pacific Fleet during the summer of 1945 was adequate, but far below the skill and effectiveness with which US carrier forces operated. Unsurprisingly, British weaknesses stemmed from a lack of experience in operating carriers on the scale and intensity that characterised Pacific operations. The Royal Navy's expertise lay in the convoy and anti-submarine techniques demanded in the Atlantic. Although the steel decks and armoured hangars of the British carriers gave them greater protection from kamikaze attacks than the wooden decks of the American vessels, their striking power was significantly inferior. Armoured

The British Pacific Fleet carrier HMS Formidable, *was twice damaged by kamikaze aircraft in 1945. In this case a direct hit next to the bridge destroyed ten aircraft, indented the steel deck by 2 feet and depressed a main beam in the hangar by 15 inches. Nevertheless, because the British placed considerable emphasis on passive defence for their carriers,* Formidable *was able to recommence air operations six hours later. (Fleet Air Arm Museum CARS F/36)*

hangars reduced the strength of carrier air groups, making it difficult to saturate enemy ground defences. Consequently the British suffered proportionately higher rates of loss than American air groups. Air operations were further hindered by the need to develop techniques for coordinating the large numbers of aircraft involved in Pacific operations, and by the initial British slowness in launching and recovering aircraft. But the gravest hindrance to Royal Navy operations was the weakness of logistic support services. Although the British managed to supply TF 57 with fuel, ammunition and replacement aircraft in 1945, continued operations, especially the invasion of Kyushu in November 1945, might have overwhelmed slender British resources. Japan's surrender avoided a potential humiliation for the British, whose participation in the Pacific war had been grudgingly accepted by Admiral Ernest King on the proviso that it could support itself.

Questions about the importance and effectiveness of the British Pacific Fleet in defeating Japan ignore the real significance of its contribution to the war in the Far East. Unquestionably, the Americans would have won the war without British forces. But to the British High Command the real issue was the political and moral requirement that Britain should bear its share of the burden in the final operations against Japan. To the American people the sight of British carriers facing Japanese suicide attacks alongside their own forces was of profound psychological importance in attitudes to Britain. The American ambassador to London summed up the situation, noting that if the British did not join the Pacific campaign, 'we will create in the United States a hatred for Great Britain that will make for schism in the post-war years'. No one understood that more profoundly than the British political and military leadership.

plunge her into political turmoil. Blockaded from the sea, bombarded by carrier- and land-based aircraft, her sea lanes choked with mines, Japan was a defeated power. The refusal of Japanese leaders to accept the Allied terms of unconditional surrender without a guarantee of the Emperor's position, led to preparations for the invasion of Japan in late 1945 and early 1946. Code-named 'Downfall', the landings in Kyushu (Operation 'Olympic') and Tokyo Bay (Operation 'Coronet') were to be conducted on a scale that the Japanese Army, lacking heavy equipment and largely ill-trained, would have been unable to resist. In the end, however, President Truman resolved to use the atomic bomb to shock the Japanese into surrender. The attacks on Hiroshima (6 August) and Nagasaki (9 August), together with a Soviet invasion of Japanese-occupied Manchuria, finally forced Japan's leaders to accept defeat. On 15 August Emperor Hirohito (1901–89) ordered his people to 'bear the unbearable'. On 2 September Japan formally surrendered to the Allied powers, the ceremony taking place on board the battleship USS *Missouri* in Tokyo Bay.

Japan's defeat stemmed from a variety of factors, not least the fact that she did not have the resources to win a prolonged war of attrition against the United States. The nature of the conflict meant that the IJN played a critical role in deciding the outcome of the war. However, the Imperial Navy's obsession with the decisive battle and its deeply flawed concept of the 'interceptive' operation meant that ultimately, despite considerable tactical skill, it failed to defend the nation that it was supposed to serve. In the face of overwhelming American strength, and the US Navy's more balanced approach to war at sea, the Japanese fleet was worn down in a series of engagements before being finally overcome. The failure to protect vital merchant shipping was a particularly serious omission, and was critical in bringing Japan to her knees.

'If nothing else, World War II proved the prodigious power of ships (sea and air) capable of operating in the third dimension. It was in that third dimension that Japan lost the Pacific War. He who lived by the sword died by the air bomb and the submarine torpedo . . . The atomic bomb was the funeral pyre of an enemy who had been drowned.'

Theodore Roscoe,
United States Submarine Operations in World War II
(1949)

ELEVEN

WAR IN THE AIR 1939–45

LLOYD CLARK

Air power came of age during the Second World War. After a protracted period of experimentation its impact was keenly felt tactically, operationally and strategically. Whether through aerial reconnaissance, close air support, battlefield air interdiction, transportation, the delivery of airborne troops or strategic bombing, the war revealed the clear advantages to be attained from the skilful use of aircraft. Those belligerents that broadly developed the use of air power and understood the investment required to sustain this resource-heavy form of warfighting over a protracted period, achieved the greatest advantages. Those states that employed a more limited form of air power directed towards a series of swift victories achieved only short-term benefits. Nevertheless, however it was used, air power was a vital ingredient in Second World War military success.

'Anyone who has to fight, even with the most modern weapons, against an enemy in complete command of the air, fights like a savage against modern European troops, under the same handicaps and with the same chances of success.'

Field Marshal Erwin Rommel, The Rommel Papers *(1953)*

THE 'BLITZKRIEG' YEARS

The way in which Germany employed air power between 1939 and 1941 provides a good example of a belligerent gaining short-term advantage from its limited use. Although the Luftwaffe was configured in a way that enabled it to carry out any role, its strength lay in supporting ground forces. 'Blitzkrieg', indeed, relied on aircraft to help create the conditions in which the Army could attain speed and momentum towards its objectives and advance with freedom. It was with such air roles in mind that the Germans prepared for war. This preparation was central to the Germans' early military successes as they had the pilots, aircraft and experience with which to defeat their enemies quickly. Poland, the Low Countries, France and Norway had all been carefully studied by the Germans during the 1930s and all eventually suffered at the hands of the Luftwaffe.

Against Poland in September 1939 the Luftwaffe attained air supremacy over an enemy who was outnumbered and flying obsolete machines. The Polish Air Force (Lotnictwo Wojskowe) possessed only 313 modern fighters and bombers, and the Army lacked large quantities of good anti-aircraft artillery. The Germans deployed 1,323 first-line aircraft, and although its attempts to destroy the Polish Air Force on the ground failed in the face of a pre-emptive dispersal to secret air strips, the Luftwaffe had adequate superiority to seize the initiative at the start of the war. With control of the skies, it concentrated on dislocating the enemy's ground forces through demoralising attacks on troop concentrations, lines of communication and command and control centres. Polish mobilisation (which depended on railway transport) was badly disrupted, and the Luftwaffe also carried out terror attacks against refugee columns and the city of Warsaw in order to break the enemy's will to resist. Despite a gallant performance which saw the Poles achieve a superior kill rate in aerial combat, the Polish Air Force could do little to interfere with German ground operations. On 17 September surviving units were evacuated to neutral Romania, from which many Polish pilots fled to Great Britain. Here they would fight with great success during the summer and autumn of 1940.

The campaign in Western Europe took a similar form to the one in Poland. Although the Western powers possessed more aircraft, they suffered from a number of deficiencies that together gave the Luftwaffe a significant advantage. French serviceability rates were poor and the miscellany of types with which they entered the war compounded the problem. German aircraft all carried a voice or morse wireless set, but many of their opponents' aircraft lacked modern communications systems.

The Junkers Ju 87 Sturzkampfflugzeug (dive bomber), or Stuka, provides one of the most powerful images of the 'Blitzkrieg' years. Over 5,700 were produced, and examples served with the Italian, Hungarian and Romanian air forces, as well as with the Luftwaffe. Despite its slow speed and vulnerability to enemy fighters, the Stuka remained in service until the end of the war, being steadily upgraded to carry heavier bomb loads, anti-tank cannon or, as in this case, cluster bomb containers. These are later model Stukas (Ju 87D series), serving on the Eastern Front.

Doctrinally, while the Germans had devoted some attention to preparing for ground support operations against pre-planned targets, and had in the Ju 87 Stuka dive-bomber the perfect instrument for delivering them, their enemies were unprepared for using air power in intimate support of land combat. The British government's decision to retain large numbers of its best aircraft for the defence of the United Kingdom also damaged the Western powers' cause in the short term, not least because French fighters were generally inferior to those of their enemy.

As in 1939, Luftwaffe strikes against its opponents' air bases on 10 May 1940 were fairly ineffective. However, by focusing its air assets at decisive points the German Air Force was able to play a vital role in the successful development of the campaign in Western Europe. On 13 May, for example, 180 Stukas attacked poorly protected French positions near Sedan on the River Meuse with their 550-pound bombs. The intense raids shattered the cohesion and morale of the defenders, who were then quickly overwhelmed by German troops who crossed the river in rubber boats. Similarly, attempts by Allied units to redeploy to counter the German blow met interdictory strikes that slowed their progress and sapped their will to fight. Airborne operations played a significant part in undermining the defence plans of the Dutch and Belgians in particular, and the willingness of the Germans to target civilians – for example, through the destruction of Rotterdam city centre on 14 May – had a devastating effect on morale. With some reason, a number of historians have suggested that it was the Luftwaffe – and not the panzer divisions – that played the decisive role in securing the German triumph of 1940.

'The gunners stopped firing and took cover. The infantry, cowering and immobile in their trenches, dazed by the crash of bombs and the shriek of the dive-bombers, were too stunned to use their anti-aircraft guns and fire. Their only concern was to keep their heads down and not move. Five hours of this punishment shattered their nerves. They became incapable of reacting to the approaching enemy infantry.'

General Edmond Ruby, quoted in William S. Shirer, The Collapse of the Third Republic *(1972), referring to the Luftwaffe bombardment at Sedan, 13 May 1940*

Future Luftwaffe doctrine and aero industry planning were heavily influenced by these victories. However, the Luftwaffe's success did not only reveal German strengths. Although poorly directed and penny-packeted British and French air attacks were easily brushed aside during the advance to the Channel; the aerial battle over Dunkirk in May and June 1940 was a very different matter. Lacking a long-range fighter and well-protected bombers, the Luftwaffe could not finish off the fleeing British Expeditionary Force, and succumbed to the quality of the RAF's Spitfires and Hurricanes in great numbers – 240 German machines were shot down, against the RAF's 177. Indeed, German losses in the campaign of May–June 1940 (1,236 aircraft totally destroyed and another 323 written off) were surprisingly heavy. Although these losses were hardly fatal, they were not sustainable and therefore could not be ignored. Having prepared for a short war with very limited casualties, the Battle of France highlighted weaknesses in the Luftwaffe that were to haunt Germany for the remainder of the war.

That Germany was neither physically nor mentally prepared for an attritional air struggle was well illustrated by the Battle of Britain in the summer and autumn of 1940. This episode underlined many deep-seated Luftwaffe vulnerabilities. In order to destroy RAF Fighter Command the Luftwaffe required a long-range fighter, an appropriate bomber and a suitable doctrine. The Germans had none of these. Although they came close to success, they suffered heavily at the hands of a tenacious and well-led RAF that gradually exploited their weaknesses.

A deceptively tranquil scene from the Battle of Britain as sergeant and officer pilots relax in front of a Supermarine Spitfire. In reality, social barriers still existed between the two types of pilot and the battle traumatised many of those who flew in it, losses among inexperienced aircrew being particularly heavy. (Illustrated London News)

THE BATTLE OF BRITAIN

The Battle of Britain was fought as a result of German's need to attain air superiority before launching Operation 'Sea Lion' – the invasion of England. Hitler felt confident after his rapid successes in France and the Low Countries, and few observers believed that Britain could hold out for long against a determined Nazi offensive. The Germans, however, had focused their air power on support of the Army rather than on strategic bombing. Consequently, they lacked a long-range heavy bomber and a fighter with the range necessary to have any significant combat time over England. Thus, operations were generally confined to London and the south-east of England. The RAF, moreover, had been preparing for a defensive battle since 1936 under the guidance of Air Chief Marshal Sir Hugh Dowding (1882–1970) and, importantly, had invested in radar. The ability to track the course and altitude of enemy aircraft 150 miles away was to help the squadrons of Fighter Command be in the right place at the right time to intercept them. This interception ability was crucial, as the RAF could boast no superiority over the Germans in quality or quantity of pilots and aircraft – at the start of the battle the Luftwaffe had 2,500 aircraft while the RAF had only 609 fighters.

The first phase of the campaign began on 10 July 1940 with German attempts to gain air superiority over the Channel. In the month of fighting that followed, both shipping and coastal towns were targeted. With some justification, it was the Luftwaffe that claimed success by early August. However, although both sides suffered heavily, the German losses were twice those of the British. This situation was fraught with problems for the Luftwaffe, for although the British were replacing their losses quickly, the Germans were not.

The second phase of the Battle of Britain began on 13 August when the Luftwaffe initially attacked various targets across south-east England, but then began to focus on RAF fighter stations. Despite some early success, the Luftwaffe continued to take heavy losses and Fighter Command held on. 'Holding on' was about all that the RAF was able to do at this stage.

Pressure grew further on the British in early September. Together with aircraft and pilot losses (in just two weeks Fighter Command lost 25 per cent of its pilots), airfield damage meant that the Luftwaffe was close to

Hugh Dowding (1882–1970), commander of RAF Fighter Command 1936–40. Dowding's pre-war struggle to improve Britain's air defences, and his careful conduct of operations in 1940, were vitally important factors in ensuring British success in the air battle that raged over southern England after the fall of France. (RMAS Collection)

attaining air superiority over Kent and Sussex. The battle was reaching its critical period and it is likely that had the Germans maintained this pressure then Fighter Command would have been defeated. But then the Luftwaffe suddenly changed tack.

Under the misapprehension that they were still some way from attaining a measure of air superiority, the Germans attempted to force Dowding's hand by bombing London. The first raid took place on the afternoon of 7 September when over 300 bombers, escorted by 600 fighters, targeted the capital. The new strategy caught Fighter Command by surprise: as a result Luftwaffe losses were light and fires burnt late into the night. As the days passed, however, it became clear that the enemy had shifted his focus to London, and with their airfields left unmolested, the RAF began to turn the tide of the battle.

On 15 September the Battle of Britain reached its climax with the RAF suffering relatively few losses as it decimated the enemy. The impact that this period had on the course of the battle was immense. As a result of the Luftwaffe's failure to crush Fighter Command, the Germans were forced on to the defensive as the RAF began to attack their invasion preparations along the French coast. Although the raids on London continued, on 17 September Hitler postponed Operation 'Sea Lion' indefinitely. By early October he knew that he had lost the battle and the invasion was formally cancelled on the 12th.

The Battle of Britain was the first decisive air battle in history. It thwarted Hitler's invasion hopes, revealed many and deep-seated German military and economic weaknesses and proved to the world that the Luftwaffe was far from invincible.

The repercussions of the Luftwaffe's failure to destroy Fighter Command were dramatic for the planned invasion of the United Kingdom (Operation 'Sea Lion'), which was eventually cancelled. The impact of the loss of valuable aircraft was also considerable. The Battle of Britain stretched Germany more than anticipated. With an economy that was only just capable of making good Luftwaffe losses rather than making it stronger, greater difficulties were on the horizon. Indeed, the fact that Britain produced 4,283 fighters in 1940 while Germany produced only 3,106 was to prove significant in a war that was becoming ever more attritional.

With 'Sea Lion' cancelled, Hitler's attention turned east. Yet even before the invasion of the Soviet Union (June 1941), German resources were increasingly diluted by attempts to consolidate north-west Europe and to overcome opposition in the Balkans, North Africa and Crete. The invasion of Crete in May 1941 relied heavily on air assets and was the last cry of German airborne warfare.

The Second World War saw all manner of airborne operations. The years between 1940 and 1945 were the brief but turbulent heyday of the large-scale airborne operation using parachute and glider forces. The Germans had developed an ability to insert troops by air during the inter-war years and their invasion of France and the Low Countries in 1940 began with an airborne assault to take objectives in advance of the ground offensive. The operations in Holland did not go as smoothly as planned, but the 'impregnable' fort at Eben Emael in Belgium was neutralised in just 20 minutes after airborne troops landed in gliders on its grassy roof. The German High Command still had to be totally convinced of the advantages of the airborne concept, however. The invasion of Crete, Operation 'Mercury', was to be its great test.

'Mercury' was launched on 20 May 1941 when airborne forces landed by glider and dropped by parachute to take various objectives on the island. Problems, however, bedevilled the attack from the outset. Shock and surprise was diminished by the fact that a shortage of transport aircraft led to two separate airborne lifts. Allied anti-aircraft fire caused a number of gliders to crash and parachutists to be scattered, and radio failure meant that the struggling airborne troops were out of contact with their commander back in Greece. Over 4,000 men became casualties out of the 22,000 deployed for the invasion. Of 530 Ju 52 transport aircraft used in the operation, 242 were destroyed or damaged. Crete was taken, but at a price so great that it severely dented Hitler's confidence in airborne warfare. Indeed, a similar operation to seize Malta in August 1942 was cancelled and no other large-scale German airborne operation took place during the war.

The resources lost at Crete were sorely missed as Germany prepared to invade the Soviet Union in June 1941. By the opening of Operation

'Of course, you know that we shall never do another airborne operation. Crete proved that the days of parachute troops are over.'

Adolf Hitler

German paratroopers wave to a Stuka as it passes overhead, Crete, May 1940. The success of the airborne assault owed much to the Luftwaffe's air supremacy over the island. Without it, the operation almost certainly would have failed. (RMAS Collection)

'Barbarossa' the Luftwaffe had recouped the aircraft losses sustained during the Battle of Britain. However, aircraft numbers had not increased and quality was already beginning to suffer. Although the Luftwaffe could boast 2,775 aircraft for the invasion of the USSR, Soviet resource superiority was significant and the Red Air Force amassed a total of 10,000 machines. Hitler, a man rarely deterred by poor odds, placed his faith in superior Luftwaffe fighting methods and the quality of his aircraft and crews. Even so, the job of defeating the Soviet Union quickly was clearly as awesome a task for the Luftwaffe as it was for the Army.

A swift victory was important for Germany because Hitler was determined to avoid being drawn into an attritional conflict. Yet although approximately 7,500 Russian aircraft were destroyed in the first thirteen weeks of the campaign, the Soviet Air Force survived. Despite causing great enemy losses and rendering important help to German ground forces, once again an under-prepared Luftwaffe could not finish the job. Operation 'Barbarossa' demanded much of German air power in numerous roles, but over such a massive front the Luftwaffe could not cope. Instead, it was stretched ever more thinly against an enemy that grew quickly from 1942 onwards.

German preparation for an attritional air war was extremely poor. This can be seen in part by the failure to put in place an infrastructure that could rapidly increase aircraft production when this was required. Such a serious disability was exacerbated by the fact that the Germans had eighty-six different aircraft models at the front. This variety overwhelmed their poorly directed and clumsy aircraft industry. German inefficiency dogged aircraft production and development throughout the war, and is illustrated by the fact that although the Luftwaffe was chronically short of aircraft, resources were consistently diverted towards projects to develop and produce the V ('Vergeltung', or 'Vengeance') weapons and the jet engine. The Germans, in short, had little understanding of what was required to fight a protracted air war.

The Soviets produced some very good aircraft during the Second World War. The Lavochkin LaGG-3, unfortunately, was not one of them. Sluggish and unmanoeuvrable, and outclassed by German fighters, its highly polished covering led to it being known to its pilots as the 'varnished guaranteed coffin'. In an effort to overcome the poor visibility from its cockpit, many pilots – as here – took to flying with its canopy open. Nevertheless, the aircraft was at least resilient, and before being phased out it performed with some effect in the ground attack role.

The Allies, on the other hand, were extremely well prepared for this sort of contest. Preparation for a protracted air conflict began during the last years of peace and saw the development of various efficient and well-directed aero industries that could rapidly expand production when required. The Allies also put crucial emphasis on the need for standardisation and for highly practical aircraft that could be easily updated when required – a decision that was to serve them well in wartime. Different air forces, of course, developed at different speeds and with differing foci. The Soviet Air Force, for example, was concerned mainly with tactical support and was consequently dominated by tactical strike aircraft such as the Petlyakov PE-2 and the superb Ilyushin IL-2.

The Soviets did not use air power as broadly as they might have, but it can be argued that they conducted a similar kind of attrition against the Germans through their ground advance as the Americans and British did through their long-range strategic bombing. Moreover, when discussing the Soviet use of air power it must be remembered that they also mounted a number of airborne operations. With 50,000 airborne troops in readiness in 1941, the potential for large operations was even greater on the Eastern Front than elsewhere. Nevertheless, apart from the success of a few raids, several poorly supported airborne assaults over the period between 1942 and 1944 achieved little but heavy casualties.

CLOSE AIR SUPPORT AND STRATEGIC BOMBING

Although the Soviets concentrated their air power on tactical support of ground forces, the British had major difficulties carrying out this role. Both over France in 1940 and again in North Africa between 1941 and 1943, the RAF showed that it had neither the aircraft, doctrine nor training to be effective in the tactical role. However, progress was made in the Western Desert and lessons were learned about what air power could achieve tactically. Eventually, a tactical doctrine was developed: gain air superiority; conduct air interdiction operations against rear zones; and attack the enemy in cooperation with one's own army. The Americans developed a similar doctrine as a result of their experiences around the Mediterranean and these principles worked well during 1944–5 in north-west Europe, where Allied ground forces enjoyed powerful close air support after control of the skies had been achieved. The destruction of the Luftwaffe was crucial in attaining this air supremacy, and once it was done the Allied ground forces could break out from their beachheads with relative impunity. It is interesting to note, however, that although successful in dislocating the German defenders, air interdiction operations ran into problems resulting from a lack of suitable aircraft with which to do the job. Although the newly introduced US Marauder and British Typhoon carried out tactical support of the armies, heavy bombers had to be used throughout northern France for interdiction purposes. These aircraft were hardly ideal, and the destruction they caused resulted in many logistical difficulties for Allied troops when they advanced inland. This problem was overcome later in the campaign by the introduction of specialist light and medium bombers, but it reveals an early Allied focus on strategic bombing rather than tactical support. It is important to emphasise, however, that tactical support could not take place unless air superiority was first attained, and the way in which this was achieved was closely tied to – and had important implications for – Allied strategic bombing.

'Then the Lord rained upon Sodom and Gomorrah brimstone and fire from the Lord out of heaven.'

Genesis 19:24

Strategic bombing was high on the list of British priorities from mid-1940, for prior to the USA and USSR entering the war it was deemed the only possible means of attaining victory. Nevertheless, bomber operations by the RAF in late 1939 and early 1940 revealed that Bomber Command was ill prepared for a major offensive. Many lessons needed to be learned. Daylight raids against enemy shipping – chiefly in the North Sea and the Baltic – and night-time leaflet drops over Germany, for example, resulted in extremely heavy British losses. These prompted a shift to night-time precision bombing of important industrial targets. However, when in August 1941 an official investigation revealed that only one-third of

'The fighters are our salvation, but the bombers alone provide the means of victory. We must carry an ever-increasing volume of explosives to Germany so as to pulverise the entire industry and scientific structure on which the war effort and economic life of the enemy depend.'

W.S. Churchill, 3 September 1940

One of the finest strategic bombers of the Second World War, the Avro Lancaster entered RAF service in early 1942. It served in several roles and in many different types of mission, and carried a heavier bomb load than any other aircraft type in the air war over Europe. Almost 7,400 were built, and some were still in operational use as late as 1954. (Jonathan Falconer Collection)

aircraft actually dropped their loads within 5 miles of their targets, a shift was made to the bombing of large towns and cities ('area bombing') with the aim of disrupting war production by terrorising, de-housing and killing the German working population.

The appointment of Air Marshal Sir Arthur Harris (1892–1984) as Commander-in-Chief of Bomber Command in February 1942 was a watershed in the campaign. Harris not only bolstered political and public support for the bomber offensive, but also made sure that the best advantage was attained from new long-range bombers like the Handley-Page Halifax and Avro Lancaster, and from new navigation and bomb-aiming technology. Together with a constant reassessment of tactics, these developments eventually led to a significant disruption of the German economy and heavier civilian losses. When RAF bombers targeted Hamburg with incendiaries in July 1943, for example, a firestorm killed almost 40,000 people.

American involvement in the European war from 1942 onwards gradually gave the bombing campaign a lift. The slow start to the US offensive was largely due to the Americans' desire to forge their own path and learn their own lessons rather than merely to follow the British. Early US daylight precision bombing raids therefore suffered heavy casualties – just like similar RAF raids before them. Casualties were so heavy – on one raid in October 1943 the Americans lost 60 out of 291 bombers – that the whole campaign was threatened unless losses decreased. As German fighters caused most of the difficulties, the Americans decided that the best course of action was to destroy the Luftwaffe. The results of this decision to create air superiority not only safeguarded Allied bombers, but also had a positive impact on the ability of the Allies to use air power in other roles as well.

The US destroyed the Luftwaffe from late 1943 onwards by attacking any target that the Germans might be willing to use aircraft to defend, and then meeting them with long-range fighters such as the P-47 Thunderbolt and P-51 Mustang. During a period of fair flying weather in late February

1944, US bombers enjoyed skies virtually devoid of German fighters. As a result, the Americans were able to devastate German factories and oil installations. Between January and June of that year 2,262 Luftwaffe pilots were killed and 3,278 German fighters were lost. Thus, by the time of Operation 'Overlord' the Luftwaffe had just 300 fighters available in France, while the Allies had some 12,000. Slowly but surely the Allies had attained massive air superiority.

Together with continued British night-time raids, the success of this new approach meant that by early 1944 the Western Allies should have been in a very good position to start a decisive bomber offensive over Germany. However, despite the undoubted advantages to be attained from such an operation, the needs of the Normandy invasion (June 1944) came first. Thus, between April and October bombers were very often employed in tactical roles. Not until the autumn of 1944 did the Combined Bomber Offensive finally begin. Although it lasted just eight months, it had an important impact on Germany's ability to sustain the war. Many industrial areas were destroyed and 6 million civilians were displaced. While it would be wrong to say that the bomber offensive devastated German war production, the economy was severely hindered and the production of tanks and aircraft fell to one-third below projected levels in 1944. These raids, moreover, had the effect of further diluting Hitler's scant front-line resources as men and materials were plundered to protect German air space. By 1943, 33 per cent of artillery production and 20 per cent of ammunition were directed to anti-aircraft activity and well over a million Germans were employed in the air defence of the Reich. The strategic bombing offensive curtailed the Germans' ability to sustain their war effort and forced them to react, in an increasingly ineffectual manner, to Allied initiatives.

The North American P-51 Mustang was probably the finest piston-engined fighter of the Second World War. With a range (with drop tanks) of 850 miles, from late 1943 it bore the brunt of deep escort tasks for the USAAF's daylight bomber raids into Germany. Mustangs flew 213,873 missions over Europe, mainly as a fighter, but also in the reconnaissance, close air support and interdictory roles. (USAF)

THE ALLIES' USE OF AIRBORNE FORCES

With air supremacy attained over north-west Europe, the Allied High Command was keen to make the most of the wider benefits that came with it – and that included mounting airborne operations. Unlike the more radical states of Germany, the Soviet Union and Italy, the United States and Britain had not immediately embraced the airborne concept at the start of the war. However, by the end of 1942 the Americans had two airborne divisions and Britain had one.

The British learned some important lessons during their first major airborne operations in North Africa in 1942, and again during the invasion of Sicily in July 1943 (when some British troops landed 40 miles from their objectives). However, such experiences led the Allies, like the Germans and Soviets before them, to question the usefulness of these techniques. Doubts still persisted when the Allies invaded Italy in

The bomber offensive, 1940–5

	British and American (USA 1942–5 only) bomber production	Bomb tonnage dropped on Axis-occupied Europe
1940	3,529	14,631
1941	4,668	35,509
1942	18,880	53,755
1943	37,083	226,513
1944	42,906	1,188,577
1945	23,554	477,051
Total	130,620	1,996,036

ALLIED BOMBING OF GERMANY

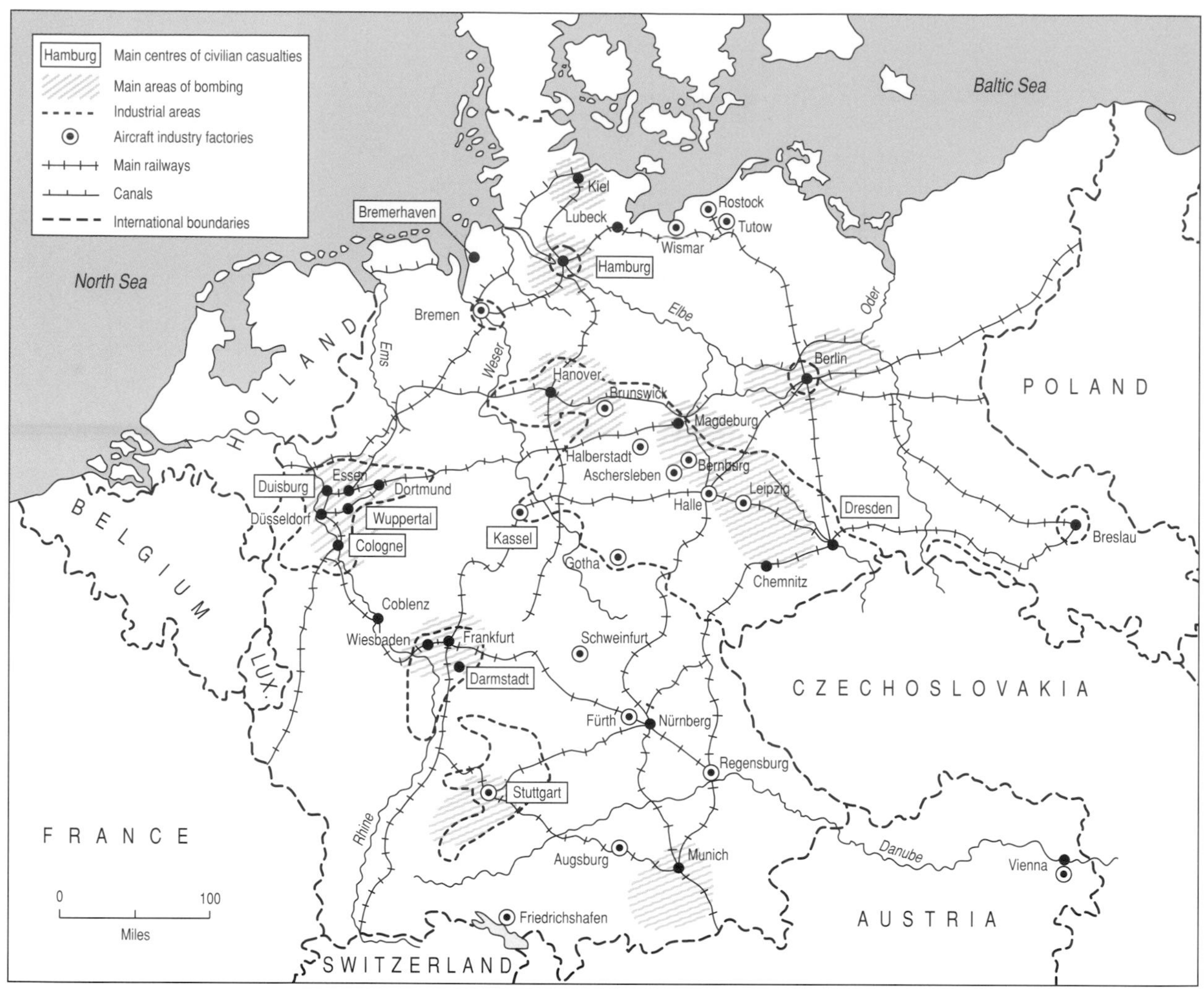

September 1943. Airborne forces were again used for this assault, but this time soldiers of the American 82nd Airborne Division managed to drop within 1 square mile and helped to get the stalled ground offensive moving again around Salerno. A successful operation was also launched on 6 June 1944 when British and US airborne troops were used to shore up the flanks of the Normandy assault, and again in August when the Allies mounted the invasion of southern France (Operation 'Dragoon').

The assaults of summer 1944, although not flawless, restored Allied confidence in airborne warfare. By September a new and ambitious operation was being devised for the newly created 1st Allied Airborne Army. Operation 'Market Garden' failed to seize a crossing of the Rhine over which British 2nd Army could advance, but the river was eventually crossed in March 1945 with the assistance of airborne troops used in a more conservative role. 'Varsity' provided a successful conclusion to Second World War Allied airborne operations, operations which gave the Allied High Command flexibility and once again illustrated the advantages they had gained from their investment in air power.

Smiling British paratroopers prepare to embark in Short Stirling transports, Fairford, Gloucestershire, 17 September 1944. These are members of 21st Independent Parachute Company, whose job it was to land twenty minutes before the assault waves in order to mark drop zones with beacons and flares. They fulfilled their task with great success, but unfortunately their skill could not compensate for the range of other problems encountered by British forces at Arnhem. (IWM CL1154)

OPERATION 'MARKET GARDEN' – THE BATTLE OF ARNHEM

Operation 'Market Garden' involved the largest airborne operation in history and aimed to end the war in Europe by Christmas 1944. To overcome the supply problems encountered by the Allies as they advanced on a broad front, the commander of British 21st Army Group, Field Marshal Bernard Montgomery, proposed to the Allied Supreme Commander, General Dwight D. Eisenhower (1890–1969), that a narrow-fronted thrust by his forces would crack open the German front and pave the way for a rapid push to Berlin. After continual badgering Eisenhower eventually agreed to his plan on 10 September and Operation 'Market Garden' was born.

'Market Garden' sought to insert airborne troops behind enemy lines in order to seize a number of vital bridges in Holland over which British 2nd Army could advance. The airborne divisions involved were the 101st US, which was to drop around Eindhoven, the 82nd US, which was to land at Nijmegen, and the 1st British (with the attached 1st Polish Independent Parachute Brigade), which was to land near Arnhem. The aim was to pave the way for the capture of the Ruhr, Germany's industrial heartland. Planning started immediately because the operation was to take place just seven days later.

After a successful first lift on Sunday 17 September things quickly started to go wrong. Although British ground forces from 2nd Army eventually reached the south bank of the River Rhine, by the time they got there the airborne troops no longer held the main road bridge and evacuation of the remaining troops back across the river was the only realistic option. The reasons for the failure of 'Market Garden' are myriad, but a number were especially important.

First, the planning process for this complex inter-Allied operation took place over the course of just seven days. Although the plan was based closely on a previous aborted operation, there were still serious difficulties in solving the massive administrative problems that the operation threw up. Indeed, time was so short that once decisions had been made, they had to be followed through. There was little chance for careful consideration or a change of mind in the light of new information. Nevertheless, the prize was massive and objectives were deemed achievable, so the operation went ahead.

One of the most crucial administrative problems that could not be solved was the number of transport aircraft required. The lack of transport aircraft negated the primary airborne advantage of speed and surprise, and rather than all the troops being transported to Arnhem on 17 September in a single lift, three separate lifts had to take place. These lifts were eventually spread out over five days because of bad weather, and resulted in the dilution of the attacking force. This problem was made worse by the fact that a significant proportion of the first-lift troops were required to defend the drop zones and landing zones for subsequent lifts. To complicate matters even more, the lifts had to take place in daylight (it was a no-moon period) and the drop zones and landing zones were up to 8 miles from the objectives because of a perceived lack of alternative sites. Thus, the defending Germans not only had the advantage of being able to assess quickly numbers of attackers and the locations of their landing zones, but also had time to build vital defensive blocking positions. As a result only 750 airborne soldiers actually got through to Arnhem road bridge, the major objective, to await the arrival of 2nd Army.

These problems might not have had such dire consequences had the enemy not been of such high quality or so heavily armed. Airborne troops are lightly equipped and lack tactical mobility. For this reason accurate Intelligence is absolutely crucial. Airborne soldiers cannot be expected to hold their own for long against a heavily armed and highly mobile enemy. Unfortunately, this is exactly the sort of enemy that the British found in and around Arnhem – Germans with self-propelled guns, tanks and cannon-armed half-tracks. The two SS Panzer divisions that British Major-General Robert Urquhart's (1901–88) men landed on amounted to around 5,000 men with some armour, and the Allies were aware of this. However, although Allied commanders did not necessarily lack information about the enemy that they faced, many did underestimate what the enemy was still capable of achieving and how quickly the Germans could reinforce Arnhem with more armour and men.

The airborne troops' situation around Arnhem against such an enemy was not helped by a lack of close air support. The fact that the RAF was unable to provide this support until six days into the battle because of other duties and the poor weather meant, quite simply, that the lightly armed airborne troops were left to fend for themselves. The lack of a battlefield air interdiction plan to cover the countryside around Arnhem also meant that the Germans were able to move reserves to the battle area. Only late in the battle were German artillery and mortars targeted to relieve some of the pressure on the beleaguered airborne troops.

Communication difficulties hardly helped. The radios used by the British were totally ineffective in the Arnhem terrain and this meant that not only was the division out of contact with headquarters outside Arnhem, but also commanders could not communicate locally. Indeed, it was precisely this problem that forced Major-General Robert Urquhart, commander of the 1st British Airborne Division, to move away from his HQ at a vital early phase in the battle to instil a sense of urgency into his attacking troops, only to then find himself cut off by the Germans.

Finally, 2nd Army, led by General Brian Horrocks' (1895–1985) XXX Corps, made slow progress up the single, raised road to Arnhem because of a tenacious German defence. German artillery successes often meant that burnt-out vehicles blocked the road. Because the ground on either side of it was unsuitable for tanks, the wrecks had to be bulldozed off before the advance could continue. The net result of XXX Corps' difficulties in reaching Arnhem was that the airborne troops had to fight for longer than expected. The men at the bridge held out heroically for five days before being overrun, while the rest of the division was withdrawn to the south side of the river when the lead elements of XXX Corps eventually reached the Rhine on D plus nine.

Of the division that had flown into battle at Arnhem, 1,484 were killed or died of wounds, 3,910 came back in the evacuation and 6,525 became prisoners of war (of whom approximately 2,250 were wounded). Although it is easy to say in hindsight that 'Market Garden' should never have taken place, it is important to remember the circumstances in which the operation was conceived, planned and conducted. With the Germans on the retreat, September 1944 was the time for a daring operation to decisively shorten the war and bold decisions had to be taken quickly if the opportunity was not to be lost. 'Market Garden' was a sensibly conceived plan, but a plan flawed in too many details to succeed.

THE PACIFIC WAR

The Allies made good use of air power in a variety of roles during the European war and this aided the ability of ground forces to advance to their objectives. However, in the Pacific War – which was dominated by naval operations – air power was even more important. It could be argued that in terms of offensive operations, aircraft changed the course of naval history by assisting in the destruction of the pre-eminence of the battleship. Signs of this were to be found even before the USA joined the war: in November 1940 British Swordfish torpedo bombers from HMS *Illustrious* damaged or destroyed three Italian battleships in Taranto harbour in southern Italy. More important, though, was the sinking of the British capital ships *Prince of Wales* and *Repulse* by the Japanese on 10 December 1941. This was the first time in history that such warships had been sunk at sea by aircraft. One of the most famous examples of an air attack on shipping, however, came on 7 December 1941 with the Japanese raid on Pearl Harbor. This not only resulted in eight battleships being destroyed or damaged, but also forced the United States into the war. The consequences of such air threats to shipping were far-reaching, and navies immediately sought to protect themselves with their own air cover. In the process the aircraft carrier came of age.

Both the Americans and Japanese understood that air power would be crucial in a Pacific war, both as a means of protection for vulnerable fleets and as an offensive tool when trying to seize clusters of small islands by exposed amphibious assaults. Thus, aircraft carriers were highly valuable assets that quickly became the target of air attacks. These attacks sought to destroy the carriers in an attempt to achieve air superiority and make the enemy fleet vulnerable. However, whereas the Americans prepared for a protracted campaign, the Japanese sought to use air power in order to side-step the need for an attritional war and to pursue the decisive battle. Admiral Isoroku Yamamoto (1884–1943), Commander-in-Chief of the Japanese Combined Fleet, thought that if the USA lost a large number of aircraft carriers, the time taken for them to be rebuilt would give the Japanese the opportunity to create an empire and develop the strength to take on and defeat any future American attacks.

In June 1942 Japanese attempts to annihilate the US fleet in a battle off Midway Island instead resulted in American aircraft destroying four

'ESSEX' CLASS FAST FLEET CARRIERS

On 31 December 1942 the USS *Essex* (CV-9) was commissioned. The lead ship in her class, the *Essex* was big and fast, displacing 27,635 tons with a maximum speed of 32.7 knots. A cruising speed of 15 knots gave her a range of 15,000 nautical miles. The size and armament of the *Essex* enabled her to absorb and inflict heavy punishment. Defensive armament consisted of 12 5-inch, 32 40mm and 46 20mm anti-aircraft guns. Offensive capabilities came from 36 fighters, 36 scout/dive bombers and 18 torpedo planes. A total of 24 'Essex' class carriers were built from 1941 to 1946, 14 of which saw active service in the war. Their blend of speed and firepower made these carriers a key component in US naval operations from late 1943 to the end of the war. Although many Essex carriers suffered heavy damage – especially from suicide (kamikaze) attacks – none was sunk. The damage suffered by the USS *Franklin* in March 1945 off Okinawa illustrates the robustness of these vessels. Two bombs penetrated her deck, causing explosions and fires in her hangars that put her out of action. However, superb damage control saved the *Franklin*, and on 20 March she was able to retire to Ulithi Atoll under her own power.

Post-war modifications enabled the Essex carriers to continue in front-line service in Korea (1950–3) and Vietnam (1964–73). The last ships were decommissioned in the early 1970s and eventually scrapped in the mid-1980s. In their long lives the Essex carriers followed the words of America's first great naval hero, Captain John Paul Jones (1747–92): 'Give me a fast ship for I intend to sail into harm's way!'

Damaged Japanese aircraft set up to serve as decoys on Aslito airfield, Saipan (Mariana Islands), June 1944. The capture of Saipan by US Marine and Army units brought Japan within range of US B-29 bombers, and led to the resignation of the Japanese prime minister, General Hideki Tojo. Not surprisingly, given the island's importance, the battle for it was savage, and involved the almost complete annihilation of its 32,000-strong garrison. (US National Archives)

valuable Japanese fleet carriers. This gave the Americans a great advantage as their enemy had thereafter to keep his battleships and cruisers away from areas that could not be supported by land-based aircraft. This episode reveals the central importance of tactical aircraft in a war conducted over vast oceans. However, it was not only the tactical use of aircraft that was important in the Pacific. Just as in Europe, the USA used air power to engage the Japanese in an attritional war in order further to weaken their overburdened war economy.

Japan was not in a good position to fight a protracted attritional war as its pre-war preparation had concentrated on waging something far shorter. In line with such thinking the Imperial Japanese Navy had a paltry 100 pilots completing training each year during the late 1930s. After a disaster the size of Midway the Japanese had great trouble replacing their lost airmen. This was not helped by a decision in 1943 to provide naval aviators for ground-based operations in the southern Pacific. By the end of that year the Japanese had lost 7,000 aircraft and crew.

Such losses required drastic action, and this inevitably led to a decline in the competence of pilots as training programmes were truncated. By 1944 the Japanese were suffering 50 per cent operational losses. Both the IJN air force and the fleet were hopelessly outnumbered (9 carriers and 450 aircraft against 15 carriers and 900 aircraft), with the Americans also using modern aeroplanes and well-trained crews. The 'Great Marianas Turkey Shoot' in June 1944, in which the Americans downed 300 Japanese aircraft for the loss of just 31 of their own, came about as a result of this disparity. During this period Japanese losses were so great that the IJN air arm became virtually impotent. By November 1944 it was forced to resort to kamikaze attacks. These suicide strikes were deemed by the Japanese to be fitting for warriors and did not require either modern aircraft or well-trained pilots. Over 3,000 kamikaze attacks were eventually launched and 49 ships – including 3 carriers – were sunk as a result. A further 280 ships were damaged. However, despite these losses the impact of the kamikaze tactic was not great and US superiority was not significantly damaged – but the policy did reveal the extent of Japanese desperation by this stage of the war.

Japanese desperation was rooted in intense supply problems that had been brought about by US submarine action which, between 1942 and 1945, decimated its merchant shipping *en route* from South-East Asia. With a shortage of raw materials and an economy that was not ready for a protracted war, Japanese industry found it increasingly difficult to supply the armed forces with what was required to sustain the fighting. Japan's backward economy was poorly directed and haphazardly organised, and industry bowed under the pressure exerted upon it. In these circumstances the production of aircraft suffered particularly badly: 53 basic naval types (with 112 variations) and 37 army designs (with 52 variations) made the job even more difficult.

The air war in the Pacific theatre revealed not only that any nation wishing to compete in a modern attritional conflict had to be well prepared, but also that it had to provide extremely high levels of quality production for the duration. As Japan found to her cost, the result of neglecting the needs of a protracted air war was a vulnerable industry and home front, which, if attacked, could seriously affect the ability of the nation to sustain its war effort.

JAPANESE CARRIER AIRCRAFT

During the 1930s the Imperial Japanese Navy designed some of the most advanced carrier aircraft in the world. The A6M 'Zero' was an innovative fighter design; its ability to turn inside and out-climb rivals gave it a decisive edge in combat. Two specialist aircraft types provided the carrier's offensive power. The B5N 'Kate' was principally a torpedo bomber, but was capable of level bombing and reconnaissance. The D3A 'Val' dive-bomber was a rugged and highly manoeuvrable aircraft. The 'Val' sank more Allied shipping in the Second World War than any other Axis aircraft type. In the early years of the war the combination of these excellent aircraft and superbly trained pilots proved critical to Japanese success. However, lack of armour and self-sealing fuel tanks led to heavy losses. By late 1943 the appearance of advanced American aircraft designs rendered the 'Zero', 'Val', and 'Kate' increasingly obsolete. Inability to replace them with new types of aircraft and to recover losses in aircrew eventually undermined the combat effectiveness of the Imperial Navy with disastrous results.

US front-line aircraft strength, 1943–5

Jan 43	3,537
Jan 44	11,442
Jan 45	17,976
July 45	21,908

Japanese front-line aircraft strength, 1943–5

Jan 43	3,200
Jan 44	4,050
Jan 45	4,600
July 45	4,100

US PACIFIC STRATEGY

The USA used air power with great success during the Pacific War and the ability of its industry to supply what was required in order to take and keep the initiative was certainly a great help in this. Indeed, whereas the Battle of Midway in mid-1942 served only to weaken Japanese offensive capabilities, within a year the Americans were able to go on the offensive when new carriers and aircraft became available.

The USA's offensive strategy was made up of two intertwined strands and air power played a key role in both. In retaking the Pacific islands, aircraft were used in a tactical role to create air superiority before amphibious assaults were launched, while in the destruction of Japan bombers were used in a strategic role to destroy the enemy's economy. This strategy worked well and the Americans advanced quickly through the Pacific as the Japanese could no longer compete in the air and their army was overrun. The US advance eventually led to the capture of the

Marianas in June 1944. These islands provided a base from which heavy bombers could carry out the destruction of Japan.

Strategic bomber operations began in late November 1944 when the B-29 Superfortresses of the US 20th Air Force targeted Japanese cities and industrial centres. Success was relatively limited at first as the skills and equipment required for high-altitude precision bombing were only gradually being acquired. Nevertheless, after a review of procedures in January 1945 the raiders, then armed with incendiaries, became increasingly successful. The devastation that these low-level night raids created was awesome. In March 1945 one raid on Tokyo resulted in a firestorm and the deaths of 100,000 people. Similar raids against scores of Japanese cities met with very limited opposition and considerable success. The impact upon Japan's ability to sustain the air war was significant: American figures point to a 43 per cent decline in Japanese aircraft engine production and an 18 per cent drop in airframe construction between December 1944 and July 1945.

It must be noted, however, that this bombing did not totally destroy Japanese morale, and resistance was still fanatical during the invasions of Iwo Jima and Okinawa in early 1945. Nevertheless, the US raids did undermine Japanese civilian resolve and the dropping of two atomic weapons on Hiroshima and Nagasaki in August had a further effect on their will to fight. But, it was the Soviet Union's land invasion of Japanese-occupied Manchuria that finally brought about surrender.

'Now I am become Death, the destroyer of worlds'. These words from Hindu scriptures entered the mind of Robert Oppenheimer, leader of the scientific team that developed the atomic bomb, after witnessing its first test on 16 July 1945. A few weeks later, on 6 August, the nightmare of atomic warfare came true for the citizens of Hiroshima, a relatively unimportant Japanese city of 350,000 people. In a few seconds, almost 80,000 of them died from the effects of blast or burns. Three days later a similar number would die at Nagasaki, the first – and so far only – victims of the use in anger of the most terrible weapons known to mankind. (IWM SC278262)

Aircraft production of the major powers, 1939–45

	1939	1940	1941	1942	1943	1944	1945
USA	5,856	12,804	26,277	47,836	85,898	96,318	49,761
USSR	10,382	10,565	15,735	25,436	34,900	40,300	20,900
Britain & Commonwealth	8,190	16,149	22,694	28,247	30,963	31,036	14,145
Germany	8,295	10,247	11,776	15,409	24,807	39,807	7,540
Japan	4,467	4,768	5,088	8,861	16,693	28,180	11,066
Italy	1,800	1,800	2,400	2,400	1,600	–	–

The Second World War saw aircraft used in a wide variety of roles. The powers that embraced air power fully and broadly were victorious. This, however, required careful peacetime preparation and a clear understanding of how to conduct a protracted air war. The Allies were late in their preparation for war, but nevertheless ensured that they could mobilise efficient and well-directed aero industries capable of producing quality aircraft in the numbers required for an attritional war. The defeated nations did not prepare in the same way. Their earlier preparation and focus on a short war led to the development of industries that were not capable of sustaining a protracted conflict or providing the sort of modern aircraft desperately required by their air forces.

The Allies found the opening years of the war difficult. The Germans, in particular, used air power to devastating effect in their early European conquests. However, by gradually developing the ability to fight an air war and then slowly attaining air superiority, Allied air power began to reach its full potential tactically, operationally and strategically. The attainment of air superiority was therefore crucial to Allied military success. As President Roosevelt said in May 1941: 'command of the air by the democracies must be and can be achieved. Every month the democracies are gaining in the relative strength of the air forces. We must see to it that the process is hastened and that the democratic superiority in the air is made absolute.' It took a number of years for this 'command of the air' to be attained, but when it came it offered an opportunity for the Allies to unleash the full force of strategic air power against Germany.

Bombers were not the decisive weapon of war that some had imagined. Even less was strategic bombing a way of circumventing the need for ground offensives. Nevertheless, the impact of the Allied bombing offensive was significant. In Germany, for example, the air war killed more civilians than all British and American casualties put together, and in Japan more people died in six months of heavy aerial bombardment than in the whole of the US war effort. Some have used such evidence to suggest that air power was decisive in the Second World War, but in reality it was far from the only arbiter of success. Air power was, however, a crucial component in the Allies' complex military machine and provided a significant driving force behind the development of the Allied strategy that eventually delivered victory.

T W E L V E

SOCIETIES IN TOTAL WAR, 1914–45

N I A L L B A R R

One of the most striking features of the twentieth century was the enormous impact of war on states, nations and peoples across the globe. Every war can be seen as a revolution and if, as Marx argued, war is the 'locomotive of history' then the First and Second World Wars are without doubt the best examples of this phenomenon.

TOTAL WAR

Between the beginning of the nineteenth century and the dawn of the twentieth, the entire nature of states within Europe changed. The capability of states to organise and control their populations had been transformed by the growth of modern bureaucracies and communications. The Industrial Revolution had vastly increased the productivity and prosperity of much of the continent. The states of Western Europe had become a powerhouse of production, mass-producing goods of all types, and technological innovation had resulted in many new devices that changed life dramatically. From the railway and blast furnace to the Singer sewing machine and the telephone, technological advances had had an enormous impact. The effect of technological change on the nature and conduct of war had been no less profound. From the magazine-fed, bolt-action rifle and the machine gun, to quick-firing artillery with high-explosive shells, the destructive power of weaponry had increased dramatically. It was estimated that a British artillery battery in 1906 could lay down in just two hours the equivalent explosive force of all the gunpowder used by Britain in the Napoleonic Wars.

Meanwhile, the Agricultural Revolution generated major surpluses of food and this bounty, combined with advances in public health, led to unparalleled population growth. The expansion in population was mirrored by the growth of national armies. During the Napoleonic Wars, from 1800 until 1815, France mobilised 1,600,000 men. This was a real achievement for a pre-industrial society, but such figures pale into insignificance next to the fact that on the outbreak of war in 1914 France could immediately put 3,200,000 men into the field – truly a nation in arms. Modern nationalism had become a powerful force in binding states and peoples together. The nation as an 'imagined community' gained real strength and emotional force during the nineteenth century through the conscious invention and rehearsal of national symbols and rituals. The impact of all these changes on the nature of war in the twentieth century was profound. Indeed, it can be argued that it was through the experiences of the First and Second World Wars that the true consequences of all these changes came into stark relief.

By 1914, given the vast scale of the armies and their voracious demands for food, fodder, clothing, ammunition, transport and supplies of all kinds, a war economy could no longer be improvised. Thus the pursuit of decisive victory in the twentieth century could not fail to involve more than just the armies, navies and air forces that fought the battles. The home front, with its reserves of manpower, labour and productivity, was intimately linked to the battle front. Civilians on farms, in factories and offices produced and administered the vast quantities of supplies needed for the fight. People were forced to accept the necessity of long working hours, sacrificing sleep, luxuries and even basic commodities to support the war effort. Many men were forced, through conscription, to serve in the armed forces – and many wives and mothers had to accept the loss of a husband, brother or son who was killed or wounded in action. Warfare in the twentieth century involved the infliction of loss, suffering and sacrifice on entire nations.

The problem was that modern industrialised warfare tended to take on its own logic. In the nineteenth century, Clausewitz had recognised the propensity of warfare to escalate towards extremes. The twentieth century demonstrated the veracity of this theory. Once a mass war had begun, it became virtually impossible to reverse, and with little possibility of a compromise peace the war had to be fought to its logical conclusion: victory or defeat. Thus, the political aims of the combatants tended to become more extreme as the conflict progressed. Britain had entered the First World War to preserve Belgium's neutrality and the balance of power within Europe, but these aims were soon altered to include the need to destroy German militarism and the threat that its alleged barbarism posed to civilisation. Germany's aims for the war were first set down by its Chancellor Theobold Bethmann-Hollweg (1856–1921) in September 1914. They included the annexation of Belgium, French Flanders and the Channel ports, and an economic union that would give Germany economic domination in Europe. Unsurprisingly, this left little room for compromise with the French and Belgians, who were not prepared to surrender a yard of their sovereign territory. With the onset of trench deadlock along the Western Front in the winter of 1914 no side had achieved its political objectives, but already the cost had been too great to accept a compromise peace. The British Expeditionary Force began the campaign in August 1914 100,000 men strong but had already suffered 90,000 casualties by the end of November. The Germans knew the First

'This would be a universal war of unprecedented scope and unprecedented force. From eight to ten million soldiers will destroy one another and in the course of doing so will strip Europe clean in a way that a swarm of locusts could never have done. The devastation caused by the Thirty Years' War telescoped into three to four years and spread over the entire continent, hunger, epidemics, the universal engagement of both troops and masses, brought about by acute need, the hopeless jumbling of our artificial trade, industrial, credit mechanisms: all this ending in general bankruptcy; the collapse of old states and their vaunted wisdom . . . the utter impossibility of foreseeing how this will end and who will emerge victorious from this struggle; only one result is absolutely beyond doubt; universal exhaustion and the creation of the conditions for the final victory of the working class.'

Frederich Engels, 1887

The Second World War saw every conceivable resource mobilised for the war effort. Here, in a scene that Hannibal might have recognised, elephants are used to haul timber for boat-building on the River Chindwin in Burma, February 1945. (RMAS Collection)

Battle of Ypres in November 1914 as the 'Kindermord' since so many former schoolboys and university students who had rushed to the colours in August 1914 were killed in their 'Ersatz' Korps. Meanwhile, the French had suffered 300,000 casualties in the 'Battle of the Frontiers'.

Such enormous effort, sacrifice and loss could only be demanded from a population to which the reasons for the war could be explained and justified. Paul Lincke's song, 'Wir müssen siegen' ('Victory must be ours'), popular in Germany at the start of the First World War, explained this phenomenon. Defeat meant ruin, humiliation, and quite possibly the extinction of a nation's government, institutions and way of life. The war required such sacrifice and effort that the needs of entire nations had to be subordinated to that one goal: victory at all costs. And continuation of the war, with all the sacrifice it entailed, meant that only complete victory could justify the cost.

In the Second World War, the political aims of the combatants were clear and gave even less room for compromise. Adolf Hitler, as Führer of Germany, had vast and far-reaching goals, particularly concerning the Soviet Union. His aim was to destroy the Soviet Union and occupy its territory up to the Ural mountains. This would create a vast German Empire in the East which would provide *Lebensraum* (living space) for a racially pure German people. The Slavic population of Eastern Europe and Russia was offered a simple choice: slavery or death. This forced the Russian people to respond with complete resistance against the Germans in order to prevent the extermination of their entire society – no matter what the cost. Even the Western Allies – Britain and the United States – adopted the policy of demanding the 'Unconditional Surrender' of both Germany and Japan at the Casablanca Conference in January 1943. There could be no compromise and the war was fought for the highest stakes.

WAR AT THE FRONT

The no-holds-barred struggle for victory was, of course, most intense in the theatres of war themselves. Every country involved in the world wars had to build, equip and train vast armies, navies and air forces in order to

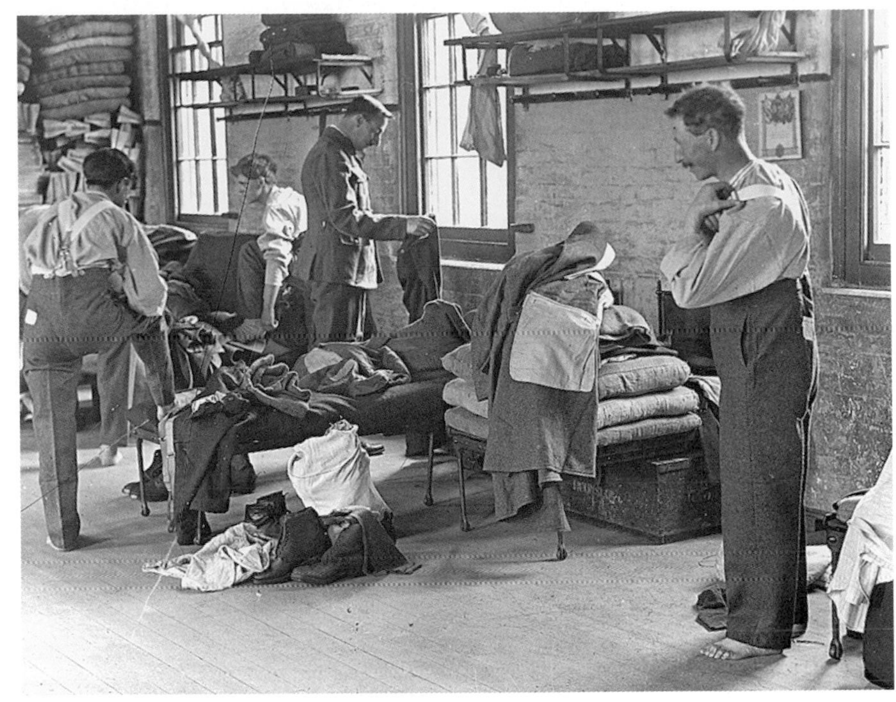

First World War British conscripts begin the transformation into soldiers. Many of the best twentieth century armies have been conscript forces, and men like these would achieve some of the most impressive victories in British military history in the summer and autumn of 1918. (IWM)

Below: *States involved in total war have often tried to harness religion to political purposes. The German Kaiser did so in 1914, and Stalin deliberately encouraged Soviet citizens in 1941 to fight for 'Holy Mother Russia', rather than for an ideology that few of them even understood. The human need for a god to whom one can look in times of trouble also led armies to take the provision of pastoral care seriously in both world wars. Here British infantry hold a communion service before launching an attack in Normandy, 10 July 1944. (RMAS Collection)*

The demonisation of one's opponent is another feature typical of total war. Ironically, although posters like this may have persuaded some Americans to enlist in 1917–18, soldiers in action often felt more affinity with their opposite numbers in the enemy's ranks than with their own civilians. (US National Archives)

survive and defeat its opponents. The recruitment of much of a nation's manhood into the armed services had an enormous social impact. Recruitment and conscription on a vast scale led to the division of whole societies into fighting men at the battle front and civilians on the home front. Particularly during the First World War this produced a whole range of tensions between the soldiers fighting and dying on the battlefields and the supposedly safe and complacent civilians at home. This sharp division of experiences also made post-war readjustment a difficult and lengthy process.

Efficient armed forces that could defeat their opponents were critical in prosecuting a total war – and, as the German Wehrmacht proved in its lightning campaigns of 1939–41, battlefield victories can transform the nature of a war. Throughout both conflicts, all combatants were involved in a constant learning process in which they struggled to outmatch their opponents in numbers, equipment, tactics and strategy – a true race to the swift. States that could not compete on these terms, such as France and Italy in the Second World War, were doomed to defeat and occupation.

However, success on the battlefield was no longer enough in itself. Wars could not be won solely with armies, navies and air forces. Economic and industrial mobilisation on a vast scale, combined with modern transport and communications, could often repair defeat on the battlefield. Since combatants were no longer simply fighting an opponent's armed forces, but also all the elements that supported the fighting front, the single decisive blow that might destroy an enemy army and lead to a clear-cut victory became virtually impossible to achieve. Wars became strategically attritional in character: a nation's armed forces, reserves and willpower were all slowly worn down in a long, drawn-out struggle. The successful conduct of war on the battlefield now had to be combined with credible war aims, far-reaching mobilisation of human, economic and technological resources, efficient management of industrial production, cordial diplomatic relations with allies and neutrals, and most importantly, the maintenance of the will to fight on the home front.

THE WAR OF RESOURCES

Every state involved in a total war had to struggle for resources – the raw materials to supply its factories, food for its people and technology to give it the edge in combat. Britain in both world wars had access to the resources of its empire and the Americas through its control of the seas, although this lifeline was threatened in both wars by German submarines. In the Second World War the Soviet Union was only able to survive the loss of much of European Russia because fresh reserves of oil, coal and ores had been opened up in Siberia just prior to 1941. The United States in

PROPAGANDA

Propaganda came to be seen as an essential support for the willpower of a nation to continue in the enormous sacrifices and effort required by total war. Conversely, all combatants indulged in propaganda to attack the civilian morale of their opponents. During the First World War much early propaganda was uncontrolled – particularly the lurid and unconfirmed reports about the German 'rape' of Belgium which circulated in Britain and France in 1914 and early 1915. None the less, these stories had a decisive impact on the Allied desire to fight against the 'evils of German militarism'. As morale began to flag during 1917, governments organised ministries of information or propaganda to press their case. Much of the 'black' propaganda that was utilised backfired, however. The fabricated story of the German 'corpse factories' where dead soldiers were turned into soap was particularly ill-judged, but Hitler considered British propaganda against Germany to have had a decisive influence in 1918.

During the Second World War all combatants organised propaganda from the outset with varying degrees of success. Joseph Goebbels' (1897–1945) German Ministry of Propaganda scored some notable early successes, and in 1940 Lord Haw-Haw (William Joyce, 1906–46) was widely listened to in Britain. However, as the war went on and German forces began to suffer reverses, Goebbels' message of ultimate German victory became discredited. One of the most celebrated cases concerned Rommel's retreat from El Alamein in November 1942. The German Propaganda Ministry reported that Rommel's army was advancing victoriously – to the west! In film production, Goebbels concentrated on producing entertainment rather than Nazi ideology (with some notable exceptions). However, his final film, *Kolberg*, about Prussian resistance to the French in 1806, simply demonstrated the excesses of the Nazi regime. The film cost an astonishing 8.7 million marks and used over 187,000 soldiers as extras (more than took part in the original battle), all in an attempt to demonstrate that a united people could resist any foe. All this effort was undertaken in 1944–5, when Germany badly needed every soldier at the front. During the conflict, the British decided to abandon most of their attempts at 'black' propaganda and instead concentrated on providing an accurate, though censored account. The BBC in particular gained a worldwide reputation for accuracy and honesty. By 1943 most of occupied Europe gained its news from the officially banned BBC World Service.

both wars was the only state that did not need to worry unduly about resources – with the wealth of an entire continent at its disposal, the USA could supply all of its wartime needs and more. Japan actually began the war in the Pacific in 1941 because of its need for raw materials, most notably oil and rubber, which it could take from Indonesia and Malaysia as part of its South-East Asia Co-Prosperity Sphere. However, Japan had the distinction of being the only combatant in either war to have its trade and industry strangled by a submarine campaign that sent most of the Japanese merchant marine to the bottom of the sea.

Nazi Germany attempted to make war pay for war. Hitler adopted a fundamentally different policy to that of Imperial Germany in the First World War. He was adamant that the German people must not be made to suffer, because he remembered the sacrifices of the First World War and knew that his popularity depended on ensuring that the home front did not have too difficult a time. While taxes rose, Hitler was careful not to increase vastly the burden on his population. Instead, his war was paid for by the rest of occupied Europe, which was plundered for its manpower, industrial resources, raw materials and food. This policy was initially very successful. With his piecemeal conquest of Western and Eastern Europe, Hitler was able to harness the full resources of the continent for his German Empire. This meant that Germany did not suffer the same shortages or difficulties that it had in the First World War. However, the aim of exploiting the riches of European Russia proved to be illusory. The Germans gained more raw materials from Russia during the period of the Nazi-Soviet Pact (August 1939–June 1941) than they were able to loot during their occupation. As the war continued and the tide turned against Germany, Hitler's state found it increasingly difficult to garner the necessary raw materials. Even though Albert Speer's programme of industrial rationalisation gathered pace during that year, which meant that German production peaked in the autumn of 1944, with the loss of Romanian oilfields and France's coal and iron deposits, the German economy was crippled.

The cost of total war: military spending as a percentage of national income, 1939 and 1943

	1939	1943
USA	2%	53%
UK	15%	55%
USSR	–	61%
Germany	32%	71%
Italy	10%	40%

The economic cost of fighting a total war was also enormous. It placed terrible burdens on countries, but almost any price had to be accepted in order to win. As early as June 1940, Britain was spending £55 million a week in fighting its war. Most countries increased taxation dramatically during wartime while also encouraging the population to subscribe to war loans and bonds which took more money out of circulation and helped to pay for the conflict. In Britain in the Second World War, towns and villages would hold fund-raising weeks to 'Buy a Spitfire' in what was essentially a form of voluntary taxation. However, no matter how much money a government raised through taxation and war loans it could never finance the total cost of such an enormous conflict. The British economist John Maynard Keynes (1883–1946) estimated the gap between British expenditure and income from taxation in 1941 at £500 million. In the First World War, Britain called in loans and borrowed money across the globe; consequently its status changed from the world's largest creditor nation in 1914 to one of the largest debtor nations in 1918. In the Second World War, Britain's gold reserves were exhausted by 1941 and the rest of the conflict had to be financed through the 'Lend-Lease' agreement with the United States, whereby British bases across the globe were leased to the United States in return for the 'loan' of military equipment, supplies and even food.

INDUSTRIAL PRODUCTION

The intimate link between the armed forces and the necessity for the complete mobilisation of industry during a total war was illuminated

The Krupps works, Essen, Germany 1912. Factories like these survived the First World War only because the belligerents lacked the means to target them effectively. The people who worked in these places, however, were less fortunate a quarter of a century later. Essen was heavily attacked by RAF Bomber Command in 1943–4, and raids in July 1943, and in October and December 1944, inflicted very heavy damage on the Krupps facilities. (RMAS Collection)

clearly by the shell crisis. This affected the British Army (and most other forces) during early 1915 on the Western Front. In September 1914, the British Liberal government under Henry Asquith (1852–1928) had instituted a rather unhelpful policy of 'Business as usual' for as long as the war lasted. But as the new Minister for War, Field Marshal Herbert Kitchener (1850–1916), discovered, *laissez faire* economics could not meet the vast orders for ammunition that he began to place with Britain's small ordnance industry. When the war continued into 1915, British production of artillery shells simply could not keep pace with the voracious demand from the Army, which needed more and more high-explosive ammunition to deal with the growing trench system. A shortage of shells meant that offensive action was difficult, and when these problems were made public by *The Times* correspondent Colonel Repington, it brought scandal and embarrassment for the government.

It became clear that without economic mobilisation, the British munitions industry could not grow at the pace necessary to feed the Army with the weaponry it needed. Asquith's government then created a Ministry of Munitions under the 'Welsh Wizard' David Lloyd George, who began to revolutionise production with the construction of huge new national munitions factories and the use of women in skilled jobs. A measure of his success is that British shell production rose from 2 million in 1915 to 17 million in 1916. Similar schemes and measures had to be adopted by all combatants in both world wars in order to feed the fighting at the front lines. The output of factories and farms built the sinews of war and economic mobilisation became just as important for the conduct of hostilities as the armies in the field.

'Modern warfare will be a war of engines. Engines on land, engines in the air, engines on water and under water. Under these conditions, the winning side will be the one with the greater number and the more powerful engines.'

Josef Stalin, 1941

The Soviets called it the 'war of machines', and the war of production reached new heights between 1939 and 1945. With their slogan 'All for the Front' the Soviets ruthlessly exploited their natural resources and manpower in producing over 78,000 tanks, 16,000 self-propelled guns and 98,000 artillery pieces. Such vast numbers were not only necessary for the intensive and fierce battles that raged on the Eastern Front, but also gave the Soviet Army an unchallenged material superiority over the Wehrmacht by 1943.

While the Soviet Union concentrated almost exclusively on the needs of the Army on the Eastern Front, Britain with its more limited reserves of manpower and industry had more diverse requirements. By 1941, Britain was not only producing equipment for its own Army (and military aid for Russia), but also building a strategic bombing fleet, constructing warships of all descriptions and large numbers of merchant ships. These demands stretched the country to the very limits of its capacity so that it became known to its people as the 'India Rubber Island'.

In complete contrast, Hitler's Germany did not mobilise fully until 1944 – when it was already far too late. After Germany's early successes there seemed to be no need to mobilise the entire German economy. Given the fractured nature of power in Nazi Germany, the *Gauleiters*, or regional governors, also curried favour with the populace by encouraging the production of consumer goods. When the Allied bombing offensive destroyed people's homes and possessions this only increased the pressure to continue the production of consumer items. Given this pressure, German production of military equipment, which was vital to win the war, was not impressive. Throughout the Second World War German industry was only able to produce 24,000 tanks – approximately the same number as Britain (which had many other concerns), while the United States built over 50,000 Sherman tanks alone. However, it was in the United States that the 'war of machines' took on an entirely new meaning. The United States never fully mobilised, yet in November 1943, the peak of wartime production, US industry was turning out six ships a day and $6 billion worth of war supplies every month. The United States was able to supply all of its own military needs as well as Lend-Lease supplies to Britain and the Soviet Union without even breaking stride.

United States Lend-Lease Aid, 1941–5 ($ million)

	To Britain	To USSR
1941–2	5,839	1,396
1943	9,031	2,436
1944	10,776	4,074
1945	4,437	2,764

Such large-scale mobilisation of industry raised complex labour and manpower issues for all combatants. While armies, navies and air forces clamoured for more men to serve in the front line, industry and agriculture could become starved of the workforce necessary to supply the services. Thus the efficient use and distribution of labour became an essential part of a war economy. The British government in the Second World War certainly adopted the most efficient system – a manpower 'budget' in which the various needs were debated and a compromise solution reached. Ernest Bevin (1881–1951), the Minister for Labour, had to take drastic steps in July 1941 since it was estimated that 2 million men and women would be required by June 1942 and there would be a deficit of over 300,000 in the manpower budget. Bevin announced his new measures on 2 December 1941: they went further than the schemes of any other combatant in mobilising the population for war. Men could be called up from the ages of eighteen to fifty-one. But all people of both sexes could be called up for national service – women were to be directed or conscripted for the first

'We must be the great arsenal of democracy.'

President Franklin D. Roosevelt, 29 December 1940

WOMEN AND THE COMBAT TABOO

All European countries have traditionally had an aversion to female service in the armed forces. During the First World War this taboo was broken – particularly by Britain which recruited over 450,000 into the Women's Auxiliary Air Force, Army and Navy. However, it was during the Second World War that the combat taboo for women was finally broken. It was Britain that again first breached this taboo on 25 April 1941 with the formation of 'mixed' anti-aircraft batteries which served at home. Even though the female soldiers served as radar and predictor operators, they were not allowed to load or fire the guns. In this way the British blurred the issue. However, the Soviet Union allowed female recruitment into the combat arms. Women served with distinction in the Soviet Air Force as fighter and bomber pilots, as infantry soldiers, artillery gunners and front-line medical personnel.

The Red Army made extensive use of women in the combat role, as this photograph of two snipers during the Second World War shows. Many served with great bravery, eighty-six being awarded the gold star, Hero of the Soviet Union medal. (US National Archives)

time in any civilised nation. Initially, only unmarried women aged twenty to thirty would be called up, with a choice between industry and the services. However, in 1942 this was changed to include unmarried women up to the age of forty. The impact of this new direction of female labour was such that in mid-1943, the proportion of the nation's women between fifteen and sixty in the forces, munitions and essential work was double that of the First World War. Yet the changes were not quite as dramatic as they seemed. If peacetime trends had continued, it is estimated that 6.75 million women would have worked outside the home, while in 1943, the estimated number of women employed was 7.5 million. Nevertheless, there were profound changes: nearly 3 million married women and widows worked during the war but only 1.25 million had been employed before the war. The full extent of British mobilisation can be judged from the fact that during the Second World War, nine out of ten single women aged between eighteen and forty, were in the forces or in industry.

All spheres of working life (with the exception of coal mining) became familiar to British women and 450,000 were in uniform by the height of the war. Although Britain probably used female labour more intensively than any other power, the Soviet Union went one step further by utilising women in the combat role. Soviet women were trained as fighter and bomber pilots, snipers, tank drivers and combat medics. Over 800,000 Soviet women, including 27,000 partisans, served in the armed forces. All gained a well-deserved reputation for courage under fire. At the same time, Soviet women who remained civilians were intensively used for labour. Women made up

48 per cent of the labour force in the oil industry alone. However, not all states utilised female labour to the same extent. Given Hitler's fixed opinions on the role of women, Nazi Germany did not utilise its reserves of female labour as efficiently as it could have, and instead made up the short-fall by using forced labour from occupied Europe and slave labour from the death camps.

FEEDING THE POPULATION: AGRICULTURE AND RATIONING

Food production was absolutely critical to the prosecution of world wars. Without the basic essentials of life, no nation could fight a total war for any sustained period. All countries engaged in hostilities had to try to feed as much of their population as possible from domestic sources and to reduce their dependence on imports of non-essential goods. In both world wars, Britain came close to defeat because of the impact of Germany's U-boat campaign – in 1917 and again between 1940 and 1943. While the defeat of the U-boat menace itself was essential, so too was increased domestic agricultural production. Measures such as 'daylight saving time' were introduced to maximise the farmers' working day and large tracts of land were put under the plough for the first time. The rural labour force suffered greatly from the needs of the Army and the female workforce grew to replace the men who had joined up. At the same time, ordinary people in the Second World War were exhorted to 'Dig for Victory' by growing their own fruit and vegetables in allotments, gardens and even city parks and squares. While such increased production could not eliminate the need for imported foodstuffs, it certainly reduced the requirement and meant that Britain did not starve. None the less, the needs of wartime meant that unrationed bread in Britain was tough and grey because the extraction rate of flour in the milling process had been increased to 85 per cent! People complained about this unattractive, 'indigestible' bread, but it did keep hunger at bay.

Helping the war effort provided a ready excuse for not eating one's greens. Here a British child helps to fill the pig bin. (IWM)

Just as the production of increased quantities of foodstuffs became vital, so did the concept of rationing available food. This meant that nations adopted a 'siege economy' in which limited stocks were shared out among the population and combined with many restrictions and price controls. In Britain, rationing was promoted as 'fair shares for all'. Yet even the extra 8-ounce cheese ration for agricultural workers in Britain introduced in 1941 caused a storm of protest from town dwellers who had to manage on 3 ounces. By and large, the British rationing system did work and the British government understood the importance of the fact that in a 'people's war' it was critical that everyone was seen to be making the same sacrifices. These measures also led to much communal eating in so-called 'British restaurants' where people could generally receive slightly more food than 'on the ration'. By 1944, over 14 million people in the Soviet Union were being communally fed every day.

RATIONING

The British rationing system introduced on the outbreak of war in 1939 was the first based on the new science of dietetics and was designed to ensure that every member of the population received a balanced diet. While bread and potatoes remained unrationed and thus formed the bulk of the population's diet, other commodities were in short supply and people received less and less of them. Luxuries such as chocolate virtually disappeared, although children were allowed a weekly sweet ration. Rationing reached its peak in August 1942 and although allowances were meagre, they were sufficient. Each adult received 1 pound of meat a week supplemented by 4 ounces of bacon or ham but only 2 ounces of butter – along with another 4 ounces of margarine. As the war went on, more and more items came to be rationed so that even tinned food and tea were regulated in this way.

The scientific basis of British rationing in the Second World War meant that the population as a whole remained healthy and fit for war work. Special measures were taken to ensure that babies and young children received the vitamins and nutrients they needed to grow – this included extra milk and a vitamin C ration in the form of blackcurrant or rosehip juice. Indeed, rationing and fixed prices meant that even the poorest people had access to a balanced diet for the first time and this actually improved the general health of the population.

Rationing in Britain also went further than in any other country. Even furniture and clothes were regulated and various coupons and 'points' were received depending on circumstances. Newly married couples were lucky enough to receive extra points to set up their new home.

Even with such an organised and efficient system, there was a thriving black market run by 'spivs' who could secure almost anything from petrol to caviar – at a price. None the less, during a 'People's War' this comprehensive system of rationing was seen as essential. The rules were seen to be fair and meant that there was an equality of sacrifice throughout the population – regardless of wealth – and this contributed greatly to the feeling of solidarity in Britain during the war.

SCIENCE GOES TO WAR

Just as the provision of basic commodities like food and raw materials assumed enormous importance during mass warfare, and the war of production became all-important, so the harnessing of scientific endeavour became crucial to winning wars. During both world wars it became necessary to build on a technical lead to maintain the edge in the conduct of war. This race was less obvious during the First World War, but it was none the less profound.

Foremost in this technological battle was the development of aircraft from very flimsy and clumsy machines into much more formidable fighting platforms. Both sides had to compete in the race to build better aircraft since inferior fighter or 'scout' machines meant the loss of air superiority and heavy casualties. The speed of development meant that one year's cutting-edge fighter became the next year's 'sitting duck'. The Allied air forces experienced this twice in the 'Fokker Scourge' of 1915 and 'Bloody April' in 1917. The British and French development of the tank was one of the main innovations of the ground war, but developments in wireless communications were also of great importance.

The Second World War was popularly seen as the war of the 'boffins' in which scientific advances affected almost every aspect of the war. The Battle of Britain (1940) revealed just how complex and dependent on technology warfare had become. Modern, monoplane fighters like the

A V-2 bombardment rocket on its trailer. Like many weapons developed by Nazi Germany, the V-2 was over-engineered and ultimately a poor use of resources. It also had a limited range (200 miles), Nevertheless, its payload (2,150lb of high explosive) and supersonic speed made it a weapon of some psychological as well as physical value. A total of 517 V-2s hit London between 8 September 1944 and 27 March 1945, killing 2,700 people. A large number were also directed at the Belgian port of Antwerp, a crucial logistics base for the Allied campaign in north-west Europe. (IWM)

Spitfire and Hurricane, which the RAF deployed, managed to defeat the Luftwaffe not simply because of the determination of their young pilots. In fact, the use of the 'Chain Home' early warning radar stations, combined with radio control centres that vectored RAF squadrons on to German raiders, constituted one of the first examples of 'system' warfare in which many elements were brought together to achieve success. The 'Battle of the Beams' during the 'Blitz', in which British scientists attempted to bend or jam the German radio signals that guided their bombers on to British cities, was also one of the first examples of electronic warfare. The constant competition to make such scientific and technological developments was evident throughout the war in the production of radar, rocketry, tanks, aircraft and, of course, the atomic bomb.

Yet just as with the more basic requirements of the war effort, efficient management and coordinated use of scientific resources were essential. In fact they were more important for success than scientific imagination alone. Nazi Germany, although famed for such dramatic inventions as the V2 rocket, guided missiles and the Me 262 jet aircraft, was incredibly inefficient in utilising its scientific resources. With hundreds of competing and overlapping agencies, German scientific effort was dissipated and few really valuable inventions came to fruition. Britain's more careful and centralised organisation of its scientific capabilities through universities and the services led to the creation of the modern science of operational analysis. At the same time, British developments such as the centrimetric radar, the proximity fuse, and the breaking of the German 'Enigma' codes had a much more profound effect on the course of the war than the more dramatic German inventions.

ATTACKS ON THE HOME FRONT

All combatants realised the importance of the home front as a key element in the war effort. As a logical extension, civilians working on the home front soon became legitimate targets – since if the enemy's home front could be attacked and disrupted, the war could be won just as quickly as through battlefield success. The first real attempt to attack an enemy's home front was the German shelling of British coastal towns in 1914. The outrage caused by these ineffectual attacks far outweighed their benefit, but none the less the German use of Zeppelins and Gotha bombers over Britain from 1915 to 1917 in an attempt to break the British will to fight was a pointer to the future. By the Armistice the British had also created an independent force of heavy bombers to raid German cities in retaliation. Far more serious in its effects during the First World War was the British naval blockade of Germany and the German response of unrestricted submarine warfare against all shipping approaching Britain.

The fate of Germany in the First World War demonstrated the sacrifices that could be forced on a nation during total war. Germany was heavily dependent on foreign imports for many products (such as coffee and sugar) that were seen as staples of the German diet, which was based heavily on protein and fats. The British blockade of Germany had begun two days before the outbreak of war in 1914, and by 1918 was strangling Germany's supplies of food, fuel and resources.

Initially Germany had not suffered badly from the blockade and this led to an unfortunate complacency. However, the German military authorities made it quite clear that the German people were expected to 'sacrifice everything for the military needs of the state'. The Central Powers as a whole were never as adept as Britain or France at managing their resources or in ensuring that available food was distributed fairly. This wastage, combined with the blockade, led to the notorious 'Turnip Winter' of 1916–17, when German civilians subsisted on the next year's seed potatoes and turnips.

By the beginning of 1918, Germany lacked almost every basic commodity its civilians needed and, ominously, was beginning to experience shortages of war material as well. Hanging over all these problems was the inefficient distribution of the available food. The total food supplies for the civilian population should have given a ration of 3,000 calories a day (which was only 10 per cent below the amount considered adequate by the Allies). However, the Food Control Board could not ensure fair distribution between the producers in the countryside and the consumers in the towns, so that for the bulk of the population, 1,500 to 1,600 calories was the norm – only two-thirds that required to maintain health. Irrespective of the quantity of food, by 1918 there was no fat, milk, meat or coffee in the dull and monotonous diet. German civilians had been forced through requisitions to give up metal door handles, window fastenings, buttons and even toy soldiers, at the same time as their houses were left unlit and unheated. Living in cold, dark homes with only the bare minimum of food to sustain them, it is no surprise that German civilian morale broke in 1918.

Conversely, the German use of unrestricted submarine warfare in 1915 and 1917 was a direct attempt rapidly to starve Britain into submission. While the Germans had planned to win the war with their Army in a land campaign, the deadlock on the Western Front meant that by 1917 they

EVACUATION IN BRITAIN, 1939–44

With the threat of mass bombing from the air, the British government set in train an enormous policy of evacuating children from what were considered the most threatened areas to the comparative safety of the countryside. The evacuation of some 1½ million children began on 1 September 1939 and the railways ran 4,000 special trains during the four days of the plan. In the evenings, after a long and tiring journey, children were allocated billets with local householders – some of whom were willing to create a home from home and some of whom were not. This mass evacuation brought many middle-class rural people into direct contact with children from poor families who had lived in the cities in conditions of desperate poverty. Finally, Britain as a whole began to understand the reality of the Depression – and its effect on children. Many were lice-ridden and clothed in worn out hand-me-downs and some had never eaten chicken or eggs before. The psychological stress on the children who had been separated from their families was underestimated at the time. None the less, although many children returned to the cities in early 1940 – just in time for the 'Blitz' – others remained in the countryside for the rest of the war, and many relished the new life which the countryside could offer. There were further evacuations in 1940 and 1944, but none could rival the first for its size and psychological and social impact on British life.

The Second World War involved terrible civilian suffering, with homes destroyed and families uprooted on a massive scale. Here French mothers take cover with their children during a British barrage in Normandy, June 1944. (RMAS Collection)

turned to the new submarine weapon to win the war. The U-boat campaign brought Britain close to disaster, but the continued sinking of neutral, and in particular American shipping, brought the United States into the war in April 1917. The escalation of violence and targets could widen wars well beyond their original boundaries.

While attacks on the home front had been serious during the First World War, developments in technology between 1918 and 1939 meant that the Second World War saw unprecedented violence being directly inflicted upon civilians. Air power theorists in the inter-war years, such as Guilio Douhet in Italy, had argued that a state's entire war economy could be destroyed rapidly using strategic bombing from the air. This theory remained unproven during the inter-war years, but the bombing of Guernica in April 1937 and Shanghai between August and November the same year demonstrated that modern bombers could have a much greater impact than had been the case in the First World War. British planners feared that in any future war, huge fleets of German bombers would lay waste to British cities in a matter of hours and that civilian panic would lead to chaos and economic breakdown.

There had been moves in the thirties to ban attacks from the air and, indeed, both Britain and Germany refrained from attacking each other's

The real face of war. Victims of the firestorm, Hamburg 1943.

THE BOMBING OF HAMBURG

The first real demonstration of the power of massed bombing fleets was the firestorm that engulfed Hamburg in July 1943. Operation 'Gomorrah' was a combined effort by RAF Bomber Command and the US 8th Air Force. It was designed to destroy Germany's largest port city and inflict thousands of civilian casualties. Germany's second city had been bombed 137 times before and so its civil defence preparations were reasonable. However, on the night of 24/25 July, 740 British bombers caused a massive blaze which the German fire services were unable to put out until 26 July. With streets choked with rubble, the fire crews had found it impossible to reach many of the fires. On the night of 27/28 July, the RAF struck again and this time its 722 bombers created a fire of such intensity over an area of 22 square kilometres that the heat reached 1,000°C. This 'firestorm' created winds of up to 150 miles an hour which smashed buildings and sucked trees and people into the flames. The German fire service was overwhelmed.

The RAF came back again on 30 July and caused yet more havoc but the final raid on 2 August caused relatively little further damage. This ten-day operation was the most destructive series of raids on any German city. Some 40,000 people were killed, another 40,000 seriously injured and 61 per cent of Hamburg's homes were destroyed. Yet even after this enormous effort to destroy Hamburg, only 10 per cent of industrial capacity was disrupted and the 1.8 months of lost industrial production were soon made up by increased output elsewhere.

Devastated apartment blocks in Hamburg.

German air raids on Britain, 1940–3

	Tonnage dropped
1940	36,844
1941	21,848
1942	3,260
1943	2,298

cities in the opening stages of the Second World War. However, the logic of attacking the national capacity and will of an opponent to wage war soon resulted in bombing civilians. This began as an accident, when some German raiders mistook their targets and tipped their bombs over the East End of London. Churchill ordered a reprisal raid on Berlin and soon, Luftwaffe bombers were targeting London and other British provincial cities in what became known as the 'Blitz' during the winter of 1940/1.

The German bombing of British cities during this period was the first sustained attack upon an enemy's industrial capacity and civilian population. And yet, although the 'Blitz' was traumatic and destructive, the German campaign did not succeed in destroying British morale or capacity to wage war. London, in particular was subjected to almost nightly raids for months, but most Londoners settled down to the 'even tenor of the Blitz'. People actually became accustomed to sleeping in shelters – or at Tube stations – and then coping with the wreckage evident the next day. The raid on Coventry on 10 November 1940, when 100 square acres of the centre of the city were destroyed, did result in a collapse in morale, but its effects were local and temporary.

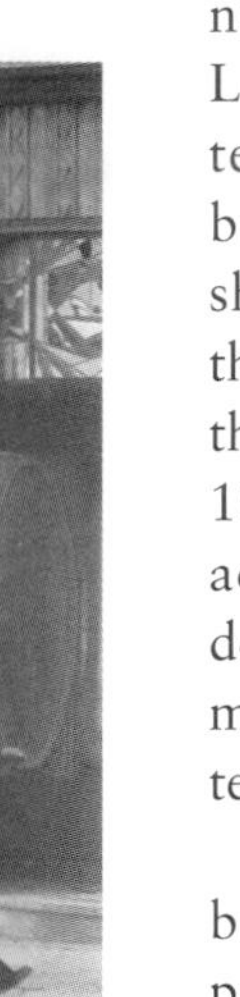

Both during and after the Second World War Nazi apologists tried to portray the conflict as a pan-European crusade against Bolshevism. This is a Waffen SS recruiting office in the French port of Calais, its doors closed after the liberation of the town by Canadian troops in September 1944. To their credit, relatively few Frenchmen responded to the Nazi call, and although a French SS division was nominally formed its strength never exceeded 7,000 men. (Robin Lumsden Collection)

Similarly, the British and American bombing offensive which gathered pace in 1942 with the RAF's first 'thousand bomber raid' on Cologne, failed to destroy German morale or industrial capacity. By 1944, the RAF and US 8th Air Force could mount round-the-clock raids with relative impunity and cause enormous destruction, but the raids on Dresden in February 1945 finally brought a reaction against the policy of targeting civilians in a total war. The United States' bombing campaign against Japan, which opened when B-29 bases were built within range of Japan after the capture of Saipan in August 1944, had a devastating impact. Within a matter of months the USAAF managed to smash Japanese industry and cause many casualties. The fire bombing of Tokyo on 9 March 1945 saw the destruction of Japan's first city and the deaths of 100,000 of its citizens. Even then, Japanese morale bent but did not break. The use of the atomic bombs on Hiroshima and Nagasaki was merely the logical extension of this terror bombing. None the less, after 1945 the world came to see that a future war fought to extremes would lead to nuclear devastation.

However, air bombardment was not the only way in which civilians could be brought directly into the war. For millions across Europe, Asia and Russia, war could be brought to them forcibly through the tragedy of occupation. Advancing armies generally drove huge numbers of refugees in their path. These columns began with the Belgian civilians who fled German occupation in 1914 and ended with the displacement of over 4 million Germans who left East Prussia in 1945. In the First World War, the German occupations of Belgium and northern France were deliberately ruthless in order to quell any attempts at resistance. By 1917 populations in the occupied area were close to starvation and encountered increasingly brutal treatment from the Germans. The Allied armies that advanced 100 miles in the autumn of 1918 were greeted not as conquerors but as liberators.

However, no matter how unpleasant the experience of occupation had been in the First World War for France, Belgium, Serbia, Romania and Ukraine, much worse was to follow in the Second World War. While German occupation forces in Western Europe were disliked by the inhabitants and could make life very hard, the situation was not as desperate as it became for millions of people in Eastern Europe. Motivated by extreme racial theories, Hitler's Germany inflicted terrible brutality on the people in its eastern occupied territories. Poland was entirely dismembered and officially ceased to exist. The Poles suffered systematic starvation and random executions throughout the war. In the Soviet Union, the German soldiers and authorities treated the population as *Untermenschen* (subhumans) who could be worked or starved to death.

Throughout Europe such harsh policies resulted in resistance to German occupation. Initially such protest was composed of passive resistance, but increasingly, bodies of guerrilla fighters were formed who began a policy of sabotage, assassination and armed resistance. This bloody undeclared war reached a height of savagery in occupied Russia. The Germans used their divisional and even army-sized anti-partisan operations as excuses to kill guerrillas and non-combatants alike.

Throughout the war, the Polish Home Army was one of the most determined and effective of resistance forces. In the summer of 1944 the Home Army even managed to snatch control of a large part of Warsaw from the Germans in a carefully planned operation which was bloodily suppressed by SS troops. Warsaw was destroyed and much of its population with it. The partisan and resistance struggle underlined the total nature of the conflict and brought untold sufferings to millions of civilians. In a very real sense there was no front line and no one was safe from the brutality of modern war.

THE OCCUPATION OF POLAND

While all countries occupied by a foreign army suffered great hardship, the Polish experience of being overrun by Nazi Germany from 1939 to 1945 was among the most terrible. Even before the Germans formally annexed Poland on 25 October 1939, over 530 towns and villages were burned and 16,376 people were killed. Unlike most countries occupied by the Germans, Poland's right to exist was denied. Germany annexed part of Polish territory but the rest was simply placed under the control of the General-Gouvernment. Nazi racial theories were first put into practice in Poland. Thousands of Poles were forcibly deported from areas earmarked for 'Germanisation' and the SS carried out a systematic programme of executing Poland's educated elite – which included doctors, lawyers and school-teachers. The Polish people received starvation rations and every day became a struggle to survive. In the face of such brutality, the Polish resistance movement became one of the most effective and best organised in Europe.

THE STRAIN OF TOTAL WAR

Both world wars were protracted struggles in which willpower, industrial might and manpower finally determined the outcome. In both conflicts, the defeated powers finally succumbed to national exhaustion. The strain of prosecuting such wars told on all the participants and combatants. Britain at

By 1944 the Germans faced a desperate manpower shortage, to which they responded by making increased use of older and younger age groups. These boy soldiers, captured by the British in June 1944, were not unusual among the forces encountered during the last year of the war. Having lived most of their lives under the Nazi regime, they often fought with fanatical bravery. (RMAS Collection)

the end of the First World War found itself transformed from a creditor to a debtor nation, with 957,000 dead and over 2 million wounded servicemen. France had been ravaged by occupation and suffered nearly 2 million dead, yet the threat of a resurgent Germany still existed. The Soviet Union in the Second World War suffered perhaps as many as 30 million dead, with vast tracts of European Russia ravaged and destroyed. Yet the cost of the war to the victors was only overshadowed by the devastation suffered by the defeated. In 1945 Germany lay in ruins, much of its population homeless and starving and its territory occupied and dismembered by four conquering armies.

The total economic, material and social cost of both world wars can never be calculated. Indeed, the human cost of the wars can never be fully known or perhaps even comprehended. The First World War cost over 9 million dead in Europe alone while the final cost of the Second World War also proved the disturbing reality that civilians were just as much a target during wartime. At least 18 million civilians were killed out of a total of perhaps 60 million dead. The psychological damage to the individuals and societies that came through these conflicts is still being felt today.

The political consequences of both wars were profound. Europe never really recovered from the First World War, and the second European 'civil war' removed Europe's pre-eminent status in the world. While the United States and the Soviet Union became the world's two dominant powers, the peoples of European colonies found their own voice through decolonisation and independence.

Such cataclysms were bound to change the shape and character of societies and peoples, and yet the social effects of total war can be overestimated. War brought greater freedom to women in many societies, an awareness of the problems of poverty and deprivation for fellow citizens and often a fierce belief that the conditions of the Great Depression must never happen again. If governments could release vast energies during wartime in ensuring that entire populations were fed, clothed and worked for the war effort, then why not in peacetime? Yet the conditions of wartime were unique and could not be replicated in peace. And, although many soldiers and civilians found the return to a peacetime existence difficult, societies across the world in 1918 and 1945 desperately craved a return to 'normality' – a peacetime existence that restored old values and social structures. At the end of both world conflicts, people certainly believed that the price of total war was too terrible to contemplate there being another.

THIRTEEN

THE COLD WAR ERA, 1945–72

SANDERS MARBLE

Was it a cold war, or a hot peace? The answer depended mainly on where you lived. If you were in either the democratic First World or most of the communist Second World, things were fine. However, if you lived in the Third World, it might have been very ugly indeed. This was because West and East deterred each other with nuclear arsenals that grew steadily into the 1980s. But mere deterrence and avoidance of fighting did not remove the causes of conflict. With both sides fundamentally, implacably opposed to the other, there was plenty of fuel to stoke fires. The nuclear weapons kept the lid on the pot. Rather than boiling over into a Third World War, the hot water spattered into a series of Third-World wars, fought between proxies, satellites or allies of the superpowers. The superpowers themselves were not exposed to the temptations and risks of escalation. The war was fought to win over 'enemy' civilians, not to gain ground. Nikita Khrushchev (1894–1971), Soviet leader from 1953 to 1964, aptly said that 'the struggle must be economic, political and ideological, but not military'.

'It is my earnest hope, indeed the hope of all mankind, that from this solemn occasion a better world shall emerge out of the blood and carnage of the past, a world founded upon faith and understanding, a world dedicated to the dignity of man and the fulfilment of his most cherished dream for freedom, tolerance and justice.'

General Douglas MacArthur, 2 September 1945

THE START OF THE COLD WAR

It had not even started out as a conflict. Within days of Hitler's invasion of Russia (22 June 1941), the West offered aid to the USSR. When the Soviets proved capable of stopping and then beating the Germans there was a tremendous upsurge of interest in and respect for the Soviet government. It had done something nobody else had. Clearly, communism had some strengths, some truth to succeed where democratic Western Europe had failed. But respect did not really translate into support of communism. Western governments worked with the Soviets, but to win the war, not to redraw boundaries in Europe for a new balance of power. As the day of Hitler's fall came closer and closer, tensions about the shape of the post-war world grew, although they remained below the surface. There was a short honeymoon after Germany's surrender that only lasted into the spring of 1946 – not even a year after the war. Stalin had pursued a traditional Russian policy of expansionism: into the Caucasus (trying to create a puppet

The Cold War, 1945–50

Feb 1945	Yalta Conference
July 1946	Bikini Atoll US atomic weapons test
March 1947	Truman doctrine of support of 'free peoples'
June 1947	Marshall Plan for European economic recovery proposed
Feb 1948	Communist coup in Czechoslovakia
June 1948	Berlin blockade begins
April 1949	NATO formed
May 1949	Berlin blockade ends
Sept 1949	First Soviet atomic weapon tested
June 1950	North Korea invades South Korea

STALIN AND KHRUSHCHEV.

Of course the Cold War looked different from the Soviet, or Russian, perspective. Immediately after the Second World War Josef Stalin and the Communist Party had a tremendous reservoir of good will: they had, apparently against the odds, defeated Hitler. Stalin brought back the stifling censorship and controls of pre-war years and channelled the people's efforts into rebuilding the country. Industrial output increased, but standards of living rose slowly because of the infrastructure that had to be rebuilt. The price was borne willingly because of the prestige of the Party and Stalin. But in his last years Stalin was returning to his paranoid purges of the 1930s, and it is well for the world he died before more millions perished.

Nikita Khrushchev emerged in 1953 as the Soviet leader, and a large part of his consolidation of power involved undermining Stalin's legacy. It was not a question of ideology: Khrushchev genuinely thought he was helping to build communism, and the state would wither away once capitalist imperialism was defeated. He did make communism more palatable: there were more consumer goods, fewer tanks (but more missiles), more homes, fewer arrests by the secret police, vast new tracts of land broken to the plough and yielding crops. He also destroyed Stalin's political legacy in an extraordinary secret speech to the Party Conference in 1956, admitting that what had formerly been described as 'capitalist slanders' against Stalin were true: their own leader had killed millions of Soviet citizens. His words sent a shock through all communist parties and embarrassed them against their foes.

But Khrushchev's energy got him into trouble. His foreign policy lurched around, winning no friends for intervention in Hungary (1956) and Cuba (1962), while his frequent shake-ups of the Party in the USSR meant a growing cadre of enemies at home. Stalin would have shot or imprisoned men he removed; ironically, Khrushchev retired them, and they lived to see his removal.

regime in northern Iran); pressing Turkey for access through the Bosphorus; gobbling up most of the Balkans (setting up puppet regimes in Romania and Bulgaria; supporting communists in Yugoslavia and Albania, backing the Greek communists); and moving into Eastern Europe as well, with regimes in Poland, Hungary, Czechoslovakia and eastern Germany. It is quite possible that Stalin would have quit after these gains, having secured a safe buffer zone for the USSR.

But mixed with normal Great Power politics was ideology. As far as the West could tell, the threat came not just from Russian expansionism (or securing of borders), but the tentacles of world communism, and ideas knew no borders. The West had yielded Stalin a sphere of influence, but had not anticipated that each of the countries within it would be put under a communist government, marching in step with Moscow. Everywhere the Red Army had gone the Soviets tried to set up a communist government – and only failed in Austria where elections were real, not staged. The West was also scared of the strength of its own communist parties. Admiration for the Russians' struggle against Nazi Germany meant more communists and more 'fellow travellers'. Furthermore, the communists had earned considerable respect for their role in anti-Nazi resistance movements throughout Western Europe. In the immediate aftermath of the war it was a close thing whether France and Italy would elect communist governments.

Out of alarm at the apparently insidious spread of communism, the USA started a policy of containment. There was no stomach in the United States for remobilisation and a fresh war against Russia, but neither was there any intention of giving in to the 'Commies'. So in March 1947 President Harry S. Truman (1884–1972) proclaimed a noble, but limited, call: support for 'free peoples who are resisting attempted subjugation by armed minorities or outside pressure'. The Americans drew a perimeter around the USSR beyond which expansion was forbidden, and into which communism was contained. At the time the struggle was largely between the United States and the Soviet Union: Western Europe was too poor, before the massive financial aid provided through the Marshall Plan took effect, to play a large role. Britain and France were struggling to rebuild their own countries, create welfare states, and deal with their fragmenting empires. Nearly bankrupt of money and low on fighting power, they ceded primacy in the struggle against communism to the USA. Britain handed over its position in Greece and Turkey, while the French asked for American support in Indo-China.

There were new ground rules for this 'war by other means'. The Soviets would not be permitted to expand their sphere of influence, but at least after 1956 the West would not try to roll it back. In Europe the battle lines were drawn for the next half-century. Winston Churchill, speaking at an obscure American college at Fulton, Missouri, gave the boundary its name: the Iron Curtain.

The world briefly settled down into an armed peace, with the Soviets busy rebuilding their devastated country and the USA reviving the West through the Marshall Plan. Then things changed. The Soviets had been agitating for better terms in Germany, but had got nowhere because they offered nothing in return. In June 1948, to squeeze the West, they cut off land access to Berlin. At first perplexed, then angry, the West reacted, but avoided direct confrontation, showing how little it wanted war even when the Americans had a nuclear monopoly. Various US generals proposed sending troops to escort trains, or bombing Soviet airbases, but instead a massive, unprecedented airlift supplied the population of a whole city for a year. The political ramifications were important: the West would not yield to Soviet arm-twisting, but this was the Soviets' first overt threat in Western Europe.

'If we retreat from Berlin, then after Berlin will come Western Germany. If we mean . . . to hold Europe against communism, we must not budge.'

General Lucius Clay, US Military Governor, in Germany, 1948

The Berlin blockade resulted in a serious Cold War defeat for the USSR. Over 2 million tonnes of coal, food and other supplies were delivered by US and British aircraft between 26 June 1948 and 30 September 1949. Here some of the city's 2.5 million inhabitants watch an American Douglas C-54 transport land at Tempelhof airport in west Berlin. (US Air Force)

NUCLEAR WARFARE AND STRATEGY

Nuclear weapons had a huge impact on the future of warfare. The idea of a 'decisive' nuclear attack was voided by MAD (Mutually Assured Destruction): if the world was a cinder, who had won? Even the 'hawks' who believed some victory was possible were left predicting friendly casualties in the tens of millions. At first the impossibility of a nuclear war was not so evident, mainly because there were not many warheads, nor were they very powerful. The USA (and thus NATO) could, in good conscience, adopt a policy of 'Massive Retaliation' in 1954: if the Soviets put a foot across the border, they would immediately be hit with everything. It looked cheap, at least in money, because conventional forces could be slashed. This argument began to crumble not only because the Soviets built up their own forces but also because it provided absolutely no flexibility.

Massive Retaliation meant that any provocation immediately resulted in a nuclear nightmare. It was the ultimate expression of brinkmanship, and bluff. Western societies (communist peoples were allowed no say in the matter) began to fear invasion less than nuclear destruction. Under President John F. Kennedy (1917–63) the mantra became Flexible Response, which proclaimed that NATO would build up its conventional forces, would not be the first to use nuclear weapons, would fight a conventional war to start with and only escalate if the communists did. It was an uncomfortable doctrine, largely because NATO was often weaker in conventional forces and thus might have to escalate, but it was never tested.

The construction of the first nuclear-powered ballistic missile submarines (SSBNs) added another means of delivering weapons of mass destruction to the existing air- and land-based systems, creating in the process the nuclear 'triad'. This is the first operational SSBN, the USS George Washington, *which carried sixteen Polaris missiles and entered service in 1959. (US National Archives)*

The reason why it was never tested, of course, was that the nuclear arsenals of the superpowers deterred war between them. However, deterrence rested on some risky assumptions. If the Soviets built up their air defences, US bombers would lose their threat and the USSR might be tempted to strike at US missile silos. Anti-Ballistic Missiles were an alarming development that threatened the whole fabric of deterrence, except that nobody could make them work; something which led both sides to negotiate them away. The switch, in the late 1960s and 1970s, from liquid- to solid-fuelled rockets meant faster reaction times, but also created a tension until both sides had them: nobody wanted to get caught fuelling their liquid-fuel rockets as enemy rockets arched inwards, so a first strike became slightly more likely. Even the idea of shifting targets from cities to missile silos, apparently a humanitarian gesture, had mad, MAD side effects. If the enemy aimed at silos, and developed missiles good enough to hit them, he might be encouraged to try, thus weakening deterrence. Later, missiles were put on submarines, so that they could lurk unseen as a deterrent, but this stimulated a frantic technical race to locate submarines through several methods (and hide them through others). There were plans to put missiles on bombers (later developed into cruise missiles) or in space. Sometimes programmes were started without much intention of full development, but just to put pressure on the enemy, or to be traded away in negotiations. All in all, nuclear strategy became a chess match, both sides trying to see several moves into the future – and hoping for checkmate.

'Deterrence is our primary mission, and peace is our profession. We have a mixed force of bombers and missiles to carry out this mission.'

US General Bruce C. Halloway, 1969

Stalin loathed his military position after Hiroshima and made the development of a Soviet atomic bomb a high priority. It was achieved, with considerable help from spies, in 1949. In a split second, the detonation of the Soviet A-bomb changed the world's diplomatic and military balance. Gradually nuclear strategy developed on both sides of the Iron Curtain. Until the mid-1960s there was the possibility of attacking first and catching the opposition's missiles or bombers on the ground. But quickly enough both sides built enough missiles and kept bombers constantly aloft so that there would always be retaliation. What ensued fully justified the acronym MAD: Mutually Assured Destruction. Nobody could guarantee to knock out the enemy's warheads, and there were enough to ensure that your own cities would be levelled.

THE COLD WAR HOTS UP

The first fighting of the Cold War was about as far from Western Europe as possible. In setting out its containment perimeter, the USA had neglected to mention Korea; the Secretary of State simply left it off his list in an important speech. This was doubly problematic, since the temporary wartime demarcation line between US and Soviet forces which had entered

A communist leaflet calls on US troops to desert during the early part of the Korean War (1950–3). The reference to good treatment was of course nonsense – in fact, both sides treated prisoners harshly. Nevertheless, 21 Americans did refuse repatriation at the end of the war, preferring to make a new life in the communist world rather than return to the USA. (IWM BF436)

WE GUARANTEE GOOD TREATMENT TO YOU

All the American officers and soldiers who already came to our side have been well treated by the Korean peoples' Army and the Chinese volunteers. They will surely be given the opportunity to be sent back to their home as soon as possible. Then they can eat the apple sauce prepared by their mother and stroke the brown hair of their wives again.

PUT DOWN YOUR WEAPONS AND COME OVER TO US. YOU WILL SURELY GET THE SAME TREATMENT. IF YOU FIGHT ON, YOU WILL DIE SHAMFULLY AND UNWORTHILY FOR TRUMAN AND MACARTHUR. THEN EVERYTHING IS GONE.

'In war there is no substitute for victory.'

General Douglas MacArthur, 1951

'Korea has been a blessing. There had to be a Korea either here or some place in the world.'

General James A. Van Fleet, 1952

'The wrong war, at the wrong place, at the wrong time and with the wrong enemy.'

General Omar N. Bradley, 1951, referring to Korea

The Cold War, 1951–9

Sept 1952	Establishment of South-East Asia Treaty Organisation (SEATO)
Oct 1952	Britain explodes its first atomic bomb
Nov 1952	USA explodes its first hydrogen bomb
July 1953	Korean War armistice
Aug 1953	USSR explodes its first hydrogen bomb
Oct 1954	West Germany admitted to NATO
May 1955	Warsaw Pact formed
Oct 1956	Soviet troops suppress Hungarian uprising
Nov–Dec 1956	Suez Crisis
May 1957	Britain explodes its first hydrogen bomb
Oct 1957	Sputnik launched
Dec 1959	First Polaris submarine enters US service

previously Japanese-controlled Korea – the 38th Parallel – had already sent mixed signals to the Soviets. It had been the line for Japanese and Russian spheres of influence before the First World War, and the Soviets may have assumed that the Americans were writing off the peninsula. They got a shock when the USA – operating through the United Nations (UN) to reduce the direct tensions – intervened rapidly after North Korean forces invaded the south in July 1950. US forces were shown to be badly out of shape at first, but soon got themselves in order and after a bold amphibious invasion at Inchon on 15 September 1950 chased the North Koreans almost to the Chinese border. The Chinese felt threatened, intervened in late November and rolled the UN forces back.

This brought a dramatic rift in US policy-making. General Douglas MacArthur (1880–1964), Commander-in-Chief Far East, spoke for an older generation of strategy that refused to compromise 'victory'. He wanted to widen the war, bring in Nationalist China and drop as many atom bombs on Red China as it took to 'save' Korea. The Truman administration took a more rational view of what constituted victory and settled for pushing the communists back and establishing a free Korea, even if it included only half the peninsula. Neither side's leaders wished to escalate to a world war. A ceasefire was negotiated in July 1953 and the Koreans are still divided after three years of war and forty-seven of suspicion and threat.

This was the dramatic part of the Cold War, but most of it was conducted by less aggressive means. With conflict too likely to escalate beyond the nuclear threshold, for most of the time the war was just confrontation. Clausewitz might have approved because the Cold War was really politics as war, rather than war as politics. Words were the main weapons, and were valued or devalued according to the source. Communism relied on such outlets as the Communist Information Bureau to spread the good news of the future of mankind. Support could be given to any group that undermined the opposition, and by any means. Politicians who opposed communism could still be on the books of the KGB as 'agents of influence' so long as they argued for sweeping changes in the West. Human rights, anti-colonialism, anti-nuclear groups, any opposition to the status quo might somehow be supported from Moscow. A 'World Conference of Intellectuals for Peace' held in Poland would mean one thing; a 'Conference of World Intellectuals for Peace' in West Germany would have a different final position because both sides played the same game. Radio Free Europe broadcast to the Workers' Paradises east of the Iron Curtain. Eastern and Western diplomats vied to make the most turgid and pointless speeches in the UN. Resolutions were drafted in the full knowledge that they would be vetoed, but the point was to force the veto rather than find any solution. The object was not to change the mind of the opposing governments, but to sap the will of the opposing population. Victory in this conflict would come not from a single lightning strike, but through a process of incremental moral attrition.

Friendly morale had to be supported too, very largely through economic gains. Capitalism claimed it was a more efficient economic system that would produce more; communism held out for more equitable distribution of goods. (Khrushchev of course claimed that communism would out-produce capitalism as well, and so 'bury' it.) Here the Americans stole a march on the Soviets through the Marshall Plan. Billions of dollars, when a billion dollars bought something, rescued the economies of Western Europe. It did no harm to the USA either, since most of the money bought American goods. The Americans extended aid to friendly governments in the Far East, in the process setting Japan on the road to where it is today. The communist counterpart was the Council for Mutual Economic Assistance, and it failed. Never more than a cloak for Soviet trade demands, it also suffered as a result of the low economic levels of some member countries. Cuba, for instance, needed virtually everything except sugar, and only had sugar to give in return.

To win hearts and minds, peaceful aid was extended. This might take the form of engineers building dams and highways, or the Peace Corps trying to reduce disease. These programmes would have been genuinely altruistic had the world not been so polarised, but the people involved were genuine volunteers. As it was, the programmes were intended not only to help the less fortunate, but to show that the donors cared, and so defuse (from the Western view) or increase (as the Soviets hoped) claims about which system was fairer.

The Red Army massively outnumbered the conventional forces of the western powers for much of the Cold War. These are Soviet T-62 main battle tanks, the mainstay of Soviet armoured units from 1965 onwards. Cheap, easy to manufacture and robust, over 40,000 T-62s were produced, with thousands being exported to the USSR's friends around the globe. (Jonathan Falconer Collection)

Aid also took less pleasant forms. Arms were sold or given wherever there was a chance of advantage, to the point where Kalashnikovs were just about everywhere. Nor was the USA slow in arming its allies. Indeed, canny governments in strategic parts of the world often had both US and Soviet arms in their arsenals.

All this effort was directed towards decisively defeating the opposing value system. But with the superpowers hemmed in by the risks of direct confrontation, it was safer to play the game through intermediaries. The Americans preferred to use military advisers to support the armed forces of their allies in a ring of containment around the USSR. The Soviets, after the Korean War, operated mainly in the Third World and sent some advisers, but also used the convenient fig leaf of communist solidarity. Thus Cuban or East German troops sweated in Africa while the Red Army stayed in Europe. (Anticipating events slightly, the Soviet method worked except on the one occasion the Red Army became directly involved: Afghanistan.)

'All diplomacy is a continuation of war by other means.'

Chon en Lai, Chinese politician, 1954

But for all the tension between the superpowers, between communism and capitalism, there were other things happening in the world. The US State Department for a long time had trouble understanding this. John Foster Dulles (1888–1959), Secretary of State between 1953 and 1959, had polarised vision: countries were either friends or enemies. In this he did little more than mirror the views of many of his countrymen, who had grown up isolated from the rest of the world and saw little reason to change. With good and evil toe-to-toe, many Americans did not appreciate the nuances of diplomacy. But Dulles' black-and-white views did little for countries that were not interested in either joining or fighting the Communist Bloc. The whole Non-Aligned Movement tried to steer an independent course between capitalism and communism, desperately trying to get the aid and expertise they needed by playing off one bloc against the other.

THIRD-WORLD WARS

Also confusing the issue were conflicts and struggles that had little to do with the Cold War. The big European empires collapsed or were given up more or less gracefully in the 1950s and 1960s. The United Nations (UN) roughly tripled in membership as various bits of empires obtained their independence. African countries generally avoided ideology better than did Asian ones, but Africa saw more civil and tribal wars, as well as factional power struggles, while Asia had more inter-state conflict.

'War has become a luxury that only the small nations can afford.'

Hannah Arendt (1906–75), 1971

Colonial wars gave opportunities to communists: they opposed colonialism for ideological reasons, and independence movements found the Eastern Bloc more than willing to provide arms. Furthermore, if the colonial power was divided at home about holding on to its colonies, dissension tended to put people of good will on the same side as communists. Probably the worst situation was in French North Africa. The now independent states of Morocco, Algeria and Tunisia were then officially part of France, legally no different from the mainland. How could they be yielded? Furthermore, the French communists were already a powerful force and the nation came close to tearing itself apart on the issue. By comparison, the British Empire sank gracefully away, despite the desires of some (led by Churchill, who said he did not become Prime Minister to preside over the demise of the Empire) to hold on. There were nasty colonial struggles, but the British managed never to antagonise the whole local population. Thus the bizarre Mau-Mau uprising of 1952–60 in Kenya (itself nothing to do with communism) was firmly quashed and terrorists in Aden (1964–7) were temporarily held off with the aid of at least some of the population. On occasion a local government would be supported against encroachments, like the Borneo Confrontation (1963–6), when Indonesia was deterred from a serious invasion by the deployment of British troops.

Although the uprising among the Kikuyu people of Kenya was suppressed by British and colonial military and police forces, without radical social, economic and political reforms the campaign would have ended in an expensive stalemate. Indeed, the prospect of independence and majority rule for the indigenous population was a crucial factor in swaying the Kikuyu away from the insurgents, and towards the colonial authorities. These are Kikuyu Guards, raised by the British as part of their counter-insurgency effort. (RMAS Collection)

On other occasions there were wars in the Third World involving countries that had little to do with the superpowers, but that none the less got caught up in their rivalry and power politics. India and Pakistan disliked each other from the moment of partition, and are still arguing over the final fate of Kashmir. Pakistan became a US client (or ally, depending on one's views) while India was in the outer orbit of the USSR. The three wars (1948, 1965, 1971) between the two

THE EFFECT OF THE COLD WAR ON SOCIETIES

Like all wars, the Cold War had a profound effect on the societies that were embroiled in it. The good news was that ministries of war became ministries of defence. The bad news was that the world lost the distinction between peace and war. There were no invasions, but there was the constant possibility of invasion. Most human beings, especially those in capitalist and communist countries, could be incinerated by nuclear weapons within about twelve minutes of a war starting. The world wars had shown that societies had to be mobilised behind their armies, but now mobilisation lasted for decades. Military service was extended to peacetime in Britain (until 1963) and the USA (until 1973); continental countries were already accustomed to this. With borders invisible to aeroplanes, and increasingly satellites, spying developed to include 'technical means' and expanded vastly, with the KGB and CIA just the headline opponents. Everybody spied on anyone they could. But without declarations of war, and with gains and losses measured in influence and inclination of third parties, defence suddenly had a new counterpart: security. Everything affected security. The health of the general population was a concern, because the armed forces needed sturdy servicemen. Education too was part of the battleground, and not just in terms of inculcating nationalism. With a struggle settling in for generations, new technologies might be decisive. Whoever fell behind might never catch up, so general education and especially science received money. Perhaps the best example was America's National Defence Education Act, raced through Congress just after *Sputnik* (1957) showed a Soviet advantage. A few years earlier, nobody would have linked education and national defence; now they were inextricable.

'No American who works for the CIA is a spy. A spy is a foreign agent who commits treason.'

Jim Keehner, CIA psychologist, 1976

A parallel development was the extension of security consciousness into domestic affairs. Spies might be anywhere, since ideology reached across borders. Communism attracted many of the best and brightest in the 1930s, and some rose to positions of importance in science, government and – embarrassingly in Britain – the security services themselves. The possibility that 'Reds' might be anywhere led to demagogues like US Senator Joe McCarthy (1908–57) whipping up frenzies that Reds were everywhere. Fortunately, the worst spy scares passed, but soon enough every civilian's peace of mind would be undermined by terrorism.

Terrorism, like nuclear waste, was a by-product of the Cold War. A minority group or fringe political group would split, and the more radical members would take their ideology seriously enough to take up arms. Since the superpowers had to be discreet, and undermine rather than overthrow their opponents, barmy groups that had languished for generations, or student radicals who never outgrew their youthful rebellion, suddenly had patrons. Alternately, relatively responsible countries might find their clients passing weapons on to someone else – from the Eastern Bloc to Libya, and then who knew where. Ironically, many of the groups that flourished for a time in the West, with dramatic programmes to overthrow Western oppression and tyranny, and which were backed by dribbles of communist aid, would have been crushed as soon as communism took over. Some were sophisticated enough to take what they could get, hoping to achieve their limited political aims and have the West still win. The problem for innocent civilians was that terrorist bombs and bullets lacked any ideology or sophistication.

had nothing to do with communism or democracy, but from Washington and Moscow they were viewed through that distorting prism. The Cypriot rebellion (1955–60) was caused by nationalism, not international communism, and for a while the tension between Greece and Turkey – ironically two NATO members – threatened to cross into war. The assorted Arab–Israeli wars (1948, 1956, 1967, 1973) did not really fit the East–West pattern either. Israel was democratic and the Arab countries generally were not, but that did not stop the West supporting various Arab governments and Israel too. Nor did it stop the Soviets trying for as much

Decolonisation, 1946–76

1946	USA gives independence to the Philippines
1947–8	Britain gives independence to India, Pakistan, Burma and Sri Lanka (Ceylon)
1949	Netherlands gives independence to Indonesia (Dutch East Indies)
1954	France begins withdrawal from Indo-China
1956	France gives independence to Morocco and Tunisia; Britain gives independence to Sudan
1957	Britain gives independence to Malaya and Ghana
1960	Britain gives independence to Nigeria, Belgium to Zaire (Belgian Congo) and France to 14 new African states
1960–6	Britain gives independence to 9 new African states
1962	France gives independence to Algeria
1974–5	Portugal gives independence to Guinea-Bissau, Angola and Mozambique
1976	Spain evacuates the Spanish Sahara

influence in the region as possible. Since the West gave support to Israel, the Soviets made most of their gains in Arab areas. But no country in the Middle East was interested in Marxism–Leninism. They wanted arms, technology and aid. Their goals were their own: all wanted to increase their influence in the region and/or prop up their regimes. Because of the strategic and economic importance of the region (the Suez Canal, warm water ports and, of course, oil) the West made common cause with some very dubious governments. The Shah of Iran (1919–80) was never likely to win a Nobel Peace Prize, Saudi Arabia had laws probably as strict as any Muslim country and the Egyptian version of democracy was quite dilute. None of this made the wars an East–West problem, although by 1973 Soviet regional influence had risen sufficiently that it came close.

Angola provides a fine example of how the Cold War distorted the real issues in some areas. The Portuguese had tried to hold on to their colonial empire, but finally had to admit that maintaining it was beyond their strength. In 1974 the Portuguese government fell, and the Army – for once left-wing – held power loosely. Decolonisation took place rapidly, and provoked a race to see who would consolidate power as the Portuguese left. There were three groups vying in Angola: the Popular Movement for the Liberation of Angola (MPLA), the National Union for the Total Independence of Angola (UNITA) and the National Front for the Liberation of Angola (FNLA). The groups had cooperated at various times and had no strong ideologies; the MPLA was furthest to the left, the USA had sometimes backed the FNLA, and UNITA was largely tribal. The Portuguese Army and USSR – strange bedfellows – for various reasons both backed the MPLA. The USA continued hesitant support for the FNLA as the State Department and CIA bickered with each other. Meanwhile, the Chinese had been backing UNITA and were joined by the South Africans – even stranger bedfellows. Then Cuban troops turned up in large numbers, any chances for a shaky government by Angolans died and a civil war still shreds the country, with nobody able to win. Neither capitalism nor communism solved anything in Angola, and more people are dead because of the involvement of both.

The most striking example of Western involvement in the Third World, and impossible to justify in East–West terms, was the Suez Crisis of 1956. At this time Britain and France were both losing influence in the world. The British Empire was being handed over as fast as it decently could be; France had just lost Indo-China, left Syria to the Syrians and was making no progress in the tangle of Algeria. Britain had given Egypt its independence (for real, rather than the nominal independence it had since 1919) and the Egyptians had not been terribly grateful. Their monarchy had failed, Colonel Gamal Abdel Nasser (1918–70) and the Army had taken over and were apparently taking the country towards socialism, and Nasser was being nicer to the USSR than previously. (Socialist governments were more acceptable in Europe than in the Third World, because apparently European democratic socialism was not liable to descend into communism: indeed, the British Labour government had played a leading role in the formation of NATO in 1949.) The situation in Egypt gave the French and British the fig leaf they needed to intervene. But they were still hesitant, and so thc invasion convoys circled while the

ISRAEL'S SURVIVAL STRATEGY, 1948–72

The creation through war of the new state of Israel between 1947 and 1949 (out of the former British League of Nations Trusteeship Territory of Palestine) not only transformed the political map of the Middle East, but it also provided a unique theatre within which the Cold War would be fought. When the United Nations voted to recognise and admit Israel in May 1948, the Soviet Union voted in favour along with the United States – the USSR judging that the existence of Israel would cause problems between the United States and its Western European allies. Both the British and the French in particular had long-term positive relations with many Arab states.

The existence of Israel united the Arab world as no other issue had done. As the British withdrew, the neighbouring states of Egypt, Syria, Lebanon and Transjordan (later just 'Jordan') attempted to wipe Israel out. Although the fighting ended in negotiated ceasefires along boundary lines in 1949, no Arab country would recognise Israel, which remained in a state of undeclared siege, and rapidly developed a political 'siege mentality' to cope.

The basic Israeli strategy for survival was laid down by its first prime minister, David Ben-Gurion (1886–1973). Israel was a tiny country with a population of only a few million people and no natural resources of any consequence. It could never afford to antagonise or confront either of the two superpowers directly. But it had to be prepared to fight any combination of neighbouring states, on the assumption that it could be attacked at any time. Particularly ominous was the threat of a 'two-front war', a simultaneous attack from both Egypt and Syria, with Egypt judged to be the greater danger. Since deterrence and prevention were vastly cheaper than actual warfare, Israel devoted considerable resources to military and political Intelligence, including its spy service, the Mossad.

'An Israeli operational initiative taken against concentrations of enemy forces, and the occupation on enemy territory of targets having a vital security significance, at a time when the enemy is mustering his forces for an attack but before he has time to actually start his offensive.'

General Allan, Israeli Defence Force, defines the 'Anticipatory Counter-Attack'

Israel's thin and pointed shape made it quite impossible to defend. Surrounded by enemy countries with larger populations, and therefore large conscript armies that were supported by technology at least as good as that which Israel could afford, the Israelis knew they would lose a long defensive war. Therefore, they decided that they must base their defence on creating enough forces with which to attack, and even on carrying out a pre-emptive attack without warning if they felt sufficiently threatened. It is a historical irony that Israel very much copied the structure and doctrines of its armed forces from those of Germany and the Soviet Union. The Israeli Defence Force (IDF) was an all-conscript force structured to mobilise fully in a day or two, ready to take the field. Once mobilised it was meant to strike heavily against the waiting enemy, exploiting what the Israelis saw as their natural superiorities in leadership, morale and familiarity with the technology of war.

To the geopoliticians and theorists of both sides in the Cold War, the Middle East held a particular significance in the structure of world power. Increasingly, after the Israeli involvement in the Suez Crisis of 1956, both Egypt and Syria moved into the Soviet camp, while Israel continued to look for support from the United States and other Western countries. Although wars of proxy were not unusual in this period, they were almost all fought at a low level of military intensity. The confrontation between Israel and its neighbours produced an irregular pattern of about one major war per decade and a number of minor skirmishes, all fought by conventional means. After their involvement in Suez convinced the Israelis of the value of armour in desert warfare, the IDF became the great exponent of classical manoeuvre warfare, including the use of aircraft in combination with tanks. The rest of the world had hardly seen a major armoured battle since the Korean War.

In terms of actual experience upon which potential conflicts between NATO and the Warsaw Pact might be planned, the Arab–Israeli Wars were almost the only game in town. By the 1960s the confrontation seemed to Cold Warriors on both sides to offer a laboratory in which equipment, theories and doctrines of warfighting could be tested without the risk of direct superpower collision. Much of Israeli strategy in particular seemed to fit neatly into American ideas of graduation and limitation in warfare, notably the belief that war should be short and decisive, but that the enemy should never be backed into a corner, and that the superpowers would exercise their political leverage to prevent their client states from being utterly defeated.

Although they needed both the political support and the arms, neither Israel nor its Arab enemies found the role of Cold War proxy comfortable. For both sides, conflict was about national survival and in no sense 'limited', except from a distant perspective. The supply of arms and equipment was also a constant source of friction between Israel and the West, leading to Israel developing its own arms industry – an astonishing achievement for a country so small.

The Israeli warfighting strategy was seriously tested just once in this period and worked brilliantly. In May 1967 the Egyptians and Syrians began to build up forces along their frontiers with Israel. The Israelis mobilised, and on 5 June unleashed a surprise air attack on Egypt and Syria, virtually destroying their air forces on the ground. Jordan joined in, together with other Arab countries that sent symbolic ground or air units to fight. But after four days' fighting Israeli armour and infantry had smashed through the Egyptian forces defending the Sinai frontier, who were now in full rout. Reaching the natural stop-line of the Suez Canal, the Israelis halted and redirected their forces northwards, taking the West Bank of the Jordan and east Jerusalem (captured by Transjordan from Palestinian territory in 1948) and the Golan Heights (captured by Syria in 1948). On 12 June, with Israeli armoured columns theoretically able to reach all three Arab capital cities, the superpowers agreed a ceasefire resolution in the United Nations Security Council. The 'Six Day War' was the greatest triumph for the Israeli military system. By the early 1970s, Israel had acquired Hiroshima-style atomic weapons in collaboration with the Republic of South Africa – something to which neither ever officially admitted – and the idea that the state of Israel might be destroyed in battle had ceased to be.

diplomats persuaded the Israelis to attack Egypt, thus allowing the European powers to intervene. How long Britain and France would have continued the 'intervention' we shall never know; the USA threatened to remove the economic support that Britain desperately needed and the inglorious episode was over in a few weeks.

Suez was a catastrophe for the West. Britain and France were humiliated in the UN and at home once the world had seen through the smokescreen of 'intervention'. It was clear the USA was the real power in the West: economic pressure alone had been enough to bring the former Great Powers to heel. What was arguably worse for the democratic cause was the wasted opportunity. For at the same time as Suez, the Red Army had defeated a genuinely popular movement in Hungary. The Hungarian people wanted freedom, and Russian tanks crushed them. The West had a priceless propaganda opportunity, but could not exploit it because Britain and France were doing things that gave the communists propaganda that was just as good. The net result was that the Middle East leaned a little more towards Moscow while Britain huddled a bit closer to the United States.

Then in 1957 the Russians launched *Sputnik*, the world's first artificial satellite. Suddenly there was a new vocabulary: the 'gap'. There was a missile gap here, another gap there. Not to be outdone, the USA poured money into science and eventually overtook the Soviets. In 1969 it became the first country to land a man on the moon (and get him back). Science had to leave its ivory tower.

In the late 1950s and early 1960s the Americans were behind in the space race, but generally ahead in aircraft. This lead prompted some overconfidence and President Dwight D. Eisenhower (1890–1969) was caught telling a direct lie. The USA was understandably not content to believe only what the Soviets said about their armed forces, and used a

Soviet premier Nikita Khruschev (far left) and US Vice-President Richard Nixon (holding microphone stand) debate the 'inevitable' collapse of capitalism, Moscow 1959. Their smiling faces barely disguise the tension that existed between the USA and USSR at this time. (David King Collection)

variety of Intelligence means, including spy planes. Because of formidable Soviet air defences, specialised planes had to be built, flying too high to be intercepted – a point of which the Americans were certain. Unfortunately, the Soviets were better than the US Air Force had allowed for, and in May 1960 shot down a U2 spy plane, even capturing the pilot, Francis Gary Powers. Khrushchev played his cards well, announcing the loss of an aircraft. The Americans denied this, then admitted it might have been a weather reconnaissance plane from Turkey that strayed across the border. Khrushchev then produced the plane, which had been shot down about a thousand miles into the USSR, and the pilot. Eisenhower could do nothing, and Khrushchev had a publicity coup, albeit of short duration.

The Berlin Wall goes up, 13 August 1961. Overnight, the one route by which those in the communist east could flee to the west was closed, terminating an exodus that had numbered 150,000 people each year. Here inquisitive west Berliners try to get a glimpse of life in the socialist nirvana beyond the wall. (RMAS Collection)

Berlin had remained a festering problem since the Airlift. It was still divided into four sectors, and nobody was willing to budge on final arrangements. The Soviets wanted it, the West would not yield and negotiations dragged on endlessly. Shortly after John F. Kennedy's election as US President in November 1960, Khrushchev increased the pressure to get the Western powers to leave Berlin, but still the West would not move. Berlin was an ulcer in the Workers' Paradise, because it allowed some of the best and brightest East Germans to escape to the West. This was deeply embarrassing. How could it be that the proletariat preferred Western inequalities to communist social justice? Overnight in

August 1961 a wall was built, ostensibly to keep Western decadence out, but it fooled few. The Wall, which helped to neutralise Berlin as a factor in East–West relations, became a lasting memorial to the human desire for freedom and opportunity.

'We stand on the edge of a new frontier – the frontier of the 1960s.'

John F. Kennedy, 1960

CONFRONTATION IN THE 1960S

The next major event to threaten international stability was the Cuban Missile Crisis (14–28 October 1962). This was probably the closest the world came to thermonuclear war. In 1959, when Fidel Castro (b. 1926) overthrew Fulgencio Batista (1901–73), the ineffective US-backed Cuban dictator, it seemed Castro's was simply another national liberation movement. But he gradually, some say inevitably, drifted towards Moscow. At first the USA did not take him too seriously; and hoped that he would remain inconsequential, or that someone would replace him. But Castro was more stubborn than the Americans had reckoned on, and they began to work on ways to replace him. The CIA developed apparently endless plots to destabilise (if not assassinate) him, and just as Eisenhower was leaving office plans were developed to back an invasion by 1,300 right-wing Cuban exiles. The USA was to provide air support but leave the ground fighting to the Cubans. Kennedy had barely taken office when the invasion began, but – thanks to last-minute cold feet – without American air support. The Bay of Pigs landing (17 April 1961) was a miserable failure, and understandably worsened US–Cuban relations. Castro was driven towards Moscow, and was accepted with open arms.

It was humiliating for the USA to have a communist out-station just 90 miles off its shores. It was also a wonderful opportunity for the Soviets to

The Cold War, 1960–9

Feb 1960	France explodes its first nuclear device
May 1960	U2 spy plane shot down over USSR; abortive East–West summit in Moscow
Aug 1961	Berlin Wall built
Oct 1962	Cuban missile crisis
April 1963	'Hotline' established between Moscow and Washington
Oct 1964	Communist China explodes its first atomic weapon
March 1965	US ground forces enter South Vietnam
Dec 1967	NATO adopts Flexible Response doctrine
Aug 1968	Soviet and other Warsaw Pact forces invade Czechoslovakia
Nov 1969	Strategic Arms Limitation Talks (SALT) begin

The Cuban Missile Crisis represented the culmination of the first period of the Cold War. Encouraged by President Kennedy's apparent lack of resolve over a series of foreign policy issues, the USSR deployed medium range ballistic missiles (MRBMs) to several sites on Cuba. These MRBMs were photographed by a US aircraft at San Cristobal, near the western end of the island. (US National Archives)

expand their influence into Central and South America, to whittle away at the old and undemocratic regimes there. The Soviets sent a few troops to Cuba, but when US spy planes detected missile installations the situation became very tense. Missiles on Cuba were a serious offensive threat because the Soviet liquid-fuel rockets of the era took too long to fuel for them to survive a US first strike. Before the missiles could be readied for launch, they would be radioactive vapour. But from the American viewpoint, the Soviets could not have put the missiles there just to waste them: they were an offensive threat. And they were only a few minutes' flight time from millions of Americans.

Kennedy acted swiftly, but cautiously. He was advised by many to bomb the missile installations before they were completed, or at least before the missiles were deployed. The Soviets must be taught a lesson, the reasoning went, and it was clear they were escalating the stakes. But Kennedy held back, and since we now know some missiles were actually in Cuba ready to fire, it is well he did. He made it clear the USA would not back down, that it considered the Soviet action to be the gravest possible provocation, and would act in whatever way was needed to prevent the missiles from reaching Cuba. A naval quarantine was declared. Khrushchev let Soviet supply ships get closer and closer before he 'blinked' and sailed them back to the USSR. The Soviets made some gains out of the affair: an American promise not to invade Cuba, and the withdrawal of some obsolete US missiles from Turkey. But Khrushchev's prestige was damaged, and so was his policy of adventurism abroad.

LEONID BREZHNEV (1906–82)

Khrushchev's replacement in 1964 was Leonid Brezhnev, a more cautious and (within the Party) more consensual man. He did less than Khrushchev, made fewer mistakes but had fewer successes. He brought a period of stability to the USSR, but since the USSR was supposed to be building communism, stability did not really fit the bill. Over time the economy slowed, which was not entirely Brezhnev's fault. Much of what Khrushchev had started was unsustainable: the New Lands that yielded rich harvests turned to dust in a series of droughts; to match a Western military build-up more tanks had to be built. Consumer goods suffered and production first stagnated, and then began to slip. But, more fundamentally, Brezhnev clamped down on his society. Censorship increased, although it had never gone away, and hints of intellectual freedom disappeared. Prospects for achieving communism, rather than the authoritarian 'State Socialism' that the USSR admitted was all it could manage against capitalist opposition, faded. The West was not being 'buried' as Khrushchev had predicted. Rather, it was flourishing. Meanwhile, the only group that did well in the USSR was the Party, since Brezhnev stayed away from the shake-ups that had unseated Khrushchev. The Cold War was set to go on for the foreseeable future and prospects within the USSR were dimming. It was typical of Brezhnev that he crushed the Czechoslovak Prague Spring movement in 1968, which had only called for 'socialism with a human face'.

At the same time the USA was creeping into involvement in Vietnam, a war that would strain the Western Alliance, nearly cripple American will to oppose the USSR in the Third World and that still has important ramifications in world politics. Nobody expected it to end that way, but nobody had any clear idea of what the USA was getting into when it started. In 1956 the French departed Indo-China, beaten and discredited, but left the country divided into a communist north and a non-communist (it would be too charitable to call it democratic) south. At first there was quiet as both sides tried to rebuild their shattered economies, but soon enough the Viet Cong began infiltrating and working to destabilise South Vietnam. As part of containment, the USA had included South Vietnam in the South-East Asia Treaty Organisation (SEATO), a feebler version of NATO, and responded to perceived communist aggression. It is unlikely

'Vietnam has the right to be a free and independent country; and in fact is so already.'

Ho Chi Minh, Vietnamese communist leader, 2 September 1945

Despite supporting the massive build-up of the South Vietnamese Army (from 220,000 men in 1964 to 416,000 in 1968), the USA bore the brunt of the fighting during the first part of the Vietnam War. Here troops of the American 101st Airborne Division deploy for operations in 1966. (USAF)

that a communist Vietnam would have been as destabilising as losing the war; US intervention raised the stakes and escalated matters. The Vietnamese were as nationalistic as most nations, and wanted their country unified, but while they did play the part of a regional power in the late 1970s and 1980s, they generally did so responsibly.

However, the USA did not take a chance on good behaviour. Initial American action was limited; it provided some military and financial aid to improve the army and the economy (and thus support for the government), but this seemed to have little effect. In many ways the USA was doing the wrong thing: it misunderstood Asia – in fact it misunderstood most of the world. A lot of the economic aid disappeared into official pockets; many conscripts in the Army of the Republic of Vietnam (ARVN) didn't care about ideology – they wanted to be at home on their farms. Once committed, the USA had to admit defeat or increase its support. More aid, more guns, more advisers joined the fray. The Air Force and Navy sent support, and it was US Navy destroyers that made the difference. They did not win the war, nor did they lose it, but these vessels ensured the USA went in with both feet. In August 1964, in what became known as the Gulf of Tonkin Incident, some North Vietnamese patrol boats apparently fired on US destroyers. It was only machine gun fire and the US ships were shelling the coast; there is also some doubt whether the Americans faked the whole thing. But at the time it was seen as an act of war against the USA. Congress rushed through the Gulf of Tonkin Resolution (only two Senators voted No) and authorised President Lyndon B. Johnson (1908–73) to increase the forces in Vietnam.

In 1965 Johnson formally committed US ground troops to Vietnam. But the US Army was not equipped with weapons or ideas for counter-insurgency. The Viet Cong (VC) ran circles around the Americans and their allies, although most of the non-communist world refused to send troops. Some promising programmes of pacification, of 'winning hearts and minds' were begun, but the US lacked the patience to see them through, and for every 'liberated hamlet' there was a corresponding free-fire zone, where it was admitted that there were no friendly civilians to kill. Eventually, through weight of numbers and overwhelming weight of firepower, the Americans began grinding down the VC and North Vietnamese Army (NVA). Then on 30 January 1968, the Tet Offensive began. Suddenly the VC and NVA attacked US and ARVN bases, cities, and troops anywhere they could be found. The American response eventually inflicted a crushing defeat on the communist forces. Since 1965 the American public had been fed a diet of optimistic official statements, from junior public relations officers all the way to the President himself. But the initial communist success seemed to show how hollow these had been; television pictures proved more potent than official briefings. Tet broke the back of US willingness to carry on the fight. Johnson was caught up in a domestic programme that blazed new ground for democracy, and his political capital was almost expended. He decided, in an unprecedented step, not to stand for re-election.

Richard Nixon won the 1968 presidential election with a very different programme. He was going back to some of the early ideas of the war: building up the ARVN and supporting the Vietnamese government. Militarily 'Vietnamization' had a little success, but politically it fell apart. In 1963 the US had permitted a military coup in South Vietnam, if not openly backing the change then not demanding the restoration of the more democratic incumbent, and everyone in Vietnam could see that it was a puppet regime. Since Nixon had just signalled that the USA would be pulling out as fast as it could without admitting defeat, there was no reason to give loyalty to the South Vietnamese government. So people didn't.

US military personnel and losses in Vietnam, 1965–71

	Military personnel	killed	wounded
1965	184,300	1,369	6,114
1966	385,300	5,008	30,093
1967	485,600	9,378	62,025
1968	536,100	14,592	92,820
1969	475,200	9,414	70,216
1970	334,600	4,221	30,643
1971	156,800	1,380	8,936

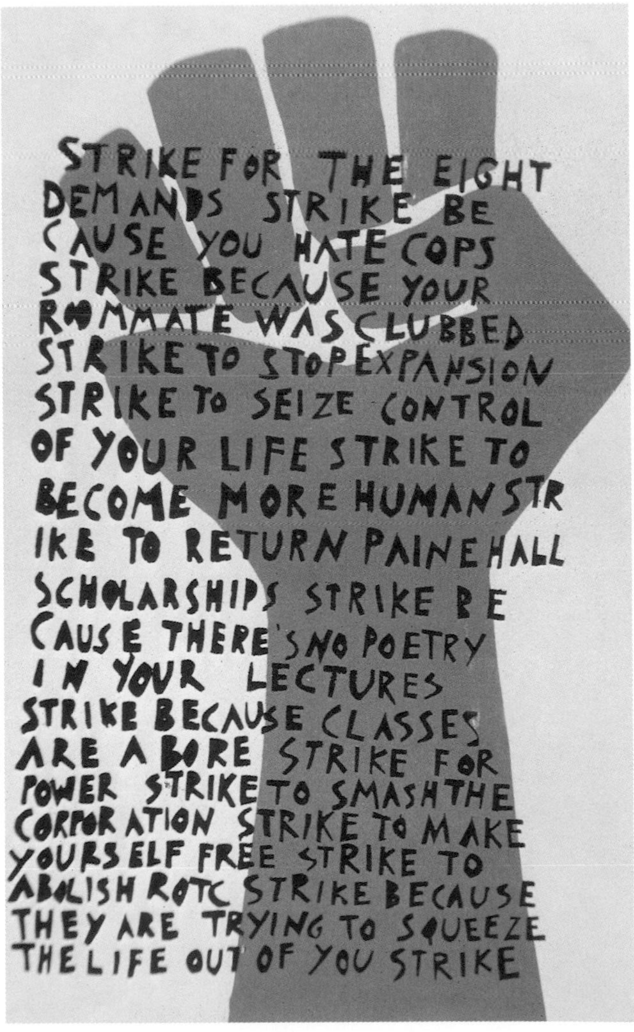

By the late 1960s American public opinion was becoming increasingly divided over the war in Vietnam, as well as over a range of other domestic and foreign policy issues. Here a poster drawn up by Harvard University students makes recommendations on how to deal with an eclectic variety of concerns.

ROLLING THUNDER

The fear of direct superpower confrontation or escalation to nuclear war coloured every action that the United States took in Vietnam. After the Gulf of Tonkin Resolution of August 1964 (described by President Lyndon Johnson as 'like granny's nightdress – it covers everything') authorised a much-expanded American commitment, the United States fell into a very similar military strategy to that which it had used to contain the war in Korea eleven years before. American ground forces in South Vietnam were greatly increased from January 1965 onwards, including the use of conscripts on a large scale for the first time. But there would be no incursions by ground troops into North Vietnam, for fear of provoking direct intervention by communist China (as had happened when the Americans invaded North Korea in late 1950), or more overt action by the Soviet Union. Instead, the American ground troops would fight a defensive war, trying to prevent North Vietnamese Army incursions into South Vietnam either through the Demilitarised Zone (DMZ) at the 17th Parallel or from the valley exits to the Ho Chi Minh Trails, the historic smuggling routes through the jungle mountains, or by assisting the Army of the Republic of Vietnam with its 'village war' against the local Viet Cong (Vietnamese communist) battalions.

'Tell the Vietnamese they've got to draw in their horns and stop aggression or we're going to bomb them back to the Stone Age.'

Curtis LeMay, USAF Chief of Staff (Ret'd), 1967

'An opponent can be bombed into surrender or even into non-existence, but he cannot be bombed into honest negotiations.'

Professor Charles Osgood, American academic, 1966

Also, as in the Korean War, the main American means of attack would be from the air. Begun in March 1965, the air campaign against North Vietnam was known by the general code-name of 'Rolling Thunder', and lasted until October 1968. Aircraft flew from South Vietnam, from bases in Thailand (refuelling in the air), and from 'Yankee Station', the position of one or two aircraft carriers off the North Vietnamese coast. It was a highly theoretical use of air power. The Americans showed considerable deliberate restraint in choosing their targets, while leaving themselves the option of escalation. They attacked only with tactical aircraft such as the F-105 Thunderchief, F-4 Phantom and A-6 Intruder, and not heavy bombers. Aircraft were not usually allowed to bomb North Vietnamese cities, especially the capital Hanoi, or to mine the harbour at Haiphong, the principal northern port. No bombing was usually allowed within 30 miles of the Chinese border, or of selected targets in case Soviet or Chinese officials were hit. Within two months of the beginning of the bombing campaign, Johnson called a short halt in order to offer the North Vietnamese the chance to negotiate. Further pauses and resumptions of the bombing followed. In the course of 'Rolling Thunder' the Americans flew about 350,000 missions and lost approximately 1,000 aircraft. At the high point of the campaign in July–December 1966, 2,600 missions were being flown each week, and 68,000 tons of bombs dropped. Various military, transportation and industrial targets in North Vietnam were struck and destroyed.

From its start, 'Rolling Thunder' was controversial. The man who authorised it, United States' Secretary for Defence Robert McNamara (b. 1916), never believed that it could succeed, and saw it more as a political tool to reassure the government of South Vietnam. Most of the North Vietnamese equipment was being made in Soviet or Chinese factories and then shipped in to the country. The North Vietnamese industrial base was tiny, easily dispersed, and not particularly vulnerable to bombing on such a scale. The pattern of bombing, irregular and often light, also gave North Vietnam time to make preparations and repairs. At the height of 'Rolling Thunder' there were more than 100,000 Chinese troops unofficially present in North Vietnam carrying out rear-area duties, and releasing North Vietnamese troops for service in the south.

The strategy of fighting a ground war of patrols and firefights against an elusive enemy in South Vietnam was controversial and unpopular; while 'Rolling Thunder' itself was unpopular both with aircrew, who felt that its restrictions did not give them a chance of victory or made them risk their lives for too little, and among those in the United States who felt that bombing – which inevitably caused civilian casualties in North Vietnam – was an immoral form of war. While only a minority of Americans at home protested against the bombing strategy, the protests became increasingly vocal as with each year bombing proved ineffective in forcing North Vietnam to give up its war in the South.

In March 1968, as part of his announcement that he would not run again for office, Johnson restricted bombing to south of the 20th Parallel, where most of the 'Rolling Thunder' raids had already taken place. In May preliminary peace talks began between North Vietnam and the United States in Paris; and in October Johnson called a total halt to the bombing of North Vietnam. 'Rolling Thunder' had caused considerable damage to North Vietnam, but it had failed in its objective of dissuading the North Vietnamese from continuing the war.

Under President Richard Nixon (1913–94), two further American bombing campaigns took place over North Vietnam. The first of these, 'Linebacker I', began in April 1972 and for the first time used B-52 heavy bombers to attack Hanoi and Haiphong, as well as to break up North Vietnamese troop movements southwards. This campaign ended in October, to be followed by the much shorter 'Linebacker II' or 'Christmas Bombing' of December 1972, in which B-52s in strength attacked Hanoi. Nixon believed that this display of force was critical in securing a ceasefire from the Paris negotiations in January 1973, enabling the United States to pull out of Vietnam.

The US Army struggled on, fighting, thanks to US successes in Tet, fewer opponents, but with troops increasingly unwilling to die in a war they knew they were not going to win. Frustrated, they shot their officers, or civilians, or just took drugs, no more able to understand the war than anyone else. Nixon had to escalate the war in some areas in order to cut back in others: bombing of the North increased, and American troops invaded Cambodia in 1970 to clear out VC base areas. Eventually, in 1973 an exhausted USA settled with the Vietnamese, claimed victory, and withdrew as fast as it could. (The brilliant satirist Tom Lehrer (b. 1928) gave up his job as a professor of mathematics at Harvard University after Henry Kissinger received the Nobel Peace Prize for, as Lehrer put it, 'invading Cambodia'.) The empty shell of the Republic of Vietnam was left to totter on until 1975.

While the USA was militarily bogged down in Vietnam, there were hopeful signs of improved superpower relations in Europe. Negotiations and cooperation, however limited, were replacing stark confrontation about everything. The new mood was called détente, and was largely the result of popular pressure on Western governments. Society had become more liberal and people had grown accustomed to the seemingly permanent rivalry. The confrontation was losing its edge and novelty, and some useful de-escalation of rhetoric took place. There were still powerful voices against meaningful compromise, and détente was more a mood than a list of negotiated accomplishments, but it was something for statesmen to do at

In one of the most paradoxical images of the Vietnam War, United States Secretary of State Dr Henry Kissenger receives the Nobel Peace Prize from the US Ambassador to Norway, London, December 1973. (Associated Press)

conferences. There were agreements on limiting nuclear arms increases, Strategic Arms Limitations Treaties (the first signed in May 1972 that would, a decade later, broaden into actual reductions), on the status of West Berlin, and on the details of how West Germany would deal with the Communist Bloc. But in all this, détente was limited to Europe: in Asia or Africa the Cold War did not become any more gentlemanly. Nor did détente mean much in Eastern Europe. In Czechoslovakia a genuinely popular movement led by reformist communists, the 'Prague Spring', was quashed by the Red Army in 1968. Again, as at the time of Suez, the West was hamstrung in exploiting the propaganda value because of the US involvement in Vietnam.

One of the main reasons for declining world support for US involvement in Vietnam was the nature of the Vietnamese government. According to its own words, the US was supporting democracy against tyranny. But too many times the West supported anti-communist tyrants against communist would-be tyrants. Even worse, when there was a genuinely non-communist popular movement for some liberalisation in the Third World, the West usually was afraid that it was in fact another tentacle of World Communism. And so they propped up existing regimes, however repressive. Even determined anti-communists could have serious concerns about some of their bedfellows, and it gave the Eastern propaganda organs plenty of ammunition. Human rights moved up the agenda, so that people like President Jimmy Carter (b. 1924) would later try to make it a centrepiece of foreign relations.

General Duong Van Minh (second right, behind microphones) announces the overthrow of the South Vietnamese prime minister, Ngo Dinh Diem, in November 1963. The military coup against Diem went ahead with the tacit approval of the Americans, who hoped that Diem's corrupt and ineffective regime would be replaced by one better able to resist the communists. Unfortunately, Minh and his successors failed to satisfy their US allies, and the incompetence of the South Vietnamese government would be a major factor in explaining the communist victory in Vietnam twelve years later. (RMAS Collection)

Nixon had undertaken to extract the USA, with whatever shreds of dignity available, from Vietnam. To repair the country's standing he engaged in power politics. A doughty anti-communist of long standing, he opened US relations with Red China. In the parlance of the day it was 'playing the China card' against the Soviets, using the Chinese as leverage. The Chinese had revealed the fractures in World Communism in 1961 when they fell out with Moscow, but that earned them no credit with the West. Nixon's ploy had very little ideology behind it. He withdrew diplomatic recognition for the strongly anti-communist but tiny Republic of China on Taiwan in exchange for the communist (but anti-Moscow) People's Republic on the mainland. Probably only someone with Nixon's credentials could have taken the political risk, for China had long had a political resonance in America that, coupled with recognising the world's most populous communist regime, would have torpedoed most politicians.

Nixon's fall had nothing directly to do with foreign policy, except that thanks to Vietnam the American people were more suspicious of their government. US foreign policy did not change, and when the Arabs struck at Israel in October 1973 the USA responded with arms shipments to Israel and by raising US forces worldwide to higher readiness to warn off the Soviets. Western Europe was coping with the repercussions of its own student radicals, and with spreading anti-establishment demonstrations and terrorism (and some pro-communist terrorism). But the USSR could take little advantage. Brezhnev was losing energy and the economy was sliding gently downhill. Outside influence of a new variety intervened, with OPEC embargoing oil to the USA; this sent the free-world economy into a tailspin, if only temporarily. Once the West managed to assuage its conscience by adding human rights to its own agenda (thus pulling the teeth of much Soviet propaganda about the Third World), the confrontation between capitalism and communism could return to being top priority.

The Cold War, 1970–3

Feb 1972	President Nixon visits Communist China
May 1972	Nixon visits Moscow; SALT I Treaty signed (including Treaty on the Limitation of ABMs, and Interim Agreement on the Limitation of Strategic Offensive weapons)
June 1972	Further SALT I agreements signed
Jan 1973	Vietnam ceasefire agreement

'Peace is a continuation of war by other means.'

General Vo Nguyen Giap, North Vietnamese military leader, 1973

FOURTEEN

THE COLD WAR ERA, 1973–91

PETER CADDICK-ADAMS

'Report first sighting immediately.' His tank topped the crest on the last words, and there opened up before him the most frightening sight he had ever seen. The open ground below, stretching to a faintly seen line of trees about two kilometres away, was swarming with menacing black shapes coming fast towards him. They were tanks, moving in rough line-abreast about 200 metres apart, less than 1,000 metres off and closing the range quickly. Another line was following behind and a third just coming out of the trees. The world seemed full of Soviet tanks.

(General Sir John Hackett, *The Third World War*)

THE RETURN OF THE COLD WAR

Although the Vietnam conflict was over for the American Army in January 1973, its shadow has hung over the US military ever since. Conscription (first enacted in 1948) ceased immediately, but over 59,000 US servicemen had been killed or were posted missing in Vietnam. While Korea had seemed to justify the US strategy of fighting limited wars – the limitation applying in a geographic sense and without the resort to atomic/nuclear weapons – the Vietnam conflict ultimately discredited this policy. Following the American withdrawal, in early 1975 the North Vietnamese resumed the offensive and overran the South with ease, while the USA could do nothing to prevent the collapse of a country that it had supported with blood from 1965. On 30 April Saigon fell.

With the Vietnam War over, the 1973–89 period was dominated by the confrontation between NATO and the Warsaw Pact. General John Hackett's best-selling book, *The Third World War* (1978), described a fictional major conflict fought in Europe between NATO and the Warsaw Pact and articulated clearly the kind of war for which both power blocs were training in this period.

Fuelled by suspicions of Western aggression towards the Soviet Union (Russia had lost at least 20 million people in a war that had ended only twenty-five years earlier), throughout the 1970s the Soviet-dominated

The Cold War, 1974–80

April 1975	Saigon (South Vietnam) and Phnom Penh (Cambodia) fall to Communists
Aug 1975	Helsinki Summit on Security and Cooperation in Europe
Sept 1977	USA and USSR agree to abide by SALT I after its expiry date
Dec 1977	USSR deploys SS–20 missiles in Europe
Dec 1978	USA normalises relations with Communist China
June 1979	SALT II Treaty signed (but not ratified by US Congress)
Dec 1979	Soviets invade Afghanistan; NATO announces deployment of Pershing and cruise missiles to Europe
Nov 1980	Ronald Reagan elected US President

Soviet inter-continental ballistic missiles on their transporters. (Jonathan Falconer Collection)

Warsaw Pact sought solace in confrontation. It built up conventional forces in Europe and developed an intermediate-range nuclear arsenal, culminating in 1977 with deployment of the SS-20 fully mobile missile system. However, the intermediate-range nuclear missile force (INF) arms race was won convincingly by NATO. It answered the Soviets in December 1979 by deciding to station 572 new Pershing II and ground-launched cruise missiles in Western Europe, including West Germany and the United Kingdom. At the same time the UK committed itself to upgrading its nuclear arsenal with the Trident D5 submarine-launched ballistic missile (SLBM) system in place of Polaris. These decisions fuelled support for the Campaign for Nuclear Disarmament (CND), then closely allied to Britain's Labour Party. Similar protest groups throughout Western Europe, which recent evidence points to having been funded partly by the KGB, held rallies, demonstrations and vigils, attracting hundreds of thousands of sympathisers, and the whole 1973–83 era was characterised by a general anti-military mood among much of the population of Western states.

In some cases this mood was linked with the final days of the anti-Vietnam demonstrations, protests against conscription in France and

The Campaign for Nuclear Disarmament (CND) saw a resurgence in Britain during the 1980s. This was largely the result of NATO's decision in 1979 to deploy Pershing and cruise missiles in Europe, but a series of crises over the next four years also gave the disarmament cause considerable momentum. Here youthful demonstrators register their protest outside an American airbase in Britain. (RMAS Collection)

Germany or a vague rebellion against authority, culminating in nihilistic terrorist groups who used violence as a weapon against what they perceived as US imperialism and aggression. In other cases these attitudes were the product of fear of war. Such protests, however, failed to divide the Western Alliance or halt the new missile deployments, and cruise and Pershing II arrived in Europe from November 1983. These missiles re-established a credible NATO ability to threaten local nuclear retaliation, short of global nuclear war. Although the Pershings could not reach Moscow, the Kremlin estimated they could strike at long-range targets in 4 to 6 minutes, much less than the 20 minutes Moscow had previously relied on to detect and react to missiles launched from the USA. This in turn affected Soviet military doctrine and strategy.

Soviet strategy was influenced by another controversial development – 'Star Wars'. This was the popular name given to US President Ronald Reagan's proposed Strategic Defense Initiative (SDI), which was unveiled in March 1983. The project called for a series of satellites orbiting the earth, capable of detecting and destroying ballistic missiles aimed at the United States. Although probably unfeasibly expensive and beyond even America's technological skill, 'Star Wars' was perceived by some in the Soviet Union as a realistic danger, a nightmare come alive that threatened to destabilise the delicate balance of terror. As if the tension over SDI was not enough, in September 1983 a Soviet fighter shot down Korean Airlines Flight 007, which had strayed over Russian territory that bristled with military installations. All those on board the airliner – 269 people – were killed. Soviet allegations that the Boeing 747 was on a reconnaissance mission have not yet been substantiated, but the episode suggested confusion and gaps in Soviet air defences, later highlighted by Mathias Rust, a German civilian who piloted a Cessna light aircraft from the West and landed it in Red Square, in Moscow.

As if to emphasise NATO weaknesses, during the 1970s the Soviet Union began to revive its doctrines of 'Deep Battle' and 'Deep Operations' from the Second World War, first demonstrated on a large scale by the Warsaw Pact 'ZAPAD 81' manoeuvres of 1981, held in the Baltic States and Poland. Together with plans in the event of war for multiple 'echelons' of Soviet and Warsaw Pact reserve forces to move through Poland and East Germany, this raised the real prospect of the Soviets breaking through NATO forces on the Central Front in a matter of days, without the need for nuclear weapons.

The NATO response, led by the United States, was to develop doctrines based on technology and skills in manoeuvre, rather than manpower, to maintain a credible conventional defence of the Central Front under the general heading of 'manoeuvre war'. The NATO version, first proposed in 1979, was known as 'FOFA' (Follow On Forces Attack). This called for NATO to develop surveillance and reconnaissance systems, such as the American E-8 J-STARS (Joint Surveillance and Target Attack Radar System) and E-3 AWACS (Airborne Warning and Control Systems) aircraft, in order to 'see deep' (a technical term) more than 100 kilometres

Ronald Reagan is seen by some commentators as a sincere but naïve idealist who permitted his officials too much leeway in interpreting his ideas. As leader of the most powerful country on Earth, he presided over a hawkish foreign policy that did much to convince the Soviets of the West's aggressive intent. Indeed, by late 1983 it seemed to many that the world stood closer to nuclear confrontation than at any time since the Cuban Missile Crisis. (Associated Press)

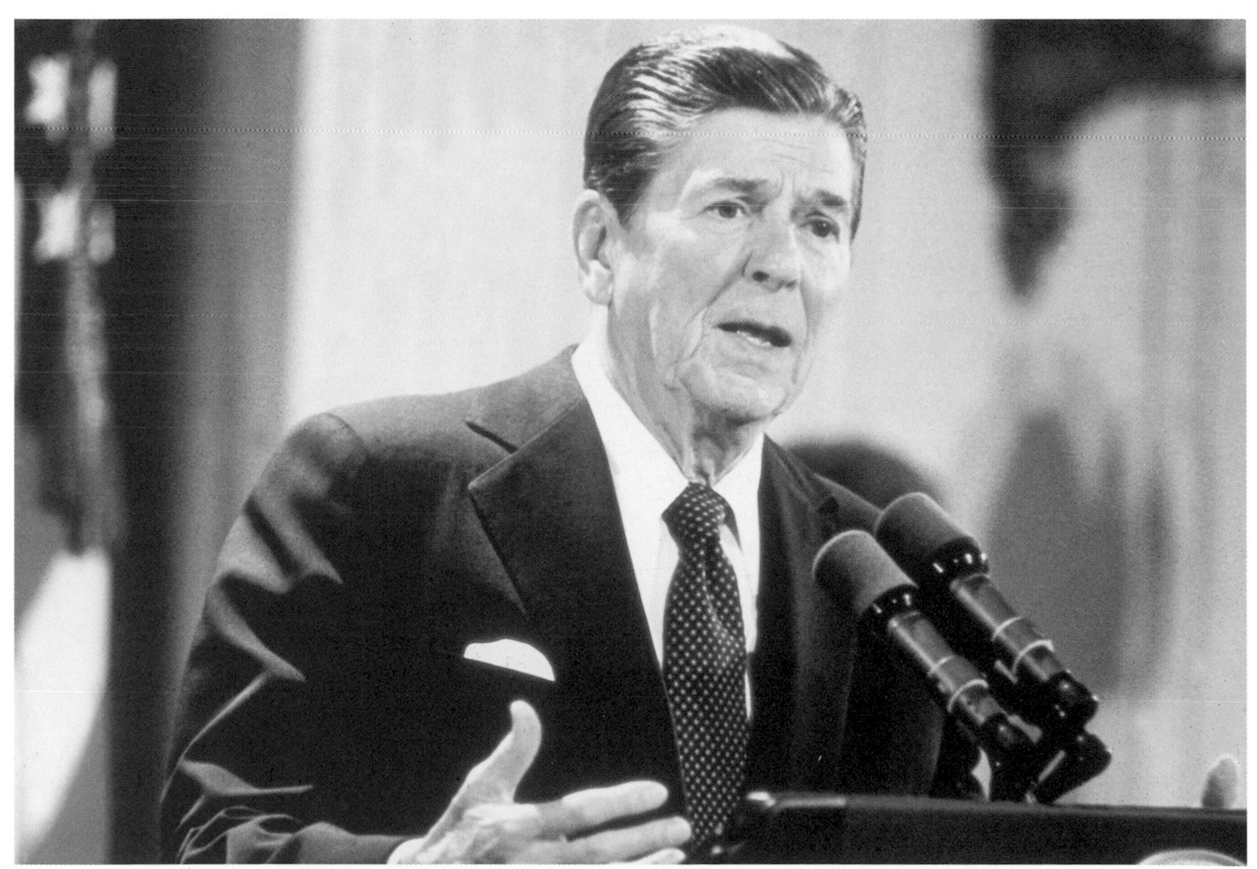

into the enemy rear positions, identifying targets on the ground and in the air respectively. FOFA then called for the capability to 'strike deep' with aircraft, missiles and even long-range artillery against the Warsaw Pact reserve echelons as they advanced, preventing them from ever reaching the battlefield.

Closely linked to FOFA and developed at the same time, but more sophisticated and unique to the Americans, was 'AirLand Battle', which was made official US Army doctrine in 1982 (a more ambitious and futuristic version known as AirLand Battle 2000, and planned as a replacement, was never implemented). The essence of AirLand Battle was that it sought to link air power together with the battle on the ground deliberately and systematically, whereas previously any benefits to the ground battle from air power had been indirect and general. As Warsaw Pact reserves approached the battlefield, and were expected to join in the fighting, American airpower would either delay or destroy them, timing this action so that it synchronised with the best moment for a decisive attack that would win the ground battle as well. In the 1980s for the first time, NATO talked about defeating an attack by the Warsaw Pact, rather than just delaying or defending against it.

Cold War stand-off: HMS Illustrious *shadows the Soviet anti-submarine cruiser* Novorissiisk *(foreground). The emergence in 1976 of the four Kiev-class vessels (of which the* Novorissiisk *was one) caused disquiet in the West, being perceived as an attempt to challenge US carrier battle groups for mastery of the oceans. In fact, the Soviet ships had no such capability, although they did carry a formidable array of missiles as well as a small mixed airgroup of helicopters and aircraft. The rise of Soviet naval power was one element in a general process that improved the potency and scale of the USSR's armed forces during the 1970s, and was intended to provide the Soviet leadership with a wider range of political and military options during the Cold War. (Royal Navy via Jonathan Falconer)*

THE WARSAW PACT

The Warsaw Pact was founded on 14 May 1955 by eight East European socialist states as a military alliance to rival NATO. It comprised Albania (which later left), Bulgaria, Czechoslovakia, the German Democratic Republic (East Germany), Hungary, Poland, Romania and the USSR. Led and always dominated by the Soviet Union, the Warsaw Pact originated as a response to the Paris Conference of 1954, which saw the formation of the Western European Union (WEU), and which resulted in West Germany being invited to join NATO (which it did in 1955). The socialist countries met in Warsaw on 11 May 1955. The Pact, which came into effect on 5 June, formally recognised what was already the case: that the Soviet Union effectively ran, trained and equipped the East European armies. Ultimately, the alliance was for the benefit of the dominant player: the Soviet Union.

Unsurprisingly, the Pact's working language was Russian, and its main organisations included a Committee of Defence Ministers, a Combined Armed Forces HQ in Moscow and a technical committee. The commonality of their equipment – mostly of Soviet design – gave the Warsaw Pact nations a potential advantage in a war over NATO, although the political reliability of their troops frequently gave cause for concern. Towards the end this commonality was fast eroding as the various states began to develop their own equipment, and even doctrine. By the time of German reunification the Warsaw Pact had become a political and military dinosaur. It was formally dissolved on 1 July 1991.

AirLand Battle also marked an important break with previous American military thinking by emphasising manoeuvre and disruption of the enemy over physical destruction by firepower. Ideas of manoeuvre warfare were also adopted in the 1980s by all the American services except the US Navy, and also by the British, along with FOFA as part of their contribution to NATO.

THE YOM KIPPUR WAR, OCTOBER 1973

'. . . this people, small as it is, surrounded as it is by enemies, has decided to live. And if we have to pay the price for living, we have to pay it.'

Israeli Premier Golda Meir, 13 October 1973

As an era seemed to close with the ceasefire signed in Paris on 27 January 1973 between the Americans and North Vietnamese, within months the Middle East erupted once more into war. The death of the Egyptian President Gamal Abdel Nasser in 1970 raised tensions in the region because his successor, Anwar al-Sadat (1918–81), was determined to restore Egypt's lost territories in the Sinai. By 1972, having failed to achieve diplomatic momentum, he began planning a military campaign in conjunction with the Syrian President, Hafiz al-Assad (1930–2000).

On the afternoon of 6 October 1973, on the Jewish Day of Atonement (Yom Kippur) and the tenth day of Ramadan, the Syrians attacked the Golan Heights. Committing five divisions to the operation, they attempted to recapture the Heights (lost in 1967) in an assault which was coordinated with an Egyptian strike in the Sinai. The two armoured brigades of Israeli Defence Force (IDF) defenders on the Golan possessed only 180 Centurion Vs and M-60s against the Syrians' 1,300 tanks, which included Soviet-supplied T-54s, T-55s and T-62s. Syrian armoured personnel carriers (APCs) advanced in close support, while concentrations of surface-to-air missiles (SAMs) and anti-aircraft guns kept the Israeli Air Force at bay.

Israeli troops under fire on the Golan Heights, October 1973. The Israelis came within an ace of defeat during the first 24 hours on their northern front, but eventually secured their positions and on 11 October launched a major counterattack towards the Syrian capital, Damascus. This was so successful that the Syrians were forced to ask their Egyptian allies to begin an offensive from the Suez Canal bridgeheads to draw Israeli troops away from the Golan. In turn, this led to the defeat of the Egyptian armoured reserves in the Sinai and the Israeli counterattack onto the west bank of the Suez Canal on 16 October. (State of Israel MOD via Colonel David Eshel)

Achieving surprise on both fronts, the round-the-clock fighting stretched the endurance of both sides' personnel to the limit. This was arguably the first time that well-matched tank crews had fought since the Second World War, and the effects of sustained combat both on the soldiers and their weapons were keenly studied abroad. The Israelis stood their ground on the Golan, sustaining heavy casualties and the loss of most of their armour, although their 7th Armoured Brigade knocked out over 500 Syrian vehicles in the northern sector ('the valley of tears') before being destroyed. The 188th Brigade inflicted similar damage in the south. Their sacrifices, however, bought time for reserve formations to be mobilised and rushed to the area, where they succeeded in halting the enemy advance.

Meanwhile, under cover of a 2,000-gun artillery barrage, the Egyptian 2nd and 3rd Armies crossed the Suez Canal with textbook precision and broke down the high sand ramparts with which the Israelis had lined their side of the canal using high-pressure water jets. Within half an hour the Bar-Lev Line was breached. This linear defensive system had been completed between January and February 1969, and consisted of widely spaced observation posts supposedly strong enough to withstand enemy artillery, supported by armoured forces in the rear. Although more than $40 million was spent on its construction, the Bar-Lev Line was easily penetrated by the Egyptians, who then ambushed the IDF armour rushing to its defence, resulting in the virtual destruction of several Israeli formations.

The Egyptians had planned their bridgehead defences to include infantry carrying Soviet-supplied RPG-7 grenade launchers, 'Sagger' anti-tank wire guided missiles, and the armoured brigades of the infantry divisions used in the canal crossing. Israeli artillery was neutralised or destroyed by the Egyptian Air Force, which fielded 240 front-line aircraft, and IDF armoured counter-attacks were soon broken up by the Egyptians, who concentrated up to fifty-five anti-tank weapons per kilometre. This particular episode underlined the vulnerability of modern armour, even when moving *en masse*, to first-generation hand-held infantry anti-tank guided rockets, a concept that originated with the German *Panzerschreck* of the Second World War.

The IDF was caught unprepared; in the absence of tank transporters, many armoured units had to move to the Sinai or Golan on their tracks, reducing track and engine life, and causing crew fatigue prior to arrival. In the rush to mobilise, some tanks were still coated in protective grease, lacking items such as field glasses and machine guns, and manned by scratch crews. The vulnerability of IDF tanks sent shockwaves around the world, leaving other armies hastily examining their arsenals and demanding quantities of lightweight throw-away anti-tank weapons.

Recovering its balance, on 14 October the IDF repulsed an Egyptian tank assault into the interior of the Sinai, and, crucially, the USA was persuaded to send replacement materiel, allowing Israel to commit her reserves. On 16 October, with American equipment arriving, an IDF assault under General Ariel Sharon (b. 1928) crossed the Suez Canal north of the Great Bitter Lake, opening a gap between the Egyptian 2nd and 3rd Armies. Meanwhile, on the Golan the Israeli counter-attack began on 10 October, pushing the demoralised Syrian forces back beyond their start line. Moroccan, Jordanian and Iraqi forces tried in vain to stem the IDF, and by the time of the UN-sponsored ceasefire on 22 October over 1,300 wrecked or abandoned Arab armoured vehicles choked the Golan Heights. Of the Arab forces on both fronts, possibly 50,000 had been killed, wounded or captured.

A week into the war, once it had analysed the reasons for its high tank losses, the IDF began to mix APC-borne infantry and artillery with armour. While the infantry closed with the troublesome Saggers and RPGs, Israeli armour engaged targets only at long range, leaving the infantry to clear the way forward. Thus the IDF had to relearn the concept of the all-arms battle in the midst of a war. The Israeli Air Force (IAF) had similar problems in overcoming the Arab air defences, which consisted of Soviet-manufactured missile batteries and guns. Using the American experience of dealing with SAM batteries in Vietnam, the IAF soon switched its attention to attacking the SAM command and control centres, thus blinding the missile batteries on their tracked launchers, and flying at very low altitude, where they could hide from the SAM radar among 'ground clutter' signatures.

By the time the ceasefire brokered by American Secretary of State Henry Kissinger took effect on 27 October, the Egyptian 3rd Army and the city

The Yom Kippur War, 6–27 October 1973

1400 hrs, 6 Oct	Egyptian 2nd Army (2, 16, 18 infantry divisions) and 3rd Army (7, 19 infantry divisions) launch attack across Suez Canal into Israeli-occupied Sinai. Syrian forces (5, 7, 9 infantry and 3 and 11 armoured divisions) attack Israeli positions on Golan Heights
6–8 Oct	Egyptians consolidate Suez brigeheads and repulse Israeli counterattacks. Israeli forces halt Syrians on Golan
9 Oct	UN Security Council fails to agree to a call for a ceasefire
10 Oct	Soviets begin airlifting supplies to Egypt and Syria
11–19 Oct	Israelis launch counter-offensive on Golan. Syrians (and other Arab forces) driven back towards Damascus
13 Oct	Egyptians transfer armoured reserves (two divisions) from west to east bank of the Suez, aiming to launch offensive to divert Israeli attention from the Golan
14 Oct	Failure of Egyptian Sinai offensive
15 Oct	Israelis counter-attack in Sinai
16–19 Oct	Israelis cross Suez Canal. Heavy fighting on east bank to keep bridgehead re-supplied
18 Oct	Israelis break out to south of bridgehead on west bank of the Suez Canal
22 Oct	UN Security Council calls for a ceasefire. Israelis encircle Egyptian 3rd Army by driving south to Suez city
24 Oct	Israel, Egypt and Syria agree to ceasefire
27 Oct	Ceasefire comes into effect

of Suez had been encircled. Despite Israeli successes in the latter phases of the conflict, the war eroded the myth of Israeli invincibility and underlined serious shortcomings in Israeli Intelligence. Israel was also at fault in miscalculating the military capabilities of its Arab neighbours, who were armed with the latest Soviet equipment, and who operated in a professional manner. Whereas air power and superior tank tactics had won the Six-Day War for Israel in 1967, it was the infantryman who emerged as the saviour of Israel in 1973.

Losses in this short but vicious conflict were high in men and equipment. The Israelis lost 400 tanks completely destroyed and hundreds of others damaged, 102 aircraft shot down and 8,000 casualties, of which 2,400 were fatal. The war had been a very close-run affair. These battles affirmed the strategic importance of the Golan Heights, which now bristles with early warning radar, IDF bases and Jewish settlements. Armour and air power doctrine was hastily revised in NATO and the Warsaw Pact, for whom the Israelis and Arabs had effectively fought a war by proxy. The Arabs fought with a Soviet doctrinal template, using modern Warsaw Pact equipment. Their obstacle crossing worked well, as did their virtual annihilation of IDF front-line armour.

Although the American and British armies had planned and executed large and complex campaigns during 1944–5, and again in Korea, the method of those operations had largely been forgotten by the early 1970s. Nuclear weapons cast a long shadow over the evolution and development of NATO ground-combat doctrine during this period and the later appearance of tactical nuclear weapons seemed only to reinforce the impotence of large-scale manoeuvres of ground forces. In short, NATO

GENERAL MOSHE DAYAN (1915–81)

Dayan had been jailed in 1939 by the British for being a member of the Haganah (the Jewish underground), but was released in 1941 to fight the Vichy French in Syria, where he lost his left eye, thereafter sporting a characteristic eye patch. As a major, he defended the Jordan Valley against a larger Syrian force at the start of Israel's War of Independence (1948–9), and emerged as GOC Southern Command at the war's end. In 1953, as its Chief of Staff, he started to rebuild the Israeli Defence Forces (IDF), instituting rigorous training, increasing the number of infantry and armoured formations, and creating an airborne elite. His reforms were vindicated in the 1956 war, when his forces routed four Egyptian divisions with minimal casualties in the Sinai.

Elected to the Knesset (Israeli parliament) in 1959, he was Minister of Defence during the Six-Day War (1967). During this conflict the Israelis destroyed the Egyptian Air Force on the ground with a bold pre-emptive strike, occupied the Sinai and West Bank and captured the Golan Heights from Syria. But criticised for the IDF's lack of preparedness at the start of the Yom Kippur War, Dayan resigned in 1974. Three years later he was appointed Foreign Minister, but he eventually resigned again over policy towards the Israel–Egypt peace process and died in 1981. Exuding a swashbuckling, piratical air (owing in part to his eye patch), the energetic and charismatic Dayan learned his trade the hard way, without formal military or staff training, and is considered the father of the IDF and its greatest commander.

'Return your swords to your scabbards but keep them ever-ready, for the time has not yet come when you can beat them into ploughshares.'

General Moshe Dayan, 1967

stagnated at every level of planning and activity below the strategic. American (and then NATO) tactical and operational doctrine began to be re-examined as a result of the effects of the weapons systems deployed in the 1973 war, ultimately with the effects described earlier in this chapter.

THE SOVIET INTERVENTION IN AFGHANISTAN

If the decade of the US military's involvement in Vietnam can be said to have undermined American faith in their military culture, the decade of Soviet operations in Afghanistan similarly challenged the apparent invincibility of the USSR's military might. Its intervention in Afghanistan, 1979–89, grew from a military coup of April 1978, which brought Nur Taraki, leader of the Marxist People's Democratic Party of Afghanistan to power. This heralded an era of forced modernisation, including comprehensive land reform, to which most of the population was opposed. The resultant series of rural disturbances led to over 10,000 civilian deaths, and in another coup in September 1979 a hard-line communist, Hafizallah Amin, seized power.

The Kremlin feared that Amin's regime would provoke a massive anti-Soviet Islamic counter-revolutionary movement on the USSR's southern borders and built up Soviet forces along the frontier. On Christmas Eve 1979 Soviet special forces seized the airport at Kabul, the Afghan capital, and three airborne divisions flew in, while four motor rifle divisions, assembled mainly from reservists in central Asia, entered Afghanistan from the north. Amin's rival, Babrak Karmal, was installed as President after a battle which saw both Amin and General Paputin, the Soviet general leading the invasion, killed.

While the USSR hoped that the new government would soon stabilise the internal situation in Afghanistan, and that Soviet troops could quickly be withdrawn, the opposite happened. World opinion was inflamed, not least by the massive flight of refugees, of whom 3½ million entered Pakistan, with another 2 million fleeing to Iran. Resistance quickly grew, based around mujahedeen irregulars. Towns were besieged and convoys attacked, while the Soviet occupation force grew to around 100,000 men. The forces of the Afghan regime rapidly disintegrated, largely through desertion. Partly as a result, the Soviet 40th Army soon lost the initiative and was reduced to garrisoning the main cities and safeguarding communications, particularly the supply line from the Soviet border to Kabul.

The Afghan mujahedeen included disparate local tribes and larger political parties based in Peshawar in Pakistan, loosely bound by adherence to Islam and hatred of the Soviets. Rather like the resistance movements that existed in Europe during the Second World War, however, Afghan religious, political and tribal rivalries militated against an effective military structure. By 1983 the Soviet forces learned how to deal with the rebels by employing extensive air power, especially helicopters.

A combination of strafing runs by MiG-21 fighter-bombers, attacks by Mil-24 Hind armoured helicopter gunships, and local assaults by troops carried in Mi-6 Hook helicopters soon forced the mujahedeen back into the hills. The widespread use of helicopter gunships underlined the utility of

Afghan mujahedeen pose with Soviet-designed SA-7 shoulder launched infra-red anti-aircraft missiles. The source of these particular weapons is unclear, and although they may have been captured from Soviet or Afghan government forces it seems more likely that they were provided by the Americans, who sent several billion dollars of aid to support the rebellion. (RMAS Collection)

this type of aircraft in modern war, and Western nations began to rewrite their doctrine to include helicopter assaults. While the Soviets developed the use of helicopter-borne troops to seize commanding heights and to cut off the retreat of the Afghan rebels, such tactics were used later by different armies in other theatres of war, including by the various factions in Bosnia.

Although the Soviets encouraged the Afghan government to recruit and use its own armed forces to guard installations and attack the mujahedeen, Red Army troops remained heavily committed, and their losses grew rapidly. In 1985, communist control extended through much of the country but was still unable to prevent the flow of weapons from Pakistan. This flow increased in 1985–6 when, concerned that resistance might flag, the United States decided to increase its aid to the mujahedeen, including the provision of Stinger anti-aircraft missiles (from October 1987). The new missiles diminished the Soviets' air supremacy, as the Hind gunships proved vulnerable to Stingers, and many observers (wrongly) saw this decision as the turning point in the war. The new weaponry undoubtedly helped to restore the military balance, but the Soviet leader, Mikhail Gorbachev, was already seeking an exit strategy from Afghanistan, and in 1986 forced the new Premier, Mohammed Najibullah, to make conciliatory overtures to the rebels, offering a cease-fire and power sharing. Nearly all the radical policies, among them land reform, were gradually abandoned and national reconciliation was actively sought.

By intervening in Afghanistan the Soviet Union had embroiled itself in an unwinnable war, which severely damaged the morale of its armed forces and caused domestic unease. In April 1988 the Soviets announced that their forces would withdraw from Afghanistan over nine months, ending on 15 February 1989, though the USSR continued to support the Najibullah regime until its collapse in April 1992. This Soviet version of Vietnam is estimated to have cost the USSR some 480,000 casualties (14,000 killed, 53,000 wounded and 415,000 sick) over the decade and proved yet again that the harsh, unforgiving land of Afghanistan is best left to its own devices.

THE IRAN–IRAQ WAR

If the Yom Kippur War can be seen in some respects as a 'Blitzkrieg' that only partly succeeded, and Afghanistan as a war against partisans, then the next major conflict to break out in the 1973–89 period seemed to many observers to resemble the attrition of the First World War. On 22 September 1980 Iraqi forces invaded Iran, triggering one of the longest, bloodiest and costliest wars since 1945. By the time the guns fell silent on 18 August 1988 the two sides had suffered widespread destruction, severe economic damage and casualties that are estimated to lie anywhere between 367,000 and a million.

Saddam Hussein's decision to exploit the instability that existed in Iran after the overthrow of the Shah (January 1979) was essentially opportunistic. However, although Saddam may have hoped for a complete collapse of the Iranian regime, which was led by the militant Ayatollah Khomeini, there is little evidence that he expected it or thought it likely. Rather, he believed that by ordering a limited offensive by only five of his twelve army divisions, he could win a quick and relatively bloodless victory that would result in minor border re-adjustments and that would deter Iran from attempts to destabilise his own power base. He probably also hoped to use such a success for propaganda purposes, especially at the meeting of the Non-Aligned Movement which was scheduled to take place in Baghdad in 1982.

However, despite halting the Iraqi offensive only a week after it started and offering to negotiate, Saddam discovered that he had started a war that he could not end. Partly motivated by anti-Arab Persian nationalism, partly by hatred of Saddam's 'heretical' regime, and partly by sheer affront at being attacked, the Iranians fought back. Although Iran's armed forces were in disarray as a result of the Revolution, the sheer size of the country and the scale of its resources made a rapid collapse unlikely, especially against an attack on the scale of the Iraqi one. Furthermore, the Iranian clerics soon grasped the fact that the war provided an excellent opportunity to consolidate their domestic position and revolutionise Iranian society. Not unless or until this changed were they likely voluntarily to end the conflict. Interestingly, despite the violent rhetoric of the Iranian clerics and the bloody battles that ensued, Iran never truly unleashed a 'total' war. Instead, her leaders generally preferred to keep their mobilisation of resources within limits acceptable to the Iranian population. Only in 1987, when the war became unpopular among ordinary Iranians, and especially among the urban poor upon whose support the clerics relied, did Iran's rulers begin to think seriously about coming to terms with Saddam. Even then, however, it took another year to bring the war to a close.

In January 1981 Iran carried out its first major counter-offensive since the beginning of the war, and by the end of the year Iraq had been dislodged from most of its strongholds in Khuzestan (in southern Iran). In a sensible strategic move, Saddam then withdrew his forces from Iranian territory and

Iranian dead near Amara, Iraq, February 1984.

redeployed them along the international border, challenging Iran either to make peace or to fight a positional, attritional war. This move, however, failed to appease the fundamentalist clerics in Tehran and on 13 July 1982, following a bitter debate within the Iranian leadership, a large-scale offensive was launched in the direction of Basra, Iraq's second city.

Thereafter, and rather predictably, the campaign degenerated into a costly and futile series of battles, as wasteful in human lives as war on the Eastern Front had been during 1941–2. Successive human waves of Iranian conscripts assaulted the Iraqi defences, only to be repulsed at a horrendous cost. It took four years of attacks for Iran to gain its first significant foothold on Iraqi territory in the Fao peninsula (February 1986), and retain it in the face of desperate Iraqi counter-attacks.

By this time international fear of an Iranian victory, with all the attendant nightmares of the global spread of Islamic fundamentalism, ensured that the rest of Europe (both East and West) armed Iraq to the teeth. The Soviet Union and France offered weapons, the US supplied military Intelligence support, while the Gulf states financed Iraq's war effort, and a million imported Egyptian workers replaced the nation's manhood in the fields and factories. These things, in fact, were instrumental in preventing Iraq's collapse.

At the same time, however, a war-weariness began to permeate the Iranian state. It was starved of international arms supplies and subjected to a punishing economic blockade. Meanwhile, discontent among the poor who had put the clerics in power and supported the overthrow of the Shah in 1979 threatened the war effort. By April 1988 Saddam Hussein fully appreciated the effect of this discontent on the Iranian war machine and ordered his troops on to the offensive for the first time in six years. Within forty-eight hours of fierce fighting the Iraqis recaptured the Fao peninsula from the demoralised and ill-equipped Iranian troops, signalling a fundamental shift in Iraq's strategic policy. A string of Iraqi military successes followed. In May, Iraqi forces drove the Iranians out of their positions in Salamchch (east of Basra in southern Iraq), and a month later dislodged them from the Majnoon Islands, held by Iran since 1985. In early July Iraq drove the remaining Iranian forces out of Kurdistan and later that month gained a small strip of Iranian territory on the central front. Moreover, the United States Navy intervened against the Iranians, who had been mining the Gulf and attacking internationally flagged oil tankers. To stay in power and prevent a collapse of his armed forces and the erosion of his power base, Ayatollah Khomeini ordered the cessation of hostilities. On 18 July 1988 Iran accepted UN Security Council Resolution 598, which effectively ended the Iran–Iraq war.

Iraq's success was not due solely to external aid. During the war Saddam's army became reasonably competent, with the 'elite' Republican Guard training in the concept of the all-arms battle. Iraqi artillery became more accurate and integrated with the needs of the infantry, and the air force trained to deliver munitions, including nerve gas, at low level. Together with missile strikes against Iranian cities and oil targets, this led to a series of successes that ended the war. The victory also established the ascendancy of Saddam's clique within the Ba'athist ruling class, which had been Saddam's main war aim after 1980, and extended his totalitarian

The opposing forces, the Iran–Iraq War (1980)

	Iran	Iraq
Population	45 million	17 million
Army (Reserves)	300,000 (300,000)	200,000 (100,000)
Tanks	1,200	2,200
Armoured personnel carriers	2,000	3,000
Air Force (aircraft)	459	530

state, though at a cost of an $80 billion foreign debt. In the final analysis Iraq's military machine had grown enormously in size and skill, and – with the exception of the Israeli Defence Force – was the best trained and equipped force in the Middle East by the war's end in 1988. Perhaps it should have come as no surprise that one of the best ways to keep such an army at the cutting edge was to use it again.

THE FALKLANDS WAR: THROWBACK TO EMPIRE

Following the wars of decolonisation from 1945 to 1970, Britain's armed forces had shrunk steadily and re-equipped to deal with two major challenges. One was the ongoing troubles in Northern Ireland, where troops had been deployed since 1969, and the other was the massive NATO commitment opposing the Soviet threat in Europe. Future war for the British Army was relatively easy to predict: the Red hordes of the Soviet Army would come galloping over the horizon and I British Corps in Germany would deploy to meet them while the Territorials and reserves mobilised. However in 1982, much to the surprise of most international military analysts, Britain became involved in a peculiar island war that was more akin to a Victorian territorial dispute than a late twentieth-century conflict.

The Falkland Islands or 'Malvinas' lie in the South Atlantic Ocean, approximately 500 miles east of Argentina, and were at different times colonised by Britain, France and Spain. From 1833 they had been a British possession, although Argentina claimed sovereignty on the basis of previous Spanish occupation. In appearance and climate, the patchwork of islands was not unlike Dartmoor or parts of Scotland – windswept peat bogs and rocky hills. Standing in Port Stanley, the capital, one might

Effective cooperation between different arms was one of the keys to British success in the Falklands War. Here the assault ship HMS Fearless *disgorges troops by landing craft and helicopter at San Carlos, May 1982. (© British Crown Copyright/MOD via Jonathan Falconer)*

certainly be forgiven for assuming that one had landed in a Scottish fishing village. The total population was just 1,800 and those outside Stanley lived in remote sheep-farming settlements.

Confident that Britain would not fight over an apparently trivial issue like the sovereignty of these islands, the Argentine military junta led by General Leopoldo Galtieri (b. 1926), which found itself in growing domestic difficulties, considered invasion.

A British defence review of 1981 resulted in plans to reduce the Royal Navy, including the withdrawal of the ice patrol vessel HMS *Endurance*, the UK's only immediate military support for the islands. This undoubtedly encouraged the Argentine government, which interpreted the *Endurance* decision as a signal that Britain was no longer interested in the Falklands. The war was triggered by the raising of the Argentine flag on the island of South Georgia (almost 1,000 miles east of the Falklands), whence some scrap-metal dealers had gone to dismantle an old whaling station. On 2 April 1982 Argentine special forces overwhelmed the tiny garrison of Royal Marines at Stanley, also capturing the island of South Georgia.

'Fear is no basis for foreign policy.'

Margaret Thatcher, 1978

The decision to mount Operation 'Corporate' to liberate the Falklands was taken early, and owed much to Prime Minister Margaret Thatcher's (b. 1925) personal determination, aided by UN Security Council Resolution 502. The operation was controlled from the Royal Navy's headquarters at Northwood, near London, and involved much of its surface fleet. Ironically, had the Argentines acted later, the RN would not have been able to mount the operation, for the 1981 defence review involved mothballing the assault ships *Fearless* and *Intrepid*, selling the carrier *Invincible* to Australia and scrapping the anti-submarine carrier *Hermes*, all of which were to play vital roles in the campaign.

A task force was assembled, eventually totalling thirty-nine warships with Sea Harrier aircraft, helicopters and chartered merchantmen. The assault troops, under Major-General Jeremy Moore (b. 1928), comprised 3 Commando Brigade (Brigadier Julian Thompson (b. 1934)) with 40, 42 and 45 battalion-sized Royal Marine Commandos and 2nd and 3rd Battalions the Parachute Regiment under command. Brigadier Tony Wilson's 5 Infantry Brigade contained 2nd Battalion Scots Guards, 1st Battalion Welsh Guards and 1/7th Gurkha Rifles. Special forces included elements of both the Special Boat Service (SBS) and Special Air Service (SAS), while the Royal Artillery furnished field and air defence artillery.

The Argentine garrison was reinforced prior to the battle to two brigades under Brigadier-General Mario Menendez, the islands' new military governor. The British used Ascension Island, just south of the Equator, as a forward base, and on 18 April the main task force, led by Rear Admiral Sandy Woodward (b. 1932) sailed south from it. On 12 April, with two nuclear submarines in the area, Britain announced a maritime exclusion zone (MEZ) around the Falklands. Soon after, on 24–6 April in appalling weather, South Georgia was recaptured by the Royal Marines and special forces without any British losses. This had marginal direct influence on the war and demonstrated the difficulties that would be encountered in assaulting the Falklands, but was an important psychological boost for the UK and cannot have helped the morale of the conscripts of the Malvinas garrison.

The Falklands War, 2 April–14 June 1982

2 April	Argentine invasion of the Falklands
3 April	Royal Marines on South Georgia overwhelmed. UN passes Resolution 502 demanding immediate Argentine withdrawal
5 April	First elements of British Task Force sail from Portsmouth
12 April	Maritime Exclusion Zone declared around Falklands
26 April	British special forces and Royal Marines recapture South Georgia
1 May	British special forces land on Falklands. RAF bombs Port Stanley airfield
2 May	*General Belgrano* sunk
4 May	HMS *Sheffield* sunk
7 May	British Task Force leaves Ascension Island
12 May	*QE II* leaves Southampton with 5 Infantry Brigade
14 May	SAS raid on Argentine airfield on Pebble Island
21 May	British land at San Carlos
25 May	HMS *Coventry* and *Atlantic Conveyor* sunk
28–9 May	Battle of Goose Green
1 June	5 Infantry Brigade lands at San Carlos
8 June	*Sir Galahad* and *Sir Tristram* bombed at Fitzroy
11 June	Battle begins for Port Stanley
14 June	Argentine forces on the Falklands surrender

The bombing of Port Stanley's airport on 1 May by an RAF Vulcan was a curious episode. The aircraft refuelled seventeen times *en route*, dropped four bombs, only one of which inflicted minor damage, an operation which was repeated on four other occasions. This was perhaps more a demonstration by the RAF to *itself* of its long reach than a militarily significant act, although the UK press seized on the strike as an expression of RAF air supremacy. But the Argentine air force would not give way without a struggle.

The naval war quickly escalated, and on 1 May aircraft from Woodward's task group attacked ground targets, while his ships came under attack from Argentine aircraft. The next day the old Argentine cruiser *General Belgrano* was torpedoed by the submarine *Conqueror* south of the Falklands, an event which remains controversial because the *Belgrano* was outside the MEZ at the time of her sinking. This, however, persuaded the obsolescent Argentine surface fleet to stay in port.

Though its navy was deterred from further intervention, Argentina's air force soon flexed its muscles. On 4 May two Super Etendard strike aircraft flying low launched sea-skimming Exocet missiles towards the *Hermes*, one of which struck the *Sheffield*, a Type 42 destroyer on radar picket duty ahead of the carrier. The ship was abandoned with twenty dead, and on 12 May the destroyer *Glasgow* was badly damaged by aerial attack and limped away for repairs. This underlined the RN's weakness: its ship-borne radar systems were inadequate against the latest missiles, there were insufficient aircraft to protect the fleet and no AWACS-type early warning aircraft were deployed. These defects could be put down to shifting defence priorities in the preceding years, but were a reminder that the RN had not seen such concerted action since the Second World War.

The Argentine pilots in their A-4 Skyhawks, Mirage III interceptors and Super Etendards continued to challenge the RN and RAF when the British landed around San Carlos on 21 May, mounting repeated attacks on the warships and merchantmen in Falkland Sound. The frigates *Ardent* and *Antelope* were sunk and three destroyers damaged. On 25 May another Type 42 destroyer, the *Coventry*, on radar picket to the north of West Falkland, was lost, together with the requisitioned Cunard container ship *Atlantic Conveyor*. The latter was loaded with vital supplies and heavy-lift Chinook helicopters, all but one of which were destroyed. Other ships were struck, but saved by poorly fused bombs that failed to explode. Menendez committed a tactical error in not moving troops to San Carlos, and as his pilots concentrated on the naval Task Force, 3 Commando Brigade was left unmolested and was able to fan out across East Falkland.

45 Commando and 3 Para pushed eastwards on foot to invest Port Stanley in a gruelling 50km march across East Falkland in atrocious weather, while 2 Para headed south to the settlement of Goose Green. On 28–9 May in a surprisingly vicious battle 2 Para assaulted the Goose Green area, losing their commander, Lieutenant-Colonel H. Jones (awarded a posthumous VC), but taking over twice their number in prisoners – some 1,200 men. The capture of Goose Green provided an important psychological lift for the Task Force, coinciding with a low point in their fortunes – the fleet was suffering catastrophic losses and 2 Para had sustained fifty-two casualties (over 10 per cent of its fighting

strength). Goose Green was equally a blow for Argentine confidence because Menendez had just reinforced it.

5 Infantry Brigade landed at San Carlos on 1 June with General Moore, who moved his two Guards battalions to Bluff Cove on the east coast by sea, the loss of Chinook helicopters on the *Atlantic Conveyor* having eroded his ability to lift troops by air. While unloading, the landing ships *Sir Galahad* and *Sir Tristram* were hit by four strike aircraft and fifty-one servicemen were killed: this was Britain's largest loss of life in a single combat incident since the Korean War. With the bulk of his forces now investing Stanley, Moore planned attacks on the high ground around it. On the night of 11/12 June 3 Para took Mount Longdon, 45 Commando captured Two Sisters and 42 Commando overran Mount Harriet, while their disgruntled comrades in 40 Commando guarded the San Carlos beachhead.

This fighting was bitter and bloody: British troops had not been exposed to such casualties within a generation. The 3 Para assault on Mount Longdon, for example, cost seventy casualties, including twenty-three dead; it earned Sergeant Ian McKay a posthumous VC. At the same time an Exocet damaged the destroyer *Glamorgan*, which was providing naval gunfire support. Overnight on 13/14 June the Scots Guards took Tumbledown Mountain at the cost of fifty-two casualties, while 2 Para stormed Wireless Ridge, supported by over 6,000 rounds of artillery fire, which kept its casualties down to eleven. The defence began to collapse: the attackers followed crowds of demoralised men into Stanley and Menendez signed a surrender document at 2100 hours on 14 June.

The war cost the British 1,032 casualties, among them 255 dead; 6 British ships had been destroyed, along with 10 Harriers and 24 helicopters. Perhaps 1,000 Argentines had been killed (368 of them in the *General Belgrano*), and another 11,400 were captured. The junta fell soon afterwards. These figures sound horrendous, but would have been considered light in any major land war fought by the Western powers, who had lost any recognition of what 'heavy' casualties mean: one day on the Somme in 1916, albeit an unrepresentative one, cost 57,450 men, among them 19,240 killed. That the war could have been averted had Britain shown clearer signs of wishing to retain the Falklands is axiomatic. Galtieri unwisely forced Mrs Thatcher to make the choice between national humiliation and a military campaign at the limit of Britain's logistic capability. A lesser-willed premier might have swallowed and taken the former course. For Thatcher there was really no decision to make.

THE MIDDLE EAST AGAIN

While the world's attention was focused on the Falklands, on 6 June 1982 Israel mounted Operation 'Peace for Galilee', designed, as Israeli Prime Minister Menachim Begin (1913–92) put it, to 'cleanse Southern Lebanon' of the Palestine Liberation Organisation (PLO) and to create a secure buffer zone against PLO guerrilla forces based in the area. At this time the eyes of the international community were concentrating on the events unfolding in Port Stanley, and worldwide protests were muted. The initial phase, code-

The Israeli Defence Forces, 1973–82

The IDF grew massively in strength after the near-disaster of the Yom Kippur War. In terms of equipment alone, the growth was as follows:

	1973	1982
Artillery brigades	0	15
Tanks	1,225	3,825
Other AFVs	1,515	4,000
Armoured personnel carriers	500	4,800
Self-propelled guns	300	958

The Cold War, 1981–91

Nov 1981	Intermediate Nuclear Forces (INF) talks begin
Dec 1981	Martial law declared in Poland
June 1982	Strategic Arms Reduction Treaty (START) talks begin
Dec 1982	Martial law lifted in Poland
Mar 1983	President Reagan announces the Strategic Defense Initiative ('Star Wars')
Sept 1983	Soviet fighter shoots down Korean airliner
Nov 1983	Cruise missiles arrive in Europe; INF talks suspended
Dec 1983	START talks suspended
Nov 1984	Reagan re-elected as US President
Mar 1985	Geneva Superpower summit
Oct 1986	Reykjavik Superpower summit
Dec 1987	Washington Superpower summit
June 1988	Moscow Superpower summit
Feb 1989	Soviet forces withdraw from Afghanistan
Dec 1989	Malta Superpower summit
Nov 1989	Fall of the Berlin Wall
Oct 1990	Reunification of Germany
Nov 1990	Conventional Forces in Europe (CFE) Treaty signed
July 1991	Warsaw Pact dissolved; START I Treaty signed
Dec 1991	Collapse of the USSR

named 'Little Pines', was aimed at the PLO, but on 9 June the Israelis put 'Big Pines' into effect and struck against Syrian troops based on Lebanese territory. Although there was some tough fighting, notably against the PLO at Beaufort Castle on 7 June, by 11 June Israeli troops had reached Beirut. There the age-old challenges of urban combat proved too much and the Israeli campaign ground to a halt in August with an American-brokered ceasefire. A multinational force of Americans, French and Italians supervised the departure of the PLO guerrillas, but Israel later occupied west Beirut. In September Lebanese Christian forces massacred hundreds of Palestinian civilians in two refugee camps in an area under nominal Israeli control, which led Britain, France and America to send peacekeeping troops to the city.

Though the British, with a long culture of peacekeeping in Northern Ireland, performed well, suicide bombers attacked the US and French contingents in October 1983, killing 78 French and 241 US troops. Thereafter, US forces abroad have always been wary of any fraternisation with the local community, having several times since suffered such attacks without warning. Such insularity only serves to fuel the stab-in-the-back culture that stems from Pearl Harbor (1941). By 1985 Israeli forces had abandoned Beirut, but maintained a security zone in Southern Lebanon, which was only abandoned in May 2000.

The IDF was probably one of the most professional and effective fighting forces during this period, yet even it proved vulnerable to a concerted Palestinian guerrilla campaign, coupled with the unpopularity of conscript service in Southern Lebanon. As with previous Arab–Israeli wars, in 1982 the superpowers watched closely to evaluate new weapons systems in combat. This was the first major use of reactive armour (on the Israeli Merkava MBT) and unmanned aircraft (RPVs – Remotely Piloted Vehicles), which were used successfully to hunt for Palestinian SAM sites. On 9 June the Israeli Air Force used a balanced 'force package' of RPVs, aircraft and missiles to seek out and destroy Syrian air defences in the Bekaa Valley. After the SAM batteries and radar systems had been knocked out, a massive dogfight developed, in which the Israeli jets prevailed by a huge margin. On the ground, the advance down the Bekaa Valley proved the value of Israeli doctrine, which taught the importance of all-arms coordination (including highly mobile artillery on call, and combat engineers forward with the armour). In 1982 IDF doctrine and tactics were very different from those used at the beginning of the Yom Kippur War in 1973. The defence analysts who in the aftermath of Yom Kippur had loudly proclaimed that the tank and the manned aircraft were dead were proved to be mistaken, but the importance of integrating armour into an all-arms combat team – lessons that had been learned painfully in both world wars – was reinforced.

THE END OF THE COLD WAR

Another development during this Cold War era was the incorporation of psychological warfare capabilities into the world's main armies. Largely because of political sensitivities, psychological warfare had several names during the twentieth century, including propaganda, political warfare and psychological operations (psyops) or information war. It encompasses activities to weaken an opponent's will, reinforce loyalty and gain the military or moral support of the uncommitted, usually through the control and management of news and information. Put simply, it is perception management, or military PR. While the West Germans maintained a battalion sending leaflets by balloon to their comrades opposite in East Germany, psyops techniques of broadcasting (in the Iran–Iraq War and Southern Lebanon) and distributing leaflets by air to rebel tribesmen (in Afghanistan) proved effective means of communication or persuasion. The success of these techniques by the British in the counter-insurgency campaign in Oman (1970–5) convinced some observers that psyops was an essential component of modern low intensity operations. Leaflets were successfully used by US forces in Grenada during Operation 'Urgent Fury' (October 1983), and in Panama in December 1989 (Operation 'Just Cause').

Perhaps the most interesting development during this period, however, concerns not a single conflict, or a strategy or doctrine. Rather, it is the elevation of special forces to near superstar status. The Soviet Union has always placed great emphasis on the use of special forces and, along with other members of the Warsaw Pact, it created a large number of *Spetsnaz* formations which would have spearheaded any assault on the West. While the British Special Air Service (SAS) had performed with panache during the Second World War, and US special forces had played an important role

Operations in America's back yard: the US invasion of Grenada, October 1983. Throughout the post-war era the USA has shown little reluctance to intervene to protect its perceived interests throughout the Americas. This operation to 'restore order and democracy' was sanctioned by Ronald Reagan in response by attempts by Cuban-backed elements to take power on the Caribbean island of Grenada, and resulted in heavy and costly fighting. (Defence Picture Library)

Mikhail Gorbachev (b.1931) did more than any single individual to create the circumstances that ended the Cold War. This photograph was doctored to remove the birthmark from his scalp, the mark having been seen by some Soviet citizens as the mark of the antichrist! (David King Collection)

in Vietnam (alongside Australian and New Zealand SAS troops), it took another event in peacetime to create the mystique. An Arab terrorist group took over the Iranian Embassy in Prince's Gate, London, in May 1980 and began negotiating in front of the world's media. With a nihilistic disregard for life, they killed one hostage, but within days black-suited, balaclava-masked SAS troopers abseiled down the front of the building, retook the embassy and killed all six terrorists, though not before another hostage was killed and others wounded. The operation was caught by the world's camera crews and considered a stunning success. Since then the British Army's anti-terrorist role has been enhanced, and many other countries have imitated the force. At an operational level this has underlined the need for special forces to be routinely incorporated into any operation, and for the world's politicians special forces provide a useful low-cost force multiplier. For Hollywood, such elite troops have create a whole genre of super heroes, capable of winning wars single-handedly.

But events in Europe in 1989 took even the myth-makers in Hollywood by surprise, and brought a long overdue end to the Cold War. As late as the 1960s the USSR could plausibly present itself as an economic success, and thus as a serious competitor to the West on more than simply military grounds. By the early 1980s, however, the Soviet economy was in serious trouble, leading to it being described as 'Upper Volta with rockets'. Under Brezhnev the Soviet economy stagnated, and the effort of keeping up a hugely expensive arms race with the United States placed intolerable burdens on the USSR. The beginning of the New Cold War in the late 1970s exacerbated the problem, as under the Carter and especially the Reagan administrations the United States pursued ambitious military programmes. The USA could easily afford them: the Soviet Union, struggling to keep up, could not. Moreover, the peoples of the Soviet Bloc were as eager as ever for personal freedom, democracy and human rights. By the time that Mikhail Gorbachev (b. 1931) came to power in 1985 reform was desperately needed.

Gorbachev's policies of *perestroika* (reconstruction) and *glasnost* (openness) were intended to reform the USSR, to make it more efficient, but they resulted in its destruction. He deserves to be remembered kindly

by history, as unlike so many great figures of the twentieth century he was ultimately a force for good. Gorbachev cooperated with Western leaders to end the Cold War, but by allowing limited freedom both within the Soviet Union and its satellite states he opened a Pandora's box. Unlike his predecessors, who had moved to crush similar liberalising movements in Hungary in 1956 and in Czechoslovakia in 1968, Gorbachev was not prepared to use force to maintain communism in Eastern Europe. As a consequence, in 1989 'people power' brought the communist regimes of the Warsaw Pact states crashing down. The defining moment was the breaching of the Berlin Wall, symbol since 1961 of a divided Germany and a divided Europe. Two years later the Soviet Union itself collapsed, the Communist Party utterly discredited and Gorbachev forced from power. The West had decisively won the Cold War.

The end of the Cold War. The Berlin Wall comes down, 10 November 1989; the scene by the Brandenburg Gate (see p. 173). (Associated Press)

FIFTEEN

IRREGULAR WARFARE, 1899–1989

EDMUND YORKE

'The guerrilla fights the war of the flea, and his military enemy suffers the dog's disadvantages; too much to defend, too small, ubiquitous and agile an enemy to come to grips with.'

(R. Taber, *The War of the Flea*)

Robert Taber's stark 1965 warning of the ominous prospects for America's regular forces if deployed against the predominantly irregular 'people's forces' of Vietnam, proved an unnervingly accurate one. It was also a chilling portent of another superpower misfortune yet to come, the Soviet Union's disastrous experiences at the hands of Afghan irregular forces during the bitter Soviet–Afghan War of 1979–89.

Before embarking on this summary of irregular conflict in the twentieth century it is important both to define the origins and meanings of this very broad term. As M.R.D. Foot observes in 'Underground Warfare' (*Encyclopaedia of Twentieth-Century Warfare*, 1989), irregular warfare (sometimes termed 'underground warfare' or, since the 1800s 'guerrilla warfare') is 'as a rule fought by weaker against stronger forces; often, although not always, with success'. The practitioners of irregular warfare, or insurgents, are generally far outnumbered by their enemies, and usually try to secure superior force at their rarely chosen points of attack, often by laying ambushes. They frequently adopt unorthodox weaponry and uniforms (including plain clothes and even the enemy's uniform), and women often participate in significant numbers and on equal terms with men. In the words of Samuel Huntington, irregular or guerrilla warfare, 'is generally a form of warfare by which the strategically weaker side assumes the tactical offensive in selected forms, times and places'.

Irregular warfare is by no means a novel form of military activity. Indeed, its origins can be traced back many centuries. The first documented evidence of guerrilla warfare is in a Hittite parchment, the *Anastus Papyrus*, in which the Hittite King, Mursilis, refers to attacks by irregulars operating at night. In the fifth century BC the ancient military theorist, Sun Tzu, also described irregular or guerrilla tactics in his *Art of War* – a text destined, as we shall see, to influence Mao Tse-tung some 2,500 years later. Instances of guerrilla warfare were frequently referred to by Roman military historians – in North Africa, Gaul, Germany and above all in Spain. At the disastrous battle of Teutoburg Forest (AD 9), the Roman Commander Varus and over three legions (27,000 men) were overwhelmed and massacred in a successful forest ambush by the irregular forces of the formidable guerrilla leader Arminius the Cheruscan. It was one of the greatest defeats in Roman military history.

In more recent times the great military strategist Carl von Clausewitz (1780–1831) highlighted the political significance of 'people's war', focusing on the role of partisans in conventional warfare. By then Clausewitz and other Western military writers had already witnessed numerous examples of irregular warfare, either during the American War of Independence (1775–83), when American militia forces fought British regulars, or the early part of the French Revolutionary Wars. Other key examples included La Vendée (1793), Tyrol (1809) and the Peninsular War (1808–14) in Spain. Indeed, it is the ferocious campaign, consisting of numerous small-scale encounters, waged by the people of Spain against occupying French armies, from which the term 'guerrilla' (small war) is derived. By 1812 up to 30,000 Spanish guerrillas were operating against the French. They enjoyed significant successes, notably in April 1812 when a group under the renowned guerrilla leader Mina ambushed and destroyed a French convoy of 2,000 troops in central Spain. Similarly, during Napoleon's great Russian campaign of 1812 irregular Russian partisan groups (which included small regular units of the Russian Army) successfully harassed the French during their retreat from Moscow. Of the nearly 500,000 French regulars who had invaded Russia barely 20,000, desperately battling against bitterly cold weather and ferocious Cossack attacks, reached the safety of France.

'Wherever we arrived, they disappeared; whenever we left, they arrived. They were everywhere and nowhere, they had no tangible centre which could be attacked.'

French officer fighting Spanish guerrillas, 1912

As in Napoleon's disastrous 1812 campaign, the decision to conduct irregular warfare is often the product of a strategic crisis when the regular forces of one side have been defeated. Alternatively, if guerrilla forces do not exist in the first place, one side may turn to guerrilla tactics in order to continue the struggle as long as possible. Having lost the ability to conduct regular operations a belligerent may also resort to guerrilla warfare in the hope that outside help may materialise, or that prolonged resistance through this lesser form of warfare may induce the victorious side to accept more lenient peace terms.

It was the latter situation that dictated the drastic change of Boer tactics during the Second Anglo-Boer or South African War of 1899–1902. Here, imperial forces led by the British generals Roberts and Kitchener implemented a 'scorched earth' and 'block-house' policy designed to deprive the highly mobile Boer commandos of space and food supplies, thereby destroying their ability to wage regular warfare. For over two years after the surrender of the Boer commander Cronje at Paardeburg in February 1900, it was the use of such irregular tactics, involving hit-and-run raids and ambushes, which enabled little more than 20,000 Boer fighters to tie down twenty times as many British and imperial troops, and despite military defeat eventually secure what proved to be a politically advantageous peace.

Before the First World War the British, by virtue of controlling the world's greatest empire, faced a large number of conflicts involving irregular forces. As with most European armies they generally succeeded militarily (as eventually against the Boers in 1902) owing to their superior technology, numbers and/or firepower. There were, however, occasional examples of disasters to dent imperial confidence. In 1842, for instance, a 15,000-strong Anglo-Indian army was virtually annihilated in the snowy passes of Afghanistan by irregular Afghan tribesmen. Similarly, the British suffered catastrophic defeats at Isandlwana and Intombe Drift in 1879 at the hands of the Zulus, and lost at Maiwand the following year, again at the hands of Afghan irregulars. Other conventional or regular Western forces also met unexpected disaster during the nineteenth century. An Italian army was destroyed at Adowa in Abyssinia (1896) and a large section of General Custer's 7th Cavalry was similarly annihilated by the Sioux at the Battle of the Little Big Horn (1876).

Such victories by irregular forces, however, were the exception rather than the rule during the pre-1914 period. Furthermore, the general superiority of Western regular armies ensured that the necessary doctrine to deal with the challenges of irregular conflicts was neglected, a problem not helped by the wide diversity of their often primitive opponents. C.E. Calwell's book, *Small Wars* (1896), was a rare attempt by a European military writer to define operational principles against irregular opponents, but many of his ideas (such as the use of defensive square formations) were already outdated in the context of contemporary European warfare. In the virtual absence of doctrine the conduct of many pre-First World War irregular conflicts was often characterised by the absence of conventional rules of warfare. This frequently resulted in extreme situations of mutual brutality. Irregular conflict was not adequately covered by the Hague or Geneva Conventions and, following a precedent maintained by the Prussian Army in France (1870–1), those caught taking part in 'acts of terror' could expect summary execution without trial. After such acts of alleged terrorism by French irregulars (*Franc Tireurs*) the wife of the German Chancellor, Otto von Bismarck, even suggested to her husband that all Frenchmen should be shot or stabbed to death, down to the smallest *enfant*.

THE FIRST WORLD WAR AND THE INTER-WAR YEARS

The First World War produced two key examples of irregular conflict where guerrilla tactics achieved notable successes against larger conventional armies. The legendary exploits of Britain's Colonel T.E. Lawrence (1888–1935), as adviser to the Arab revolt against Turkey (1916–18), can be seen as a small but significant watershed in the development of irregular warfare. For the first time Lawrence added a political, social and psychological dimension to the tactical inheritance of guerrilla war. His achievements in assisting a loose confederation of Arab

Thomas Edward Lawrence (1888–1935). Lawrence was an enigmatic figure whose exact contribution to the success of the Arab revolt remains in dispute. Nevertheless, partly as a result of his book Seven Pillars of Wisdom, *and partly because of the success of the film* Lawrence of Arabia, *he has found an important place in the pantheon of guerrilla leaders. (IWM Q60212)*

tribesmen in hit-and-run raids against Turkish road and rail communications (notably at Aqaba in July 1917) remain controversial, but it has been argued that in purely strategic terms the campaign tied down up to 50,000 Turkish troops and, by distracting the Turks from their main British enemy, represented a significant benefit to the latter's cause. Indeed, with Lawrence's help Imal Faisal's (1883–1933) Bedouin tribesmen reached Damascus before the British General Edmund Allenby's (1861–1936) imperial forces, as Turkish power in the region rapidly collapsed. By late 1917 Lawrence had played a part in successfully welding together an admittedly small (around 10,000 men), but highly mobile and well-equipped irregular striking force.

'If you can wear Arab kit when with the tribes you will acquire their trust and intimacy to a degree impossible in uniform.'

T.E. Lawrence, 1917

By contrast the more prolonged campaign waged by German irregular forces under the command of General Paul von Lettow-Vorbeck

(1870–1964) against the British in German East Africa has, until recently, received much less attention. For over four years from November 1914 to November 1918, Lettow-Vorbeck's mixed German-Askari force persistently outmanoeuvred a vastly superior conventional British imperial army. Like many irregular army commanders, Lettow-Vorbeck only developed his guerrilla tactics by trial and error. When his first conventional skirmishes with the British proved too costly in men and supplies he dismembered his *Schutztruppe*, or 'bush army', into small units, often of fewer than ten men, who were sent on special raiding missions. He generally faced inferior quality and inexperienced imperial troops, and although he frequently lacked food and water supplies, he survived four years of long treks through deserts and bush, occasionally even crossing international boundaries into Portuguese East Africa. He only surrendered at Abercorn, Northern Rhodesia, after he had been informed of the Armistice. To the surprise of his British captors his forces at the time of his surrender consisted of only 156 Europeans, 1,168 Askari and 3,000 African carriers.

'There is almost always a way out, even of an apparently hopeless position, if the leader makes up his mind to face the risks.'

Major-General Paul von Lettow-Vorbeck, East African Campaigns (1957)

Compared to Lawrence, Lettow-Vorbeck has received little recognition for his achievement as an irregular army commander. This was probably because he lacked Lawrence's personal charisma and flare for publicity, but Lawrence's campaign achieved more fame because he also took the trouble not only to record his experiences, but to formulate theories of irregular warfare. As several commentators have pointed out, Lawrence's seminal work, *Seven Pillars of Wisdom* (1926), for the first time established a crude theoretical basis for an irregular mode of warfare. Lawrence stressed, for instance, the importance of morale and propaganda in a guerrilla struggle and its essentially political nature – 'we had won a province when we had taught the civilians in it to die for our ideal of freedom'.

Possibly due to Lettow-Vorbeck's successes and their experience of earlier imperial irregular conflicts, the British at least were beginning to recognise the potency of challenges from hostile irregular forces. From 1915 to 1918, for example, the British kept 30,000 troops in north Egypt, far away from the key fighting fronts, because they feared that the Senussi tribesmen of Libya might attack the crucial lifeline of the Suez Canal.

By the 1930s the face of irregular war was already beginning to change. While Lenin regarded irregular or guerrilla aspects of the Russian Civil War (1917–21) as merely a substitute for conventional war, and only one of many means by which the Revolution might be spread or effected, the Chinese communist leader Mao Tse-tung (1893–1976) brought in a new dimension. His 1938 treatise, *On Protracted War*, advocated three novel tenets that gave guerrilla warfare new potential. First, there was the admission that guerrillas alone could not win. Mao therefore envisaged a progressive effort to create regular forces while irregulars waged their hit-and-run tactics. At a later stage guerrillas/irregulars and regulars would together coordinate a campaign against the enemy. Both styles of fighting and both styles of organisation were needed to win. Second, and equally important, Mao demanded a mammoth effort in organising popular political and moral support for guerrillas and regulars. The entire population had to be enlisted in one organisation or another. The Chinese leader envisaged a symbiotic

'A rising of the masses of the people needs no justification. What has happened is an insurrection, and not a conspiracy.'

Leon Trotsky (1879–1940)

Trotsky was wrong. The Bolshevik Revolution of November 1917 was based on a conspiracy. For years, Bolshevik revolutionaries had built up small clandestine groups within the Russian Army, in factories and in the countryside. Like cancer cells, they had rotted the 'body' of Russian society from within. In 1902 V.I. Lenin (1870–1924) had published *What is to be Done?* in which he argued for a highly disciplined, well-motivated revolutionary party which would organise the masses. Lenin's party, from which anyone who disputed his version of Marxism was purged, helped to produce the Bolshevik victory in 1917. The Imperial Russian system had already collapsed, the victim of defeat in war and internal unrest; Lenin capitalised on that unrest to seize power.

Lenin was born Vladimir Ilyich Ulyanov. His elder brother was executed in 1887 for revolutionary activity. This had a profound impact on the seventeen-year-old Lenin, who was already influenced by the writings of Karl Marx (1818–83). In 1895 Lenin was exiled to Siberia by the Tsarist authorities, where he finished an important work, *The Development of Capitalism in Russia*. In 1900 he went into a different form of exile in Switzerland. Three years later the Russian Social Democratic Workers Party met in London, where factions fell out. Lenin's became known as the 'Bolsheviks' (or the majority party).

In the first decade of the twentieth century Russia was in turmoil. It rapidly industrialised, with associated social unrest as peasants left the countryside to work in factories in the cities. Many peasants, who had been serfs until 1861, still lived in conditions of extreme hardship. Many intellectuals were alienated from the autocratic regime of Tsar Nicholas II (1868–1918). Russia's defeat at the hands of Japan in 1904–5 prompted an abortive revolution.

Things seemed better by 1914; but the outbreak of the First World War brought fresh military defeat, occupation of Russia's territory by her enemies, and more misery for the masses. In such circumstances revolutionaries thrived. Far away in Switzerland, Lenin was involved in a Socialist Conference that set up a new revolutionary organisation, the Communist International. By March 1917 the authority and prestige of the Tsar had collapsed and he was overthrown in a liberal revolution. The new moderate government kept Russia in the war against Germany. In a cynical move to gain short-term advantage, the German authorities allowed Lenin to return to Russia, travelling through their territory in a sealed train. On arriving in Russia in April 1917, Lenin, ably aided by Trotsky, began to plot to overthrow the Provisional government.

Thanks to their highly disciplined members and effective organisation, the Bolsheviks had a firm base in the cities, but the 'October Revolution' of 1917 (which took place in November by the Western calendar) took the form of a coup, a seizure of power, not a spontaneous uprising. The Bolsheviks occupied the old Winter Palace in Petrograd (St Petersburg), the main centre of government, and other key objectives. Over the next three years the Bolsheviks fought ruthlessly to hang on to power in the face of determined efforts to get rid of them, including a major civil war and intervention by states such as Britain and the USA. By the time of Lenin's death in 1924 it was clear that the Union of Soviet Socialist Republics would survive.

Bolshevik Red Guards pose in Petrograd, October 1917. One doubts whether the original owner of what appears to be a rather luxurious car had donated it to the Red cause with particularly good grace. (David King Collection)

Mao's communists both suffered and benefited from having a range of enemies deployed against them. Here the Kuomintang leader Chiang Kai-Shek (centre) is flanked by the warlords Yen Hsi-shan (right) and Feng Yu-hsiang (left). (David King Collection)

relationship, the guerrillas being 'fish' and the people the 'water' in which they swam. It did not matter if the cause was truly desirable among the people; mass support was so vital that coercion and orchestrated hatred directed at selected scapegoats was encouraged from the start. Finally, Mao's scheme depended on the belief that the war would be a long one requiring considerable sacrifice and with no promise of quick victory. Notions about not holding ground, concentrating for actions and dispersing immediately after had been germane to irregular warfare long before Mao. The Chinese communist leader simply preserved what was orthodox and added facets, such as developing support structures among the peasantry, that gave this ancient form of armed conflict a modern potency.

By contrast, the European or Western powers – with few exceptions – continued to fail to appreciate the changing nature of irregular or guerrilla warfare. In the Easter Rising of 1916 and the Anglo-Irish War of 1918–21, the British failed to recognise the clear indications of a future politically motivated insurgency. In the 1916 Easter Rising, in a failed embryonic attempt at urban guerrilla warfare designed to eject the British from Ireland, the massively outnumbered 'Irish Volunteers' were brutally suppressed. The execution of their captured leaders only served to arouse strong Irish and Irish-American sympathy for what had initially been a weakly supported rebellion. Later, during the protracted Anglo-Irish War the British relied mainly on crude coercive tactics with the extended use of military support to the civil power. In confronting the Irish Republican Army (IRA), the small

Understandably apprehensive, a group of communists await execution after the failure of the 'Autumn Harvest' uprising, 1927. (David King Collection)

MAO TSE-TUNG AND THE LONG MARCH

Mao Tse-tung (or Mao Zedong) was one of the most significant figures in world history in the twentieth century. Founder of the Communist People's Republic of China, he was one of the greatest theorists and practitioners of revolutionary warfare. Mao was born in 1893 into an educated peasant farming family in Hunan province. An intellectual, in 1918 he started work as a library assistant at the University of Beijing where he read the works of Karl Marx. In 1921 Mao was one of the founders of the Chinese Communist Party (CCP). Mao's genius was to take the ideas of Soviet Marxism and apply them to the situation in China, where the vast bulk of the population lived on the land. In an appropriately agricultural metaphor, Mao wrote: 'We communists are like seeds and the people are like the soil. Wherever we go, we must unite with the people, take root and blossom among them.' Like Clausewitz, Mao believed that war was a political instrument: as he famously remarked, 'Political power grows out of the barrel of a gun.'

Mao Tse-tung (1893–1976). This photograph was taken during the Long March (October 1934–October 1936), during which the main Chinese communist force slowly moved from the south-east of the country to the northern province of Shensi.

For six years the CCP uneasily coexisted with Chiang Kai-Shek's (1887–1975) ruling Kuomintang (nationalist, or KMT) Party. But in 1927 the CCP staged the 'Autumn Harvest' uprisings in response to a purge by the KMT. These were bloodily suppressed. Mao and the CCP then built up strongholds in the mountains, but in a series of campaigns KMT forces put the communists under severe pressure. Ruthless but effective counter-insurgency operations by Chiang Kai-Shek's forces of some 700,000 men threatened to destroy the communists once and for all. By 1934 Mao had risen high within the CCP, and he was instrumental in carrying out the so-called 'Long March'.

The Long March has passed into Chinese folklore as the greatest epic in the history of the CCP. The 100,000-strong Red army fought its way through KMT positions, taking heavy casualties in the process, and retreated some 6,000 miles across south-west China to northern Shensi province. The Reds crossed eighteen mountain ranges and twenty-four rivers. The KMT forces pursued them, harassing the communists on the ground and from the air. Nevertheless, after thirteen months the Reds reached their destination. Their numbers were reduced by about 50 per cent, partly through casualties and partly because cadres had been left behind to revolutionise the population *en route*. The Long March was one of the greatest feats of endurance in military history. It bought the CCP a breathing space, but it was lucky that Chiang's subordinates, having chased the communists to Shensi, ignored orders to conduct a vigorous offensive against the battered revolutionary forces.

In 1937 the Japanese invaded China and the KMT and CCP patched up a truce. In 1946, after the defeat of the Japanese, the Chinese Civil War recommenced. Mao had made good use of the intervening period and the KMT were defeated in three years. The respite bought by the Long March was a major factor in Mao's victory.

military arm of a national political movement, they showed inflexibility and made fundamental errors, such as the crude attempt to use veterans recruited from the Western Front as auxiliaries to the Royal Irish Constabulary. The often brutal and indiscriminate retaliation by these 'Black and Tans' against the 3,000-strong IRA, whose main weapon was not partisan warfare but individual assassination, drove many waverers into the arms of the Republican movement. By 1921 a war-weary Britain had reached a compromise peace. Just as Lawrence, and to a lesser extent Lenin, provided Mao with inspiration, so the IRA campaign of 1916–21 was to inspire others, notably the 1950s EOKA campaign led by George Grivas (1898–1974) which was designed to drive the British out of Cyprus.

On the eve of the Second World War it was clear, therefore, that the *modus operandi* of irregular or guerrilla warfare in pursuit of victory was beginning to change. For centuries, irregular warfare had been organised merely as a response to alien occupation and was only completely understood in terms of the support of conventional armies against an opponent's lines of communication. In 1939, as Mao's campaign against the Japanese was already illustrating, irregular war was developing into something more than simply a tactical method. In stark contrast, the attitudes of regular army commanders had scarcely changed. Army general staffs continued to show virtually no interest in irregular warfare and the various military academies saw no reason to include courses on it in their curriculum. Irregular war was perceived as half brigandish or sheer banditry, altogether a messy business best left outside the confines of regular armies and their commanders. Thus in the 1930s at least one German writer considered it would endanger the country's war effort, for the very reason that its methods were so diametrically opposed to the traditional German way of waging battle.

Orde Wingate (1903–44) was a capable theorist and practitioner of guerrilla warfare. Before the Second World War he helped to organise 'special night squads' against Arab insurgents in Palestine, and in 1941 he led a guerrilla force that helped to drive the Italians from Abyssinia. However, he is most commonly associated with the 'long range penetration' groups, or Chindits, who operated with mixed success against Japanese lines of communication in Burma in 1943–4. Ambitious and unstable, Wingate attempted suicide on one occasion and was killed in an air crash in March 1944. (RMAS Collection)

This is not to say that individual officers had not gained valuable experience in inter-war irregular conflicts. Major-General Orde Wingate's (1903–44) experiences in combating the Arab Revolt in Palestine (1936–7) undoubtedly helped him to plan the great Chindit operations against the Japanese in occupied Burma from 1943 to 1944. There was also the odd voice in the wilderness, warning of what was to come. Although mainstream British theorists, notably Sir Charles Gwynn (*Imperial Policing*, 1934) and H.J. Stimson (*British Rule and Rebellion*, 1937), still relied almost solely on coercive tactics as a solution to minor insurgencies (e.g. conflicts with tribal irregulars on the Indian North-West Frontier) one British commentator, Major B.C. Dearing, published in 1927 an illuminating essay on 'Modern Problems of Guerrilla Warfare'. With astonishing foresight, in this essay he both pointed at developing forms of irregular war and hinted at ways of combating it. Dearing noted, in particular, the political implications of counter-insurgency, especially the influence of domestic public opinion as a brake on those powers who would otherwise have acted with the same ferocity as on past occasions. He also highlighted the development of modern weapons which favoured the guerrilla more than those operating against him; weapons that could be readily concealed and lent themselves to the first principle of guerrilla warfare – rapid contact and equally rapid dispersion. In populated areas, Dearing noted, there were wide opportunities for guerrillas to 'make propaganda to destroy property and to deliver attacks with great ease'. In this context the task of the army became essentially a police role. Dearing also stressed the likelihood of guerrilla insurgents targeting the financial rather than the military resources of a great power, as the Cuban rebels had done with success in 1898 and as the IRA attempted to do through its bombing onslaught on the city of London in the early 1990s. However, such predictions were the exception, not the rule, in the inter-war period.

THE SECOND WORLD WAR

The irregular resistance or partisan campaigns directed against German and Italian occupation forces in the Second World War confirm this period as a watershed in the development of irregular war as a means of achieving success against conventional or regular armies. Resistance in the specifically German-occupied territories ranged from a refusal to read Nazi newspapers to all-out organised armed struggle. Resistance fighters provided military Intelligence for the Allied cause, printed anti-Nazi propaganda and sabotaged the economic war effort. Most significantly, partisan warfare aimed at destroying lines of supply and communications and creating a general climate of insecurity, thus compelling the Axis powers to divert some of their forces from the main theatres of war.

The various Second World War partisan campaigns showed for the first time that forms of irregular war, if waged in a certain way and politically geared to a concept of national resistance (with appropriate organisation), could be a large-scale and consistently successful means of securing victory or partial victory against ostensibly superior conventional armies. Two cases of partisan warfare will serve to illustrate this point.

Yugoslavia between 1941 and 1945 was the scene for an intricate irregular resistance war against Axis occupation. As M.R.D. Foot points out ('Underground Warfare'), Croat, Serb, Slovene and Montenegrin nationalists pursued divergent aims, the Croats perhaps most atrociously (the fanatical pro-Nazi Ustasha movement establishing the murderous 'Independent State of Croatia' in 1941). Roman Catholic Croats, Orthodox Serbs and Muslims were at odds and there was a restive Albanian minority. Aside from these local and regional divergences, there were two major rural-based resistance movements, one headed by General Dragoljub Mihailović (1893–1946), who looked to the Royal Yugoslav government in exile, the other by Josip Broz (1892–1980) under his alias – Tito.

Unconsciously replicating the Chinese pattern, Tito welded his resistance army into a cohesive national liberation force. By 1943 he had

Marshal Tito (in light uniform) reviews Yugoslav Army of National Liberation partisans on the Adriatic island of Vis, 1944. Tito's forces benefited from vast quantities of Allied material aid, as well as extensive air support from British and American squadrons based in Italy. By mid-1944 his forces were much stronger than his main domestic rivals, the Croatian Ustashe and Mihailovic's Serbian Chetniks. However, with few exceptions, until the very end of the war his forces could not beat German troops in open combat, and it took a massive Soviet invasion of Serbia in autumn 1944 to guarantee a rapid end to the Yugoslav civil war and the consolidation of communist power in Belgrade. (David King Collection)

created from desperate bands of fighters a type of guerrilla force radically in advance of anything yet encountered. As John Ellis observes (*From the Barrel of a Gun*, 1995) Tito did not simply aim to fight a defensive military struggle against a foreign invader. Rather, he used the struggle as a political catalyst from which would emerge a new type of state founded upon new ideas of social justice. Tito saw that he must advance beyond the old parochial defensive concept of guerrilla warfare – 'we must not let the enemy force us by clever tactics onto the defensive; the spirit of our groups must be offensive, not only in the attack but in defence as well'. At times Tito would fight the Axis forces in head-on battles, even when this was suicidal – notably during the Fifth German Offensive (May–June 1943) when the partisan 3rd Division was almost wiped out while guarding the rear of Tito's retreating units. Indeed, such was the impact of these tactics that by 1943 the German High Command admitted that it no longer faced 'bandit' warfare, but that a new front had been opened in south-east Europe. By employing large military units, widening his class and ethnic support (including Slavic minorities other than Serbs) and entirely centralising or regularising control through commissars and party cells, and by holding towns and setting up miniature states in liberated areas, Tito easily outmatched his rival, Mihailović. Tito's cause was also undeniably aided by the excessive German coercive responses which involved all-out war against the civilian population, including shooting all partisans and treating their sympathisers with great brutality. By the end of the war Tito's multi-ethnic army numbered over 800,000 fighters (among them many women) and claimed 450,000 'fascist dead'. The latter number was clearly exaggerated (as with many other partisan statistics), not least given the fact that the total number of Axis occupation forces never exceeded 467,000!

Nevertheless, no other irregular or guerrilla struggle in occupied Western Europe ever approached the intensity of that waged in Yugoslavia. In other countries, resistance movements such as the *maquis* of south-west France never really got off the ground until the armies of Russia, the USA or Britain began to intervene. This was partly a reflection of terrain as, for instance, the low-lying lands of Holland and Denmark provided little scope for large-scale partisan warfare.

However, comparable in terms of scale to Yugoslavia was the partisan campaign fought against the invading Axis forces within the USSR from 1941 to 1945. The first appearance of partisans in the battle for Russia occurred shortly after the start of Operation 'Barbarossa' (June 1941). But, they were largely ill-organised and ill-trained. It was not until the Germans had advanced hundreds of miles across a 1,500-mile front that partisan bands began full-scale operations. Within a year, bands behind German lines were stalling transport, interrupting communications, destroying supplies and taking a steady toll of German lives. As the author Brooke Mclure observes in *Modern Guerrilla Warfare* (1962), 'so effective were these "irregulars" that a German Army of more than 100,000 troops was unable to keep clear the arterial supply routes to the front'. However, their cause among the people was again reinforced by the typically brutal nature of Nazi reprisals, which included mass hangings of suspected partisans and their supporters. As early as September 1941 Generalfeldmarschall Wilhelm Keitel (1881–1945), Hitler's Chief of Staff, had issued the notorious 'Keitel Befehl' permitting the execution of 50 to 100 'communists' for every German soldier killed by partisans, a policy enthusiastically carried out by the Waffen SS and Wehrmacht security divisions. Partisans often retaliated by torturing captured German soldiers to death. While such measures and countermeasures contributed to the unprecedented barbarity of this particular conflict, the Soviet partisan groups never achieved the potency of Tito's forces. In the traditional or general pattern of guerrillas acting more as auxiliaries to the Soviet conventional forces, they were strictly controlled and confined to harassing tactics. Moreover, there were huge internal divisions which the Nazis were able to exploit by recruiting local volunteers from anti-Soviet nationalities in, for example, Ukraine, Latvia, Lithuania and Byelorussia. Some partisan groups, such as the 'Ukrainian Insurgent Army', actually fought both fascist and communist as it soon became clear that both were equally oppressive totalitarian regimes.

Thus the Second World War set a precedent for a new and more potent mode of irregular conflict. Before the war, established military techniques had seemingly made regular armies almost invincible, and irregular or guerrilla groups could only hope to challenge them in exceptional circumstances. The Second World War was a turning point; Europe's marked decline, combined with the fatal weakening of the colonial powers, both undermined the confidence of the European ruling classes and led to deep economic and political unrest. In turn, this created a revolutionary situation the world over. In the Far East, for instance, the initial Japanese victories over the old colonial powers of Britain, Holland and France had a marked and immediate catalytic effect on their subject colonial peoples. In these conditions, following such a major shift in the global balance of power (with two new superpower rivals each anxious to sponsor surrogate movements or client states), it was possible for determined groups to find support for an all-out assault against the established powers by other than political means. Once it had been demonstrated that suitably organised irregular armies could achieve impressive results – as in Tito's Yugoslav campaign and Mao's victories over the Japanese before 1945, and, later, against the Chinese nationalist armies in 1949 – they were bound to be emulated.

THE COLD WAR YEARS

Major colonial struggles, 1945–1990

1945–9	Indonesia (vs. Dutch)
1946–54	Indo-China (vs. France)
1954–62	Algeria (vs. France)
1961–74	Guinea-Bissau (vs. Portugal)
1961–76	Angola (vs. Portugal)
1962–74	Mozambique (vs. Portugal)
1966–90	Namibia (vs. South Africa)

It was the old European colonial powers who were the first to reap the whirlwind. As Ian Beckett and John Pimlott have succinctly observed in *Armed Forces and Modern Counterinsurgency* (1985), 'traditional colonial policing was simply no longer appropriate in meeting insurgency that was now firmly based on revolutionary political ideology and which often eschewed direct military action against the security forces for political indoctrination amongst the population'.

In post-war Palestine, for instance, a virtually bankrupt and war-weary Britain swiftly retreated following a brief but bitter war of attrition waged against them by Jewish extremist gangs which culminated in the 1946 bombing of the King David Hotel in Jerusalem. The British had mistakenly equated the Arab Revolt with this new post-war Jewish insurgency, which was politically inspired by the terrible lessons of the Holocaust. The British paid the penalty of trying and failing to confront a new form of urban irregular warfare (as practised by the Irgun and Stern terrorist groups) with old style pre-war coercive tactics.

Although the end of the Second World War and the 1949 Chinese Revolution heralded a new era of irregular warfare that might be termed 'national liberation' or 'revolutionary war', this was not, in the immediate post-war years, the dominant mode of irregular warfare. In fact, during the first three decades after 1945 no two irregular wars were necessarily alike. As Walter Laquer confirms in *Guerrilla* (1985), 'radicals fought conservatives, national minorities pursued separatist policies and the conflicts frequently took the form of guerrilla or quasi-guerrilla war'. Some, as in Palestine, pre-dated the Second World War in origin, some were boosted or catalysed by it, with resistance movements switching their focus (as in Greece, Malaya and the Philippines) once the territories concerned were no longer occupied by the wartime invaders. Some of these wars were short, others protracted; some ended with the victory of the insurgents, others with their total defeat. While the Greek and Malayan insurrections were communist-inspired and led, the Kikuyu-led Mau Mau rebellion against British rule in Kenya was in the time honoured tradition of an anti-colonial uprising.

From a purely military perspective the pattern of these irregular conflicts was also highly variable. In Greece and Indo-China the communists transformed their guerrilla groups into militias and even regular army units of brigade and division strength. In Indonesia the rudiments of a regular army had emerged during the war. The Greeks and the Indo-Chinese communists received key support from neighbouring communist countries; the 'Huks' fighting the Americans in the Philippines were given no such assistance. While in Greece irregular warfare was largely mountain-based, in South-East Asia it took place mainly in jungles and forests.

The French, deploying old-style coercive tactics, rapidly succumbed to the Chinese-influenced rural revolutionary Viet Minh in Indo-China, culminating in total humiliation at Dien Bien Phu (1954). But the British led the way in developing counter-insurgency tactics to contain this new phenomena of irregular war. In the Malayan Emergency (1948–60) Britain became the first Western power to win such a revolutionary-inspired conflict, combining selective and flexible military counter-strokes with a political 'hearts and minds' campaign. The challenge had been formidable. Chin Peng, the Malayan Communist Party leader, had clearly modelled his campaign on Maoist strategy. Basing himself in the jungle, he hoped first to liberate the rubber estates along its fringes. Then he intended to extend his control into the neighbouring villages until he had an area in which he could establish a people's republic, and to which he could bring his guerrillas from the jungle to be trained and equipped for big battles in the

British troops move through undergrowth in pursuit of a wounded communist guerrilla, Malaya 1952. British counter-insurgency was highly effective in breaking the link between the mainly ethnic Chinese insurgents and the population. However, it should be said that the British benefited from favourable circumstances in Malaya, and contrasting their success with American failure in Vietnam is at best artificial. (ref: CFP582, © British Crown Copyright/MOD)

COUNTER-INSURGENCY

The emergence of insurgency as a major force in the twentieth century was paralleled by the development of counter-insurgency (COIN). Just like the Marxist–Leninist and Maoist form of insurgency, some schools of COIN, especially the British, placed as much emphasis on political aspects of conflict as on purely military ones. The British school grew out of a pragmatic response to the types of colonial small wars that British forces engaged in before and after the Second World War. The British Army had a long tradition of colonial policing that produced a body of informal doctrine. Making a virtue out of necessity, the British made much use of local troops, a policy that continued into the post-1945 period.

When, after 1945, Britain was faced with a rash of ideologically based (nationalist- and often communist-inspired) insurgencies in her imperial possessions, the Army updated its heritage of colonial policing to face the new situation. Several broad themes can be identified in the British approach: cooperation between the military and civil authorities; minimum use of force; tactical flexibility; an emphasis on Intelligence and winning the 'hearts and minds' of the population (the two things are inextricably linked) to isolate the insurgents from the people, the insurgents then being destroyed; and political reform to remove the grievance that caused the insurgency in the first place.

This approach was not always followed. In the Anglo-Irish War (1918–21) and in the Amritsar massacre in India (1919) British forces used heavy-handed methods that were politically counterproductive and indeed caused a backlash from public opinion at home. In other campaigns British methods, which relied on winning over the uncommitted middle ground to the side of the government, simply did not work. In Palestine (1945–8) and Aden (1964–8) the British decisively lost the 'competition in government'. In Malaya (1948–60), in the rebellion in Kenya in the 1950s, and in Dhofar (1970–5), however, the British method of combining military and political action proved highly successful. In the 1990s, the British approach to COIN, suitably modified, proved to be a successful basis for conducting peace support operations (PSO) in places such as Bosnia.

> *'It is by combined use of politics and force that pacification of a country and its future organization will be achieved. Political action is by far the most important.'*
>
> *Marshal Joseph Gallieni's instructions to French forces occupying Madagascar, 22 May 1898*

The French can claim to have invented modern counter-insurgency as far back as the 1830s and '40s. Attempting to quell resistance in Algeria, French forces developed a mixture of political and military action. In the later nineteenth century this approach was developed into a strategy that later became known as *tâche d'hûile* or oil stain, the idea being that French control and 'civilisation' gradually spread throughout an area, the administrators following the soldiers. In contrast to the pacific imagery of *tâche d'hûile*, the French never hesitated to apply strong-arm military methods if they were thought necessary. Their strategy was applied with varying degrees of success in Indo-China and Madagascar as well as North Africa.

After 1945, the French, like the British, faced a range of ideologically driven enemies. From 1946 to 1954 the French campaigned against Ho Chi Minh's (1890–1969) Viet Minh fighters in Indo-China. Against the Viet Minh's Maoist-inspired tactics and strategy, traditional French COIN proved inadequate. The French won some victories at the military level but lost the battle for political support. In 1954 a French attempt to defeat the Viet Minh in a conventional battle at Dien Bien Phu ended disastrously. This destroyed any shred of credibility the colonial regime may have had and undermined support at home. France was almost immediately faced with another major insurgency, this time in Algeria (1954–62). As a consequence of the defeat in Indo-China some French Army officers had begun to develop a new doctrine for COIN, which became known as *guerre revolutionnaire*. Based on an inversion of Marxist revolutionary theory, this was a highly politicised strategy that employed psychological warfare and sometimes torture, as well as conventional military and political approaches to COIN. By the late 1950s the Algerian insurgents had been militarily defeated, but by using methods that led to a backlash in liberal democratic France. When Charles de Gaulle (1890–1970), recently installed as French President, offered Algeria independence, some French units mounted an unsuccessful coup – a foray by the military into the political sphere that was in many ways the logical outcome of *guerre revolutionnaire*, and which led to the doctrine being discredited.

open. The final stage would be to challenge and beat the British Malayan government in conventional warfare. It was a campaign successfully defeated by a coordinated politico-military response in which Sir Robert Thompson's (1916–92) famous 'five principles' – advancing the need for a clear political aim on the part of the government, the need to adhere to the rule of law, the need for a consolidated plan, the need to establish secure base areas and the need to destroy the political infrastructure of the insurgents – proved the recipe for victory. As Pimlott and Beckett have, however, noted, the keynote of the subsequent British approach has always been flexibility – 'whereas other countries . . . have slavishly followed the fashion established in Malaya of separating the population from the guerrilla by means of resettlement, the British themselves have recognised that indigenous societies are not necessarily socially or economically "right" for resettlement'.

The main British COIN campaigns

1945–8	Palestine
1948–60	Malaya
1952–60	Kenya
1955–9	Cyprus
1962–6	Brunei/Borneo
1964–7	Radfan/Aden
1969–	Northern Ireland
1970–5	Dhofar

In campaigning against the irregular communist forces of the Huks in the Philippines (1945–58), the Filipino regular army (assisted by US special advisers) also learned to moderate an early coercive policy. The 'carrot and stick' approach of pursuing the Huks into remote areas while army engineers built new roads, bridges, canals, schools, clinics and 'liberty wells' was a triumph – 'the socio-economic hearts and minds programme effectively eroded popular support for the Huks' (Beckett and Pimlott).

Unfortunately, the apparent failure of the American military to follow through such lessons largely accounts for the greatest military victory achieved by predominantly irregular forces against the West's most powerful regular army. The crushing defeat of the American Army in Vietnam (1965–73) represented the high-water mark of mainly irregular forces pursuing revolutionary war tactics. The United States Army demonstrated inadequate flexibility; its over-reliance on heavy bombing raids and large static fire bases with insufficient emphasis on socio-economic initiatives – aside from 'protected hamlets' – proved an unmitigated disaster. Despite the continued optimism displayed by the American Commander-in-Chief, General William Westmoreland (b. 1914), over 500,000 American GIs were, for instance, unable to prevent communist Vietcong insurgents overrunning the US Embassy in Saigon during the 1968 Tet offensive. British advice, based on Malayan experience, was patently ignored ('We don't tell you how to run Malaysia and you don't tell us how to run Vietnam', was President Johnson's heated riposte), while US tactical inflexibility was perhaps summed

Winning hearts and minds the American way. An underprivileged US citizen (13 per cent of the American population was black, yet blacks composed 28 per cent of US combat troops in Vietnam, and 45 per cent in airborne units, as shown here) sets fire to the home of an underprivileged Vietnamese citizen during a counter-guerrilla operation. (Defence Picture Library)

up in the memorable remark attributed to one American general: 'I will be damned if I will permit the US Army, its institutions, its doctrine, and its traditions to be destroyed just to win this lousy war.'

Thus, time and time again during the 1950s, 1960s and 1970s, Third World irregulars or guerrilla forces confronted conventionally armed and regular forces and on more occasions than not, emerged victorious. Aside from the Franco-American debacle in Indo-China, French, Belgian and Portuguese colonialism in general proved particularly vulnerable, mainly because (unlike the British) these nations had failed to provide an indigenous class with a stake in the survival of the colonial regime. Algeria gained independence from France and Angola and Mozambique from Portugal after prolonged, irregular and largely rural-based guerrilla campaigns. In some cases, colonial regimes did not even wait to confront their enemies. The precipitous and irresponsible abandonment of the Congo by Belgium in 1960 left a legacy of massacres and political chaos that has contributed to the destabilisation of the area today. Occasionally, colonial regimes even lacked superior manpower. In the Rhodesian conflict (1965–80) lack of numbers led the hard-pressed regime to develop a 'fire force' concept to offset lack of resources through a concentration of firepower and mobility.

'It does not matter how small you are if you have faith and a plan of action.'

Fidel Castro, 1959

Western-supported governments were not alone in experiencing severe trials at the hands of specifically Marxist-inspired insurgents. In 1959 Fidel Castro's irregular, vastly outnumbered, largely rural-based guerrillas rapidly triumphed over the corrupt Batista regime in Cuba, after the latter was effectively abandoned by the USA. In Rod Pascall's words, 'By the mid-1970s communist guerrilla warfare gave alarming indications of invincibility.'

From the Cuban Revolution (1956–9) emerged a key revolutionary exponent of the art of irregular or guerrilla warfare – Che Guevara (1928–67). Drawing on his experiences in the struggle against Batista, Guevara developed a model of Latin American revolution which asserted that in the countryside elite irregular forces working from an 'insurgent centre' (the 'Foco Insurreccional') could mobilise the people without (as Mao had taught) the careful development of a separate and parallel political organisation. However, this theory proved less successful than the Cuban campaign and, after a brief but unhappy excursion in 1965 to assist with the Kinshasa rebellion in Zaire (now the Democratic Republic of Congo), he disastrously sought to bring his own brand of revolution to Bolivia. Here his small guerrilla band was hunted down and he was killed by US-trained Bolivian forces in 1967. It was a rare setback for Marxist revolutionary warfare in the three post-war decades.

'One does not necessarily have to wait for a revolutionary situation: it can be created.'

Ernesto 'Che' Guevara, Guerrilla Warfare *(1961)*

By 1970 the picture of irregular conflict had been further complicated or 'coloured' by the emergence of the spectre of full-scale urban guerrilla warfare. The increasing urbanisation of global society during the post-war period had facilitated the spread of this mode of warfare and it proved particularly problematical for Western democracies during the 1970s and 1980s. Its potential had already been demonstrated in 1944 when Belgian resistance fighters had used urban guerrilla tactics to thwart German sabotage operations, thereby ensuring that the vital Antwerp docks were handed over intact to the Allies. As mentioned earlier, during the Irish and

CASTRO AND GUEVARA

Fidel Castro and Ernesto 'Che' Guevara occupy ambiguous places in the pantheon of twentieth-century revolutionary guerrilla leaders. Castro (born 1926) was an inspiring leader who achieved an astonishing victory over the forces of the Cuban dictator Fulgencio Batista. Landing in Cuba in 1956 with only eighty-one followers, he suffered a military setback very early on in the campaign and was forced into the mountains. In the first year of revolution Castro enjoyed little success, but thereafter he gathered increasing backing, his supporters representing shades of political opinion that ranged from moderates to hard-line Marxists. On New Year's Day 1959 Batista fled and Castro entered Havana as victor. In retrospect, the Batista regime was rotten to the core and ripe for destruction: it was corrupt, badly ruled, and the army was largely demoralised. Guevara (1928–67) failed to recognise the peculiar circumstances of the Cuban Revolution, and instead drew upon his experiences to formulate the Foco theory of insurgency, which led to his defeat and death in Bolivia.

Although he did not set out to be deliberately hostile to the United States, Castro pursued left-wing policies that ultimately led to a rupture with the USA. Castro eventually declared himself a communist and turned to the Soviet Union for support. For the next two decades Cuba was a supporter of Soviet-backed revolutionary movements in many parts of the world.

Castro is, at the time of writing, still in power in Cuba, having long survived his Soviet sponsor. Guevara achieved enormous popular fame in his lifetime, which has scarcely diminished even though his Focoist theories have been discredited. Thanks to the musical *Evita* and the posters that adorn student walls, he remains a twentieth-century icon.

Fidel Castro (far left) and Che Guevara (third left) march through the streets of Havana, 5 March 1960. The occasion is the funeral procession for victims of an explosion allegedly caused by US intelligence services. (Associated Press)

Carlos Marighela (1911–69), author of the Minimanual of Urban Guerrilla Warfare *(1969). Marighela believed in the old revolutionary concept of the 'propaganda of the deed', the belief – dismissed by Marx and Lenin – that small groups could create revolutionary conditions by acts of violence. More of a tactician than a strategist, Marighela's work was widely read and imitated by those on the extreme Left with a taste for anarchic violence. The* Minimanual *itself was plagiarised by a number of groups, notably the Provisional IRA in the early 1970s. (RMAS Collection)*

Palestinian crises of 1916–21 and 1945–8 respectively, urban extremist terrorists had demonstrated a crude form of city-based irregular warfare, but it was in the 1960s that radical student protests revealed a new enthusiasm for urban defiance of established regimes.

The strategy of urban guerrilla warfare was based on recognition of the fact that the political and military economic centre of power was in the great conurbations, and that it should be attacked there, not from the periphery. One of the first advocates was the Spanish-born Abraham Guillen, an 'anarchist-Marxist' who settled in Uruguay. His conception did not exclude cooperation with rural 'militzias', but he did maintain that in highly urbanised countries revolutionary battles ought to be waged in urban areas, 'for the revolutionary potential is where the population is'. His theories were developed further by a Brazilian, Carlos Marighela (1911–69), who focused on the provocation of the conventional/regular enemy by highly trained 'firing groups' of no more than four or five people with hit-and-run tactics from all directions, for example in the form of bank raids. This would take place in a familiar urban environment where the ultimate aim would be to compel the enemy to 'transform the political situation into a military one'. Such theories inspired many other

'It is necessary to turn political crisis into armed conflict by performing violent actions that will force those in power to transform the political situation of the country into a military situation. That will alienate the masses, who, from then on, will revolt against the army and the police and blame them for this state of things.'

Carlos Marighela

irregular movements in South America, including the violent left-wing Tupamaros movement which conducted an unsuccessful guerrilla campaign (1968–72) against the Uruguayan government.

During the 1970s and 1980s Western governments also entered into fierce confrontations with these urban guerrilla groups. The West German government faced a ferocious campaign waged against them during the 1970s by the twenty-strong Baader-Meinhof terrorist group. The latter's essentially destructive effort did not ignite a 'social blaze', and nor did that of the Red Brigades in Italy, but both did achieve an enormous concentration of police effort against them. Indeed, both organisations' political impact was far in excess of their military capability, as West Germany and Italy were forced partially to suspend democracy and to introduce martial law measures. In Northern Ireland after 1970, 20,000 British regular troops confronted an increasingly sophisticated and largely urban terrorist group, the Provisional IRA, which – despite the recent ceasefire – is still recognised as the most potent terrorist group in Europe, both in terms of structure and operational capacity.

Ironically, by the late 1970s and early 1980s the 'guerrilla worm' had turned. Marxist regimes themselves began either falling to or being besieged by guerrilla revolutionary movements. Regular or conventional armies in communist Nicaragua, Ethiopia, Angola, Afghanistan, Mozambique and Vietnamese-occupied Cambodia became engaged in counter-insurgency activities themselves against a wide variety of irregular armies. Thus, the USSR in her declining years faced her own 'mini-Vietnam', a prolonged ten-year campaign confronting Afghan mujahedeen irregulars who, with American support and mountain cover, inflicted heavy casualties upon Soviet regular forces. By 1989 Soviet forces had evacuated the country, their losses amounting to over 14,000 dead and 460,000 sick and wounded – casualties that had serious domestic political repercussions and contributed to the downfall of communism. In the event, these Marxist regimes had proved as inept in dealing with insurgents as had the Western-supported or Western governments a few decades earlier.

The twentieth century saw a dramatic change in the character and scale of irregular conflict. Although, as Walter Laquer has observed, 'the retreat into urban terror, noisy but politically ineffective, is not a new departure but, on the contrary, the end of an era', the plethora of repressive regimes which continue to thrive in the post-Cold War era suggest that Maoist guerrilla warfare remains, in the words of Pascall, 'a logical choice for those seeking to overthrow a government'. It is perhaps still a truism that, as Mao himself once said, 'guerrilla strategy is the only strategy possible for an oppressed people'.

'Everybody dances or nobody dances.'

Slogan of the Tupamaros movement in Uruguay

SIXTEEN

THE GULF WAR AND THE FUTURE OF WAR

WARREN CHIN

'In our day wars are not won by mere enthusiasm but by technical superiority.'

V.I. Lenin, 1918

One of the central themes of this book has been an analysis of how technology has changed the conduct of war and the role it has played in allowing belligerents to pursue the goal of decisive victory. Looking back over the last hundred years it is evident that the basic political and economic conditions – created to a large extent by technology – have made it more difficult to achieve this goal. The failure of the Great Powers to accomplish a rapid and decisive victory in 1914, and Germany's inability to achieve a similar outcome against Russia in 1941, demonstrate the resilience of the modern industrialised state. A more extreme example of this complex and contradictory relationship is the situation created by nuclear weapons. Although there have been instances where technology has assisted rather than hindered the achievement of a rapid and decisive victory, examples are few and far between. Furthermore, the reasons for the success of such operations often went beyond the imbalances in technology between the opponents. But such results have not held back the drive to find the perfect weapon. Even during the Cold War the military–industrial complex continued to see technology as a means to secure victory. Thus, in the 1970s and 1980s the Americans used technology as an essential feature of both nuclear and conventional warfighting doctrines that envisaged the achievement of victory in a war against the Soviet Union.

The quest for decisive victory through technology continues even in the midst of a diminished threat to the West in the post-Cold War world. In fact, if anything, the search is intensifying and will continue to do so for the foreseeable future. Western armed forces are under increasing pressure to ensure that, if they are used, the outcome will be clear-cut and decisive. This pressure stems from the changing attitudes both of governments and their electorates towards the use of force. The reasons for this are complex, but of fundamental importance is the fact that for the West these conflicts are not perceived as being like traditional wars. They are not fought to protect or expand the vital interests of the state; neither are they wars of national survival. Today, it can be suggested, Western military operations are often designed to support the achievement of humanitarian goals, rather than the calculations of traditional power politics. As a result there is a general feeling that while carrying out such operations is laudable, they should not result in loss of life among the military personnel deployed. There is also an expectation that such actions should be concluded quickly. The moral overtones of these conflicts produce a further complication in that the operation needs to be conducted in such a way that only the guilty suffer. The media's coverage of the operation and expert assessment of its conduct impose further pressure to ensure that the application of force is quick, decisive and discriminate.

'An arms race is a race with no finishing post. There is no ultimate military weapon.'

Sir Solly Zuckermann, British scientist, 1965

The general perception that force can be used as though it were a surgeon's scalpel was reinforced, and perhaps even created, by one key event: the Gulf War (2 August 1990 to 28 February 1991). Indeed, it has even been claimed that the manner in which this war was conducted by the Americans represented a 'Revolution in Military Affairs' (RMA). The technology that defined and characterised this RMA provided the equipment needed to fight and win decisively. So one-sided was the Gulf War that its conduct was compared to a video game: it was remote, impersonal, controllable, and only the space invaders were killed. The Gulf War and the debate that ensued created an expectation of how future war would be fought.

A more sceptical view would be that we have seen this all before. The opening stages of the Franco-Prussian War (1870–1) were also held up as the 'paradigm', the pointer to the future of modern war. As a result, Europe's Great Powers operated on the assumption that the next major war would be quick and decisive. Unfortunately, the actual outcome was the First World War (1914–18), a horrific bloodbath that cost the lives of millions. This happened, in part, because people learned the wrong lessons from the past and ignored wider changes that were taking place within the state, society, the economy and industry. The danger is that we are making the same mistake today as our predecessors did in the period leading up to 1914. Current and future political and economic conditions appear to be reinforcing the general trend for wars to become longer, not shorter. A lively discussion has emerged on whether the West is preparing for the war it would like to fight, rather than the war it will have to fight in the future. The purpose of this chapter is to examine this debate and consider whether the West is preparing to fight the wrong kind of war. In addressing this issue it is necessary to examine what was new about the Gulf War and explore the broader strategic context within which wars are likely to happen. Through this analysis it should be possible to make a more accurate assessment of how relevant current thinking on the RMA really is.

THE LEGACY OF THE GULF WAR

The Gulf War came as a great surprise to the world. Not only was the Iraqi attack on Kuwait unexpected, but so too was the apparently unorthodox way in which the American-led Coalition subsequently fought and defeated the invaders. At the time of the crisis comparisons between the two forces

The Gulf War chronology, Aug 1990–Jan 1991

2 Aug 1990	Iraq invades Kuwait: UN Security Council passes Resolution 660 condemning invasion
6 Aug 1990	American representatives meet Saudi leaders in Riyadh: UN Security Council passes Resolution 661, imposing economic embargo on Iraq
7 Aug 1990	US deployment to Saudi Arabia begins (Operation 'Desert Shield')
10 Aug 1990	Arab League agrees to send forces to defend Saudi Arabia
25 Aug 1990	First complete US unit deploys along Saudi–Kuwait border
10 Sept 1990	USA appeals to NATO allies for assistance
14 Sept 1990	Britain announces deployment of forces to Saudi Arabia
15 Oct 1990	Deployment of US VII Corps from Germany agreed
29 Nov 1990	UN Resolution 678 authorises use of 'all necessary means' to implement previous resolutions
12 Jan 1991	US Congress authorises President Bush to use force to implement Resolution 678
16/17 Jan 1991	Operation 'Desert Storm' begins

suggested that a battle between them might be bloody and protracted. Iraq had the sixth largest air force in the world, with over 770 aircraft operating from 123 airfields scattered throughout Iraq and Kuwait. In addition, it possessed a formidable air defence system, consisting of over 16,000 radar-guided and heat-seeking surface-to-air missiles (SAMs) organised across 150 sites. Mixed in with these were nearly 4,000 anti-aircraft guns. It was estimated that the density of SAMs and anti-aircraft artillery deployed around Baghdad was seven times greater than the air defence surrounding the North Vietnamese capital of Hanoi during the conflict in Vietnam. Before the start of the air war Coalition planners predicted heavy losses, fearing that between 10 and 15 per cent of the aircraft used in the campaign might be destroyed. Approximately 1,700 aircraft made up the Coalition air force, and based on these projections, the Coalition was expected to lose between 170 and 230 of them.

The Iraqi Army represented an even more formidable obstacle. In January 1991 it was believed to have a strength of 1.1 million men, with over 7,000 tanks, 11,000 pieces of artillery, nearly 350 multiple rocket launchers and 110 surface-to-surface missile systems. After eight years of war with Iran, the Iraqi Army was thought to be battle-hardened and expert in fighting defensively. To make matters worse, it had been given five months in which to prepare its defences in Kuwait and, according to satellite imagery, it used this time to great effect, erecting sandberms, anti-tank ditches filled with oil and an elaborate system of trenches. The Coalition numbered 540,000 troops and did not have the three-to-one numerical superiority believed to be required by an attacking force. There were also fears that the Iraqis would use chemical weapons as part of their defence. Perhaps not surprisingly, estimates of combat losses likely to be incurred during a land war were even more depressing than those for the air campaign. Predicted casualties for an offensive into Iraqi-occupied Kuwait ranged from 20,000–30,000 killed and wounded to a shattering 100,000 casualties.

Subsequent events, however, proved these assessments to be spectacularly wrong. The Coalition lost 34 aircraft throughout the entire war and only 150 of its soldiers were killed in land operations. However, the war was notable not simply because the Coalition achieved victory with so few casualties. Equally important was the scale of destruction inflicted on the Iraqi Army. Post-war assessments made by the US theatre command (CENTCOM) estimated that the Iraqis suffered 20,000 killed and 60,000 wounded. In addition, over 86,000 Iraqi troops surrendered. General Norman Schwarzkopf, commander of the Coalition, described this outcome as the 'perfect victory'.

Why, then, was the Coalition able to defeat the Iraqi war machine with such ease? Various factors were put forward to explain the Coalition's success. However, the attentions both of experts and the general public were dominated by one particular phenomenon: the air campaign. In the immediate aftermath of the war there was a general impression that air power had created the conditions for victory in the Gulf War. Of greater long-term importance was the belief that if air power had been freed from the shackles of having to support the Coalition's land forces, it might have won the war on its own.

AIR POWER IN THE GULF WAR

The idea that air power is the decisive weapon of war is not new. Even in the 1920s and 1930s its proponents argued that future wars would be won solely through the application of air power. But to their surprise, strategic bombing in the Second World War did not result in the instant surrender of Germany and Japan. Neither did it bring about the quick collapse of the North Koreans during the Korean War (1950–53), and it certainly did not result in the rapid capitulation of the North Vietnamese during the American intervention in Vietnam (1965–73). The inability of air power to achieve a decisive victory during the Vietnam War was particularly striking, given that the Americans dropped over 6 million tons of explosives on North Vietnam and its forces fighting in South-East Asia.

Yet advocates of air power were not put off by the disaster of Vietnam. In fact, they were able to draw some reassurance from certain aspects of this conflict. For example, the capability of the United States Air Force (USAF) was significantly improved as a result of technical developments during the war. Of particular importance was the development of smart (laser and TV-guided) bombs. There were also notable successes in the air war, perhaps the most important of which was the 'Linebacker II' operation in December 1972. The significance of this was that for the first time in the war the USAF was allowed to conduct a full-scale strategic bombing campaign against North Vietnam's vital military, industrial and transport infrastructure. The only important constraint was the need to avoid substantial civilian casualties, and this was addressed through the extensive use of smart bombs. As a result the North Vietnamese government negotiated a peace settlement with the United States that it had hoped to avoid. In the eyes of some commentators, 'Linebacker II' demonstrated what air power could achieve if given the operational freedom to fight the war as the USAF saw fit.

'Linebacker II', 19–30 December 1972

Tactical aircraft sorties	1000+
B-52 sorties	740
B-52s lost	11
B-52 crewmen killed, captured or missing	66
North Vietnamese MiG fighters destroyed	8

An American officer, Colonel John Warden, developed these ideas further into a coherent doctrine. While at the USAF Staff College, Warden wrote a critique (1988) of the air campaign in Vietnam. In his view the USAF had not identified North Vietnam's critical vulnerabilities, and had been bombing the wrong targets for most of the war. Too much effort had been invested in attacking the North Vietnamese Army and its supporting infrastructure, and not enough bombs had been directed at the North Vietnamese state. He believed that air power could be the decisive arm in war if it attacked the following targets in a specific order of priority:

1. the political leadership and command and control of the state;
2. sources of power generation, petrol storage facilities and centres of military production;
3. the transport infrastructure;
4. psychological operations;
5. the armed forces of the state.

'Any person, thing, idea, entity or location selected for destruction, inactivation, or rendering non-usable with weapons which will reduce or destroy the will or ability of the enemy to resist.'

US Air Force definition of 'Military Target', Fundamentals of Aerospace Weapons Systems

Warden called this prioritised list of targets 'inside-out warfare'. He envisaged a focus of resources on attacks against the political and state apparatus. These would then spread out from the centre towards the industrial base, power stations and the transport system. Of least importance were attacks against the enemy's armed forces, which were generally to be left to wither on the vine.

Consequently, the debacle of Vietnam contributed to the emergence of new aerial weaponry and the development of a coherent doctrine on the application of air power, elements which were to come together in the Gulf War. Clearly, tangible evidence of this can be seen from the equipment used in 1991. However, less obvious is the impact of Warden's concept of 'inside-out warfare' on the Coalition air campaign. It is clear that Warden played an important role in the early stages of planning the air war, and that his concept of how the war would be fought conformed closely to his own beliefs regarding the use of air power; indeed, in one of the revised plans he did not even list the Iraqi forces in Kuwait as a target. It is also clear that his 'Instant Thunder' plan provided the framework around which the eventual air campaign was based. Although Warden was forced to return to Washington after he presented his ideas, members of his staff were incorporated into the special group responsible for developing the master plan for the air war. Their plan demonstrated a close resemblance to Warden's concept. The only notable addition was the inclusion of the Iraqi Army, in particular the Republican Guard, in the target list.

A parallel development that came to the fore in 1991 was the use of information systems capable of instantly providing a vast amount of data on the enemy to the theatre commander and his subordinates. Thus, through the use of satellites, the Coalition was able to build up a complete picture of the Iraqi deployment. It was able to monitor weather conditions and, more importantly, it could navigate its forces through the almost featureless landscape of the desert. It even had the ability to detect a missile launch from the surface. It was also possible for the Coalition to track the movement of Iraqi forces in the air, on land and at sea using a variety of airborne surveillance systems. In addition, the Coalition was able to listen to Iraqi radio communications and, where necessary, jam them or use them to target enemy command and control facilities. Target acquisition on the battlefield was also enhanced through the use of information-gathering systems such as thermal imaging. The establishment of this 'information-rich environment' increased the effectiveness of air power still further by providing real-time data on the exact location of Iraqi forces and other targets.

It was the combination of these systems that allowed the Coalition to establish air supremacy over Iraq and Kuwait within ten days of the start of the air war (the night of 16/17 January 1991). Command and control of Iraq's air defence was carried out by a French-designed computer system known as 'Kari' (which is 'Iraq' spelt backwards in French). The heart of this facility was the Air Defence Operations Centre (ADOC) in Baghdad. It was responsible for creating a complete picture of the air war over Iraq and for establishing priorities for all air defence engagements. Subordinate to the ADOC were the regional sector operations centres (SOCs), and beneath this layer were numerous intercept operation centres (IOCs), which provided local air defence control.

Through the use of surveillance carried out by aircraft fitted with electronic listening systems, the USAF was able to locate and analyse the

A Royal Air Force Boeing E-3 Sentry AWACS. Systems like AWACS are integral to the Revolution in Military Affairs, which relies upon the very rapid collection of information, its equally rapid processing into Intelligence and the use of this Intelligence to deliver precision strikes to achieve decisive military results. Nevertheless, AWACS aircraft are crewed by human beings, and the system is not infallible. During the Gulf War, for example, a failure to provide US Navy F-14 combat air patrols with the frequencies on which AWACS operated almost allowed Iraqi Mirage jets, carrying anti-ship missiles, to launch strikes against American ships in the Gulf. With 5,000 crew on board each of the US aircraft carriers, the results could have been catastrophic. (Defence Picture Library)

AWACS AND J-STARS

The Boeing E-3 Sentry is an airborne warning and control system (AWACS) which provides an all-weather surveillance, command, control and communications capability. It contains a rotodome antenna that is over 9 metres in width, mounted on twin pylons on the rear fuselage of the aircraft. It is operated by a crew of seventeen and can remain airborne for up to eleven hours. During the Gulf War, USAF AWACS operated from Riyadh in Saudi Arabia and Incirlik in Turkey. American and Saudi aircraft flew over 840 AWACS sorties, remaining in the air for over 5,000 hours and providing radar surveillance and control for more than 120,000 Coalition combat and support flights. They also assisted in shooting down thirty-eight Iraqi fighters. This system was of vital importance in providing the Coalition with a transparent picture of the air space over both Iraq and Kuwait.

Complementing the AWACS was the Boeing E-8 Joint Surveillance and Target Attack Radar System (J-STARS). This was designed for battlefield surveillance, peace support operations, and verification of treaty agreements. It has a crew of twenty-one and can remain airborne for over twenty hours. First developed in the 1980s by merging separate USAF and US Army research projects, it was still undergoing trials when the Gulf War began; nevertheless, it was deployed to Saudi Arabia in November 1990. J-STARS provides the operator with a terrain map over which all moving objects can be tracked. It is able to identify which objects are vehicles rather than animals, and it even has the power to identify whether the object is a tank, truck or armoured personnel carrier. It traces the movement of these vehicles, providing the operator with a real-time picture of enemy movement in the theatre of operations and on the battlefield. It can also work out traffic flow and is able to predict likely choke points where the enemy will be vulnerable to attack. It is the ground equivalent of the AWACs, providing a complete picture of the movement of enemy land forces. The commander thus has an almost perfect picture of what the enemy's forces are doing.

'Kari' air defence system and identify the location of the ADOC in Baghdad, as well as the regional SOCs and the local IOCs. On the first night of the war US special forces helicopters, using a satellite system of navigation known as the global positioning system (GPS), were able to guide Apache helicopters to the location of Iraqi forward radar observation sites. These were then attacked using Hellfire anti-tank guided missiles. Almost simultaneously, Stealth bombers flew through the now blind Iraqi forward air defence to attack SOCs in the south. Meanwhile, in Baghdad the ADOC and other command and control facilities were attacked by thirty Stealth bombers and fifty-four cruise missiles. A critical flaw in the 'Kari' system was that once the ADOC was destroyed none of the SOCs could communicate with each other to coordinate a defence. This allowed the Coalition to attack and destroy each sector in isolation using either cruise missiles or Stealth bombers. Once the SOCs and IOCs were inoperative Iraq's air force also became redundant, because it relied on the command centres to provide information to enable its aircraft to intercept the enemy.

Iraqi SAMs were also effectively neutralised. Drones designed to mimic the radar profile of a fighter were flown over Iraq's air defences in an effort to get the operators to track the drones with their radar. EF-111 Raven aircraft then jammed the radar signal, forcing the SAM operators to use maximum power so that they could continue tracking the drones. Anti-radiation missiles then used the radar emissions to guide themselves on to the position of the SAM battery, destroying it. So effective was this method of attack that by the third day of the air war Iraqi radars remained switched off.

Opposite: *A McDonnell AH-64 Apache attack helicopter. In the early morning of 17 January 1991 nine US Army AH-64s of 101st Airborne Division (Air Assault) fired the first shots of the Gulf War, destroying two early warning radar sites in southern Iraq. Later in the war Apaches were used extensively against Iraqi ground forces, apparently with considerable success. However, more recent experience with the AH-64 has called its utility in other environments into question. This was especially true during NATO operations against Yugoslavia in 1999, when Apaches were deployed to Albania, only to discover that they were unable to fly over the region's mountains when fully loaded. (Defence Picture Library)*

CONVENTIONAL AIR-LAUNCHED CRUISE MISSILES

The conventionally armed air-launched cruise missile was the product of an American research programme to develop an unmanned decoy in the 1960s. Recognising the potential of the system, the USAF expanded this project to create a long-range, low-altitude nuclear-armed missile. A variant of this system armed with a conventional warhead was introduced in 1986. This was known as the Conventional Air-Launched Cruise Missile (CALCM). This version of the cruise missile family carries a 1,000-pound warhead containing steel balls. The missile has a range of about 680 miles and relies on inertial guidance to locate its target. It constantly checks its course while in flight by comparing a map in its computer memory with the actual terrain under its flight path. It is extremely accurate and will fall within a radius of 15 metres of its designated target. This weapon is launched from a modified B52 bomber. While in transport to its target all of its systems are inert. After take-off, navigation details are transferred from the B52 to the cruise missile every sixty seconds. Later versions of this weapon used GPS to guide the missile. Of the 323 cruise missiles launched by the US Navy and USAF during the Gulf War, 90 were CALCMs. A more powerful version of the CALCM, armed with a 3,000-pound warhead, was used against Iraq during Operation 'Desert Fox' in 1998.

THE EF-111 RAVEN

The EF-111 is a converted bomber designed to conduct electronic warfare. Carrying a pilot and electronic warfare officer, its function is to jam enemy early warning and SAM radars so that fighter aircraft are able to engage and destroy the enemy's SAM defence. The EF-111 first saw active service in 1986 when four participated in a US air attack against Libya in retaliation for its support for acts of terrorism against US personnel in Europe. It was also among the first aircraft deployed as part of 'Desert Shield' (the defence of Saudi Arabia). The EF-111 played a vital part in 'Desert Storm' and eighteen aircraft flew over 1,300 operational sorties during the campaign. It was able to supply stand-off long-range electronic jamming of enemy radar by flying in friendly air space and, with the aid of other electronic warfare aircraft, create a jamming barrier to mask friendly air activity. It could also provide direct assistance to aircraft operating over the battlefield in support of ground operations.

The EF-111A 'Sparkvark' played a vital role in jamming and confusing Iraqi electronic defences during the Gulf War. However, like many of the high-tech tools of modern war, the EF-111's usefulness in conflicts other than war is open to question. In particular, in a world where peacekeeping, intervention operations and counter-insurgency represent the principal roles for 'first world' armed forces, and in which negotiating skills, empathy, the ability to speak foreign languages and good judgement are at a premium, the EF-111 can be seen as having little to offer. Nevertheless, the fact is that armed forces are reluctant to give up such weapons voluntarily, and there is every reason to believe that systems like this will be a focus for defence spending during the twenty-first century. (US Department of Defense)

With the suppression of Iraq's air defence system, the Coalition was free to carry out its strategic air campaign. Eight types of targets were attacked: the political leadership; weapons of mass destruction; ballistic missile launchers; command and control facilities; electrical power; refineries; key bridges; and railways. It was estimated that these operations were extremely effective, with attacks against the transport infrastructure resulting in the destruction of thirty-seven road bridges and nine important railway bridges. Serious damage was claimed to have been inflicted on a further nine road bridges stretching across the Tigris and Euphrates rivers, and it was calculated that attacks against Iraqi lines of communication reduced the flow of supplies into Kuwait from 75,000 tons to only 16,000 tons per day. Air power was also effective in shutting down 88 per cent of the Iraqi national grid, and serious damage was inflicted on eleven of its power plants, resulting in an 80 per cent reduction in its electricity generating capacity. The USAF also judged that they made nearly 90 per cent of Iraq's oil refining capacity inoperative.

Air power also played a vital role in preparing the battlefield for the Coalition's planned ground offensive. The goal of the Coalition air force was to reduce the Iraqi Army's tanks, artillery and armoured vehicles by 50 per cent before the land war began. Estimates made just before the launch of ground operations indicate that they came close to achieving this objective. Approximately 39 per cent of Iraq's tanks, 32 per cent of its armoured vehicles and 47 per cent of its artillery, it was claimed, had been destroyed by 23 February 1991. It was also believed that the air campaign caused the psychological collapse of the Iraqi Army and that this explained why it put up so little resistance. Overall, between 17 January and 24 February 1991 Iraqi forces in theatre fell from 336,000 to 200,000 men, of whom it was gauged that over 86,000 deserted before the ground war started. It was also speculated that the morale of those who remained was poor. Certainly, it seems that many Iraqi soldiers and officers decided to surrender at the first opportunity.

Finally, it was argued that air power also made a vital contribution to the fighting on the ground between 24 and 28 February 1991. It was estimated that Coalition aircraft were responsible for the destruction of 450 tanks, 220 armoured vehicles, 353 artillery pieces and over 950 trucks. The role of ground forces seemed to be to act as an auxiliary to air power; their function being to sweep up the rubble left behind by the Coalition air force.

Such an analysis suggested that the Gulf War marked a shift in the decisiveness of war from the ground to the air. In the past, victory had been achieved by troops on the ground defeating an opponent in a

The 'Highway of Death'. As Iraqi forces withdrew from Kuwait towards Basra on 26 February they came under heavy attack from air, and later ground, forces. Hundreds of vehicles, many of them civilian ones stolen from Kuwait, were destroyed. However, relatively few Iraqis were in fact killed, most preferring to escape on foot rather than stay with their vehicles. Furthermore, the Coalition failed to prevent large parts of the Republican Guard escaping from the KTO. Following the cease-fire, these forces played a vital role in suppressing anti-Saddam revolts in southern and northern Iraq, causing some in the West to ask if the war had been a military triumph but a political failure. (ref: G69/23/1, © British Crown Copyright/MOD)

succession of battles that generated operational (that is, campaign-level) and eventually strategic victory. In the Gulf War, however, tactical success in battle seemed to be dependent upon long-range strikes launched by air forces, naval aviation and guided missiles throughout the theatre of operations, supported by a comprehensive surveillance and information network capable of providing a total picture of the battlefield and the air space above it. The main lesson of the Gulf War appeared to be that the land battle was no longer the only way to secure victory.

THE AIR CAMPAIGN: LEARNING THE WRONG LESSONS?

'Organizations created to fight the last war better are not going to win the next.'

General James M. Gavin (1907–87)

'Before a war military science seems a real science like astronomy. But after a war it seems more like astrology.'

Dame Rebecca West, British writer

Operation 'Desert Storm' serves as a paradigm for future military operations. In future wars between relatively evenly matched opponents it is assumed that military action will begin with offensive air and space operations by both sides. It is also anticipated that there will be no clearly defined 'front line' and that space will emerge as a decisive theatre of operations. The initial targets in this air and space war will be the enemy's C4I(BM) (command, control, communications, computers, Intelligence and battlefield management systems), with both sides seeking to blind their opponent while preserving their own C4I(BM). In the future the first objective will to be gain control of the electronic air waves, the second will be to establish air supremacy and the third will be to conduct deep strikes against the enemy's strategic and operational centres of gravity; those objectives which, if destroyed, will do fundamental damage to his ability to fight effectively. Most important is the belief that, since strategic objectives can be destroyed through air and space attacks, victory will be achieved without the seizure and occupation of territory by ground forces.

This style of war has considerable appeal to Western states. First, and most important, it suggests that it is not necessary to commit ground troops to achieve victory. This means that the war can be fought without suffering any friendly casualties. Second, because of the accuracy of the weaponry involved, it should be possible to apply force to key military targets in a discriminate fashion and thus avoid killing innocent civilians, something that is politically controversial in the West.

However, although the RMA appears to offer a persuasive solution to the security problems confronting the West, it is not without its difficulties. In particular, some of the claims made about the RMA are highly questionable. The first and most obvious issue is cost. In the immediate aftermath of the Gulf War it was generally assumed that nearly all the munitions fired were high-technology smart weapons. In fact, subsequent analysis revealed that only a small proportion fell into this category. Barely 7 per cent of the munitions fired were precision-guided and, most surprisingly, the US Navy fired only 282 cruise missiles. The advantage of this mix of weapons was that the air campaign cost only \$1.3 billion. Although this is a considerable sum of money it was estimated that if the Coalition had used nothing but smart munitions then there would have been a tenfold increase in the cost of the air war. There can also be a significant difference between the likely cost of the munitions

Initial hopes that the Coalition air campaign would require only five or six days to be effective proved highly optimistic. Increasingly attacks came to rely less on 'smart' weapons, which relatively few aircraft were able to operate, and more on 'dumb' bombs like these. Even then, human error could reduce the latter's destructive effect. Many B-52 strikes, for example, were directed hundreds of yards from their intended targets because of mistakes in allocating grid references. Nevertheless, the cumulative effect upon the Iraqis' morale of incessant air bombardment was significant, and tens of thousands of them deserted or surrendered at the first available opportunity because of the air attacks. (RMAS Collection)

Cruise missiles like this US Navy Tomahawk can hit targets hundreds of miles from their launch point. However, sometimes this proved a distinct disadvantage for the Coalition. Most notoriously, when a laser guided bomb struck the Al-Firdos bunker in Baghdad (which was believed to be an Iraqi communications centre) on the night of 12/13 February 1991, hundreds of civilians who were sheltering there were killed. The devastating public relations implications had the effect of immediately ending all attacks on Saddam's administrative means of controlling the Iraqi population, with the long-term result that it was easier for Iraq's ruler to remain in power after the war was over. (RMAS Collection)

Attacks on the Iraqi air force were fairly successful, leading to the destruction of 290 of its 724 fixed-wing aircraft. Many were destroyed in their hangars – some of which had been hardened to withstand the effects of nuclear weapons – by precision guided munitions. Here a British officer poses on top of a heap of rubble within one such building in southern Iraq. (RMAS Collection)

used and the damage inflicted on the opponent. For example, in September 1996 the Americans fired cruise missiles to the value of $50 million to destroy Iraqi air defences in the south of the country. Yet within two weeks the sites were operational again.

There is also considerable doubt that the air campaign was as decisive as was first assumed. For example, attacks on Iraq's political leadership did not result in its paralysis. The problem, it seems, was not that the weapons did not hit their targets, but that they were aimed at the wrong sites. The lack of good 'human Intelligence' (that is, spies) within Iraq made it difficult for air planners to know what to target in order to paralyse the enemy's leadership. Attacks on Iraq's command and control infrastructure were also less effective than had been previously thought. This was because the Iraqis built an enormous amount of spare capacity into their telephone network so that, even though badly damaged by bombing, it was still possible for the government to communicate with its forces in Kuwait.

The operational effectiveness of the air campaign has also been brought into question. For example, it now appears that air power was not able to cut off and isolate Iraqi forces in Kuwait. Contrary to the assumptions of the air plan, the Iraqis were able to repair damaged bridges quickly. They also set up pontoon bridges and diverted traffic along indirect routes into Kuwait. As a result, the Iraqis were able to restore their supply lines more rapidly than the Coalition anticipated. This failure might also explain why, in the final phase of the land war, the Coalition air force was unable to stop the escape of a large part of the Iraqi Army (especially the Republican Guard) back into Iraq.

The USS Nimitz *returns to the United States after operations in the Gulf, 1997. The nuclear-powered, 93,000-ton* Nimitz *entered service in 1975. Together with the Americans' thirteen other aircraft carriers, she forms the backbone of US global maritime power, allowing the USA rapidly to project its influence over a wide area without relying on the goodwill of other states to provide air bases. Nevertheless, the vast cost of building and maintaining such ships (the* Nimitz *carries 90 aircraft and over 5,000 crew), together with their alleged vulnerability to attack, has focused increased attention on much cheaper alternatives. In particular, the late 1990s saw considerable discussion about 'arsenal ships', low-profile vessels relying on stealth technology for their protection, carrying hundreds of long-range missiles that would utilise satellite technology and automatic systems – rather than large crews – to be targeted and fired. For various reasons, however, the future of these new designs is uncertain, and recent decisions by the French and British to build large aircraft carriers indicate that the days of such vessels are not yet over. (Defence Picture Library)*

The greatest single failure of the air war and its information systems, however, was the inability of the Coalition to prevent Iraq from firing Scud missiles against Saudi Arabia and Israel. This was in spite of the fact that a large number of resources were diverted to this mission; more air strikes were launched against Scuds than were carried out to suppress Iraq's SAM defences. The Scud hunt highlighted a number of problems. Of particular importance was the time it took to transfer information from the satellites that identified the launch of a Scud to the fighter-bombers allocated to find and destroy the missiles. It was especially difficult to find Scuds fired from mobile launchers, and the Iraqis generally had enough time to move and then hide the vehicle. Even when fighter pilots saw a launch they still found it extremely difficult to locate the actual launcher. Thus, out of forty-two pilot sightings of a Scud being fired from a mobile platform, only eight led to an actual attack on the launcher (and there is no evidence of any of these being destroyed). A significant problem was that the Iraqis also went to great lengths to construct decoys. These were so good that, according to UN weapons inspectors sent into Iraq after the war, it was impossible to tell the difference between the fake and the real thing. No doubt this explains why the Coalition air force claimed to have destroyed three times the number of Scuds actually possessed by Iraq. The inability of the Coalition to find and target the Scuds once they had been launched allowed the Iraqis to keep firing Scud missiles virtually until the end of the war.

Even the damage inflicted by air power on Iraqi ground forces, both before and during the ground war, has been contested. For example, the CIA disagreed with damage assessments which stated that air power came close to destroying 50 per cent of Iraqi heavy equipment. Its assessment indicated that the actual figure was closer to 25 per cent. It is also clear that Iraqi forces were able to lure fighter aircraft to attack decoy tanks and armoured vehicles, and that when equipment was attacked but undamaged, setting fire to tyres was often enough to give the impression that it had been destroyed. It is certainly true that the amount of damage inflicted against the Republican Guard was considerably less than pilots claimed. Assessments indicate that only 24 per cent of Guard equipment was destroyed by air attack. This is a very low figure given that pilots described the area occupied by the Republican Guard as a 'target-rich environment'.

It is not just that the Coalition air campaign was less effective than had been assumed. More disturbing are claims that by trying to build on the perceived technological success of the Gulf War the West is preparing for the wrong type of war. The most obvious illustration of this problem lies in the conservative application of this technology by the armed forces. Worryingly, change seems to be conceived primarily in terms of how far the RMA supports existing military systems and equipment, and there appears to be little interest in the wider effects of the information revolution which we are currently experiencing, or the possible repercussions this will have for the security of the state. Thus, 'information warfare' is generally seen as a battlefield force multiplier, and little is said about how the armed forces intend to deal with the pervasive threat of what might be termed pure 'cyber war'. This would involve attacks which do not target the opponent's armed forces, but instead

The Gulf air campaign, 1991

Number of days	43
Strike aircraft used	1,500
Total sorties (of which strike sorties)	112,000 (53,000, or 47%)
Strikes against 'strategic' targets	18,000
Strikes against 'tactical' targets	35,000
Weapons expended % smart weapons	225,000 7
Cruise missiles fired	323
Tonnage of bombs dropped	88,500

'This is my prediction for the future – whatever hasn't happened will happen and no one will be safe from it.'

J.B.S. Haldane, British scientist

concentrate on vulnerable computer communications systems used extensively by government, the military and business. The current RMA also ignores other areas of scientific advance, such as developments in biotechnology and the plethora of biological weapons that might be developed as a result of inventions in this field.

THE CHANGING STRATEGIC CONTEXT AND THE RMA

A more immediate concern is the fact that the RMA is oblivious of another revolution that is taking place at this very moment. So profound is this revolution expected to be that it is affecting both the sources of conflict and its character. This revolution is not based upon technology, although the latter will have some bearing on its development, but on economic, social and political developments. It does not rely on high technology: in fact, it can be extremely primitive. It involves a form of violence that does not discriminate between the soldier and the civilian, and ethical and legal constraints on the conduct of war do not apply. Finally, this kind of conflict is not waged by what the West would recognise as legitimate political organisations with the right to use force, and there is little evidence of any formal military organisation. In short, this kind of conflict is reminiscent of Thomas Hobbes' state of nature in which human life is 'nasty, brutish and short'. As such it is more reminiscent of warfare in the distant past than the alleged vision of the future described earlier in this chapter.

The premise upon which this interpretation is based is that the nation state is becoming less powerful. Internal and external forces that cause tensions between groups within all states are undermining them. Changes in technology have helped to increase the exposure of national economies to the effects of the international market. As a result, there have been winners and losers both between and within states. The most obvious manifestation of this trend is the further concentration of wealth among the most affluent states and within them. These trends favour the already affluent economies of the West, which are in a better position to deal with increasing differences in the living standards of the rich and the poor caused by the information revolution. More importantly, such states will be able to capitalise on the generation of new sources of wealth creation that are being produced by this revolution. Unfortunately, as a result of these changes, less-developed states could find that they become economically marginalised. Their labour-intensive industries will not be able to compete with the West's new methods of production. Similarly, agriculture might also be undermined by the emergence of new techniques and technologies produced in Western laboratories. The increasing impoverishment of less-developed states will make it difficult to satisfy the needs of their people.

This situation is likely to be exacerbated by a significant increase in the world's population, which now stands at over 6 billion. By 2025 it is predicted that this will expand to perhaps as much as 14.5 billion, with most of the growth taking place in countries whose governments do not

Opposite: *British Royal Marines in Sierra Leone, 2000. Typical of the 'New World Disorder' that characterised the 1990s, Sierra Leone's problems were ostensibly addressed in 1999, when the UN deployed a peacekeeping force (UNAMSIL) to assist in the implementation of a peace agreement reached between the country's warring factions. Unfortunately, problems with the clarity and robustness of the UN mandate, 'mission creep', logistics weaknesses and poor Intelligence and command and control led to an increasingly unstable environment and a drawing of UNAMSIL forces into open conflict against the main rebel group, the RUF. In turn, this precipitated a British intervention in May 2000 that successfully deterred an RUF attack on the capital of Sierra Leone, Freetown, and helped improve the security situation. Although later withdrawn, British forces were subsequently recommitted to help train the country's own army, and to deal (successfully) with a hostage crisis. At the time of writing Sierra Leone remains in a condition of uneasy peace, with proposals to increase the UNAMSIL presence to over 20,000 men. However, whether or not the UN has the will to support yet another protracted peacekeeping mission, with dubious prospects of long-term success, is very much open to question. (Defence Picture Library)*

SIERRA LEONE PORTS AUTHORITY
TARGRIN FERRY TERMINAL
welcome to
SIERRA LEONE

have the resources to cater for such an increase. It is anticipated that the inability of states to meet the basic needs of their burgeoning populations will undermine their legitimacy and credibility. As a result, it is expected that people will turn away from the formal state apparatus to other forms of religious, political, social and cultural organisation, and even to organised crime. It is also feared that such groups will blame the West for their plight and that attacks against Western interests will increase. It is possible that these elements will seek to capture the wealth of the West for themselves, and access to technology (in particular the computer) could help them achieve this goal. It is important to recognise that technological development is a double-edged sword and that it can also make the West more, rather than less, vulnerable. The most immediate problem in this domain is the rise of international crime and, related to this, drug trafficking. The activities of these groups not only threaten to hijack control of the state apparatus of the nations from which they originate, but also represent a threat to the internal security of Western democratic states.

The problem for the West is that the nature of the wars generated by these conditions is creating a conflict environment that exposes their critical vulnerabilities while negating their strengths. One important author, Martin van Creveld, suggests that there has been a gradual trend towards this style of war over the last fifty years. So far the West has not formulated an effective strategy for dealing with it. In the past, Western armies were impotent because of their very dependence on technology. They were too capital-intensive, relied too much on a slow and cumbersome logistics tail, possessed an equally slow and cumbersome system of command and had the wrong balance between fighting forces and support troops. Even worse, their weapons did not perform effectively in the harsh environments in which they had to operate. Unfortunately, the current RMA merely reinforces these trends.

It is also feared that if Western forces do become involved in these wars they will probably have to fight in an urban setting. This assumption is based on a projection that, by 2025, the majority of the global population will live in cities. By then there are expected to be twenty 'mega cities' each with a population in excess of 11 million. Military intervention by the West will not be able to bypass these urban sprawls. They will be centres of power and wealth, possessing the infrastructure required to gain effective control of the surrounding area and the country as a whole. The problems of fighting in an urban environment were clearly demonstrated to the Americans in Mogadishu (Somalia) in October 1993. Urban warfare will be an environment in which the application of high technology is of limited value; a fact clearly demonstrated by the failure of the latest American electronic listening and surveillance systems to detect and find the Somalian warlord Farah Aideed. It will also be a landscape in which it will be extremely easy for an ill-equipped force to inflict casualties on even the best-trained and best-equipped Western force. Unfortunately, maintaining control of a city requires men on the ground in large numbers; a commodity that most Western armies do not have. However, even if they do, concerns over casualties will prohibit their deployment. Such forces are lucrative targets for those who oppose

Western intervention. Obviously the easiest way to get rid of Western troops is to kill them, even in relatively small numbers. Political pressure back home will then force the intervening state to withdraw its forces. This was Farah Aideed's strategy in Somalia.

For states locked in a cycle of poverty, one way out is to industrialise. However, the drive to modernise also creates security problems for which the RMA has no solution. Perhaps the most important of these are environmental issues such as the depletion of the ozone layer and the problem of global warming. It is feared that these trends could have disastrous consequences for the environment and ultimately even for the survival of mankind. Most alarming is the prospect that global warming will result in increases in temperature and decreases in rainfall. This phenomenon could affect food production in many of the most densely populated parts of the world; for example, rice production in Asia. Changing temperatures will also have an impact on marine life and this could mean existing fish stocks might become even more depleted. It is also possible that as the ice caps melt sea levels will rise. Consequently, there is a danger that saline water could spoil such fertile areas as the Nile in Egypt. A more alarming concern is that, as 70 per cent of the world's population lives within 100 miles of the sea, any significant rise in sea levels will have a disastrous impact on human life. It is difficult to see how the current RMA will deal with this threat to the existence of mankind.

TOWARDS A VISION OF FUTURE CONFLICT

The antithesis of this 'doomsday' view of the future might suggest that although some change is desirable in terms of how military power is used, it is questionable whether this change needs to be revolutionary. For example, it is not entirely clear that we are actually going to witness the collapse of the state, and that intra-state conflict will be the order of the day. Thus, the current batch of failed states may simply have occurred because they were artificial entities created as a result of imperialism and superimposed on people who could not identify or relate to the system. Such states were unlikely to survive under even the most fortuitous circumstances. Moreover, it appears that most ethnic and religious minorities aspire to have their own nation state. The future could therefore see the creation of smaller but also more homogeneous states, rather than a world of failed states.

'If sunbeams were weapons of war we would have had solar energy long ago.'

Sir George Porter, British chemist, 1973

It is also possible that the world will not be torn apart because of the differences in wealth between nations and within them. Economic deprivation does not lead inevitably to rebellion and conflict. Neither is it entirely clear that global warming is a man-made phenomenon, rather than a natural process, or that the outcome will be as disastrous as predicted. The scientific community has not achieved a consensus on the issue.

Moreover, even if a rather depressing picture of the future is accepted, it is reasonable to assume that inter-state wars will continue to occur, and that conventional and indeed high-tech forces will play a prominent role in the resolution of these conflicts. In fact, it could be argued that the future

The Royal Navy's new amphibious operations ship HMS Ocean *exemplifies the changing role of naval forces in the post-Cold War security environment. With little direct threat to most of the major naval powers, emphasis has moved from ocean warfare to force projection and littoral operations using seaborne forces. This shift is associated with the increased willingness of many states to intervene in war-torn areas and humanitarian crises, bringing peace or material relief. The importance of amphibious forces in these types of operation was demonstrated by the Americans in Somalia (December 1992) and by the British in Sierra Leone (2000). In the latter case the 20,500-ton HMS* Ocean *proved a potent military threat and valuable diplomatic asset as she poised offshore with 12 helicopters and over 500 Royal Marines and their heavy equipment. (Defence Picture Library)*

will be dominated by wars fought between, rather than within, states. In view of the predicted shortage in resources, caused in part by increasing population, it seems all too likely that states desperate to ensure the survival of their populace will fight to increase their share of the finite resource base.

It is also too simplistic to argue that conventional high-technology weaponry will be useless in irregular warfare. There may be real advantages in using this equipment in such conflict environments. The most obvious is that the substitution of technology for manpower overcomes the politically sensitive problem of casualties. This provides Western states with at least one alternative to doing nothing – an option that, in the face of a looming humanitarian war, could prove costly to a government whose electorate is demanding action. A case can also be made that the possession of such kit has been effective in post-Cold War intra-state conflicts. For example, it is argued that air power played a decisive role in convincing the Serbs to agree to a ceasefire in Bosnia, a process that culminated in the Dayton Agreement in late 1995. NATO forces responsible for the implementation of this agreement also rely on high-technology equipment both to protect their own forces and to deter the Serbs. It is also argued that disasters like the US intervention in Somalia might have been avoided if more equipment had been deployed in-theatre. Of particular importance here is the controversial decision made by the US government in August 1993 to reject the request of the US commander in Somalia to deploy M1 tanks to Mogadishu. Had these tanks been available it is possible that US forces would not have suffered the casualties that they did two months later.

More significant evidence of the potential success of high-technology warfare, and in particular the importance of air power, was apparently demonstrated in NATO's war to stop Serbia from ethnically cleansing the province of Kosovo of its local Albanian population in 1999. After an air campaign that lasted seventy-eight days and in which 22,000 bombs were dropped, Serbian forces finally agreed to withdraw from Kosovo. In the immediate aftermath it was assumed that air power had won the war. This is extremely important because it apparently represents the first example of air power not just playing a vital part in the outcome of the war, but being the decisive arm. In this sense it represents the realisation of a long-nurtured dream stretching back over seventy years. It also provides confirmation of the increasing dominance of air power in modern war. Just as important is the fact that this war was won with relatively few 'friendly' or civilian casualties being incurred as a result of the air operation.

Has technology therefore provided Western armed forces with the means of securing a decisive victory in what is the messy and confused environment of intra-state violence? Unfortunately, there is no straightforward answer to this question. On paper at least, Kosovo appears to provide evidence that reaffirms the West's faith in technology.

A British Scimitar light tank, part of the United Nations Protection Force (UNPROFOR), passes a BBC Land Rover in Bosnia, 1993. The presence of independent media organisations and freelance journalists in conflict environments is something to which armed forces have had to adjust very quickly in the post-1945 era. Potentially worrying from the point of view of security, and often possessing communications systems that are the envy of even the world's most modern armies, the media can also be viewed as a useful tactical and operational tool in peacekeeping and similar environments. This was particularly well demonstrated during the 1990s in the former Yugoslavia, where the ability of soldiers to develop good relationships with journalists often had beneficial consequences for peacekeeping and peace enforcement missions. (RMAS Collection)

The air campaign against Yugoslavia, 1999	
Number of days	78
Strike aircraft used	214 (start of war) 535 (end of war)
Total sorties (of which strike sorties)	35,000 (13,000, or 37%)
Strikes against 'strategic' targets	6,000
Strikes against 'tactical targets	7,000
Weapons expended % smart-weapons	23,000 65
Cruise missiles fired	310
Tonnage of bombs dropped	11,500

However, more recent analysis of the damage inflicted on Serb forces in Kosovo indicates that the Serbian Army was virtually untouched by the air war. Does this negate the arguments of those who believe that air power won the war? Supporters of the air campaign argue that air attacks against the Serbian Army in Kosovo were irrelevant, and that it was the strategic air campaign against Serbia's political and economic infrastructure that was most important. This created pressure that Slobodan Milošević, the Serbian leader, could not ignore. Moreover, it could be argued that more high-technology equipment might have achieved a vast improvement in the damage inflicted on the Serb Army in Kosovo. Thus, instead of using manned fighter-bombers flying at over 15,000 feet to ensure they did not become casualties, an alternative solution might have been to use armed unmanned aerial vehicles (UAVs). These could fly at high speed at low level and engage targets at will.

However, if the effectiveness of air power and the RMA are accepted then how is the successive failure of US military action against Iraq since the 1991 Gulf War to be explained? A good example of this failure was Operation 'Desert Fox' (15–18 December 1998). This action was launched in response to the Iraqi government's refusal to comply with UN demands that its observers be allowed to inspect all weapons production and storage facilities in Iraq, and had two aims. The first was to destroy Iraq's known weapons storage and production facilities. The second was to cause the collapse of the Iraqi government. Quite clearly, the application of air power failed to achieve the second of these goals and even though Iraq's defence industrial production and storage facilities were damaged, the reconstruction of this capability was not prevented. In fact, because UN weapons inspectors were forced to leave, there is now no effective means of monitoring Iraq's production of weapons of mass destruction. Thus, in this case neither the threat nor the actual application of air strikes achieved the aims of the UN.

Why then did long-range precision strikes fail in 'Desert Fox' but succeed in the case of Kosovo? There are two possible answers. First, 'Desert Fox' lasted only three days compared to the campaign against Serbia, which lasted seventy-eight. Second, in the case of Serbia, the initial failure of the air war to achieve an early resolution resulted in increasing political tension within NATO as its credibility was undermined because of its failure to save the Albanian Kosovars. Fears that NATO might collapse if it failed to defeat the Serbs made it increasingly likely that NATO ground forces in the Balkans would be committed to the war. In the case of 'Desert Fox' there was no such threat and this limited the ability of the United States to coerce Iraq.

For the West the future of war is likely to see the continuing development of a long-range precision strike capability. Western governments view this as a cost-effective solution to their security problems. However, the possession of this capability does not guarantee success in war and, as with other technological quick fixes from the past, conflict will also be affected by economic, political and social changes. These forces are already altering both the character of war and the nature of the threat to the West. In these circumstances the future importance of technology as the arbiter of success in war remains highly debatable.

'It is not possible to regard our race with anything but alarm . . . From primeval ooze to the stars, we killed anything that stood in our way, including each other.'

Gore Vidal (b. 1925), American writer, 1970

NOTES ON THE CONTRIBUTORS

EDITORS

Dr Simon Trew BA is a Senior Lecturer in the War Studies Department at the Royal Military Academy Sandhurst (RMAS). He is a specialist on the Second World War in the Balkans and author of *Britain, Mihailović and the Chetniks, 1941–42* (Macmillan). He has contributed to several other published works, and appears regularly in documentaries on the History Channel.

Dr Gary Sheffield MA is a Senior Lecturer at King's College London, and a former member of the RMAS War Studies Department. He is currently based in the Defence Studies Department at the Joint Services Command and Staff College, where he also acts as Land Historian for the Higher Command and Staff Course. He is a specialist on the First World War and author of numerous works, most recently *Leadership in the Trenches: Officer – Man Relations, Morale, Discipline and the British Army in the First World War* (Macmillan).

CONTRIBUTORS

Dr Stephen Badsey MA (Cantab) FRHistS is a Senior Lecturer at the RMAS, and a Senior Research Fellow of De Montfort University, Bedford. He is a specialist on military theory and on media presentations of warfare. He has made numerous appearances as a historian on television and in the press, and has written or contributed to over a dozen books on warfare, most recently as editor of *The Hutchinson Atlas of World War II Battle Plans* (Helicon).

Dr Niall Barr MA is a Lecturer at the Joint Services Command and Staff College, and a former member of the War Studies Department at the RMAS. He is a specialist both on the history of the British Legion and the North African Campaign of 1940–3. He is currently researching a book on Bernard L. Montgomery and the 8th Army.

Tim Bean MA is a Senior Lecturer at the RMAS. He is a specialist on eighteenth-century naval warfare, amphibious operations, and the Red Army during the interwar years. He has contributed to several published works, most recently as editor of *Forests and Seapower: The Timber Problem of the Royal Navy 1652–1862.*

Dr John Buckley is Lecturer in History and War Studies at the University of Wolverhampton. He is a specialist on air power, and author of *The RAF and Trade Defence 1919–1945*. His most recent book is *Air Power in the Age of Total War* (UCL Press).

Peter Caddick-Adams is a former army officer and member of Cranfield University's Security Studies Institute, based at the Royal Military College of Science, Shrivenham. He is a specialist on the First World War, and among his publications is *By God they can Fight! A History of 143rd Infantry Brigade 1908–1995.*

Dr Warren Chin MA is a Defence Studies lecturer at the Joint Services Command and Staff College, and a former member of the War Studies Department at the RMAS. He is a specialist on British Defence Policy and has contributed to a number of published works.

Lloyd Clark MA is a Senior Lecturer at the RMAS. He is a specialist both on the First World War and airborne warfare, and has contributed to a range of military publications, most recently as author of *History of the First World War* (Hutchinson).

Dr Stephen Hart MA is a Senior Lecturer at the RMAS. He is a specialist on the Second World War in Europe, and author of *Montgomery and 'Colossal Cracks': The 21st Army Group in North-west Europe, 1944–45* (Praeger). He has also co-written several works on the German Armed Forces of the Second World War.

Professor Andrew Lambert MA PhD FRHistS is Professor of Naval History in the War Studies Department at King's College, University of London, and a former member of the War Studies Department at the RMAS. He is a specialist on both naval warfare and the Crimean War, and author of numerous books, among them *The Crimean War: British Grand Strategy against Russia 1853–1856*, *The Last Sailing Battlefleet: Maintaining Naval Mastery 1815–1850* and *War at Sea in the Age of Sail 1650–1850* (Cassell).

Dr Sanders Marble MA is a graduate of the College of William and Mary, Virginia, and King's College London. He is a specialist on the British Army of the First World War, and is currently Senior Historian for the eHistory.com internet site.

Stephen Walsh MA is a Senior Lecturer at the RMAS. He is a specialist on the Second World War on the Eastern Front, and author of *Stalingrad: The Infernal Cauldron* (Simon & Schuster). He is currently researching the career of Marshal of the Red Army Konstantin Rokossovsky.

Dr Andrew Wiest MA is Associate Professor in the Department of History at the University of Southern Mississippi, Hattiesburg, and a former visiting member of the War Studies Department at the RMAS. He is a specialist on both the First World War and Vietnam, and author of *Passchendaele and the Royal Navy*. His most recent work, as co-editor with Dr Geoffrey Jensen, is *War in the Age of Technology*.

Dr Edmund Yorke MA is a Senior Lecturer at the RMAS. He has published widely in defence, Commonwealth and African affairs. His most recent work includes co-editorship of *The New South Africa* (Macmillan) and co-authorship of *Mafeking: The Story of the Siege* (Covos-Day).

INDEX